continued inside back cover

PSYCHOTHERAPY

An Eclectic Approach

PSYCHOTHERAPY

An Eclectic Approach

SOL L. GARFIELD
Washington University

A WILEY–INTERSCIENCE PUBLICATION

JOHN WILEY & SONS, New York • Chichester • Brisbane • Toronto

Library of Congress Cataloging in Publication Data:

Garfield, Sol Louis, 1918–
  Psychotherapy, an eclectic approach.

  (Wiley series on personality processes)
  Includes bibliographical references and index.
    1. Psychotherapy. I. Title. [DNLM: 1. Eclecti-
cism. 2. Psychotherapy. WM420.3 G231p]

RC480.G37   616.8'914   79–17724
ISBN 0–471–04490–3

Printed in the United States of America

10 9 8 7 6 5 4 3 2

Series Preface

This series of books is addressed to behavioral scientists interested in the nature of human personality. Its scope should prove pertinent to personality theorists and researchers as well as to clinicians concerned with applying an understanding of personality processes to the amelioration of emotional difficulties in living. To this end, the series provides a scholarly integration of theoretical formulations, empirical data, and practical recommendations.

Six major aspects of studying and learning about human personality can be designated: personality theory, personality structure and dynamics, personality development, personality assessment, personality change, and personality adjustment. In exploring these aspects of personality, the books in the series discuss a number of distinct but related subject areas: the nature and implications of various theories of personality; personality characteristics that account for consistencies and variations in human behavior; the emergence of personality processes in children and adolescents; the use of interviewing and testing procedures to evaluate individual differences in personality; efforts to modify personality styles through psychotherapy, counseling, behavior therapy, and other methods of influence; and patterns of abnormal personality functioning that impair individual competence.

IRVING B. WEINER

University of Denver
Denver, Colorado

v

Preface

I have tried in this book to present my views of psychotherapy and the psychotherapeutic process. As indicated in the first chapter, several factors have led me to try to organize my thoughts and reflections on what, at times, has appeared to be a rather chaotic state of affairs within the field of psychotherapy. The sheer proliferation of diverse schools and procedures with their respective claims for validity has been one important factor. The sometimes apparent contrast between the stated theoretical position of therapists and what they actually do in therapy has been another factor. For many years, also, I have been impressed by the potential importance of certain underemphasized features of psychotherapy that appear common to most psychotherapies but receive little emphasis in most presentations of psychotherapy. For such reasons, I felt it worthwhile to attempt some integration and organization of my views concerning psychotherapy.

In addition to the reasons mentioned above, I was also motivated by the pattern in most books on psychotherapy to either adhere to a particular theoretical orientation or to present a brief survey of a variety of psychotherapeutic approaches. I have found neither type of book really adequate for instructing students who are beginning their study of psychotherapy. One type presents only a single theoretical view; and the other emphasizes the unique features of several schools of psychotherapy without any attempt to synthesize or delineate their possible common factors.

As a consequence, I have tried to present a view of psychotherapy based, in some instances, on my own experience, that includes emphases and procedures drawn from a variety of approaches. This being essentially what most psychotherapists appear to do in practice, it would seem desirable to acknowledge this in a forthright manner and to attempt to portray psychotherapy in this way—hence the book's subtitle, "An Eclectic Approach."

I have tried to present the features and procedures of psychotherapy that I believe are common to most psychotherapies, as well as some from other approaches that I think are potentially useful. The bases for selection are the empirical literature, where relevant, and my own experience as a teacher and practitioner of psychotherapy. Others, of course, might well view the subject differently and come up with a different presentation. This is to be expected, for we are far from having solid answers to all of the important questions pertaining to the psychotherapeutic process. Nevertheless, it is the author's view that the time is more propitious than it has ever been to attempt an eclectic presentation of psychotherapy, crude though such an attempt may necessarily be.

I have drawn on a variety of empirical findings as well as on the views of many investigators and workers in the field of psychotherapy. Because some areas have been investigated more thoroughly than others, my recourse to research data on the various topics covered has consequently been varied. This is reflected in the degree of documentation among the various chapters and the relative reliance on other sources such as personal experience. I have tried, however, to indicate the varied bases for the statements made. I have also used the terms "client" and "patient" interchangeably, to reflect the usage among the different professions engaged in psychotherapy. It is my hope that the present work will be found to be useful in the training of psychotherapists and mental health counselors and of interest also to experienced therapists. Finally, I want to acknowledge my gratitude to Washington University for a sabbatical leave that allowed me the time and freedom to write a first draft of this book in London; to my wife Amy, who saw that I was not disturbed; and to Marie McDonnell who faithfully transcribed my written drafts into acceptable typed form.

SOL L. GARFIELD

St. Louis, Missouri
July 1979

Contents

CHAPTER 1

Introduction

Several reasons have motivated me to prepare the present book. One was a need to attempt some organization of my own thoughts, observations, and experiences in the area of psychotherapy. After working in this domain for over 35 years, I felt a personal need for crystallizing my own views. A second reason was the proliferation of therapeutic approaches so evident in recent years, with conflicting and untested theories and procedures in abundance. A recent publication of the National Institute of Mental Health, for example, refers to the existence of over 130 different forms of psychotherapy (Report of the Research Task Force of the National Institute of Mental Health, 1975). Such diversity, besides being bewildering, also raises some basic and intriguing questions concerning what psychotherapy really is, or to put it another way, what are the essential processes which lead to change or satisfaction in psychotherapy? Does one school of thought have a more correct view of these fundamental processes, or are all approaches essentially either viewing different parts of the elephant, or characterizing similar phenomena in crude and different ways? In a related manner, one notes varying emphases on cognitive approaches, behavioral approaches, relationship approaches, and "feeling" approaches (Binder, Binder, and Rimland, 1976; Morse and Watson, 1977). Is one more beneficial than another? Are some better with certain types of individuals or with certain types of problems than with others, and, if so, how do we tell which is which? Or is the tremendous diversity of psychotherapies simply an expression of the relative immaturity of the field and a sign of our collective ignorance? This is certainly a provocative issue and one that has interested me for many years.

A third reason, which has also influenced my own views of psychotherapy, is the current status of research in the field of psychotherapy. Although there has been a noticeable increase in the quantity and sophistication of research in this area, there have been relatively few conclusive or spectacular findings and a disturbingly high frequency of inconsistent findings (Garfield and Bergin, 1978). Admittedly, research in psychotherapy

1

is difficult and complex. However, the payoff from research in terms of its influence on practice has been discouragingly low. The possible reasons for this can be discussed later in more detail. Nevertheless, many of the inconclusive and inconsistent findings are provocative and appear to have some implications for our views concerning psychotherapy.

Another observation that has had an impact on my own thinking about psychotherapy is the difference between what people say and what they do. In my own experience, there have been rather frequent discrepancies between what therapists have said about a particular session in psychotherapy and what appeared to have taken place on the basis of a recording of the session. Apart from the obvious occurrences of memory loss and subjective distortion on the part of the therapist, there is also the problem generated by the exclusive use of concepts and abstract words in particular schools of psychotherapy, as well as in psychotherapy generally. If the therapist uses such terms as transference, resistance, affect, defensiveness, relationship, and insight, to name a few, then there may be serious problems in communicating what behaviors, cognitions, and affects are actually being described and what specific interactions actually took place.

The above factors have been important in my attempts to understand what appears to occur in the psychotherapeutic interaction. They have been manifested, in one guise or another, in discussions I have had about psychotherapy, in my teaching and supervision in this area, and in several postdoctoral workshops I have conducted on issues in psychotherapy. The present book is an attempt to come to grips with these problems, as well as to present a reasonably organized view of psychotherapy for those who are interested students or practitioners. The work is labelled "An Eclectic View" to indicate that the author is not an adherent of a particular school or system of psychotherapy. Beyond this, the term eclectic does not have any precise meaning (Garfield & Kurtz; 1977). What it does not signify for the present volume is a presentation simply of a number of different approaches or schools of psychotherapy. Rather, it represents an attempt to order what appear to be significant variables or phenomena in psychotherapy with recourse to research data wherever possible. Personal beliefs or hunches of the author will be identified as such whenever they are presented.

Although the term psychotherapy is frequently used to denote a particular type of therapy or treatment in contrast to other therapeutic modalities, it more realistically refers to a class of therapies; the psychological therapies. Although psychotherapy can be distinguished from pharmacotherapy, electric shock therapy, and the like, it should be kept in mind that there are many different types and forms of psychotherapy, and to refer to psychotherapy as one type of uniform process is to distort the situation unless we speak only in the vaguest manner possible. Kiesler (1966, 1971) has referred to this as the "uniformity myth" and includes, in a similar manner, statements which discuss generalized views of "the patient" and "the therapist". It is well to keep this point in mind, even though it will be necessary at times to refer to the generalized terms of client, therapist, and therapy.

Although something more will be said later about selected schools, or orientations within psychotherapy, a few points can be made here. First, it can be noted that whereas the best known and most popular orientations such as psychoanalysis and its derivatives and behavior therapy have had a marked influence on the developments within the field, it appears that a majority of practitioners do not follow any particular school exclusively, or limit themselves to the procedures of just one theoretical orientation. For example, in a recent survey of 855 clinical psychologists, over half of them indicated that they were eclectics (Garfield and Kurtz, 1976). Thus while much of the published works and training in psychotherapy appears to be very much "school" oriented, the devoted adherents of these schools constitute less than a majority of those engaging in psychotherapy.

A second point is that when a psychotherapist chooses to follow a given orientation, he does so primarily on bases other than scientific evidence. Many of the different approaches to psychotherapy have carried out little or no research to demonstrate the efficacy of their approach. Consequently, when an individual chooses to be a Freudian, a Jungian, an Adlerian, or an Existentialist, he does so on some other basis than the demonstrated efficacy of the approach in question. Either the person was trained in a particular orientation, received his own personal therapy from a therapist of a particular school, or for other personal reasons selects a specific type of psychotherapy as his preferred one.

A third point to keep in mind is that a designation or naming of a particular type of therapy does not necessarily tell one what specific operations are used in therapy. In other words, two therapists who label themselves identically may not actually perform in therapy in identical ways. They may utilize similar descriptive terms and theoretical constructs, but they may interact with given clients in quite different ways. Thus one cannot take school designations at face value if the actual operations in psychotherapy are the focus of interest.

Finally, as alluded to earlier, in spite of the different descriptions of the therapeutic process provided by the various schools of psychotherapy, we are still far from certain as to what processes or procedures actually produce either positive or negative changes in the patient or client. Each orientation tends to construe and to describe what actually occurs in psy-

chotherapy in somewhat different ways and in different theoretical terminology. Consequently, when all of them claim to be effective therapies, it
is difficult to discern clearly what variables in the therapeutic approach
actually produce change. Do the various psychotherapeutic approaches
secure the desired changes by different means, or are they simply using
different theoretical terms to describe what may be similar but unclearly
understood phenomena? This is an important and complex question which
will be discussed in more detail in later sections of the book.

As might be inferred from the previous references to the diversity of
psychotherapeutic approaches which currently exist, there has been a
decided growth in this area. Most of this growth has occurred in fairly
recent years, particularly in the United States where psychotherapy generally has been relatively well received. There are undoubtedly a number
of reasons for this state of affairs. One reason appears to be related to a
more benign attitude in recent years toward psychological disturbance, or
"mental illness" in general. Another related factor was the decision taken
by the federal government to provide funds for training and research in
mental health in order to more effectively meet the needs of our people.
The report of the Joint Commission on Mental Illness and Health (1961),
authorized by the United States Congress, was instrumental in this regard
and contributed to increased funding for mental health services. Partly as
a result of ensuing legislation, as well as the creation of the National Institute of Mental Health earlier, there followed an enormous expansion of
training in the basic mental health professions and in the creation of outpatient clinical facilities. One of the basic services emphasized in this development was that of psychotherapy. This was particularly true in the
period immediately following World War II. The ataraxic drugs had
not yet been developed for use with mental patients, and the newly expanded professions of clinical psychology and psychiatric social work had
psychotherapy as their sole or primary treatment. As a result, in the 25 to
30 years after the war, there was a considerable expansion in the availability of psychotherapeutic services, and psychotherapy tended to be the
main form of treatment in the outpatient mental health clinics. There also
appeared to be an increased public acceptance of psychotherapy as a
therapy for psychological disorders, particularly among the middle and
upper classes of our society.

As a result of these developments, as well as the related awareness of
the extent of the problems of psychological and emotional disturbance, the
field of psychotherapy expanded considerably. In the absence of other
proven treatments for mental disorders, and in the belief that such disorders are primarily the result of psychological variables, psychotherapy

was seen as a promising, or as a possible, treatment for a great variety of disorders and undesirable behaviors. In addition to the more traditional view of psychotherapy as a form of treatment for the psychoneurotic disorders promulgated by Freud, psychotherapy began to be advocated for a variety of conditions and social ills, including the psychoses, alcoholism, delinquency, psychosomatic illnesses, learning disabilities, and the like. Although some individuals viewed this development as a considerable overselling of the potential effectiveness of psychotherapy, it did reflect the enthusiasm that at least some practitioners of psychotherapy exhibited. Although it is probably fair to say that there is a somewhat more constrained view in evidence today, there is still considerable diversity among psychotherapists concerning the effectiveness of psychotherapy for various types of disorders. This probably varies to some extent with the professional identity and theoretical views of the individual practitioner. It may be well, therefore, to discuss in the following section the individuals who are the providers of psychotherapeutic services.

THE PSYCHOTHERAPIST

At the present time there are many routes toward becoming a psychotherapist. This is due to the fact that there is no specifically designated or recognized profession of psychotherapy. Rather, there are many professions which include psychotherapy as one of their professional functions. This situation is the more or less fortuitous result of previous historical developments. In the not too distant past, when deviant behavior was linked with evil spirits and sin, society's designated "healers" were either the state or the church. Deviates were either incarcerated or subjected to various rituals, some of which, such as being doused in water or burnt at the stake, were rather severe treatments indeed. With the advent of more modern times and with various advances in the field of medicine, deviant behavior began to be viewed as possibly organic in origin and was conceptualized as illness, specifically as mental illness supposedly due to possible dysfunction of the brain and the central nervous system. In the latter part of the 19th century, largely but not solely due to the development of psychoanalysis by Freud, some of the disorders without any clearly discernible organic causes began to be viewed as psychologically caused. Psychoanalysis provided both a theoretical explanation of neurotic disorders and a psychological means of treatment. Both the fact that such disorders were seen as illnesses and the fact that Freud was a physician tended toward the designation of psychotherapy as a form of medical therapy, even though Freud's own theoretical views were not well received by his medical colleagues. Freud (1926) himself did not believe that psychoanalysis should be viewed as a medical form of treatment, or be restricted to physicians. In fact, he believed that medical training was, at times, an impediment to the successful practice of psychoanalysis. However, this view of Freud's was not accepted by his followers in the United States, overwhelmingly psychiatrists, who stated that conditions here were very different from those in Europe, and that a great many "quacks" would be attracted to psychoanalysis if it were not restricted to physicians.

Consequently, in the first two or three decades of this century, psychotherapy, although still a modest development and dominated to some extent by psychoanalysis, was largely viewed as being within the province of medicine. Clinical psychology, for example, was primarily concerned with the use of psychological tests, and psychiatric social workers were occupied with casework. Although there were individuals in these latter professions who did engage in psychotherapy to some extent, and there were individuals engaged in counseling of an educational and vocational nature, the total number involved appears to have been small. In a similar fashion, although there were some rather well-known "lay analysts," they were few and far between.

This situation has changed noticeably in the last 25 years. As part of the postwar development mentioned earlier, there was a large increase in the number of persons trained to be clinical psychologists, psychiatric social workers, and psychiatric nurses, as well as psychiatrists. In addition, a number of other specialties such as counseling psychology, pastoral counseling, school psychology, and educational counseling also provided at least some training in counseling and psychotherapy. Furthermore, in the last decade or so, a variety of new types of mental health workers with less formal training have also appeared on the scene, all eager to provide psychological services of one kind or another. As a result, there are individuals with varying types and amounts of training in psychotherapy who, in some fashion or other, are functioning as psychotherapists.

Since the backgrounds and training of the more traditional mental health professions are probably known to most readers, these groups will be described only briefly. Psychiatrists are first trained as physicians, and although they receive some instruction in interviewing and possibly psychotherapy during their medical school period, their main training occurs during their psychiatric residency or in specialized additional training after that. Training in psychotherapy, however, is not a primary or exclusive emphasis during the psychiatric residency, but it is only one of many types of experiences provided, and the amount of time or emphasis devoted to it will vary depending upon the particular residency center. The psychiatric resident, among other things, will also be provided instruction in pharmacotherapy, neurology, the psychiatric examination, and psychopathology, as well as the opportunity of managing a ward of patients. Thus psychotherapy training will only constitute a part of the psychiatrist's instruction during the three-year period of the residency. Because of this, a number of psychiatrists who are primarily interested in psychotherapy go on to take additional training in a psychoanalytic, or other type of psychotherapy training institute. The psychiatrist who has completed his psychiatric residency may later go on to take his Boards in the specialty of psychiatry. However, these specialty examinations attempt to appraise the candidate's knowledge in the basic areas of psychiatry, and they in no way certify competency in psychotherapy per se.

The training of the clinical psychologist in the United States, although quite different from that of the psychiatrist, has certain broad similarities in outline. The student, after completion of college, during which period he will have taken a sequence of basic courses in psychology, enrolls in a doctoral program in clinical psychology. Although this program is usually described as a four- or five-year program, most students require a longer period of time to complete the program. Until very recently, all of these programs were Ph.D. programs administered through the university graduate school and the Department of Psychology. As such, there were certain general features common to most programs. Following general guidelines recommended at several national conferences on training (Raimy, 1950; Hoch, Ross, & Winder, 1966), these graduate programs stressed basic areas of general psychology, personality theory, psychopathology, diagnostic testing, research, and psychotherapy. Over the years, the emphasis on testing has diminished, whereas that on psychotherapy has increased. This has paralleled the increasing importance of psychotherapy as the primary activity of clinical psychologists (Garfield and Kurtz, 1976).

The training of clinical psychologists is thus quite different from that of the psychiatrist, although psychotherapy is included, in varying degrees, in the training of both disciplines. Although basic medicine and the use of drugs are essential features in the training of the psychiatrist, that of the clinical psychologist emphasizes basic psychology, and research competence. They merge together in terms of a common interest in psychopathology and psychotherapy, but each has its own basic traditions, values, and emphases. Whereas psychiatrists, as physicians, are more inclined to view psychological disorders as diseases or illnesses, psychologists tend more to view them as learned patterns of behavior, or habit disorders. Furthermore, because of the emphasis on research in their training, much of the research in the field of psychotherapy has been carried out by psychologists.

The pattern just described has been characteristic of the training of clinical psychologists in the United States since 1950 and is still the dominant pattern, although different programs have emerged in the last few years. Among these are the doctor of psychology programs given in a few universities and the creation of professional schools of psychology (Pottharst, 1970). In these programs the traditional training in research in order to complete a doctoral dissertation is greatly reduced or omitted, even if the degree awarded is the Ph.D. Instead, more practicum work in diagnosis and psychotherapy is provided. These developments are still too recent for one to appraise them adequately.

The training of the psychiatric social worker and the psychiatric nurse also differs noticeably from that of the psychiatrist and clinical psychologist. Most psychiatric social workers receive their training in a two-year program within a graduate school of social work, whereas the psychiatric nurse may receive a comparable period of training in a graduate program of nursing education. Again, each field has its own traditional emphases which need not be spelled out here. The total amount of training generally, and in psychotherapy specifically, will tend to be less intensive, or of shorter duration, than that of the other two professions mentioned previously, unless it is augmented by additional specialized training. Whereas social workers will work in outpatient facilities and hospitals, with some even going into private practice, nurses tend to work in hospital settings.

Besides the members of these traditional professions, there are many others who also perform some type of psychotherapeutic function (Garfield, 1977). Bearing some resemblance to the programs in clinical psychology are the doctoral programs in counseling and school psychology. Although the former traditionally have emphasized working with less severe or "normal" problems of adjustment, and the latter have been concerned with a variety of educational, as well as adjustment problems of children in the schools, both receive some training in psychotherapy or counseling and engage in such activities. However, in addition to these programs, there are many master's level programs in counseling, school psychology, and guidance, as well as in clinical psychology which provide more limited training in psychotherapeutic procedures. Besides these, there are pastoral counselors, marriage counselors, growth enhancement specialists, encounter group leaders, psychodramatists, as well as a host of others such as indigenous mental health workers, mental health associates, and the like (Garfield, 1969; Cowen, Gardner, and Zax, 1967). There is no need to go into any detailed exposition on this matter. Our purpose here is merely to illustrate the large numbers of individuals with varying types of educational backgrounds and training who may be involved in some form of psychotherapy whether it be called counseling, psychotherapy, growth experience, or what have you. In the absence of legal definitions of what psychotherapy is, and what training is required in order to engage in it, we do have somewhat of an unusual and confusing situation. The fact of the matter is that psychotherapy is not the exclusive domain of any single profession. Rather, in some guise or other, it is practiced by a great variety of individuals and professions. Although an individual may be licensed or certified to practice medicine, law, clinical psychology, or the occupation of beautician, there are no current provisions for regulating the practice of psychotherapy, except as it is related to the regulation of a recognized profession.

WHAT IS PSYCHOTHERAPY?

At this point it may be well to attempt to give the reader some general description or definition of psychotherapy, fully recognizing that it may be difficult to capture the diversity of views and practices of this field. Basically, psychotherapy consists of the interaction between two individuals, although more than two can be involved. One of the individuals, the client or patient, is the one who is seeking help for a problem that either he, some other individual or agency, or the therapist deems potentially helped by psychotherapeutic intervention. The other participant is obviously the person designated as the therapist, who supposedly has the training and personal resources to help the disturbed client. The interaction between the two participants is mediated primarily by verbal means, although bodily gestures, movements, and displays of affect also enter in. Psychotherapy thus appears to be largely a verbal interaction between two people, a therapist and a client, by means of which the former somehow attempts to help the latter to overcome his difficulties. Since verbal interactions go on between two people in many other types of interpersonal situations, one may well ask what is unique about this particular relationship or interaction, and what is there about it which somehow is potentially capable of helping a person to surmount his problems, and to improve his personal adjustment. Although the bulk of this volume is really directed to this issue, a few preliminary answers can be provided.

Although most sophisticated individuals have some conception of psychotherapy or particular psychotherapies based on their reading and other experiences, the average person may have a somewhat hazy or distorted view of what is involved. Some may tend to see the psychotherapist as similar to any other "doctor" and expect the therapist to tell them what is wrong and what needs to be done. Others, similarly, may expect the therapist to take only a few sessions in which to diagnose their difficulties and prescribe the appropriate remedy or remedial action. Some individuals may be quite skeptical of how "just talking" can in any way help them. Still others may expect the therapist to hypnotize them or in some fashion to read their minds and do something unusual. The preconceptions or expectancies that the patient brings to the therapeutic situation may thus be of some importance in terms of how therapy proceeds, particularly when these are not congruent with those of the therapist.

In many traditional forms of psychodynamic and relationship therapy, psychotherapy has been viewed as an opportunity for the individual client to explore aspects of himself that he has tended to keep from awareness, and which, theoretically, are factors in his disturbance. Whereas the therapist is there as a guide and to provide support, it is the client who must be willing to engage in what is viewed as the difficult work of self-exploration and the facing up to the negative events in his past and current life that have produced his present difficulties. Although this is a somewhat oversimplified view, it does convey one view of the therapeutic process, and one which has been a dominant view in past years. Even in some more recent variants of psychotherapy, the burden of the work for improved adjustment is placed upon the client. The client's subjective discomfort, and his motivation for change, must be such that he is willing to undertake and persevere in the sometimes arduous task of self-exploration and subsequent modification of current behaviors. Although it is, of course, easy to place all of the responsibility and blame for change or lack of change on the client, there is, clearly, some truth to the view that the client must be an interested and active participant in this process. Even in more directive therapies such as behavior therapy or rational-emotive therapy, where the client is given instructions and tasks to perform by the therapist, he will have to be an active and cooperative participant if any change is to take place (Marks, 1978). However, in the latter instances, there will be more structure and direction provided by the therapist.

Psychotherapy, then, is an interaction between the therapist and client that utilizes verbal means, but in which there are more structured roles for both participants than in many other interactions in which personal matters may be discussed. The client has to be actively involved and also be willing to discuss matters of a highly personal or confidential nature. In many instances, the topics to be discussed may be ones which are highly upsetting to him, and which he is hesitant to discuss with others. The therapist, in turn, also has a special role to play which helps to make the interaction a somewhat special one. He is supposedly an expert in the area of handling psychological distress and performs in the socially designated role of mental healer. Because of this, he is one to whom the client can turn for help, and to whom he can confide his difficulties. To the extent that the therapist is perceived as a knowing and trusted individual who will not judge the client as others might do, the client may more readily confide and expose himself to the therapist. As a result, a rather close relationship may develop between therapist and client, with the latter being able to explore himself more readily, follow the leads of the therapist, and be willing to try to change.

Whereas the above description may be most descriptive of more traditional or relationship forms of therapy, many of the general features described would also appear to apply, to some degree, to other forms of psychotherapy. Regardless of the type of therapy offered, the client is usually asked to describe his difficulties, the situations in which his problems are manifested, previous attempts to deal with them, and why he seeks therapeutic help at this time. The client is thus asked to give a frank account of his/her problems, which may be of a highly personal nature. The therapist, regardless of orientation, must inspire some degree of trust and confidence in the client if the client is to come forth willingly with such information and to continue in therapy. Furthermore, if the client perceives the therapist as an accepting person and as one promising some hope for improvement in the future, or as indicating that the client's problems are in no way unusual, the client will tend to see the therapist in a positive light. He will tend to look forward to his sessions and to place some positive value on his psychotherapy and on the new relationship with the therapist.

To some extent, therefore, the psychotherapeutic situation or relationship is a somewhat special one which may allow certain processes to occur. The highly confidential nature of the interaction, the role of the therapist as an interested and understanding expert, the discomfort or motivation of the client for possible change, and the close relationship which may develop between the two participants, are all aspects which may help to make this situation unique and potentially therapeutic. We will explore the complexities of the therapeutic interaction in much greater detail later.

THE AVAILABILITY OF PSYCHOTHERAPEUTIC SERVICES

Since we have made reference to the psychotherapist, it is worth making some mention at this point to those who seek some type of psychological help and the settings in which these are provided. A great variety of people, from all social strata and backgrounds, experience psychological distress of some sort or other and, in various ways, seek help for their difficulties. A source frequently sought for help with such problems is the family physician or, in the case of children, the pediatrician. In many instances, the individual may have some complaints which appear to be somatic or rather vague or diffuse in nature. The family's doctor is thus a first source of contact. If the discussion with the physician and/or medication, plus the passing of time, appears to alleviate the individual's complaints, no further treatment usually will be required. However, if there is no improvement and the symptoms come to be viewed as primarily psychological in nature, then the patient may be referred to a mental health professional or agency, depending on the experiences, predilections, or personal contacts of the referring physician.

In the case of children who are manifesting difficulties or behavioral disturbance in school, a somewhat different pattern may be followed. In some situations, after a report from the school, or conference with school officials, the parents may take their child to their pediatrician, consult the latter about a referral, or directly seek psychological help. In most instances, probably, the child may be referred by the teacher to the school counselor or psychologist. After some evaluation, the child may be seen by these school personnel for some type of psychological help, or recommendations will be made to the parents for appropriate referral elsewhere. In some cases, the family's minister or priest may be consulted and some type of consultation provided. This also may lead to some type of direct pastoral counseling, or to a referral elsewhere.

Although the above are significant sources of both service and referrals, with the increased public knowledge in recent years about psychological disturbances and the greater availability of resources for help with such problems, larger numbers of individuals appear to seek such help on their own or on the advice of friends who have themselves received such services. This is particularly true of the better educated individuals who are not only more knowledgeable about mental health problems and resources, but also appear to have a more positive attitude about seeking and receiving psychological help. Although attitudes toward "mental illness" have undergone some change in recent times, individuals in the lowest socioeconomic classes tend more frequently to associate shame with psychological symptoms, and to resist receiving help for their problems until the situation becomes quite acute or severe (Hollingshead and Redlich, 1958).

Another source of service and referral is made up of a variety of social and public agencies. These include social service and welfare agencies, the courts, institutions for delinquents, the aged, the physically handicapped, and other comparable agencies. Within the heterogeneous populations served by these agencies and institutions, there are manifested the usual variety of psychological disorders. Some of these institutions may be able to provide some direct service for these problems, but in many cases the individuals afflicted will be referred to more specific mental health agencies. In general, although the economic status of the individual involved may determine the type of referral made, public agencies will most likely refer their cases to other comparable agencies, whereas private practitioners such as the family physician may refer more frequently to other private practitioners.

Individuals who are seen as having psychological difficulties, therefore, may go through some sort of screening process before they finally make contact with a potential psychotherapist. A certain number will wind up with psychotherapists who are in private practice. These generally are those who are able to pay the rather substantial fees involved or who have health policies which cover such services. A large number will seek out, or be referred to, a variety of outpatient clinics in which generally the fees for service are more moderate or where the fee is determined by the patient's income. Some clinics are attached to hospitals, some to university psychology departments, some to medical schools, some are primarily community mental health centers, and some provide services specifically for children. Some may also specialize in providing one type of psychotherapy, or are geared toward a specified type of population. The Veterans Administration in the United States, for example, has a network of clinics and hospitals for military veterans. Psychotherapeutic services are also provided in both general and psychiatric hospitals.

The types of psychotherapeutic services which are offered in these institutions and situations may vary greatly. In some, the psychotherapy offered may consist of only a few interviews oriented around the current crisis, whereas in others, notably the private practice of psychoanalysis, the therapy will last for several years. In some situations the focus will be on individual therapy, whereas in others it will be on a group of individuals or a family. Who will provide the psychotherapy will also vary. In private practice it is generally individuals in the more traditional mental health professions who have completed their training and have chosen this style of professional career. In clinics, hospitals, and medical schools which are involved in training, a significant amount of the psychotherapy performed will be done by those in training—clinical psychology interns, psychiatric residents, and social work trainees. In some agencies, the personnel may be made up almost exclusively of individuals of one profession, whereas in others the staff may have a strong interdisciplinary composition. In many universities and colleges, such services are provided for students in the university counseling center or student health service.

There are thus a variety of services, at varying levels of quality, in existence for those who are in potential need for such services. The distribution and availability of services, however, varies with the personal resources and knowledgeability of prospective clients and with their location. Large urban centers such as New York and Los Angeles have large numbers of professional psychotherapists available while rural settings have considerably fewer such resources available. Important training centers for mental health personnel also contribute to the availability of such services at relatively modest cost.

THE FOCUS OF THE BOOK

Now that some introduction to the general field of psychotherapy has been presented, we can briefly describe what will be covered in the pages that follow. The main purpose of the book is to present a somewhat systematic description of what is entailed in psychotherapy as understood and described by a particular participant-observer. The objective of the author is to attempt some integration of the findings and observations in this field, paying attention to empirical data wherever possible. On a comparative basis, psychotherapy is as yet a relatively young and undeveloped field, and one in which research investigations have constituted only a relatively recent development. As has been pointed out earlier, the field has been characterized by a variety of schools and theoretical viewpoints, and much of the published material has consisted of presentations of these viewpoints primarily at a clinical level. The present volume will not duplicate such previous efforts or be a presentation of brief descriptions of selected schools of psychotherapy. Rather, the attempt will be made to provide some coherent description of the psychotherapeutic process and the roles and activities of the participants involved, as well as discussing problems of research and the gaps that exist in our current knowledge. The presentation will be eclectic in that attention will be paid to ideas and contributions from different viewpoints as they are deemed by the writer to be of value in explaining and understanding the processes of psychotherapy. An attempt will also be made to synthesize or redefine processes and procedures that have been given somewhat different designations and explanations by the different orientations in psychotherapy.

It is the author's hope, therefore, that the present volume will give the reader a comprehensive and meaningful view of psychotherapy and of the processes involved in this particular form of therapy. It is also hoped that this particular presentation will prove useful to the student or practitioner of psychotherapy, regardless of his particular professional identification or eventual theoretical allegiance.

REFERENCES

Binder, V., Binder, A., and Rimland, B. *Modern therapies.* Englewood Cliffs, N.J.: Prentice-Hall, 1976.

Cowen, E. L., Gardner, E. A., and Zax, M. (Eds.), *Emergent approaches to mental health problems.* New York: Appleton-Century-Crofts, 1967.

Garfield, S. L. New developments in the preparation of counselors. *Community Mental Health Journal,* 1969, *5,* 240–246.

Garfield, S. L. Research on the training of professional psychotherapists. In A. Gurman and A. Razin (Eds.), *Effective psychotherapy: A handbook of research.* New York: Pergamon Press, 1977.

Garfield, S. L. and Bergin, A. E. (Eds.), *Handbook of psychotherapy and behavior change,* 2nd ed. New York: Wiley, 1978.

Garfield, S. L. and Kurtz, R. Clinical psychologists in the 1970s. *American Psychologist,* 1976, *31,* 1–9.

Garfield, S. L. and Kurtz, R. A study of eclectic views. *Journal of Consulting and Clinical Psychology,* 1977, *45,* 78–83.

Hoch, E. L., Ross, A. O., and Winder, C. L. (Eds.), *Professional preparation of clinical psychologists.* Washington, D.C.: American Psychological Association, 1966.

Hollingshead, A. B. and Redlich, F. C. *Social class and mental illness: A community study.* New York: Wiley, 1958.

Joint Commission on Mental Illness and Health. *Action for mental health.* New York: Basic Books, 1961.

Kiesler, D. J. Some myths of psychotherapy research and the search for a paradigm. *Psychological Bulletin,* 1966, *65,* 110–136.

Kiesler, D. J. Experimental design in psychotherapy research. In A. E. Bergin and S. L. Garfield (Eds.), *Handbook of psychotherapy and behavior change.* New York: Wiley, 1971.

Marks, I. Behavioral psychotherapy of adult neurosis. In S. L. Garfield and A. E. Bergin, (Eds.), *Handbook of psychotherapy and behavior change,* 2nd ed. New York: Wiley, 1978.

Morse, S. J. and Watson, R. I., Jr. *Psychotherapies: A comparative casebook.* New York: Holt, Rinehart, and Winston, 1977.

Pottharst, K. E. To renew vitality and provide a challenge in training—The California School of Professional Training. *Professional Psychology*, 1970, *1*, 123–130.

Raimy, V. (Ed.), *Training in clinical psychology*. New York: Prentice-Hall, 1950.

Report of the Research Task Force of the National Institute of Mental Health. *Research in the Service of Mental Health*. DHEW Publication No. (ADM) 75–236. Rockville, Md.: 1975.

CHAPTER 2

Some Traditional Emphases and Orientations in Psychotherapy

Without going into the ancient history of healing procedures and practices, we can note that the first organized system of psychotherapy, which has exerted a considerable influence on the field, was that of psychoanalysis, the contribution of Sigmund Freud (1938). Since probably most readers have some acquaintance with the history and development of the psychoanalytic movement (Freud, 1938), there is little need for any detailed account. Instead, we can concentrate on some of the major aspects of this system that have had an important influence on the development of psychotherapy.

Freud's views of psychotherapy were influenced by the scientific and cultural trends of his time, as well as by his own clinical experience and attempts at theoretical formulations. Particularly important were his experiences with patients classified as cases of hysteria. After earlier experience with the use of hypnosis and cathartic methods, he gradually abandoned these procedures and developed the now classic procedures of psychoanalysis. These procedures or techniques of psychoanalysis were, of course, very closely intertwined with his developing notions of human personality and abnormal behavior. His views of repression, unconscious motivation, psychic determinism, and psychosexual development clearly influenced his therapeutic approach. Neurotic symptoms were viewed as manifestations of underlying conflicts the individual had repressed because they were painful and disturbing. Based on his experience with previous therapeutic procedures, Freud believed that even what appeared to be successful attempts at removing the patient's symptoms would be of short duration and that other substitute symptoms would subsequently appear. The underlying unconscious conflict was viewed as the real problem, and until this was uncovered and resolved, no lasting improvement would result. Some means had to be secured, therefore, of bringing these unconscious conflicts to the patient's awareness if positive results were to be secured. This, however, from the psychoanalytic point of view, was not a simple matter.

Because the ideas, affects, or strivings that the individual had repressed were initially very painful to him, it was not to be expected that they could easily be brought forth by the patient. Not only had the patient repressed the material and developed or utilized various defenses against their appearance in consciousness, but he appeared also to resist the attempts of the analyst to help him overcome his difficulties. This apparent paradox was explainable by means of psychoanalytic theory. Any direct attack on a patient's problems or defenses would be resisted in a number of ways because the individual experienced this as personally threatening. Any person who was utilizing psychic energy and a defensive structure to avoid facing material which was threatening to his ego would be expected to try to ward off any attempts made to actually expose such material and thus to avoid experiencing the pain which might result. Such defensive maneuvers in therapy by the patient might be manifested by being late to therapy sessions, refusing to cooperate with the analyst, dropping out of treatment, talking about trivia in the therapy sessions, and similar phenomena. Freud termed these behaviors as resistances.

As a consequence of this, as well as the fact that Freud believed, with some justification, that attempts to break down defenses and reveal unconscious material too quickly could be traumatic for many individuals, the analytic process had to take time. The process obviously had to be geared to the particular patient in terms of his own level of adjustment and his particular problems.

The primary procedure that Freud finally devised, and which by now is reasonably well known and identified with psychoanalysis, was that of free association. In this procedure, the client is requested to lie down on a couch with the analyst sitting back of her and outside of her direct line of vision. The client is instructed to relax and to allow her thoughts to flow freely, verbalizing whatever comes to mind. It is hypothesized that in such a relaxed state the client might more freely verbalize her associations, and that eventually they would indicate or lead to problem areas. For the most part, the analyst was to intrude as little as possible in order to facilitate the flow of material from the client, but he was there to observe hesitations, blockings, sudden changes in the associations, and the like. At appropriate times, comments and interpretations might be offered by the analyst, but the emphasis was on the production of associations by the client. The analyst's role, particularly in the early stages of therapy, was to facilitate the patient's free associations.

As therapy progressed, initially on an almost daily basis, the relationship between analyst and patient deepened and, at times, certain characteristic patterns of response to the therapist were manifested by the patient that Freud designated as transference reactions. In some instances the client, frequently a female one, would admit to being in love with the analyst, a situation that Freud at first found disconcerting and unanticipated. At other times, the client might show just the opposite type of reaction and accuse the analyst of being a hateful person and of not being really interested in her case. From the psychoanalytic point of view, these responses were seen as distortions on the part of the patient. The latter was not actually responding to the analyst as a real person, but instead was responding to the analyst as a substitute or father figure, with patterns or affects not allowed to be expressed to the real persons in the patient's previous experience. The patient was thus transferring such responses on to the analyst and perceiving him in a personally determined or distorted manner. Although this was considered to be a more or less typical phenomenon in psychoanalysis, individual analysts could conceivably influence the patient by how they responded to her and interacted in the therapy sessions. It was for such reasons also that it was deemed important that the analyst have some understanding of his or her own personality and not intrude it unnecessarily in the analytic session.

Although a positive transference might be viewed positively as a factor that helped motivate the patient to continue in therapy, it could not continue indefinitely if progress were to be made, and, of course, the same was true for instances of negative transference. Sooner or later, the client had to understand what the real situation was, and in this process the analyst tended to offer the client some interpretation of what was taking place. This was not as simple as it sounds, for the client might resist the interpretation offered by the analyst. The latter, however, would persist in this task, pointing out a number of associations or occurrences which tended to support his point of view. Although how this process actually worked has not been clearly delineated, the process of interpretation has received considerable emphasis in psychoanalytic writings. It is considered of decided importance in resolving transference problems, overcoming resistances in therapy, and in providing insight and understanding to the client about his underlying problems. Consequently, we will say a few more words about the matter of interpretation here and offer some more general comments about it later in the book.

The matter of the timing and accuracy of interpretation in psychoanalytic therapy have been particular topics of discussion (Hammer, 1968). Whereas an accurate and well-timed interpretation is viewed as facilitating the process and progress of psychotherapy, an inaccurate or premature interpretation may not only be nonconstructive, but is also thought to possibly retard therapy or be harmful to the patient. On the positive side, if the client accepts the interpretation offered by the analyst, it may signify that the client has enlarged his awareness of what problems are causing him difficulties, that a particular impasse in therapy has been resolved, that the interpretation probably was valid, and that the client is responding positively to the activities of the therapist. On the other hand, if the interpretation is faulty or poorly timed, not only are the converse of the previous events likely, but the resistance of the patient may be increased, and in some instances the individual may become more disturbed. That is, the premature confrontation of the patient with threatening material that he is incapable of accepting, may lead to a more serious disintegration or level of disturbance. The patient is essentially confronted with realities with which he is not yet able to cope. Interpretation, consequently, is considered to be an important aspect of psychoanalysis, and one which demands considerable skill and sensitivity on the part of the analyst if therapy is to proceed satisfactorily.

There are two other aspects of psychoanalytic therapy that have been important components of the therapy. These are the attaining of insight on the part of the client and "the working through." Freud believed that one of the essential requisites for improvement was the attainment of insight, and understanding by the client, of his underlying difficulties. Although this was viewed as a rather long and difficult process, it was considered essential for real progress. Only when the patient understood what was back of his disturbed behavior, was he gradually able to modify his behavior along more constructive channels. Instead of reacting in ways which were derived from earlier misunderstood and distorted experiences, he could then react more appropriately and realistically. Just as a client may react in therapy to the analyst as if he were her father, so many of the current behaviors outside of therapy are believed to have been determined by earlier experiences instead of the current realities. By gradually recovering some of these earlier and repressed experiences and understanding them for what they were, the client is able to enlarge her awareness of self and gradually react in a more mature and realistic manner. The interpretations offered by the analyst pertaining to the recall of dreams as well as to the associations and behaviors manifested in the therapy sessions were an important means of helping the patient to obtain insights into her behavior. Again, insights were more meaningful and readily obtainable when the patient was ready and prepared for them and the interpretations of the analyst were appropriately given.

"The process of the working through" that took place in the later stages of therapy is more difficult to desciibe. Contrary to some views, insights were not obtained usually in a dramatic "aha" or "eureka" manner. Rather, it consisted of a more continuous and repetitious process of learning until the patient had fully accepted and integrated the insight, or a number of related understandings and insights (Wolberg, 1954). The knowledge gained from therapy had to be worked through and assimilated. From this it might be inferred that how the client viewed the analyst, and how persuasive the latter was, would be important aspects of this process.

What has been described above in brief form constituted some of the main concepts and procedures in the system of psychoanalysis developed by Freud. It was the first truly comprehensive and systematic form of psychotherapy, and although it was not at first well received by Freud's medical colleagues in Vienna, it soon became the most influential school of psychotherapy. Apart from the fact that Freud attracted many zealous disciples from many parts of the world and that institutes, journals, and organizations were formed to give the movement greater unity and strength, there were no other competing systems of sufficient vitality to rival it. Most of the other emerging orientations tended to be the products of former followers of Freud, but none of the latter appeared to offer as comprehensive a system as that of Freud, or to be as good an organizer as Freud. Furthermore, Freud was an astute clinician and observer, as well as a most facile writer, and his system clearly became the dominant one for many years. Although the peak of popularity for psychoanalytic thought appears to have been reached in the 1960s, much of current psychotherapeutic work reflects the analytic emphasis, and, as we will note in later discussions, a number of Freud's observations and formulations appear to be valuable in understanding the process of psychotherapy.

OTHER RELATED EMPHASES

Although a number of the earlier followers of Freud and adherents to psychoanalysis later parted company from the mainstream of psychoanalysis, and several have been viewed as important figures in the history of psychotherapy, none of them had as large an impact or influence on the field as Freud. Although Jung and Adler were probably the best known of Freud's earlier disciples who later went their separate paths, neither one was as influential as Freud. Furthermore, both of these men's interests were wide and were not concerned primarily with therapeutic procedures per se.

Somewhat similar comments can be made about such figures as Horney (1939) and Sullivan (1953) in this country. Although Sullivan's influence was at first limited to those who had direct contact with him as a teacher, his primarily posthumous writings gave his views some following among a smaller group of psychotherapists. Horney was a more popular writer, but her works dealt in a more general way with personality and the neuroses, and to a much lesser extent with psychotherapeutic technique. To a great degree, the work of these individuals, although drawing some adherents, did not really supplant the influence of psychoanalysis on the field of psychotherapy. A number of practicing psychotherapists may have modified some of their views and procedures in some ways as a result of these newer views, particularly in giving greater significance to social forces as factors in disturbed behavior and in emphasizing the relationship between the therapist and client, but basic analytic procedures appeared to be primary. There was no new structure or system that could be viewed as a complete substitute for that of Freud's. There were some changes influenced by other factors, as well as by these newer views, but these did not necessarily imply significant modification of basic therapeutic concepts. For example, many therapists who were not admitted or did not seek entrance to the formal psychoanalytic training institutes did not follow the orthodox procedures of psychoanalysis. They did not require their patients to recline on a couch or to come for therapy as frequently as five times per week. Instead, the patient was seated on a chair and appointments would be made for two or three sessions per week, or even once a week if the therapist had unfilled time and the patient could only afford weekly visits. Sometimes, practical necessities, it appears, may override strongly held theoretical views.

Nevertheless, although some modification in procedures took place and some changes occurred also in theoretical views and emphases, many basic postulates of Freud's were adhered to by psychotherapists designated as psychodynamic. These included the concepts of repressed unconscious conflicts, transference, resistance, and the important place of interpretation and insight in psychotherapy. For example, although Horney took exception to Freud's emphasis on biological factors as opposed to social ones in neurosis, as well as his conceptions of psychosexual development and feminine personality, she still accepted the view of unconscious motivation and internalized conflicts as factors in neurotic disorders. Similarly, although Sullivan disagreed with Freud on several issues and developed some of his own concepts and terms, he, too, accepted a basic psychodynamic view of personality disturbance. To this extent, therefore, there was a basic similarity among these views, in spite of their differences. In most instances, this spoke to an exploratory and uncovering process in therapy in which some attempt was made to bring forth repressed material and to provide insight to the client. Although the interpretations among the different groups might differ, and the corresponding insights derived by the various groups of clients also might differ, the actual processes or procedures in therapy appeared more similar than otherwise. Thus while some therapists might label themselves as Freudians, some as Sullivanians, or interpersonal therapists, and some as followers of Horney, they might all refer to themselves as analysts or as carrying out psychoanalytically or psychodynamically oriented psychotherapy. They would, in most instances, also differentiate so-called supportive therapy from the more intensive uncovering, or insight producing, therapy characteristic of most of their clinical work.

Mention has been made here of psychoanalysis and psychodynamic therapies in general, because their emphases have had a decided influence on the theories and practice of psychotherapy. Many of the concepts have been used by therapists who would designate themselves as eclectic therapists. Furthermore, the analytically oriented therapists undoubtedly constituted a significant percentage of all trained therapists, and in the period following the World War II, representatives of this orientation had positions of leadership in many departments of psychiatry and in clinical psychology programs in this country. For example, one survey of clinical psychologists in the United States in 1960 reported that 41 percent of the sample studied identified themselves as following Freudian, Neo-Freudian, or Sullivanian viewpoints (Kelly, 1961). We shall also make additional references to some of these psychodynamic concepts and procedures in later discussions of the psychotherapeutic process.

THE CLIENT-CENTERED EMPHASES

A somewhat more divergent contribution comes from the work of the well-known clinical psychologist, Carl Rogers, and the client-centered school. In the late 1930s, Rogers became dissatisfied with the traditional emphases in psychotherapy and developed his own approach, which at first was called "nondirective" counseling and psychotherapy (Rogers, 1942). A later volume was titled "Client-Centered Psychotherapy" and this designation has continued as the designation of this particular orientation (Rogers, 1951).

There are several emphases in this approach which are worthy of note here. Initially, Rogers reacted negatively to the overly traditional "expert" role of the psychotherapist. Because of the potential similarity to the common roles of the physician and lawyer, the client, consequently, may expect the therapist to do something for him or to tell him what to do. If, in fact, one takes the view that the client himself has the capacity for self-exploration and change, then the traditional helping role is rather a hindrance to the emergence and facilitation of this process. This was one of the reasons that Rogers at first referred to his therapy as nondirective, and in later writings deemphasized the techniques of therapy and stressed instead the personality of the therapist and the client's capacity for change. To a certain extent, also, he tended to place greater emphasis on the feelings of the participants, rather than on the attainment of insight and cognitions.

In more recent years, the main emphases have been on the therapeutic conditions necessary for positive movement and change in psychotherapy (Truax and Carkhuff, 1967; Truax and Mitchell, 1971). Although Rogers has continued his emphasis on the potential capacity of the individual to change, the basic therapeutic conditions stressed have in actuality been characteristics of the therapist. Condensed from an initial list of six conditions (Rogers, 1957), the three that have received the most attention and research are: empathy, nonpossessive warmth, and genuineness or congruence. From the client-centered point of view, these are the sufficient and necessary conditions for change by means of psychotherapy. A therapist who manifests these attributes will facilitate personal growth and positive self-exploration on the part of the client, whereas therapists who are deficient in these qualities may not only impede therapeutic progress, but may actually make the client worse (Rogers et al., 1967).

Although therapists of other persuasions have sometimes been critical of Rogers for implying that only his approach centers on the client, it is true that Rogers' emphasis is somewhat different. He does believe in the person's implicit capacity to change and has studiously avoided any directive procedures such as expressing disapproval of client behaviors or giving advice in any form. The therapist's task is to respond accurately, sensitively, and empathically to the communications and underlying feelings of the client. Furthermore, whereas other therapeutic viewpoints have also mentioned the importance of empathy, warmth, and genuineness on the part of the therapist, none have given them the central importance accorded to them by the client-centered school, nor have they received the intensive study and research characteristic of this orientation. In this connection, it can be mentioned that some of the signal contributions of Rogers and his followers have been the early systematic study of psychotherapy, the introduction of tape recorded therapy sessions for purposes of research, and the general emphasis on research and its importance for improving the practice of psychotherapy. These individuals were in many ways the significant pioneers in research on psychotherapy—tedious and difficult though the work is. In any event, the importance of the qualities of the therapist in his interactions with the client for the progress of therapy, which has been emphasized by the client-centered school, has general implications for all psychotherapists.

COGNITIVE AND BEHAVIORAL EMPHASES

Among the more recent contributions to the field of psychotherapy are those that have come from the behavioral and cognitive orientations. Derived initially from the work of Pavlov on conditioning, and then from the later developments in learning theory, the behavioral approach has been probably the most important recent development in psychotherapy. Whereas some individuals, particularly in Europe, tend to differentiate psychotherapy from behavior therapy and imply that one practices either one or the other, there are a significant number of psychotherapists in the United States who tend to utilize procedures from both approaches (Garfield and Kurtz, 1977). In the present volume, behavior therapy will be viewed as one approach, or one form of psychotherapy.

The behavioral approach contributes emphases that, in many respects, are quite different from the more traditional approaches already mentioned. In contrast to the psychodynamic orientations, the behavioral therapists do not conceptualize or place any emphasis on unconscious motives and conflicts, and generally want nothing to do with such inferred hypothetical constructs. Rather, as their name implies, they prefer to place their emphasis on behavior. The manifestations of the client's difficulties are not to be viewed as symptoms of an underlying conflict, but instead, are to be seen for what they are, namely, disturbed or deviant patterns of behavior. Furthermore, the latter are seen as learned behaviors and as the product of faulty learning. The individual has acquired his/her fears, phobias, compulsions, and avoidant behaviors, and what has been acquired by means of learning can be modified by the proper application of the principles of learning. In essence, what has been learned can be unlearned, and there is no reason to postulate unconscious mechanisms and the like when what is involved can be more simply and economically handled by the principles of learning. Thus behavior therapy appears to be based on postulates and views that are rather the opposite of those advanced by the psychodynamic psychotherapists.

There also appear to be some important differences between the views held by client-centered therapists and those held by the behavior therapists. The role of the therapist is theoretically quite different in these two approaches. The behavior therapist clearly takes on the role of the expert healer. In addition to taking a comprehensive history from the client concerning his current complaints, the initial appearance of the disturbing behavior, the conditions under which the client's behaviors (symptoms) are more pronounced and the like, the behavior therapist generally tends to direct the therapy. He may give the client instructions in how to relax, list exercises to practice at home, instruct him in how to visualize particular experiences, and help him to construct a hierarchy of feared situations. In behaving in this fashion, the behavior therapist clearly resembles the physician and other expert healers, and is certainly not behaving in a non-directive role.

The behavior therapists have tended to focus on a thorough evaluation of the client's problems and in devising a therapeutic or remedial plan that appears appropriate for the specific case. In contrast to the client-centered and psychodynamic schools of psychotherapy, they have paid relatively little attention to the personality or personal qualities of the therapist. Such therapist variables as genuineness, empathy, and warmth receive scarce emphasis from the behavior therapist, except where positive social reinforcement is deemed necessary, and it is then viewed within a learning theory framework and perceived differently. Nevertheless, although such therapeutic conditions or therapist variables are not emphasized in the behavioral scheme of things, one must not assume that behavior therapists lack such qualities or perform in a cold and mechanistic manner. Most of them do not, and in one study in which these therapist conditions were appraised in a group of psychoanalytic therapists and a group of well-known behavior therapists, not only did both groups of therapists manifest relatively high levels of these conditions, but on some variables the behavior therapists actually exceeded their psychoanalytic counterparts (Sloane, et al., 1975). As was mentioned earlier, it is more important to examine what therapists actually do, than what they say they do.

A significant contribution of the behavioral therapists is their attempt to systematically appraise the client's problem, to formulate the problem in behavioral terms as explicitly as possible, and then to devise a specific therapeutic program for the individual client. Reasonably, one could say that, more than in most other forms of psychotherapy, the activities of the therapist are determined by this appraisal of what is required in a given case. Whereas a client-centered therapist would listen to the client and in all instances attempt to express or convey empathy, warmth, and genuine-ness—the essential therapeutic conditions—the behavior therapist, after appraising the client's problem, would have to decide on what specific pro-cedures should be utilized. Although he might use certain preferred proce-dures such as relaxation and systematic desensitization with a large number of cases, the specific fear hierarchies used most often would be developed for the particular client. Furthermore, other techniques might be used such as behavioral rehearsal, assertive training, and the like, depending on the problems involved. The tasks in therapy, and the appraisal of progress, are more clearly defined in behavioral terms and thus are more easily under-stood by the client, as well as being more readily and clearly evaluated. These emphases in behavior therapy, as might be inferred, have not been well received by many therapists of other persuasions, particularly the psy-chodynamic, humanistic, and relationship-oriented therapists, although this appears to be changing (Birk and Brinkley-Birk, 1974; Feather and Rhoads, 1972; Marmor, 1971). The research emphasis of the behaviorists, their publication of positive results, and the relative brevity of the treat-ment as compared to many others, have all contributed to the impact be-havior therapy has had on the current therapeutic scene.

The recent development of cognitive emphases in several psychothera-peutic approaches is also of some related interest. Examples here are the rational-emotive school of psychotherapy developed by Albert Ellis (1962) and the cognitive approach described recently by A. T. Beck (1976). In these and related approaches, the cause of disturbed behavior is believed to be faulty thinking or cognitions on the part of the client. The client is unhappy or depressed because he possesses faulty beliefs. These in turn lead him to have false expectations about himself and others, and, conse-quently, he experiences failure and unhappiness. For changes to occur, the client's false or distorted beliefs must be given up and more realistic ones acquired. Cognitions thus receive relatively more explicit emphasis in these approaches to psychotherapy than they do in most others. The actual role of the therapist and the procedure he follows will also differ from those of other orientations as a consequence. In contrast to the Freudian approach, a rational-emotive therapist will be more active in directly calling the atten-tion of the client to his false beliefs and his need for ridding himself of them. Various other instructions and directions may also be given to the client, including suggestions for actually performing certain activities in the client's life situation outside of the consulting office. The differences between such cognitive therapists and those who adhere to a client-centered point of view should be apparent without further comment.

Although cognitive therapies appear to have been developed independently by therapists who became dissatisfied with the effectiveness of analytically oriented therapy, they have appeared to move more closely in the last few years to some rapprochement and amalgamation with behavioral therapies and procedures. Thus one finds some mention of rational-emotive or cognitive behavioral therapy (Meichenbaum, 1977), and Beck (1976), among others, clearly acknowledges the use and value of behavioral procedures. Several individuals, primarily trained as behavior therapists, have conducted studies comparing behavioral and cognitive procedures in psychotherapy and have devised new approaches which attempt to incorporate aspects of both behavioral and cognitive therapy (Goldfried, 1971; Mahoney and Arnkoff, 1978; Meichenbaum, 1972). Although a good deal of this research is limited by being based on small numbers of subjects and by using college students as experimental clients, the work is interesting and innovative in that it attempts to use procedures from two different orientations. It suggests the possibility that one may be able, in a somewhat systematic fashion, to utilize procedures from more than one school of psychotherapy to improve the effectiveness of psychotherapy. Other suggestions along this line also have begun to appear in recent literature (Feather and Rhoads, 1972; Wachtel, 1977; Woody, 1968).

SOME ADDITIONAL EMPHASES

The procedures and emphases discussed in this chapter, and the orientations from which they have been derived, appear to the present writer to be among the most significant that have been developed in the field of psychotherapy, both theoretically and in terms of therapeutic procedures. Before discussing them further, however, mention can be made of some other emphases which appear to have had less impact on the psychotherapeutic scene, at least from a professional point of view. Although some of these developments may be viewed as differing significantly, one from the other, they are included together here for what appear to be somewhat similar emphases, although the writer's lack of expertise and sophistication with regard to these approaches may account for this view.

One such development is that of the humanistic and existential forms of psychotherapy. Although such terms often lack precise definitions and mean different things to different people, they represent approaches that are more concerned with philosophical views of man and his experience, and less with techniques and empirical findings. Binswanger (1956), Frankl (1965), and May (1958) are representative contributors to this point of view. Although such writers tend to be concerned with the human individual's existence and the experiencing of his present reality as he exists and interacts with his world in the here and now, some, such as Frankl (1965) in particular, have discussed specific techniques of therapy that, although designated differently, closely resemble techniques described by such a vastly different approach as behavioral therapy (Garfield, 1974).

Although some client-centered therapists have also placed considerable emphasis on the client's current awareness of his experience, or the process of experiencing (Gendlin, 1961), this type of emphasis is most typical of the existentialists. In fact, a study comparing the views of client-centered therapists with those of other orientations indicated that client-centered therapists resembled an eclectic group of therapists more than the humanistic or existential therapists (Garfield and Kurtz, 1975, 1976). However, there is some similarity in the common emphasis on becoming aware of one's own feelings and experiences and being in touch with them. Because of the philosophical orientation of the existentialists and their emphasis on such concepts as "existence" and "being," it would seem that this approach would appeal mainly to clients who themselves are partial to such views— namely, relatively well educated and culturally sophisticated individuals. This, however, is a conjecture on the part of the writer, since he is unaware of any studies on this matter.

A somewhat different development, but one which is included here because of its emphasis on the free expression of feelings and the current reality of the here and now, is exemplified in such approaches as Gestalt therapy and the encounter movement. Particularly in that variant of the group encounter which has been called the marathon group, which functions continuously for a few days or over a weekend, is there a heavy emphasis on emotional interactions, being open with one's feelings, and free expression of such feelings and affects. The fact that these forms of therapy or interaction are conducted in groups may facilitate the level of emotional expression and emotional contagion which appears to characterize many of these groups. At the same time, however, it is evident that the therapist, or group leader, does try to stimulate and foster such emotional arousal and expression, although there are differences among individual therapists in this regard (Lieberman, Yalom, and Miles, 1973).

Although there is some difference of opinion as to whether encounter and marathon groups ought to be viewed as psychotherapy, or as simply a group enhancement activity for "normal" people, a significant number of professional psychotherapists do engage in this type of activity. Furthermore, a number of individuals with various types of psychological difficulties seek out such groups as a means of overcoming their difficulties.

Apart from these reasons, there are other reasons for calling attention to this development here. One is the already mentioned emphasis on the expression of emotion and feeling. To the extent that affects are an important part of human experience and appear to play an important role in various types of adjustment difficulties, they should also be of some consequence in psychotherapists' efforts aimed at ameliorating such difficulties. Sheer talk is not necessarily therapeutic, and many accounts in the psychoanalytic literature have stressed the fact that purely intellectual understandings or insights on the part of the client do not appear to be very effective (Alexander and French, 1946; Wolberg, 1954). If there is to be movement and progress in psychotherapy, it appears that the client must also be emotionally involved. Otherwise, therapy becomes primarily an intellectual exercise. The emphasis on the emotional aspects provided by the encounter and related movements would thus appear to be of some potential value, even though one may feel that such an emphasis by itself is not sufficient, that it may be overdone, or that in some cases, it is potentially dangerous.

Another aspect of the marathon procedure that seems worthy of consideration pertains to the possible gains which theoretically might result from utilizing a massed type of therapy. In the marathon groups, where supposedly high levels of emotional interaction and expression are reached, it would seem reasonable to ask if this is due, in large measure, to the prolonged continuous periods of interaction. In more conventional forms of therapy, the client may be seen once or twice a week for periods of approximately 50 minutes. Because of these shorter and spaced periods of therapy, the interaction may be less intensive and therapy, therefore, may produce less emotional arousal. Although this is purely speculative, it does appear plausible. Considerations somewhat related to this were also mentioned by Freud in concluding that daily meetings of analyst and client were required if maximum benefits were to be obtained. On the other hand, many therapists feel that time is required to try out what is learned during therapy and to integrate such learning. What research is available on this issue tends to be rather inconclusive (Bednar and Kaul, 1978).

APPRAISING THE DIFFERENT EMPHASES

The newcomer to the field of psychotherapy must at times be slightly bewildered by the great array of psychotherapies, all claiming to be successful, and all providing different paths to the same goal. Besides those already mentioned, there are numerous other varieties of psychotherapy that, of necessity, must be omitted here (Binder, Binder, and Rimland, 1976; Bry, 1972; Harper, 1975; Morse and Watson, 1977). How does one choose from this vast diversity of offerings? How does one know which form of psychotherapy is best? If some comprehensive and standardized test were made in which all of the psychotherapies were compared on a common criterion with comparable groups of subjects, one might have at least some possible answers to these questions. However, this has not been done, and there does not now exist an agency such as the Federal Food and Drug Administration to test the potency and potential harmful effects of the diverse psychotherapies. There is not even a Consumer's Union available in this area! The only potential guide is the research literature and, besides its being widely scattered and deficient in many respects, the truth of the matter is that most of the psychotherapies in existence have reported little or no research.

It would appear, then, that most psychotherapists follow a particular form of psychotherapy or select their therapeutic procedures on bases other than research evidence. No systematic study of this process has ever been made. Consequently, one can only offer some conjectures about what appears to take place, based on personal experience and observations, as well as one study of eclectic clinical psychologists (Garfield and Kurtz, 1977).

Some psychotherapists appear to be influenced by the particular approach emphasized during their training, either undergraduate or graduate. In the former case it appears to be a somewhat fortuitous occurrence since students at that stage have relatively little knowledge about the field. During their professional, graduate, or postgraduate training, students generally become more selective, choosing a school or program which is in line with their current preferences. This is probably most likely where a specific institution is known for fostering a particular viewpoint. In such instances, individuals may be attracted to a particular viewpoint for a variety of personal reasons. Either one theoretical viewpoint is intellectually attractive, it appears in accord with one's own personal experience, one has been greatly influenced by an individual of a given persuasion, or the individual's own therapy has made a deep impression on him. After the individual has completed his professional training, he may also modify his views and therapeutic procedures on the basis of his own practice or as a result of attending professional meetings, special institutes, participation in a group, and the like. The individual's personality may also influence how he responds to a particular orientation, and how he interprets it and adapts it to his own practice. No two therapists of the same school necessarily function in psychotherapy in exactly the same manner (Glover,

1955; Lieberman, Yalom, and Miles, 1973; Luborsky and Spence, 1971).

In numerous discussions with individuals engaged in psychotherapy, many of them have said that they follow a particular orientation or have evolved procedures which suit them personally. In many instances, also, there is an implication that they are using procedures which they have found to be more effective than others. On the other hand, it appears also as if therapists are utilizing an approach which they find personally gratifying, and these two aspects are not necessarily identical. For example, some doctoral students have told me that they prefer one type of therapy over another because it is more interesting and exciting than another, or that they deem one specific form of therapy as being rather boring. They do not make any reference to the effectiveness of the respective therapies, but rather to the personal satisfaction secured from using one approach over another—and attempts that are made to have them become more concerned with the former matter are not always successful.

Thus there are many different reasons for individuals choosing certain approaches to psychotherapy, and personal predilections and fortuitous circumstances appear to be as frequent as considerations of proven merit. Whereas this appears to be a current reality, there is an obvious need to try to order, appraise, and integrate those procedures that appear to be similar in many of the different approaches or that, on the basis of experience and research, appear to have some therapeutic merit. This, essentially, is the goal of the present volume, and the preceding pages have been an attempt to highlight different emphases which have been important in the development of psychotherapy, as well as illustrating some of the wide differences in orientations and procedures. Taken at face value, the various emphases discussed would appear so different that it would appear extremely difficult, if not impossible, to reconcile them into some ordered fashion. Although this is undoubtedly true to some extent, and staunch believers of any view will not be swayed, the task may not be as impossible as it appears to be. In order to do this, however, it is essential to try to look impartially at a given concept and to examine what it means operationally. One who has been indoctrinated into perceiving a given phenomenon in a specified way may find it difficult to change and perceive matters in a different light. We know from studies of attitude change, as well as from our work in psychotherapy, that it is not an easy matter to change people's views and perceptions, particularly where a person's emotions and personal security are involved. However, change is possible, and it also provides the basis for possible progress. Consequently, the task appears worthy of the effort, although the goal may not be completely attained.

A few examples of what is involved may be appropriate here. On a very broad level, we have discussed different approaches to psychotherapy that seem to emphasize a different aspect or aspects of human experience. At least in their written formal presentations, some approaches emphasize behavioral means of effecting change, some stress cognitions as the important avenue to change, and others appear to focus on affective experiences as the crucial variables in psychotherapy. On the surface, these varying approaches appear to be stressing very different pathways to a common goal. However, these different conceptualizations of what occurs appear to be overly generalized or focused abstractions of what actually takes place. The human being functions as a total organism, and it is highly doubtful that one can focus exclusively on cognitions without in some way involving behaviors or affects simultaneously or in some interactive manner. Verbal communications from one individual to another are not simply intellectual messages, although they can be in some instances. They can, however, cause an individual to become angry, frightened, or elated, as well as causing him to strike another person, to run away, or to faint and lose consciousness. Verbal communication can be a rather powerful means of inducing changes in people, although there is much that we still need to learn about how to use it for constructive purposes in psychotherapy.

In a similar fashion, whereas client-centered therapists have emphasized the importance of the therapist's empathy, warmth, and genuineness and have performed most of the research in this area, one cannot state that other therapists do not display or incorporate such attributes in their therapeutic work with clients. Although behavior therapists have paid scant attention to such therapist attributes in their publications and research, at least one important study, utilizing scales developed by client-centered therapist researchers, has shown that high levels of these attributes were manifested by behavioral therapists in their therapy with actual clients (Sloane et al., 1975). In other words, although adherents of a given orientation may make little or no reference to particular variables or procedures in their formal writings, this does not signify that the variables in question are not being utilized by these therapists. A given theoretical system appears to develop from the particular observations and conceptual formulations of an individual as he tries to organize his particular views of the phenomena in question. He attempts to make them fit together and become a coherent system. Once a particular stance or frame of reference is adopted, it will influence the observations and formulations of the individual involved. The individual, of necessity, will have to be selective, and concepts which appear to be grossly different or in opposition to the basic concepts held will be slighted or discarded. Consequently, some aspects of psychotherapy will tend to be emphasized by one school and given little or no mention by another.

It is also quite likely that essentially similar phenomena may be described and designated in somewhat different ways by some of the orientations in psychotherapy, as well as receiving different emphases. For example, the particular system of psychotherapy called psychodrama (Moreno, 1946) utilized role playing on the part of the therapist and patient for many years before other therapists made use of this procedure. It appeared later in the writings of behavior therapists under the designation of "behavioral rehearsal." Similarly, one can note the same type of procedure described by an early behaviorist, and by a more recent existentialist. Knight Dunlap, writing over 40 years ago, described a procedure which he termed *negative practice*. This had to do with attempts to correct persistent errors in typing. If an individual frequently typed "TEH" instead of "THE," instructions to consciously type "TEH" appeared to correct the error. In a similar way, Frankl (1965) describes the conscious and deliberate use of a procedure by which a patient focuses deliberately on the behavior she wants to avoid, and terms this "paradoxical intention." Other examples of this type could also be secured.

A final point to be considered here is the fact that despite such different formulations and emphases, all of the different varieties of psychotherapy claim to be successful. None of them claim to be less effective than the others, and I have yet to hear a psychotherapist tell me that his own psychotherapy was an inferior form of psychotherapy. This is a phenomenon that has intrigued me for many years, and that has clearly influenced my own views on psychotherapy (Garfield, 1957, 1974a and b). It deserves some further comment here, although it was referred to earlier.

Although it is conceivable that each of the different varieties of psychotherapy represent a unique and different means of effecting positive change in client behaviors, it is also likely that the factors emphasized by the different approaches are either similar operationally, or *are not* the crucial variables responsible for change. In other words, although one school emphasizes insight, another desensitization, and yet another empathy and warmth, it is conceivable that these variables as postulated are not the crucial ones. Rather, there may be other variables or components of these variables which are common to most of the psychotherapies, but which receive little attention and emphasis in the different theoretical formulations. One example may suffice for the present, although this topic will receive more attention in a later section of the book.

Let us take the matter of insight for illustrative purposes. Insight into one's underlying problems is considered important by most psychodynamically oriented therapists. However, what is insight and how is it acquired? An understanding of one's underlying problems is derived by verbal interactions with a therapist and will be influenced by the latter's own theoretical views. Consequently, the insights obtained from a psychoanalyst will be quite different from those obtained by followers of Alfred Adler or Karen Horney. In the first instance, it is likely that the individual will gain insight into his sexual or aggressive conflicts deriving from earlier stages of his psychosexual development. Such an insight would very likely not be obtained from an Adlerian therapist. Instead, in such therapy the client possibly would be given an understanding of the importance of his role in the family, his feelings of inferiority, and his attempts to compensate for these feelings. The followers of Horney would seem to provide still another type of insight for their patients—yet all the patients would supposedly benefit from these very different insights.

It is possible, therefore, that it is not the specific "insights" secured by the patients which are in fact therapeutic, but something else. Furthermore, whatever this something else is, it would appear to be similar among the three different approaches mentioned. If we look more closely at this situation, we can at least hypothesize that perhaps one common aspect is that the therapist provides the patient with some explanation for his difficulties. It would appear, hypothetically, that what is told the patient is not of particular import since each of the patients is told something very different. However, the explanation provided and apparently accepted by the client appears to be of some therapeutic value. Apparently then, being given some explanation of one's problems by an interested expert in the role of healer may be the important common aspect of these divergent therapies (Frank, 1971; Torrey, 1972). This, of course, is not to say that this is all there is to psychotherapy or that an understanding of one's difficulties is the crucial variable. It is simply an attempt to illustrate how some of the emphasized theoretical postulates of differing schools of psychotherapy may be viewed from a different perspective, and also the possible importance of some potential common attributes of psychotherapy when looked at in this way.

Even the behavior therapists, who say practically nothing about insight in psychotherapy and would feel that it is of no consequence in their therapy, can be shown to have something in common with the orientations referred to in our illustrations previously. The behavior therapists who use systematic desensitization generally provide the client with some understanding of the procedures to be used and their rationale. To this extent, therefore, they also provide the client with some insight and understanding of how his problems have developed and how therapy can be expected to modify his current behavior. Although not insight in the traditional psychoanalytic sense, to the extent that such procedures provide the client with an understanding of his difficulties, they may serve a similar function.

Because of what has been discussed in the preceding pages, it does not seem wise at this point in the history of psychotherapy to present only one system of psychotherapeutic procedure, or to cling too tenaciously to any fixed views. At the same time, a simple cataloging of a number of different therapeutic systems, while interesting, does not give any really clear or coherent understanding of the psychotherapeutic process. It is the latter that we will at least strive for in the remainder of the book.

REFERENCES

Alexander, F. and French, T. M. *Psychoanalytic therapy.* New York: Ronald, 1946.

Beck, A. T. *Cognitive therapy and the emotional disorders.* New York: International Universities Press, 1976.

Bednar, R. L. and Kaul, T. J. Experiential group research: Current perspectives. In S. L. Garfield and A. E. Bergin (Eds.), *Handbook of psychotherapy and behavior change,* 2nd ed. New York: Wiley, 1978.

Binder, V., Binder, A. and Rimland, B. *Modern therapies.* Englewood Cliffs, N.J.: Prentice-Hall, 1976.

Binswanger, L. Existential analysis and psychotherapy. In F. Fromm-Reichman and J. L. Moreno (Eds.), *Progress in psychotherapy 1956.* New York: Grune and Stratton, 1956, pp. 144–148.

Birk, L. and Brinkley-Birk, A. W. Psychoanalysis and behavior therapy. *American Journal of Psychiatry,* 1974, *131,* 499–509.

Bry, A. *Inside psychotherapy.* New York: Basic Books, 1972.

Ellis, D. *Reason and emotion in psychotherapy.* New York: Lyle Stuart, 1962.

Feather, B. W. and Rhoads, J. M. Psychodynamic behavior therapy. I. Theory and rationale. *Archives of General Psychiatry,* 1972, *26,* 496–502.

Frank, J. D. Therapeutic factors in psychotherapy. *American Journal of Psychotherapy,* 1971, *XXV,* 350–361.

Frankl, V. E. *The doctor and the soul,* 2nd ed. New York: Alfred A. Knopf, 1965.

Freud, S. The history of the psychoanalytic movement. In *The basic writings of Sigmund Freud.* New York: Modern Library, Random House, 1938.

Garfield, S. L. *Introductory clinical psychology.* New York: Macmillan, 1957.

Garfield, S. L. *Clinical Psychology: The study of personality and behavior.* Chicago: Aldine, 1974a.

Garfield, S. L. What are the therapeutic variables in psychotherapy? *Psychotherapy and Psychosomatics,* 1974b, *24,* 372–378.

Garfield, S. L. and Kurtz, R. Clinical psychologists: A survey of selected attitudes and values. *The Clinical Psychologist,* 1975, *28,* 4–7.

Garfield, S. L. and Kurtz, R. Clinical psychologists in the 1970s. *Amercian Psychologist,* 1976, *31,* 1–9.

Garfield, S. L. and Kurtz, R. A study of eclectic views. *Journal of Consulting and Clinical Psychology,* 1977, *45,* 78–83.

Gendlin, E. T. Experiencing: A variable in the process of psychotherapeutic change. *American Journal of Psychotherapy,* 1961, *15,* 233–245.

Glover, E. *The technique of psychoanalysis.* New York: International Universities Press, 1955.

Goldfried, M. R. Systematic desensitization as training in self-control. *Journal of Consulting and Clinical Psychology,* 1971, *37,* 228–234.

Hammer, E. R. (Ed.), *Use of interpretation in treatment.* New York: Grune and Stratton, 1968.

Harper, R. A. *Psychoanalysis and psychotherapy: 36 systems.* Englewood Cliffs, N.J.: Prentice-Hall, 1959.

Harper, R. A. *The new psychotherapies.* Englewood Cliffs, N.J.: Prentice-Hall, 1975.

Horney, K. *New ways in psychoanalysis.* New York: W. W. Norton, 1939.

Kelly, E. L. Clinical psychology—1960: Report of survey findings. *American Psychological Association, Division of Clinical Psychology Newsletter,* 1961, *14*(1), 1–11.

Lieberman, M. A., Yalom, I. D., and Miles, M. B. *Encounter Groups: First facts.* New York: Basic Books, 1973.

Luborsky, L. and Spence, D. P. Quantitative research on psychoanalytic therapy. In A. E. Bergin and S. L. Garfield (Eds.), *Handbook of psychotherapy and Behavior Change.* New York: Wiley, 1971.

Mahoney, M. J. and Arnkoff, D. B. Cognitive and self-control therapies. In S. L. Garfield and A. E. Bergin (Eds.), *Handbook of psychotherapy and behavior change,* 2nd ed. New York: Wiley, 1978.

Marmor, J. Dynamic psychotherapy and behavior therapy. Are they irreconcilable? *Archives of General Psychiatry,* 1971, *24,* 22–28.

May, R. Contributions of existential psychotherapy. In R. May, E. Angel, and H. F. Ellenberger (Eds.), *Existence: A new dimension in psychiatry and psychology.* New York: Basic Books, 1958, pp. 37–91.

Meichenbaum, D. Cognitive modification of test anxious college students. *Journal of Consulting and Clinical Psychology,* 1972, *39,* 370–380.

Meichenbaum, D. (Ed.), *Cognitive behavior modification: An integrative approach.* New York: Plenum, 1977.

Moreno, J. L. *Psychodrama, Vol. 1* (2nd rev. ed.). New York: Beacon House, 1946.

Morse, S. J. and Watson, R. I., Jr. *Psychotherapies. A comparative casebook.* New York: Holt, Rinehart, and Winston, 1977.

Rogers, C. R. The necessary and sufficient conditions of therapeutic personality change. *Journal of Consulting Psychology,* 1957, *21,* 95–103.

Rogers, C. R., Gendlin, E. T., Kiesler, D. J., and Truax, C. B. *The therapeutic relationship and its impact: A study of psychotherapy with schizophrenics.* Madison: University of Wisconsin Press, 1967.

Sloane, R. B., Staples, F. R., Cristol, A. H., Yorkston, N. J. and Whipple, K. *Psychotherapy versus behavior therapy.* Cambridge: Harvard University Press, 1975

Sullivan, H. S. *The interpersonal theory of psychiatry.* New York: W. W. Norton, 1953.

Torrey, E. F. What western psychotherapists can learn from witchdoctors. *American Journal of Orthopsychiatry,* 1972, *42,* 69–76.

Truax, C. B. and Carkhuff, R. R. *Toward effective counseling and psychotherapy.* Chicago: Aldine, 1967.

Truax, C. B. and Mitchell, K. M. Research on certain therapist interpersonal skills in relation to process and outcome. In A. E. Bergin and S. L. Garfield (Eds.), *Handbook of psychotherapy and behavior change.* New York: Wiley, 1971.

Wachtel, P. L. *Psychoanalysis and Behavior Therapy.* New York: Basic Books, 1977.

Wolberg, L. R. *The technique of psychotherapy.* New York: Grune and Stratton, 1954.

Woody, R. H. Toward a rationale for psychobehavioral therapy. *Archives of General Psychiatry,* 1968, *19,* 197–204.

CHAPTER 3

*Client Variables in Psychotherapy**

In attempting to understand the psychotherapeutic process, it is apparent that there are three main variables that may influence what takes place. These are the client or patient, the psychotherapist, and the interaction between these two participants in therapy. The social and environmental factors that impinge on the client also constitute a variable of some importance in some instances, but we will be concerned primarily with the other three variables. Important influences on the client will tend to be viewed as pertaining to the client variable where possible.

Since the primary focus in psychotherapy is the client and the problems he or she is experiencing, it is well to devote attention to this important participant early in our presentation. Some general mention was made of the consumer of psychotherapeutic services in the first chapter, but here we will examine the client's attributes and participation as they pertain more specifically to the process and outcome of psychotherapy.

A great deal has been said and written about the client in psychotherapy, and a number of studies have been carried out which have attempted to relate client attributes to other selected variables in psychotherapy (Garfield, 1978). To the extent that findings from research investigations are replicated, we have a reasonably firm basis on which to draw conclusions. In this fashion, as is true in other fields of knowledge, clinical hypotheses and folklore can be supported or found wanting. Because research in psychotherapy is complex and of relatively recent vintage, there are many areas that, as of now, have received scant attention. Where research findings are available, we shall attempt to refer to them in our discussion of the client, as well as other variables. In other instances, the lack or need of research will be noted and the author's own views clearly identified.

As indicated in Chapter 1, a variety of individuals with many different types of problems seek out psychotherapeutic help on their own or are referred through various channels. Depending on the circumstances of a

* This chapter is based in large part on the author's review of the research literature on this topic that was published previously (Garfield, 1978).

given situation, the individual may wind up seeing a psychiatrist or clinical psychologist in private practice, or a therapist from any one of a number of professions in a clinic or hospital. Within limits, psychotherapy has been emphasized as a treatment modality for patients diagnosed roughly as neurotic or with personality disorder in outpatient settings, although medication may also be used in cases of depression and severe anxiety. In the case of individuals considered to be psychotic, ataraxic and other drugs often are relied upon, although psychotherapy may also be utilized as well for some patients. Thus, to a certain extent, psychotherapy tends to be emphasized as a treatment modality with patients who are not the most seriously disturbed.

Apart from degree of disturbance, clients can also be characterized in a number of other different ways. Some of the characteristics that have been considered of possible significance and have been investigated to some extent are sex, age, social class, race, education, degree of discomfort, intelligence, psychiatric diagnosis, motivation for therapy, and a variety of personality characteristics. Some of these attributes, such as sex, are reasonably easy to appraise in a reliable manner, and age can be studied as a quantitatively continuous variable. However, when one attempts to deal with such inferred client characteristics as motivation for therapy and personality dimensions, the resulting investigation is beset by many difficulties which need not be spelled out at present. Even such a widely used designation as psychiatric diagnosis suffers from limited reliability (Garfield, 1974). Consequently, on some of these topics we may expect to find differences in the various reports in the literature and to encounter some difficulty in securing reliable generalizations.

Before we proceed to examine more specific client characteristics and their relationship to different aspects of psychotherapy, one additional point should be made. In any presentation of a complex phenomenon, it is usually desirable to discuss the separate component parts which make it up. However, it is important to realize that such an analysis cannot fully describe the reality of the total phenomenon or process. In psychotherapy, the client's attributes and behaviors are influenced to an important extent by those of the therapist, and the reverse is also true. However, in analyzing the interaction that takes place, it appears necessary at first to focus on the individual participants and their particular roles and contribution to this interaction. Thus when we examine client variables in relation to such criteria as outcome or continuation in psychotherapy, we should keep in mind that such findings have been secured from a particular group of clients who received psychotherapy from a given group of therapists. In any given instance, however, the particular results secured for a client conceivably could have been influenced to some extent by the particular therapist involved. Nevertheless, such findings do provide us with some useful information about what actually occurs in the day-to-day clinical practice of psychotherapy. For such reasons we shall first review representative findings on client variables in relation to selected aspects of psychotherapy. Although these findings will not inform the reader about how to conduct psychotherapy, they should be of value to him in helping him to understand, in a general way, some of the problems and realities of psychotherapy as it currently takes place. Some of the findings may even be quite surprising—for what occurs in clinical practice may not be quite the same as what is frequently depicted in some of the writings and popular presentations about psychotherapy, or even what a practitioner believes based on his own limited experience.

THE SELECTION AND ACCEPTANCE OF CLIENTS FOR PSYCHOTHERAPY

Most of the reports on who is selected for psychotherapy tend to come from studies of clinics and from community surveys. There is relatively little information concerning clients treated by private practitioners, although there are a few limited surveys of individuals seen by psychoanalysts. It appears very likely that there are important differences in the populations served by the therapists in these different settings. On the basis of some reports at least, the clientele of the private practitioners of psychoanalysis is made up disproportionately of individuals of the higher socioeconomic and educational levels (Hamburg et al., 1967; Knapp et al., 1960), and one can assume that there is a high degree of selectivity in the patients accepted for such treatment. Community clinics and outpatient departments in hospitals, while having some variation in selection criteria, will generally have a less selected group of patients (Garfield, 1978; Kadushin, 1969). In any event, let us proceed to a review of some of the findings in this area.

The first point that can be made is that not all individuals who apply for treatment receive psychotherapy. In addition, not all who are actually offered psychotherapy accept it, a finding that many beginning and interested students find hard to understand. In three reported earlier studies, approximately one-third or more of the individuals coming to a clinic and judged to be in need of psychotherapy refused the treatment after it was offered to them (Garfield and Kurz, 1952; Rosenthal and Frank, 1958; Weiss and Schaie, 1958). More recently, Marks (1978) also reports that of several hundred patients offered behavioral therapy at the Maudsley Hospital, 23 percent refused the offered therapy. In two studies of outpatients at Boston City Hospital, approximately 40 percent of the patients failed to show up for their scheduled first appointment (Raynes and Warren, 1971a and b). On the basis of such reports, one can anticipate that in most outpatient settings, a relatively large number of patients who have been scheduled for psychotherapy will decline this opportunity by failing to keep their appointments. Thus perhaps surprisingly, there will be a significant number of clients who appear in clinical settings who will actually reject psychotherapy when it is offered to them.

Several studies have investigated some of the possible factors related to this nonacceptance of psychotherapy, although there do not appear to be any reports of interviews with such individuals concerning their reasons for refusing psychotherapy. A significant relationship between acceptance on the part of the client and client income, and also between acceptance and rated level of client motivation, was secured in a study by Rosenthal and Frank (1958). In one other study, a significant correlation was reported between lower socioeconomic status and the failure of the client to keep his initial appointment (Yamamoto and Goin, 1966), but in another study no significant findings were secured for such variables as sex, education, or age (Noonan, 1973). It was also noted in the latter study that those who failed to keep their first therapy appointment tended to present their problems in a vague and evasive manner as compared with those who kept their appointments. Although the evidence is not conclusive, there appears to be some relationship between social class variables and failure to accept psychotherapy.

A related aspect pertains to those who appear at clinics but who are not offered psychotherapy. Several studies have reported a positive relationship between social class indices and acceptance for psychotherapy (Brill and Storrow, 1960; Cole, Branch, and Allison, 1962; Rosenthal and Frank, 1958; Schaffer and Myers, 1954). Somewhat comparable findings have been reported for those clients who are referred for psychotherapy as compared with referral for other types of treatment (Bailey, Warshaw, and Eichler, 1959; Lubin et al., 1973). In the study by Lubin et al. (1973), patients with some college education and relatively higher occupational ratings were more frequently assigned to psychotherapy than were individuals with less than 12 years of education and lower rated occupations. In another study of a walk-in clinic, a significant relationship was reported between low socioeconomic status and the frequency of receiving drugs rather than psychotherapy (Shader, 1970).

Several other investigations have also indicated a relationship between social class indices and the type of therapy received. This was clearly shown in the now classic study by Hollingshead and Redlich (1958) of New Haven where long-term psychoanalytic therapy was provided primarily to the middle and upper classes. A survey of mental health activities in Boston also showed that the patients of private psychiatrists are a highly selected group, being predominantly women who have had some college education (Ryan, 1969). Similarly, in New York City, Kadushin (1969) found that social class differentiated the applicants to various clinics and that "the more closely affiliated a clinic is with the orthodox psychoanalytic movement, the higher the social class of its applicants will be" (Kadushin, 1969, p. 51).

It would appear, therefore, that there is some selectivity in terms of what types of individuals are selected for psychotherapy and that socioeconomic factors play a role in this selection. Furthermore, there also appear to be degrees of selectivity in terms of the nature of the clinic or source of the psychotherapeutic service offered, as well as, perhaps, in the type of treatment offered. Consequently, generalizations about psychotherapy clients in general must be cautious ones in the light of variations in selectivity among the different clinical settings. We shall postpone any further consideration of client attributes per se until we have examined some additional aspects of psychotherapy which have relevance for this topic.

THE PROBLEM OF CONTINUATION IN PSYCHOTHERAPY

One of the intriguing phenomena in psychotherapy, which first attracted my attention almost 30 years ago, was that a number of patients, with evident need for psychotherapy, failed to keep their appointments after only a few interviews. They simply dropped out of therapy. Although my colleagues at the Veterans Administration Clinic, in which I was working, did not appear to pay much attention to this phenomenon, I found it both mystifying and perplexing. Such an occurrence was rarely mentioned in the books on psychotherapy. Instead, psychotherapy tended to be described as a rather long process, and despite client resistance and negative transference, it seemed to result in a happy and harmonious ending. This, clearly, was not my own experience with a moderate number of patients, and as a result, I decided, with the aid of a colleague, to carry out a study on all of the cases which had been terminated since the inception of the clinic. The results, based on analyzing over 1,000 case files and published in 1952, were quite interesting (Garfield and Kurz, 1952). Although the clinic staff saw themselves as doing psychoanalytically oriented intensive therapy, the median number of interviews of the 560 cases on whom adequate data were available was actually six interviews. In other words, by the sixth interview, half of the patients had prematurely terminated their therapy. Furthermore, almost 43 percent of the patients discontinued before the fifth interview, and only 8.8 percent remained for 25 or more therapy sessions. This was a startling finding as far as the clinic staff was concerned, although, in searching the literature, I did find a few studies published in the preceding 4 years with comparable results.

Since that time, there have been a number of additional studies reported which have tended to support these findings, and a review of these data are available elsewhere (Garfield, 1978). It appears to be a reasonably reliable fact that a large number of individuals who begin a course of psychotherapy, terminate their therapy after only a few interviews. Furthermore, this pattern of premature termination is found in Veterans Administration clinics, in psychiatric clinics, in medical schools, in state and community clinics, and probably in private practice as well, although there have been very few reports from the latter source.

Although the writer is aware that he probably has a greater interest in this problem than most psychotherapists, a few additional studies are worth mentioning. One is a previous report by the National Center for Health Statistics (1966) concerning the clients who consulted a psychiatrist during a 12-month period. The average number of visits was 4.7. Ediuson (1968), in a review of the literature, concluded that "30 to 65 percent of all patients are dropouts in facilities representing every kind of psychiatric service." Two quite recent studies of urban mental health clinics also show a high dropout rate. In one based on three such centers, 37 to 45 percent of the patients terminated therapy after the first or second interview (Fiester and Rudestom, 1975), and in another, 43 percent terminated before the fourth interview (Craig and Huffine, 1976).

Such findings rarely have been given much attention in most treatises on psychotherapy, yet they are important data. Therapists should have some knowledge of them so that their expectations about the length of psychotherapy are within the bounds of reality. Too frequently, therapists in training have the expectation, derived from diverse sources, that psychotherapy generally is going to be a rather long process and that the client also shares this expectation. Thus when the student in training, in spite of the attempts made to assign "good teaching cases," is faced with the sudden and unexpected departure of his client, he is profoundly disappointed, to say the least. For many years this problem tended to be slighted, but it has received increasing attention in recent years, and as a result, some attempts have been made to improve this situation (Garfield, 1978; Heitler, 1976). Reference to this work will be made in later sections of the book. Now it is pertinent to examine the problem of early termination further by reviewing what types of clients or client variables may be related to early discontinuation.

A large number of studies examining a variety of variables have been reported. Since the studies in this area have been evaluated in a recent review by the present writer (Garfield, 1978), no detailed review will be presented here. Rather, we shall review briefly only those findings that appear to be of potentially greatest importance, mention some of the major conclusions, and refer to illustrative studies.

Those variables that appear to show the most reliable relationship to continuation in psychotherapy are again social class variables, even though the findings are by no means uniform or consistent. A majority of the studies in this area, using such criteria as the Hollingshead Index of Social Class, occupational status or level of education, have found a positive relationship between these indices and continuation in psychotherapy. A greater proportion of those in the lower socioeconomic groups and of lower educational accomplishment drop out of therapy earlier than do their counterparts from higher socioeconomic and educational levels (Garfield, 1978). Individuals with a better education may not only be better informed and more sophisticated about psychotherapy, but to the extent that they are more similar to their therapists in cultural background and verbal communication, an easier and more comfortable relationship between therapist and client may result. As a consequence, upper class clients may appear to their therapists as more suitable for and more highly motivated toward psychotherapy, as well as being able to perceive psychotherapy as a desirable form of therapy.

Whereas social class variables have shown a relatively consistent relationship to continuation in psychotherapy, a number of other variables that have been studied in this regard have demonstrated little or no such relationship. Sex of client, for example, has been investigated in a number of studies. Most of the results have revealed no significant differences between males and females in terms of premature termination (Affleck and Garfield, 1961; Craig and Huffine, 1976; Frank et al., 1957; Garfield and Affleck, 1959; Grotjahn, 1972; Koran and Costell, 1973). In four other studies, males were reported as more frequent continuers in psychotherapy, although, in some, only a small proportion of the total variance could be attributed to the sex of the patient (Brown and Kosterlitz, 1964; Cartwright, 1955; Rosenthal and Frank, 1958; Weiss and Schaie, 1958). Although the results appear to be somewhat mixed, it does not seem that the sex of the client is a significant predictor of continuation in psychotherapy.

Age is another client variable that has received some attention in clinical writings on psychotherapy, although with little reference to continuation. Whereas some therapists appear to prefer younger patients, the research that has been done does not indicate that age is significantly related to remaining in therapy (Affleck and Garfield, 1961; Cartwright, 1955; Frank et al., 1957; Garfield and Affleck, 1959; Rosenthal and Frank, 1958; Rubinstein and Lorr, 1956). Where age was found to differentiate between those who continue in psychotherapy from those who did not at a statistically significant level, the mean difference in age was less than 2 years, and this is of little value for practical purposes (Sullivan, Miller, and Smelzer, 1958).

Another variable that has been investigated is that of psychiatric diagnosis or patient classification. In general, the diagnosis of the patient has not been found to bear any significant relationship to premature termination (Affleck and Garfield, 1961; Bailey, Warshaw, and Eichler, 1959; Garfield and Affleck, 1959; Lief et al., 1961; Pope, Geller, and Wilkinson, 1975; Rosenthal and Frank, 1958). Thus neither sex, age, nor psychiatric diagnosis appears to be a significant client variable where predicting continuation in psychotherapy is concerned. More recently, race has also been investigated as a possible variable in this connection. However, the problem is a complex one and is often confounded with socioeconomic variables. At present, there do not seem to be sufficient and clear cut data upon which to base any reliable conclusions (Garfield, 1978; Sattler, 1977).

Another set of client variables which has received rather considerable attention pertains to the personality attributes of the client. These have been investigated by a variety of psychological tests and clinical measures. Because of the great variety of techniques used to appraise client personality variables, as well as the numerous methodological problems involved in this research (Garfield, 1978), we will have to limit our discussion to a few general observations. Before doing so, however, a few comments on research in this and related areas should be presented.

Earlier, the point was made that clinics and practitioners may vary with regard to the selectivity of their patients. As a consequence of this, as well as of other factors, samples of patients used for research purposes may not be comparable. Consequently, the consistency of results and the possibility of meaningful generalization from the results obtained are also limited. If the measures used to appraise client characteristics lack reliability or validity, similar problems will be apparent. Furthermore, if premature termination or continuation in psychotherapy is defined differently in various studies, the comparability of results is also hindered. It is possible, too, for any one of a number of reasons, that the results obtained in any single investigation may be due to chance or to some particular bias or selectivity. In the complicated domain of psychotherapy, any one or all of such possible occurrences may take place and, unfortunately, have taken place. As a result, one tends to find a moderate amount of conflicting findings in the literature and failures to replicate earlier findings. As a consequence, while it is important to keep abreast of the research in one's area of work, it is also equally important to evaluate the adequacy of this research. One procedure which the author strongly recommends is to treat any single research report as a preliminary report until the findings have been replicated, unless, of course, an analysis of the study reveals such significant deficiencies that the results can be safely discarded without any concern over replication.

In any event, let us proceed with our brief discussion of client personality attributes and continuation in psychotherapy. The Rorschach Test, for example, was used in a number of earlier studies with rather inconclusive results. The same can be said of the MMPI and several other tests. Sullivan et al. (1958) initially secured some significant results on some of the scales of the MMPI, but, to their credit, continued with two cross-validation attempts and failed to replicate their initial findings.

Probably the most impressive research in predicting continuation in psychotherapy was conducted several years back in the Veterans Administration by Lorr and several of his colleagues (Lorr, Katz, and Rubinstein, 1958; McNair, Lorr, and Callahan, 1963; Rubinstein and Lorr, 1956). They used a short battery of tests and questionnaires and attempted to replicate their work on several fair sized samples of veterans. They were able to secure predictive multiple correlations in the neighborhood of .40 which exceeded the base rates for continuation in therapy by about 15 percent, a fairly respectable achievement in this difficult area. A recent study with a different group of subjects failed, however, to replicate these earlier results (Stern, Moore, and Gross, 1975). Because of differences in defining remainers, as well as sample differences in these studies, it is difficult to draw any definite conclusions.

Besides the appraisal of certain personality attributes by tests, a number of other client attributes have been investigated, including suggestibility, anxiety, motivation, expectancies concerning therapy, perseverance, and the like. In many instances the results of individual studies were never replicated, or were not supported. The clients' motivation for psychotherapy, for example, is one attribute which has been emphasized as an important one in many clinical discussions. However, this view has received support in one study (McNair et al., 1963), but has failed to be supported in three others (Affleck and Garfield, 1961; Garfield, Affleck, and Muffley, 1963; Siegel and Fink, 1962). One of the possible explanations in this and related instances is that a psychotherapeutic construct may be used without any precise meaning or definition. Clinicians may refer to a given construct and assume that they all mean the same thing by it, and researchers may use quite different methods of evaluating the supposedly same phenomenon.

The expectations which the client may have about psychotherapy have also been of interest with regard to the problem of continuation. Although a number of well educated individuals may be quite knowledgeable about psychotherapy and have realistic expectations about what is to take place, including the respective roles of client and therapist, many other individuals may not. Beginning therapists may overlook this aspect or fail to give it the attention it would appear to deserve. Consequently, when seeing a new client during the initial interview, they may not inform the client sufficiently concerning how psychotherapy will take place, how long it may take, or how it may help the client with his current difficulties. They also may not devote adequate time to ascertaining the client's own expectations about therapy or in clarifying them in understandable and unambiguous language. If the client's expectancies are seemingly incongruent with what appears to be occurring in therapy, he or she conceivably could become dissatisfied and withdraw from therapy. If the client expects that the therapist will diagnose his difficulties in short order and then tell him in one or two interviews what needs to be done to rectify his situation, he may be quite dissatisfied to see that the therapist tells him little or nothing, but simply wants him to keep talking about himself. A study of patients' expectations about psychotherapy reported some years ago may be of interest here (Garfield and Wolpin, 1963).

In this study, 70 patients, who were referred for outpatient psychiatric treatment, and who had no previous treatment of this kind, were asked to complete a detailed questionnaire prior to being assigned for treatment. The median level of education for this group was 12 years. On one item these patients were asked to select from a number of possible treatments the one which they thought was the preferred treatment for their particular complaints. In contrast to the findings for several earlier studies, 88 percent of these individuals selected psychotherapy as their treatment of choice, and a majority of them indicated emotional factors as being of some importance in their difficulties. In addition, they indicated that an understanding of one's personal difficulties would be of help with regard to their improvement. Thus on the basis of their response to these items, these patients appeared to display a positive attitude toward psychotherapy and seemingly had some understanding of it. Nevertheless, on other items their views were quite at variance with those held by most of their therapists. Over one-third of the group thought the therapy sessions would last 30 minutes or less. They apparently had not heard of the "50-minute-hour" and were basing their estimates on the time usually spent with other medical healers. Furthermore, 73 percent anticipated that they would be showing some improvement by the fifth therapy session, while 70 percent expected psychotherapy to be completed by ten sessions or less. Although the last prediction, as we have noted earlier, is a fairly accurate one for the majority of patients in psychotherapy, it was not the view held by the professional staff who saw psychotherapy as requiring a larger number of sessions.

In two studies of patient expectations about therapy and continuation in therapy, those who terminated early differed in certain ways from those who remained. In one (Heine and Trosman, 1960), the terminators emphasized the seeking of medication or diagnostic information along with passive cooperation with the therapist, whereas remainers were more inclined to stress collaboration and help in changing behavior. In the other study (Heine, 1962), terminators more frequently expected to receive advice on their problems during the initial interview, whereas continuers more frequently expected the therapist to be permissive. In both instances, those who continued in psychotherapy had expectancies about therapy which were more congruent with those of the therapist than was the case with those who discontinued therapy. A somewhat similar finding was reported in a study of 40 lower class patients (Overall and Aronson, 1962). Whereas these patients, in general, expected a "medical psychiatric" interview, with the therapists in an active supportive role, those whose expectations were least accurate were significantly less likely to return for treatment.

Thus while client expectations may be of some importance with regard to continuation, the reference to the congruence of client and therapist attitudes emphasizes again that psychotherapy involves the interaction of its principal participants. How the therapist views the client in terms of his own expectancies may also affect the process of psychotherapy. If the therapist feels that the client lacks motivation for psychotherapy, is hostile or demanding, and wants the therapist to be the active participant in therapy, conceivably, he may feel that the client is a poor case and indirectly, or even directly, influence the client to leave therapy. Unfortunately, there has been very little investigation of this matter. However, there are a few studies that appear to be of some relevance on this point.

In one study, ratings made by therapists after the second session of group therapy indicated that the therapists' estimates of their ability to empathize with a client, their positive feelings toward the client, and their evaluation of the client's ability to form a therapeutic relationship were all related to continuation in psychotherapy (Rosenzweig and Folman, 1974). In another study, the therapists' positive feelings toward clients and their prognoses for treatment were related to continuation, although this was not the case with ratings of psychopathology (Shapiro, 1974). Although these studies are concerned with the perceptions and evaluations of psychotherapists, they do pertain to client attributes as perceived by therapists in the therapy situation. They do not, however, tell us about the relative influence of each of the participants on the specific interaction which occurs, or how this process develops. In other words, are the attributes and behaviors of the client the primary factors leading to continuation, or do they act as initial stimuli which cause the therapist to react in certain ways which, in turn, influence the client in how he perceives therapy and subsequently reacts? It seems reasonable to believe that the personal attributes of the client do play a role in continuation, but that the process may be influenced positively or negatively by the personal qualities of the therapist and his manner of responding to the client.

Before concluding this section, it seems worthwhile to add a few words about one feature of the psychotherapy patient that was mentioned earlier, namely, the patient's motivation for treatment. As indicated, this attribute lacks a precise definition, and studies designed to evaluate its importance for continuation in psychotherapy have largely failed to produce positive results. Nevertheless, many therapists believe it is an important aspect when making an initial appraisal of the client. What, then, do they mean by motivation? In terms of more traditional analytically oriented therapies, the term *motivation* appears to refer to the client's willingness to explore himself, to face up to the negative components of his personality, and in general to endure the painful process of recapturing previously repressed and conflictual material. In other words, he or she is willing to endure and cope with the rather strenuous demands of a long-term type of therapy. By contrast, those individuals who desire a speedy amelioration of symptoms by the therapist are seen as lacking in motivation. Although this appears to be the core of the concept of motivation for therapy, other aspects also may be involved. Since frequent visits over a long period of time are expensive, motivation is also viewed in terms of the individual's willingness to make the necessary financial sacrifices involved. Many analysts since Freud have emphasized the importance of the client's paying a fee and making some sacrifice for his analysis to be effective. The writer even recalls one psychotherapist colleague who told him he was increasing a patient's fee in order to increase his motivation to work harder in therapy.

Besides this characteristic of self-sacrifice and the desire to face the stresses of psychotherapy on the part of the patient, it would appear that other aspects of the client may also, at times, become associated with motivation. The client's interest in receiving psychotherapy, his respect and admiration for the therapist, his willingness to accept the therapist's values and frame of reference, as well as his obvious cultural and intellectual qualities, may all enter into the therapist's appraisal of the client's motivation. The type of symptoms or complaints that are presented may also play a role. A client who emphasizes somatic complaints is less likely to be seen as motivated for psychotherapy than one who readily accepts the view that his symptoms are psychological in origin. Defensiveness on the client's part can also be related to a lack of motivation, although it can also be viewed in terms of other constructs pertaining to the personality of the client.

As a result of the many possible meanings attributed to clients' motivation by different therapists, it is not surprising that attempts to utilize ratings of motivation by therapists have not produced very promising results. When general concepts are used without some specific type of operational or behavioral definition, conflicting or ambiguous results might be expected. In this connection it is interesting to mention a secondary finding noted in three different studies in three quite different clinical settings. In one report of private patients, it was noted that those patients who completed the MMPI at the beginning of therapy continued to remain in therapy significantly more than those who did not complete the MMPI (Wirt, 1967). Somewhat similar results were secured in a second study in a university outpatient clinic (Dodd, 1970). A third report, based on patients in group therapy, also mentioned that those patients who failed to complete a group of questionnaires prior to therapy dropped out of therapy significantly more than those who completed the questionnaires (Koren and Costell, 1973). It would seem on the basis of these results, that those clients who complete some type of personality questionnaire at the initiation of therapy are more likely to remain in therapy. At this level, the generalization appears reasonable and warranted. However, when we attempt to conceptualize the operation of questionnaire completion into such terms as compliance, persistence, determination, or motivation, then we may either distort the actual operation somewhat, or allow new meanings or operations to envelop the term selected. This may occur with many of the concepts used in psychotherapy and is obviously not limited to the concept of motivation.

In concluding this section it can be stated once more that premature termination is a problem in psychotherapy that has been studied in relation to a number of different variables. Of the variables reviewed, those pertaining to social class appear to receive the most support. This empirical relationship, however, does not provide us with any specific reason for its occurrence. The greater mutuality of expectations about therapy and the greater similarity of values between therapists and clients have been some of the explanations offered, as well as the attitudes therapists display toward clients of the different classes. Whereas the first mentioned explanation has received some research support, the evidence for the latter appears more limited (Myers and Schaffer, 1958; Lerner and Fiske, 1973). It can be noted, too, that IQ, which usually shows a positive correlation with social class, has also been reported to relate to continuation in several studies (Affleck and Mednick, 1959; Auld and Eron, 1953; Gibby et al., 1954; Hiler, 1958). It should also be mentioned that most of the studies on this topic have involved more or less traditional verbal psychotherapy. Comparable reports concerning behavior therapy are not available. It is possible that this may be due in part to the differences between these two types of therapy. Behavior therapy appears to be a relatively briefer type of therapy, and the client is usually given a more explicit explanation of what is to occur. The behavior therapist also plays a very active role in directing the treatment. If these deductions are valid, they may provide us with a basis for a better understanding of some of the reasons for premature termination and allow us to modify our procedures accordingly. A discussion of such attempts will be provided later when the initial stages of psychotherapy are presented. Now let us turn our attention to the matter of client variables in relation to improvement in psychotherapy.

CLIENT VARIABLES AND OUTCOME IN PSYCHOTHERAPY

Whereas it would appear important for the client to continue in psychotherapy if the course of treatment is to be completed, the ultimate goal of treatment is the improvement of the client. If the client continues in treatment for a long period of time and shows no change or even gets worse, he or she would indeed have done better to terminate earlier. However, although positive change and the reduction of discomfort are the common goals of all therapies, none have really claimed to be 100 percent effective. What most claim is that they help most people, or that they are more effective than other types of therapy. Although most people may show positive change, there are those who either show no change, or change for the worse. Since the client is a principal participant, we would expect that client differences may affect outcome.

In discussing client variables and outcome, some attention should be given first to the difficulties inherent in appraising this possible relationship. In addition to the matter of appraising client variables, there is also the difficult problem of evaluating the outcome of psychotherapy. For some therapists the reduction or disappearance of the client's symptoms or disordered behavior will suffice as the criterion for evaluating outcome. For others, however, the symptoms are merely the surface indications of the more basic problems and other considerations will have to be considered. Still others have emphasized the client's self concept as a basic consideration in evaluating outcome in psychotherapy. It is thus evident that some of the different variants of psychotherapy would appraise different client attributes when attempting to evaluate outcome.

Besides possible differences in criteria of outcome, there is also the matter of how the different outcome criteria are appraised or measured. In actuality, although a variety of outcome measures have been used, many of the same measures have been used by psychotherapists of different theoretical persuasions. Among the most popular have been therapists' judgments or ratings of improvement, client evaluations of treatment, ratings by independent judges, tests, behavioral tasks and a variety of questionnaires. While our primary concern here is not with the methodological and research issues pertaining to the evaluation of outcome in psychotherapy, the matter of outcome is of such importance that a few of the significant problems in this area will be mentioned. One pertains to the value or validity of the measures used. For example, if a therapist judges a patient to be "very much improved," what changes have actually taken place and how much confidence can be placed in this judgment? Another problem pertains to the agreement or lack of agreement between different judgments or measures of improvement.

What appraisal of outcome does one make if a therapist judges a given client to be improved but the client feels there has been no significant change, a not uncommon finding in psychotherapy research (Garfield, 1978). How does one interpret a positive change on one criterion and no change on another supposedly equally important one? These, it should be noted, are not simply rhetorical questions. Several studies have secured rather low agreement among different criteria used to appraise outcome (Cartwright, Kirtner, and Fiske, 1963; Garfield, Prager, and Bergin, 1971; Hornstein, Houston, and Holmes, 1973; Keniston, Boltax, and Almond,

1971; Sloane et al., 1975). Therapists' judgments of outcome also appear to be more favorable than other criteria, a finding which is not difficult to understand. Finally, apart from the lack of agreement obtained with appraisals of outcome derived from different sources, there is also the related problem of comparing overall judgments of improvement made at the end of therapy with scores or ratings based on the difference between appraisals made at the beginning and the end of therapy. In the former instance, judges or raters may not recall accurately the initial status of the patient, or may be unduly influenced by the client's overall level of functioning. A client who is only mildly disturbed at the beginning of therapy and changes relatively little may still be judged to be greatly improved at the termination of therapy in comparison with more disturbed clients since the former is functioning at a higher level. Because of such considerations, we can anticipate that deriving reliable generalizations about what kinds of patients respond well to psychotherapy will not be a simple matter.

The first broad group of client variables to be reviewed will consist of social class and demographic variables, and our review will be brief since only a relatively small number of studies have been reported. In general, unlike the trend for continuation, there does not appear to be any important relationship between social class and outcome in psychotherapy (Garfield, 1978; Lorion, 1973; Luborsky et al., 1971). Thus whereas the lower class client may be more likely to drop out of therapy, once he or she remains in therapy, the outcome obtained is not noticeably different from that of other groups of clients. Education appears to show a somewhat more positive relationship to outcome, although it is not a consistent finding, and in many of the studies, therapists' ratings have been used as the criterion and sample size has been small (Garfield, 1978).

The results reported on the variables of sex and age also do not show any significant relationship to outcome. Although some psychotherapists, including Freud (1950), have believed that the older patient is less flexible, less educable, and consequently less fit for therapy, there are no reliable data to indicate that the outcomes secured with such individuals are significantly different from those secured with younger individuals (Garfield, 1978).

The largest number of studies on client variables in relation to outcome have been concerned with personality variables, and because of their diversity, it is not easy to present a concise summary of the results obtained. Like the studies mentioned in the previous section, many have been based on different psychological tests or batteries of tests with varying groups of clients. As a result, there are a number of conflicting and unreplicated findings which will not be reported here. A review of such findings are available elsewhere (Garfield, 1978; Luborsky et al., 1971; Meltzoff and Kornreich, 1970). Instead, some illustrative findings and issues will be presented.

One of the more general findings or conclusions reported in some studies was that those clients who were the least disturbed or had the greatest degree of personality integration or ego strength tended to show the greatest degree of improvement (Luborsky et al., 1971). There were, however, several studies that either failed to obtain such results or which secured the opposite results (Prager and Garfield, 1972; Stone et al., 1961; Truax et al., 1966). After reviewing some of the studies in this area, Truax and Carkhuff (1967) advanced the hypothesis that patients with the greatest "felt disturbance," evaluated by means of self-report question- naires, and with the least overt or behavioral disturbance are the individ- uals who actually improve the most. Although this view was congruent with some clinical views, it has not been adequately investigated or con- firmed. Before commenting on this further, however, we can examine a few representative recent studies.

In one study it was reported that there were no differences between im- proved and unimproved patients in initial ratings of "ego weakness," but that the two groups differed on nurses' ratings of the patients' manifest level of distress (Jacobs et al., 1972). However, the latter finding appears limited since similar ratings by the therapists, other staff members, and the patients themselves bore no relationship to outcome—a problem re- ferred to previously.

In the interesting study by Sloane et al. (1975) comparing the effective- ness of behavior therapy and psychoanalytic therapy, some differential results were secured for the two types of therapy. As measured by the MMPI, the less disturbed patients did better in the psychoanalytically oriented psychotherapy, whereas behavior therapy obtained similar results regardless of the degree of patient disturbance. In this instance, the type of therapy also appeared to be of possible importance with regard to patient degree of disturbance and outcome. Unfortunately, studies of this type have been a rarity.

The long-term project conducted by the Menninger Foundation also reported a positive correlation between ego strength and a global measure of improvement for patients who received psychoanalysis or psycho- analytically oriented long term therapy (Kernberg et al., 1972). The cor- relation obtained was not very high ($r=.35$), and the appraisals of ego strength were relative to the population studied. However, if we were to take these results and those of the previous study and generalize, perhaps somewhat dangerously, we might state that ego strength or degree of personality integration may be related to outcome in psychoanalytic therapy, but not necessarily in behavior therapy. Such a conclusion would be of interest if further research would in fact support it.

Frank (1974), one of the leaders in psychotherapy research and one of the wisest observers of the psychotherapeutic scene, believes that patient variables are the most important factors in long-term improvement. In his own research program, he found that symptoms of anxiety and depression tended to improve the most and somatic complaints the least. Anxiety has also been mentioned by others as a positive prognostic indicator in psychotherapy (Kernberg et al., 1972; Luborsky et al., 1971), although inconclusive results have been reported as well. The type and severity of client anxiety must also be considered, as well as the situations which appear to produce it. Those who display anxiety in relation to their current situation or stress, or in other words, situational rather than chronic anxiety, may secure more positive results (Smith, Sjoholm, and Nielzen, 1975).

Two scales of ego strength have also been used in research on psychotherapy. The Barron ES Scale, after an initially positive report (Barron, 1953), has not proved useful (Garfield, 1978). The results with the Rorschach Prognostic Rating Scale (Klopfer et al., 1951) have been somewhat more positive, although one-third of the studies have secured negative results. The utility of this scale, however, is limited by the type of norms provided and by the fact that the scale's success does not exceed the conventional improvement rate of about 67 percent.

Without going into great detail, it appears likely that conclusions concerning the relationship of degree of client disturbance or ego strength to outcome is to an important extent influenced by how outcome in psychotherapy is appraised. This point, alluded to earlier, was illustrated clearly in a paper by Mintz (1972), and developed also in a recent publication by the present writer (Garfield, 1978). In essence, the proposition is that where global judgments of therapy outcome are made by therapists *at the conclusion of therapy,* there exists a high probability of a positive relationship between degree of personality integration or adjustment of the client at the initiation of therapy and outcome. In other words, the less disturbed clients secure the most favorable ratings at the termination of therapy. In contrast, where patient improvement is appraised by the amount of difference between test scores or ratings obtained at the beginning of therapy and those obtained at termination, such a relationship will not be secured, and the results may favor the more disturbed client. The issue is a complex one, and I shall do my best to explain it as clearly as possible.

First, let us consider the goals of therapy. Although "cure" is frequently mentioned in medicine, it has appeared less frequently in the area of psychotherapy. Positive change or improvement tend to be the more commonly used terms. However, although practically all of us would agree on client improvement as the goal of therapy, we might differ on how much or what type of change would constitute improvement. Related to this, there has frequently been a stated or implied goal of psychotherapy to the effect that the client's overall personality functioning should be enhanced at the completion of therapy. Thus apart from the patient's specific complaints, there is usually some attention paid to his or her level of functioning. Consequently, when a therapist makes an evaluation of a client's progress at the end of therapy, he is likely to be influenced by the client's overall level of adjustment, as well as by what problems have been helped as a result of therapy. A client who enters therapy at a relatively high level of integration and functioning appears more likely to receive a high rating of improvement, whereas an initially much more disturbed client who has shown as much or more improvement, but who still functions at a lower level than the other client will tend to receive a lower rating. The therapist thus may be influenced more by the client's overall adjustment at the end of therapy than by actual improvement over the course of therapy. As a result, the better adjusted clients would appear to secure the most positive results. Furthermore, if the goal of therapy is some norm of personality adjustment that ideally should be obtained by all patients undergoing psychotherapy, then, again, those patients who are better adjusted to begin with are most likely to be the ones who come closer to this goal.

On the other hand, if the *amount* of change resulting from psychotherapy is the actual criterion, and differences between pre and post levels of functioning are measured, the results and conclusions may be quite different. Methodological issues are clearly of importance here. Individuals who, at the beginning of therapy, are relatively little impaired would be near the top of some normative scale of adjustment and would have much less room to move up in this scale than would one who is much further down the scale. To look at it another way, those individuals who are most disturbed deviate the most from the mean level of adjustment manifested by most individuals, or the statistical norm of adjustment. In terms of statistical probability they have the greatest likelihood on retesting of regressing or moving toward the mean, and, thus, of exhibiting greater change than those individuals who are already closer to the mean. As a result, if amount of change is the criterion of outcome, then those who are most disturbed at the outset of therapy are likely to show the largest gains. As already mentioned, all types of results have actually been reported in varying degrees, and the interpretation of these results have also differed. Luborsky et al. (1971), in their review of this literature, conclude that those individuals with the best personality assets secure the most favorable results in psychotherapy. Meltzoff and Kornreich (1970) and the present writer (Garfield, 1978), in evaluating this literature, reach a more cautious and less positive conclusion, namely, that the results are influenced by the criteria and methods of evaluating outcome, and essentially that the issue remains open. Whereas those individuals who begin therapy at relatively high levels of personality adjustment may be expected to function at termination at higher levels than those who initially are most disturbed, one cannot state that the former show the greatest degree of improvement. Such patients may also be "better" patients to work with and more gratifying to their therapists, and may be viewed as more "responsive" to psychotherapy, but this is something different from the amount of change. It is also likely that the better integrated patients respond better to analytically oriented therapy than the more disturbed patients, as suggested by the results of the studies by Sloane et al. (1975) and by Kernberg et al. (1972), although one must be cautious in drawing conclusions. It is time, however, to proceed to a discussion of other client variables in relation to outcome.

Although successful results in psychotherapy have been reported with clients with a wide range of intellectual ability, a number of studies have appeared to indicate a positive relationship between intelligence and outcome. In the review by Luborsky et al., (1971) 10 of 13 studies are listed as showing a positive relationship between intelligence and outcome with correlations ranging from .24 to .46. Meltzoff and Kornreich (1970), however, review 15 studies of which only 7 show a positive relationship between intelligence and outcome. They also conclude that high intelligence is not a necessary condition for positive outcome in psychotherapy, although it might be of greater importance in some psychotherapies than in others.

There are a few points that can be made about this issue. If psychotherapy does involve learning, a view subscribed to not only by the behavior therapists, then it is reasonable to assume that some minimal amount of intelligence is required for successful performance in psychotherapy. However, no precise amount has yet been specified or demonstrated as the required amount, although it would appear that psychotherapists on the whole prefer clients who possess high intelligence, as well as other desirable qualities (Schofield, 1964). It does appear on the basis of some reports that analysts and related therapists select patients who rank high on this variable, although it is also correlated and intertwined with such other variables as education, occupation, income, and social class generally (Hamburg et al., 1967; Kadushin, 1969; Knapp et al., 1960). The research data on this matter, however, do not allow one to make any categorical statements. Even if one placed more confidence in the positive results secured and ignored the inconclusive findings, the magnitude of the correlations obtained is rather low. If a correlation of .30 were to be taken as a representative finding, it would still account for less than 10 percent of the variance. Consequently, a therapist should not place undue emphasis on intellectual ability, although he or she might find it more pleasurable to interact and to discuss psychotherapeutic concepts with highly intelligent individuals.

Another topic of interest already referred to in the section on continuation is that of client expectancies. In the past this tended to refer to the expectancies the client had about therapy and his expectations of being helped. It was hypothesized that those who had high expectations of being helped might actually do better than those who had negative expectations. Frank and his colleagues were among the earliest to emphasize this and related views and to conduct some studies of expectations and outcome (Frank, 1959; Frank et al., 1959; Rosenthal and Frank, 1956). More recently, the behavior therapists in particular have reported studies in which they have tried to manipulate client expectancies experimentally. Several critical reviews of this area have appeared in published form (Lick and Bootzin, 1975; Morgan, 1973; Wilkins, 1971, 1973).

As mentioned, it was stated by Frank and his coworkers that the client's expectancies about therapy would influence outcome and that the greater the client's distress or need for relief, the greater the likelihood of obtaining change. This received some support from other studies (Friedman, 1963; Goldstein, 1960; Goldstein and Shipman, 1961; Lennard and Bernstein, 1960; Lipkin, 1954). Since these earlier studies, there has been a continuing interest in the problem, and a more critical view of it. Positive results were reported by some (Uhlenhuth and Duncan, 1968), but a lack of positive findings were secured by others (Piper and Wogan, 1970; Tollinton, 1973). Furthermore, many of the investigations which secured positive results have received some criticism in recent reviews (Perotti and Hopewell, 1976; Wilkins, 1973). It has been pointed out that, in many studies, expectancies have not been actually measured but inferred, and that self-reports have been used to appraise both expectancies and outcome. How expectancies are appraised is of some importance, for in one study significant correlations were secured between high expectancy ratings and self-report measures of outcome, but not between expectancy ratings and a behavioral measure of outcome (Wilson and Thomas, 1971).

The work on the creation of expectancy "states," carried out primarily by behavior therapists, has also produced conflicting results and brought forth criticism of the research performed. Wilkins (1973) in particular has raised a number of critical issues concerning this research and believes that there is currently insufficient evidence to support the construct of expectancy with regard to therapeutic outcome. Two other reviewers, although also critical of this work, come to somewhat different conclusions. Lick and Bootzin (1975) believe that although deficiencies in previous research preclude any firm conclusions, the data suggest that therapeutic instructions in systematic desensitization are of some importance. Perotti and Hopewell (1976), however, do not feel that the initial client expectancies for possible improvement that have been the focus in most studies have much impact on outcome. However, they do state that the beliefs a client has during therapy that he is improving and is able to handle, in better fashion, situations which were upsetting previously, are of some importance. In other words, expectancies derived while undergoing therapy are the more significant ones.

Although the research data and issues on client expectancies may not inspire a strong degree of confidence in the utility of the construct, it does seem as if some of the difficulty is because it has been defined in different ways or not defined at all. In some instances it has been used with reference to the client's beliefs about the success of treatment. In other instances it has been used to designate the expectations a client has concerning the potential effectiveness of a given therapist. It would appear on the basis of historical accounts of successful quacks in the past, that such expectations may have played a role in their success (Jameson, 1961). Whether we approve of such activities or not, if a variable has some potential influence on outcome it should be noted. Finally, as mentioned earlier, client expectations have also been mentioned in relation to such features of therapy as the client or therapist role in therapy, the length of therapy, the procedures to be used, and the like. If we are going to understand more fully the possible significance of the expectancies of the patient, more attention in research will have to be paid to specifying the type of expectancy under investigation, as well as considering the possible interactive effects of different kinds of expectancies. Consequently, in later discussions of the psychotherapeutic process, an attempt will be made to be both cautious and specific when discussing the possible importance of the expectations of the participants.

A few other topics of possible interest with reference to client variables and outcome can be reviewed briefly before ending this chapter. One concerns the possible importance of the fit between client and type of therapy.

In one study, for example, two groups of clients were exposed to two types of therapy (Abramowitz et al., 1974). The clients were classified as "externals" or "internals" in terms of their locus of control as measured by the Rotter I-E Scale. The therapies were designated as "relatively directive" and "relatively nondirective." The findings suggested that externally oriented clients did better with the directive therapy, whereas the internals performed more successfully in the nondirective therapy. In another study subjects with a fear of snakes were presented with a videotape of four therapists who illustrated four different types of therapy: systematic desensitization, an encounter therapy, rational-emotive therapy, and a combination of modeling and behavioral rehearsal (Devine and Fernald, 1973). The subjects rated their therapeutic preferences and then were assigned to a preferred, nonpreferred, or randomly selected therapy. Although there was no difference in the overall effectiveness of any of the different forms of therapy, subjects receiving a preferred treatment exhibited significantly less fear than those who received a random or nonpreferred type of therapy. These results suggest the importance of examining the possible interaction effects between type of therapy and client attributes.

There have also been scattered investigations of client qualities which have been thought to be important in psychotherapy. These have included such attributes as relatability, attractiveness, and likability. However, it would seem that although these terms are used clinically, they need some operational definition before we really know what is meant by them or can investigate their significance. Nevertheless, they may reflect aspects of psychotherapy that are important. Two studies have found a relationship between therapists' ratings of client likability and their ratings of client prognosis (Ehrlich and Bauer, 1967; Garfield and Affleck, 1961). Furthermore, in the first study listed, patients who were rated as less likable were three times more likely to be placed on multiple drug regimes than those who received high ratings. In addition, the therapists' ratings of improvement were positively correlated with these ratings. The problem here, of course, is determining whether likability influences prognosis or whether patients who are judged to be good candidates for psychotherapy are better liked.

The matter of client-therapist similarity or complementarity has also been discussed in the clinical literature, as well as receiving some research attention. Although some psychotherapists may have strong opinions on this matter, the research results are too conflicting and questionable to form a basis for any reasonable beliefs (Berzins, 1977; Garfield, 1978). As Berzins (1977) has noted after reviewing this topic in some detail, "there is at present no organized body of knowledge that could serve as an effective guide for implementing matching strategies" (p. 222).

Although it appears obvious that the personal qualities of the patient should be of some significance in psychotherapy and in the type of outcome which is secured, the problem is not as simple as it appears, at least from the standpoint of securing stable results by means of research. The range of client attributes is large, and how they are appraised or evaluated also varies greatly. For such reasons, as well as other methodological ones, replication of findings has not been easy to obtain. It is also difficult to try to order and integrate such a diversity of results. This is particularly true of personality variables. Thus while we can state with at least some confidence that such variables as social class, age, and sex are of little significance as far as outcome is concerned, conclusions about the importance of the client's degree of disturbance, motivation, likability, and expectations concerning therapy have to be hedged with considerable caution. Although this may be disappointing, it does help us to be more realistic about our clinical knowledge and beliefs, and, hopefully, in the long run, will help us in seeking and obtaining warrantable views of these variables.

REFERENCES

Abramowitz, C. V., Abramowitz, S. I., Roback, H. B., and Jackson, C. Differential effectiveness of directive and nondirective group therapies as a function of client internal-external control. *Journal of Consulting and Clinical Psychology,* 1974, *42,* 849–853.

Affleck, D. C. and Garfield, S. L. Predictive judgments of therapists and duration of stay in psychotherapy. *Journal of Clinical Psychology,* 1961, *17,* 134–137.

Affleck, D. C. and Mednick, S. A. The use of the Rorschach Test in the prediction of the abrupt terminator in individual psychotherapy. *Journal of Consulting Psychology,* 1959, *23,* 125–128.

Auld, F., Jr. and Eron, L. D. The use of Rorschach scores to predict whether patients will continue psychotherapy. *Journal of Consulting Psychology,* 1953, *17,* 104–109.

Bailey, M. A., Warshaw, L., and Eichler, R. M. A study of factors related to length of stay in psychotherapy. *Journal of Clinical Psychology,* 1959, *15,* 442–444.

Barron, F. Some test correlates of response to psychotherapy. *Journal of Consulting Psychology,* 1953, *17,* 235–241.

Berzins, J. I. Therapist-patient matching. In A. S. Gurman and A. M. Razin (Eds.), *Effective psychotherapy: A handbook of research.* New York: Pergamon Press, 1977, pp. 222–251.

Brill, N. Q. and Storrow, H. A. Social class and psychiatric treatment. *Archives of General Psychiatry*, 1960, *3*, 340–344.

Brown, J. S. and Kosterlitz, N. Selection and treatment of psychiatric outpatients. *Archives of General Psychiatry*, 1964, *11*, 425–438.

Cartwright, D. S. Success in psychotherapy as a function of certain actuarial variables. *Journal of Consulting Psychology*, 1955, *19*, 357–363.

Cartwright, D. S., Kirtner, W. L., and Fiske, D. W. Method factors in changes associated with psychotherapy. *Journal of Abnormal and Social Psychology*, 1963, *66*, 164–175.

Cole, N. J., Branch, C. H., and Allison, R. B. Some relationships between social class and the practice of dynamic psychotherapy. *American Journal of Psychiatry*, 1962, *118*, 1004–1012.

Craig, T. and Huffine, C. Correlates of patient attendance in an inner-city mental health clinic. *The American Journal of Psychiatry*, 1976, *133*, 61–64.

Devine, D. A. and Fernald, P. S. Outcome effects of receiving a preferred, randomly assigned or nonpreferred therapy. *Journal of Consulting and Clinical Psychology*, 1973, *41*, 104–107.

Dodd, J. A retrospective analysis of variables related to duration of treatment in a university psychiatric clinic. *Journal of Nervous and Mental Disease*, 1970, *151*, 75–84.

Ehrlich, H. J. and Bauer, M. L. Therapists' feelings toward patients and patient treatment and outcome. *Social Science and Medicine*, 1967, *1*, 283–292.

Eiduson, B. T. The two classes of information in psychiatry. *Archives of General Psychiatry*, 1968, *18*, 405–419.

Fiester, A. R. and Rudestam, K. E. A multivariate analysis of the early dropout process. *Journal of Consulting and Clinical Psychology*, 1975, *43*, 528–535.

Frank, J. D. Problems of controls in psychotherapy as exemplified by the psychotherapy research project of the Phipps Psychiatric Clinic. In E. A. Rubinstein and M. B. Parloff (Eds.), *Research in Psychotherapy*. Washington, D.C.: American Psychological Association, 1959, *1*, 10–26.

Frank, J. D. Therapeutic components of psychotherapy. A 25-year progress report of research. *The Journal of Nervous and Mental Disease*, 1974, *159*, 325–342.

Frank, J. D., Gliedman, L. H., Imber, S. D., Nash, E. H., Jr., and Stone, A. R. Why patients leave psychotherapy. *Archives of Neurology and Psychiatry*, 1957, *77*, 283–299.

Frank, J. D., Gliedman, L. H., Imber, S. D., Stone, A. R., and Nash, E. H. Patients' expectancies and relearning as factors determining improvement in psychotherapy. *American Journal of Psychiatry*, 1959, *115*, 961–968.

Freud, S. On psychotherapy. In *Collected Papers, Vol. 1*. London: Hogarth Press and the Institute of Psychoanalysis, 1950, pp. 258–259.

Friedman, H. J. Patient-expectancy and symptom reduction. *Archives of General Psychiatry,* 1963, *8,* 61–67.

Garfield, S. L. *Clinical psychology: The study of personality and behavior.* Chicago: Aldine, 1974.

Garfield, S. L. Research on client variables in psychotherapy. In S. L. Garfield and A. E. Bergin (Eds.), *Handbook of psychotherapy and behavior change,* 2nd ed. New York: Wiley, 1978.

Garfield, S. L. and Affleck, D. C. An appraisal of duration of stay in outpatient psychotherapy. *Journal of Nervous and Mental Disease,* 1959, *129,* 492–498.

Garfield, S. L. and Affleck, D. C. Therapists' judgments concerning patients considered for psychotherapy. *Journal of Consulting Psychology,* 1961, *25,* 505–509.

Garfield, S. L., Affleck, D. C., and Muffley, R. A. A study of psychotherapy interaction and continuation in psychotherapy. *Journal of Clinical Psychology,* 1963, *19,* 473–478.

Garfield, S. L. and Kurz, M. Evaluation of treatment and related procedures in 1216 cases referred to a mental hygiene clinic. *Psychiatric Quarterly,* 1952, *26,* 414–424.

Garfield, S. L., Prager, R. A., and Bergin, A. E. Evaluation of outcome in psychotherapy. *Journal of Consulting and Clinical Psychology,* 1971, *37,* 307–313.

Garfield, S. L. and Wolpin, M. Expectations regarding psychotherapy. *Journal of Nervous and Mental Disease,* 1963, *137,* 353–362.

Gibby, R. G., Stotsky, B. A., Hiler, E. W., and Miller, D. R. Validation of Rorschach criteria for predicting duration of therapy. *Journal of Consulting Psychology,* 1954, *18,* 185–191.

Goldstein, A. P. Therapist and client expectation of personality change in psychotherapy. *Journal of Counseling Psychology,* 1960, *7,* 180–184.

Goldstein, A. P. and Shipman, W. G. Patient expectancies, symptom reduction, and aspects of the initial psychotherapeutic interview. *Journal of Clinical Psychology,* 1961, *17,* 129–133.

Grotjahn, M. Learning from dropout patients: A clinical view of patients who discontinued group psychotherapy. *International Journal of Group Psychotherapy,* 1972, *22,* 306–319.

Hamburg, D. A., Bibring, G. L., Fisher, C., Stanton, A. H., Wallerstein, R. S., Weinstock, H. I., and Haggard, E. Report of Ad Hoc Committee on central fact gathering data of the American Psychoanalytic Association. *Journal of the American Psychoanalytic Association,* 1967, *15,* 841–861.

Heine, R. W. (Ed.), *The student physician as psychotherapist.* Chicago: The University of Chicago Press, 1962.

Heine, R. W. and Trosman, H. Initial expectations of the doctor-patient interaction as a factor in continuance in psychotherapy. *Psychiatry*, 1960, *23*, 275–278.

Heitler, J. B. Preparatory techniques in initiating expressive psychotherapy with lower-class, unsophisticated patients. *Psychological Bulletin*, 1976, *83*, 339–352.

Hiler, E. W. Wechsler-Bellevue Intelligence as a predictor of continuation in psychotherapy. *Journal of Clinical Psychology*, 1958, *14*, 192–194.

Hollingshead, A. B. and Redlich, F. C. *Social class and mental illness: A Community Study.* New York: Wiley, 1958.

Horenstein, D., Houston, B., and Holmes, D. Clients', therapists' & judges' evaluations of psychotherapy. *Journal of Counseling Psychology*, 1973, *20*, 149–153.

Jacobs, M. A., Muller, J. J., Anderson, J., and Skinner, J. C. Therapeutic expectations, premorbid adjustment, and manifest distress level as predictors of improvement in hospitalized patients. *Journal of Consulting and Clinical Psychology*, 1972, *39*, 455–461.

Jameson, E. *The natural history of quackery.* London: Michael Joseph, 1961.

Kadushin, C. *Why people go to psychiatrists.* New York: Atherton, 1969.

Keniston, K., Boltax, S., and Almond, R. Multiple criteria of treatment outcome. *Journal of Psychiatry*, 1971, *8*, 107–118.

Kernberg, O. F., Bernstein, C. S., Coyne, R., Appelbaum, D. A., Horwitz, H., and Voth, T. J. Psychotherapy and psychoanalysis: Final report of the Menninger Foundation's psychotherapy research project. *Bulletin of the Menninger Clinic*, 1972, *36*, 1–276.

Klopfer, B., Kirkner, F., Wisham, W., and Baker, G. Rorschach prognostic rating scale. *Journal of Projective Techniques*, 1951, *15*, 425–428.

Knapp, P. H., Levin, S., McCarter, R. H., Wermer, H., and Zetzel, E. Suitability for psychoanalysis: a review of 100 supervised analytic cases. *Psychoanalytic Quarterly*, 1960, *29*, 459–477.

Koran, L. M. and Costel, R. M. Early termination from group psychotherapy. *International Journal of Group Psychotherapy*, 1973, *23*, 346–359.

Lennard, H. L. and Bernstein, A. *The anatomy of psychotherapy: Systems of communication and expectation.* New York: Columbia University Press, 1960.

Lerner, B. and Fiske, D. W. Client attributes and the eye of the beholder. *Journal of Consulting and Clinical Psychology*, 1973, *40*, 272–277.

Lick, J. and Bootzin, R. Expectancy factors in the treatment of fear: Methodological and theoretical issues. *Psychological Bulletin*, 1975, *82*, 917–931.

Lief, H. L., Lief, V. F., Warren, C. O., and Heath, R. G. Low dropout rate in a psychiatric clinic. *Archives of General Psychiatry*, 1961, *5*, 200–211.

Lipkin, S. Clients' feelings and attitudes in relation to the outcome of client-centered therapy. *Psychological Monographs*, 1954, *68* (Whole No. 372).

Lorion, R. P. Socioeconomic status & traditional treatment approaches reconsidered. *Psychological Bulletin*, 1973, *79*, 263–270.

Lorr, M., Katz, M. M., and Rubinstein, E. A. The prediction of length of stay in psychotherapy. *Journal of Consulting Psychology*, 1958, *22*, 321–327.

Lubin, B., Hornstra, R. K., Lewis, R. V., and Bechtel, B. S. Correlates of initial treatment assignment in a community mental health center. *Archives of General Psychiatry*, 1973, *29*, 497–504.

Luborsky, L., Chandler, M., Auerbach, A. H., Cohen, J., and Bachrach, H. M. Factors influencing the outcome of psychotherapy. *Psychological Bulletin*, 1971, *75*, 145–185.

Marks, I. Behavioral psychotherapy of adult neurosis. In S. L. Garfield and A. E. Bergin (Eds.), *Handbook of psychotherapy and behavior change*, 2nd ed. New York: Wiley, 1978.

McNair, D. M., Lorr, M., and Callahan, D. M. Patient and therapist influences on quitting psychotherapy. *Journal of Consulting Psychology*, 1963, *27*, 10–17.

Meltzoff, J. and Kornreich, M. *Research in psychotherapy*. New York: Atherton Press, 1970.

Mintz, J. What is "success" in psychotherapy? *Journal of Abnormal Psychology*, 1972, *80*, 11–19.

Morgan, W. G. Nonnecessary conditions or useful procedures in desensitization: A reply to Wilkins. *Psychological Bulletin*, 1973, *79*, 373–375.

Myers, J. K. and Schaffer, L. Social stratification and psychiatric practice: A study of an outpatient clinic. In E. G. Jaco (Ed.), *Patients, physicians and illness*. Glencoe, Ill.: The Free Press, 1958.

National Center for Health Statistics. *Characteristics of patients of selected types of medical specialists and practitioners: United States July 1963–June 1964*. Washington, D.C., Public Health Service Publication No. 1000, Series 10, No. 28, 1966.

Noonan, J. R. A follow-up of pretherapy dropouts. *Journal of Community Psychology*, 1973, *1*, 43–45.

Overall, B. and Aronson, H. Expectations of psychotherapy in lower socioeconomic class patients. *American Journal of Orthopsychiatry*, 1962, *32*, 271–272.

Perotti, L. P. and Hopewell, C. A. *Expectancy effects in psychotherapy and systematic desensitization: A review*. Paper presented at the Seventh Annual Meeting of the Society for Psychotherapy Research, June 18, 1976, San Diego, California.

Piper, W. E. and Wogan, M. Placebo effect in psychotherapy: An extension of earlier findings. *Journal of Consulting and Clinical Psychology*, 1970, *34*, 447.

Pope, K. S., Geller, J. D., and Wilkinson, L. Fee assessment and outpatient psychotherapy. *Journal of Consulting and Clinical Psychology*, 1975, *43*, 835–841.

Prager, R. A. and Garfield, S. L. Client initial disturbance and outcome in psychotherapy. *Journal of Consulting and Clinical Psychology*, 1972, *38*, 112–117.

Raynes, A. E. and Warren, G. Some distinguishing features of patients failing to attend a psychiatric clinic after referral. *American Journal of Orthopsychiatry*, 1971a, *41*, 581–589.

Raynes, A. E. and Warren, G. Some characteristics of "drop-outs" at first contact with a psychiatric clinic. *Community Mental Health Journal*, 1971b, *7*, 144–151.

Rosenthal, D. and Frank, J. D. Psychotherapy and the placebo effect. *Psychological Bulletin*, 1956, *53*, 294–302.

Rosenthal, D. and Frank, J. D. The fate of psychiatric clinic outpatients assigned to psychotherapy. *Journal of Nervous and Mental Disease*, 1958, *127*, 330–343.

Rosenzweig, S. P. and Folman, R. Patient and therapist variables affecting premature termination in group psychotherapy. *Psychotherapy: Theory, Research and Practice*, 1974, *11*, 76–79.

Rubinstein, E. A. and Lorr, M. A comparison of terminators and remainers in outpatient psychotherapy. *Journal of Clinical Psychology*, 1956, *12*, 345–349.

Ryan, W. (Ed.), *Distress in the city*. Cleveland: The Press of Case Western Reserve University, 1969.

Sattler, J. M. The effects of therapist-client racial similarity. In A. S. Gurman and A. M. Razin (Eds.), *Effective psychotherapy. A handbook of research*. New York: Pergamon Press, 1977.

Schaffer, L. and Myers, J. K. Psychotherapy and social stratification. *Psychiatry*, 1954, *17*, 83–93.

Schofield, W. *Psychotherapy, the purchase of friendship*. Inglewood Cliffs, NJ: Prentice-Hall, 1964.

Shader, R. I. The walk-in service: An experience in community care. In T. Rothman (Ed.), *Changing patterns in psychiatric care*. New York: Crown, 1970.

Shapiro, R. J. Therapist attitudes and premature termination in family and individual therapy. *The Journal of Nervous and Mental Disease*, 1974, *159*, 101–107.

Siegel, N. and Fink, M. Motivation for psychotherapy. *Comprehensive Psychiatry*, 1962, *3*, 170–173.

Sloane, R. B., Staples, F. R., Cristol, A. H., Yorkston, N. J., and Whipple, K. *Psychotherapy versus behavior therapy*. Cambridge: Harvard University Press, 1975.

Smith, G. J. W., Sjöholm, L., and Nielzén, S. Individual factors affecting the improvement of anxiety during a therapeutic period of 1½ to 2 years. *Acta Psychiatrica Scandinavica*, 1975, *52*, 7–22.

Stern, S. L., Moore, S. F., and Gross, S. J. Confounding of personality and social class characteristics in research on premature termination. *Journal of Consulting and Clinical Psychology*, 1975, *43*, 341–344.

Stone, A. R., Frank, J. D., Nash, E. H., and Imber, S. D. An intensive five-year follow-up study of treated psychiatric outpatients. *Journal of Nervous and Mental Disease*, 1961, *133*, 410–422.

Sullivan, P. L., Miller, C., and Smelser, W. Factors in length of stay and progress in psychotherapy. *Journal of Consulting Psychology*, 1958, *22*, 1–9.

Tollinton, H. J. Initial expectations and outcome. *British Journal of Medical Psychology*, 1973, *46*, 251–257.

Truax, C. B. and Carkhuff, R. R. *Toward effective counseling and psychotherapy*. Chicago: Aldine, 1967.

Truax, C. B., Tunnell, B. T., Jr., Fine, H. L., and Wargo, D. G. The prediction of client outcome during group psychotherapy from measures of initial status. Unpublished manuscript, Arkansas Rehabilitation Research and Training Center, University of Arkansas, 1966.

Uhlenhuth, E. and Duncan, D. Subjective change in psychoneurotic outpatients with medical student therapists. II. Some determinants of change. *Archives of General Psychiatry*, 1968, *18*, 532–540.

Weiss, J. and Schaie, K. W. Factors in patient failure to return to clinic. *Diseases of the Nervous System*, 1958, *19*, 429–430.

Wilkins, W. Desensitization: Social and cognitive factors underlying the effectiveness of Wolpe's procedure. *Psychological Bulletin*, 1971, *76*, 311–317.

Wilkins, W. Expectancy of therapeutic gain: An empirical and conceptual critique. *Journal of Consulting and Clinical Psychology*, 1973, *40*, 69–77.

Wilson, G. T. and Thomas, M. G. Self-versus drug-produced relaxation and the effects of instructional set in standardized systematic desensitization. *Behavior Research and Therapy*, 1973, *11*, 279–288.

Wirt, W. M. Psychotherapeutic persistence. *Journal of Consulting Psychology*, 1967, *31*, 429.

Yamamoto, J. and Goin, M. K. Social class factors relevant for psychiatric treatment. *Journal of Nervous and Mental Disease*, 1966, *142*, 332–339.

CHAPTER 4

The Psychotherapist

The psychotherapist is obviously an important variable in psychotherapy, and while the therapist will essentially be the focus in much of what follows in later chapters, it is important to offer first some general comments and observations about the therapist's role, training, personal qualities, and impact on the patient.

We might begin by asking: what are the qualities which appear to be necessary in order for an individual to become an effective therapist? It would appear that he or she should possess certain personal attributes. We might all agree that a basic attribute would be a deep interest in people combined with a humane desire to help them with their psychological difficulties. While this might appear to be a basic and desired characteristic, by itself, it would not necessarily be sufficient. All of us know some individuals who are characterized as "do-gooders" and who want to help humanity, but at the same time appear to be quite troubled themselves. Some persons with good intentions, by intruding into the affairs of other people, oftentimes do more harm than good. We might, therefore, also state that the individual contemplating a career which involves psychotherapy should also possess some reasonable degree of personal adjustment, so that he or she is not overly hampered by personal difficulties which might adversely influence the therapeutic work with disturbed individuals.

In addition to these qualities, we would also anticipate that the would-be therapist should be someone who is sensitive to the feelings and communications of the client, displays some warmth and interest in the client, and is a good and sympathetic listener—at least up to a point. The therapist also has to explain things to the patient at various times and perhaps provide some direction for the patient. Consequently, the therapist should be able to communicate clearly and effectively. If the therapist has to communicate effectively to the client, he or she must not only be a good listener, but must know what to communicate. This, in turn, presupposes some knowledge—in this instance, a knowledge of personality and abnormal behavior, as well as of psychotherapeutic procedures. If the therapist is to acquire and retain this knowledge, he must also be a good learner and this, in turn, implies that he must be possessed of at least some minimum degree of intellectual ability.

In addition to these personal qualities deemed as desirable for the psychotherapist, a few others have also been mentioned. One of these is that the therapist should be a person who commands the trust and respect of the client. If initially the therapist does not inspire the confidence of the client, not only may this affect the expectations which the client has about being helped by the therapist, but he or she may also be more likely to terminate early and/or to seek help elsewhere. The matter of trust also appears to be of particular importance in psychotherapy, since the client is expected in most therapies to confide his personal thoughts and feelings to the therapist, no matter how horrible he may believe they are. If such a process of self-disclosure is in fact to take place, it would appear that the therapist needs to be someone in whom the client can have the utmost trust.

Whereas the personal requisites of the psychotherapist mentioned above have been cited frequently in many different expositions on psychotherapy and would appear to reflect some consensus of opinion on this topic, other attributes or specialized knowledge have also been advocated as desirable or essential by particular individuals or groups. There is little to be gained by reviewing these proposals in any detail for they are based on the beliefs of individuals derived from their own particular professional training and their experience as influenced by their specific professional affiliation. As mentioned in the first chapter, most practitioners of psychotherapy are selected and educated initially as members of a given mental health profession. They are trained to be physicians, psychologists, and social workers primarily, and only secondarily as psychotherapists. For many obvious reasons, their loyalities, their professional society memberships, and their own views are influenced to varying degrees by their professional training and allegiances. As a result, it is not surprising that individual psychotherapists with different professional training and experience may emphasize certain specific requisites for the psychotherapist, particularly in terms of skills or training, which reflect their own background. In the absence of any empirical test of the actual validity of these postulates, they must be regarded strictly as personal views or hypotheses.

In support of the preceding statement we can refer briefly to the report of an interdisciplinary conference arranged to discuss the ideal training of psychotherapists and the possible recognition of a profession of psychotherapy (Holt, 1971). Although the conference participants were decidedly psychoanalytic in their orientation, the professions of psychiatry, clinical psychology, and psychiatric social work were represented. In reading this report one cannot help but be impressed by the extent to which most of the participants were influenced by their own training and professional affiliation. Thus apart from some agreement on the desired personal qualities of the therapist already mentioned, psychiatrists believed that some type of medical training was desirable for all psychotherapists, as well as some experience in hospital emergency rooms, and so forth. Some of the psychologists, on the other hand, expressed the view that all psychotherapists should have training in general psychology and psychological testing. Clearly, these appear to be opinions that have been determined by the professional training and affiliations of the participants and not by any operational or functional analysis of the psychotherapeutic process.

PERSONAL THERAPY FOR THE PSYCHOTHERAPIST

A similar point can be made with regard to another long standing issue in psychotherapy. This pertains to the necessity for the psychotherapist to undergo some personal therapy of his own. Influenced by the views of Freud and the psychoanalysts, many psychotherapists have taken the position that some type of personal psychotherapy should be a basic prerequisite for most, if not all, psychotherapists. The rationale advanced for this view is that the therapist needs to have an intimate knowledge of himself. He needs to be aware of his own areas of conflict and how he responds to others, so that his own personality and his own problems will not unnecessarily intrude on the psychotherapeutic work with the client. This appears to be a reflection or adaptation of that old adage: "Physician, heal thyself." A related reason for undergoing personal therapy is that, by this means, the therapist will himself experience the process and be able to empathize better with the client and to understand how the client may experience psychotherapy. To this extent he or she may be a more sensitive and understanding therapist, as well as a more objective and discerning one.

For such reasons, as well as personal ones, a large number of therapists have secured personal therapy and have also recommended it as an essential training experience for all future psychotherapists. Some, in fact, believe that it was the single most important part of their training in psychotherapy. It is also a requirement of most psychoanalytic institutes and postgraduate psychotherapy training centers, as well as being recommended in other types of training programs. Yet, although such views are strongly held by many psychotherapists, some opposite views are also held (Holt, 1971). One objection made is that the individual who undergoes personal therapy may be overly influenced by the viewpoints of his own therapist and by his own personal experience. Since many of the analytic and post-graduate centers specify that the candidate's therapist must be a member of their institute or approved by them (Rachman and Kauff, 1972), there is a certain amount of indoctrination involved. One particular orientation is stressed to the exclusion of others. In addition, most of the arguments on either side of this question are based on personal convictions rather than on any kind of systematic investigation. By and large, we really have little evidence on which to base any firm conclusions as to whether or not personal therapy makes a person a better therapist. In the final analysis, one would want to appraise the therapeutic outcomes of therapists who had received personal therapy with a comparable group of therapists who had not.

Although no definitive studies on this matter have been reported, a few reports pertaining to it are available and may be worth mentioning. First of all, several surveys of clinical psychologists in the United States have shown that a large number of them have undergone some form of personal psychotherapy. In one survey 57 percent indicated that they had had personal therapy (Lubin, 1962), whereas in another the number exceeded 64 percent of the sample (Goldschmid, Stein, Weissman, and Sorrels, 1969). In a more recent survey of 855 members of the Division of Clinical Psychology of the American Psychological Association, 63 percent stated that they had received some personal therapy (Garfield and Kurtz, 1975).

Henry, Sims, and Spray (1971) conducted a study of professional psychotherapists and also found that a majority of their therapists had received some form of personal therapy. In their sample the percentages of therapists who had not undergone personal therapy were as follows: Clinical psychologists, 25.2 percent; psychiatrists, 34.6 percent; social workers, 35.7 percent; and psychoanalysts, 2.5 percent. It is also interesting to note that in this sample of psychotherapists, a number of them had had more than one psychotherapy experience. Among the psychologists, 41.2 percent had had more than one psychotherapy experience, whereas 52.3 percent of the analysts had had a similar experience. These findings thus support the belief among psychotherapists that personal therapy is a desirable experience for psychotherapists.

In the survey by Garfield and Kurtz (1975) the respondents were asked if they would recommend that all clinical psychologists undergo personal psychotherapy. Of the respondents, 45 percent said "yes,'" 38 percent said "no," and approximately 17 percent were undecided. On another item, the sample was asked to rate the importance of personal psychotherapy as a prerequisite for the work of the clinical psychologist. Almost 36 percent rated personal psychotherapy as very important, with 26 percent rating it to be of moderate importance. It is possible that these figures might have been higher if psychotherapy per se were considered instead of the broader area of clinical psychology. When the responses to this item by those who had had personal therapy were compared with those who had not, the former were significantly more positive concerning the importance of personal therapy. In another comparison, it was shown that 65 percent of those who had had personal therapy recommended it for all clinical psychologists as contrasted with only 10.5 percent of those who had not. A further analysis also revealed a strong relationship between the theoretical orientations held by the sample of respondents and their attitudes toward personal therapy. Generally, those with analytic and Neo-Freudian orientations held the most positive views of personal therapy, while the behavioral and learning theory orientations were the least positive.

It would appear then that one's view concerning the importance of personal therapy as a prerequisite for becoming an effective psychotherapist is very much influenced by one's theoretical views and whether or not the individual himself has undergone personal therapy. As indicated earlier, data on this issue are practically nonexistent although a few studies, most of them quite limited, have been reported. In one of the pioneer attempts to secure some data pertaining to this problem, Strupp (1955) compared the responses of analyzed and nonanalyzed therapists to cards containing brief paragraphs of patient statements taken from psychotherapy interviews. Although Strupp felt that some of his hypotheses concerning differences in the type of response between the two groups were partially confirmed, certain methodological deficiencies in the study, as well as in the size and experience of the two samples, seriously limit any conclusions being drawn.

In the report of a conference on training in psychotherapy, Derner (1960) also made reference to some data he had collected on a small number of students in training. He compared the eight students rated by supervisors as being the best therapists over a period of four years with those eight who were ranked as the poorest therapists over this period and was surprised to note that, in each group, half of the students had had personal therapy and half had not. The ratings of therapeutic competence were thus found to be unrelated to whether or not the therapist had had personal therapy.

In another small study, the hours of personal therapy received by therapists appeared to show an unexpected negative relationship to three criteria of patient change: the Depression and K scales of the MMPI and changes in the therapists' ratings of client disturbance (Garfield and Bergin, 1971). Although no significant tests were performed because of small sample size, the clients of the therapists who had not had personal therapy showed the largest changes on all of the criterion measures. Furthermore, those therapists who appeared to be better adjusted or less disturbed on certain personality measures also seemed to secure the most change in their clients. These findings have to be viewed cautiously since individuals undergoing therapy themselves may be more introspective and self-critical, but they suggest the possible importance of the therapist's own level of adjustment in relation to effectiveness in psychotherapy, rather than the significance of personal therapy.

Finally, reference can also be made to a study by Katz, Lorr, and Rubinstein (1958). In this study therapists' ratings of patient improvement in two subsamples of 58 patients each bore little relationship to whether or not the therapist had had a personal analysis. Although the criterion used to evaluate improvement in this study leaves something to be desired, it is interesting that the therapists' years of experience were correlated significantly with the ratings of improvement.

Before concluding our discussion of personal therapy for the psychotherapist, some additional findings from the study by Henry et al. (1971) are worth mentioning. One concerns the amount of personal threapy received by the therapists in this study. A majority of them received therapy that lasted from 4 to 7 years, ranging from 57 percent of the psychiatrists to 84 percent of the psychoanalysts. Personal therapy of this kind is decidedly time-consuming and expensive, and one may ask whether the experience is commensurate with the investment made. Responses to such a question, of course, may be made on both personal as well as professional grounds. In the investigation by Henry et al. (1971), the therapists were asked to indicate their satisfaction with their personal therapy on a three point scale. With psychoanalysts and psychiatrists, 36 percent, as compared with 46 percent of the psychologists indicated unqualified satisfaction with their personal therapy; 35 percent of the psychoanalysts, 18 percent of the psychiatrists, and 19 percent of the psychologists indicated qualified satisfaction; and 29 percent of the psychoanalysts, 46 percent of the psychiatrists, and 35 percent of the psychologists indicated that they were not satisfied with their personal therapy. These results speak mainly to personal satisfaction with therapy and not directly to the value of such personal therapy on one's effectiveness as a psychotherapist.

The limited data on the relative importance of the therapist's personal therapy as a variable in psychotherapy do not allow one to draw any hard and fast conclusions. However, what data exist do not appear to lend any strong support to the widely held view concerning the importance of personal psychotherapy for effectively conducting psychotherapy. As in other areas of psychotherapy, more systematic and definitive studies are sorely needed.

ADDITIONAL CONSIDERATIONS

We have thus discussed some general qualities which appear to be desirable for the psychotherapist and have also paid some critical attention to the issue of personal therapy as a possible prerequisite for the psychotherapist. As has been emphasized several times already, many of the desirable qualities are based on the beliefs and attempted formulations of a variety of workers in this field. At various times, particularly in terms of conferences or reports devoted to the training of mental health professionals, various lists of the necessary qualifications for entry into the profession have been promulgated (e.g., American Psychological Association, 1947; Holt, 1971; Holt and Luborsky, 1958; Raimy, 1950). Frequently these lists of desired qualifications appear to represent the most highly prized human qualities and virtues. Students who are considering a future career in these professions and who read the recommended personal qualities may not only find themselves rather depressed at their own inability to meet the stated criteria, but they may well wonder if any person who is merely mortal is capable of doing so. An illustration is available from a report of an American Psychological Association Committee on Training in Clinical Psychology (1947). The following were listed as the desirable qualities sought in clinical psychologists: 1) superior ability; 2) originality and resourcefulness; 3) curiosity;)4 interest in persons as individuals; 5) insight into one's own personality characteristics; 6) sensitivity to the complexities of motivation; 7) tolerance; 8) ability to establish warm and effective relationships with others; 9) industry and ability to tolerate pressure; 10) acceptance of responsibility; 11) tact; 12) integrity and self-control; 13) sense of ethical values; 14) broad cultural background; and 15) deep interest in psychology, especially the clinical aspects.

Qualities similar to those just mentioned have also been suggested for psychiatrists (Holt and Luborsky, 1958). Although no one would decry the attempt to set high standards for any profession, and the work of the psychotherapist would indeed appear to require personal qualities of a high order, it is well to recognize that the attributes listed represent an idealized version of the professional person as well as the aspirations of the profession. It is thus understandable that groups concerned with setting high standards for their professions would strive for standards which reflect the abstracted ideals they associate with their work. Although it is desirable to set lofty goals for oneself and one's profession, it is also important to relate such goals or ideals to some empirically tested standards of performance. Apart from the difficult task of actually attempting to define and appraise the abstract qualities deemed desirable for the profession of psychotherapy, it is also of decided importance to demonstrate that such selected qualities actually are related to the high levels of performance desired. To a large extent this task has not been adequately fulfilled. Let us, therefore, examine some of the work which has been done on the selection of clinical psychologists and psychiatrists for graduate and post-graduate education, as well as more directly related studies of the qualities of psychotherapists in relation to their performance in psychotherapy.

One of the pioneer studies in this area was a large scale investigation sponsored by the Veterans Administration shortly after World War II on the selection of individuals for the graduate programs in clinical psychology cooperating with the Veterans Administration. At this time, there was a critical shortage of trained mental health personnel and the Veterans Administration (V. A.) was faced with the enormous task of caring for the large number of psychiatric casualties entrusted to them at the conclusion of the war. Among other developments, the V. A. entered into cooperative arrangements with selected graduate departments of psychology to help select and train individuals to become clinical psychologists, thereby providing a potential pool of psychologists for their own clinics and hospitals. In addition, funds were provided for a research project on the selection of clinical psychologists.

This project, administered by Lowell Kelly, was a unique project in that prospective trainees from many universities came to the University of Michigan where they were intensively studied by means of tests and interviews (Kelly & Fiske, 1951). All of the popular psychological tests were used, as well as in-depth interviews, group exercises, observations, and a final integrative appraisal by experienced clinical psychologists. These selective measures were later correlated with successful completion of the program and ratings of clinical performance during training at V. A. field stations. On the whole, the results of this large scale enterprise were disappointing. Very few of the predictive measures bore much relationship to the various criteria used, and the highest correlations obtained were in the neighborhood of around .30. Although there have been numerous conferences on the training of clinical psychologists since that time, as far as this writer knows, there have been no similar attempts to appraise and predict successful performance in clinical psychology.

A somewhat similar attempt to study the characteristics of psychiatric residents in training in relation to performance in the clinical situation was carried out at the Menninger Clinic and reported in some detail by Holt and Luborsky (1958). This study was more psychoanalytically and clinically oriented, perhaps, than the one reported by Kelly and Fiske, but in general the results were not more promising. Thus although leaders in a particular mental health field may demonstrate some agreement in what they believe are the desirable or necessary attributes for the successful performance of their special area of skill, attempts to appraise these attributes and relate them to functional criteria of performance have generally been disappointing.

It is possible to criticize the two studies mentioned previously on certain counts. In the investigation concerning clinical psychologists, the students had been selected for admission to graduate study by different university departments of psychology in terms of their own criteria and selection standards. In most instances the criteria are deemed to pertain to successful completion of an academic, as well as clinical program, leading to the Ph.D. degree, which is essentially a research degree. That is, the students were not selected solely on the basis of becoming psychotherapists or clinicians. Intellectual and academic criteria were involved to a great extent in their initial selection before they were evaluated at Ann Arbor. The criteria of successful performance at both the university and the clinical training site undoubtedly left much to be desired and varied from setting to setting.

In the study of the psychiatrists in training, other factors also have to be considered. Although all of the psychiatric residents received their training and evaluation in one large center with one central administration, the group was already a highly selected one. Initially, they had been admitted to different medical schools on the basis of the latter's academic requirements, and all of the residents, of course, had successfully completed their medical school training and then their medical internship. The basic criteria in these instances were not psychiatric or psychotherapeutic ones, but ones deemed important generally for the practice of medicine. They were then later selected for admission to the highly sought after residency program affiliated with the Menninger Clinic where ostensibly psychiatric criteria were used. As in the Michigan project, the results were also influenced by the procedures used for selection and evaluation. The criteria of performance, as in many studies of this type, tended to be the ratings provided by supervisors rather than the actual outcomes secured in psychotherapy. Thus one could say that both of these important projects were not directly concerned with the selection and performance of psychotherapists per se, although without doubt, the majority of the subjects in these two studies were later involved with psychotherapeutic activities.

More directly related to the matter of therapists' qualities and performance in actual psychotherapy with clients have been the studies carried out by the client-centered therapists. These have investigated what have been designated as the necessary and essential therapeutic conditions for positive outcome in psychotherapy. As mentioned previously, these were termed empathy or accurate empathy, non-possessive warmth, and genuineness or congruence on the part of the therapist (Truax and Carkhuff, 1967). Empathy referred not only to the ability of the therapist to accurately gauge and understand the feelings which the client was experiencing and trying to express, but also the ability to communicate this understanding to the client. Non-possessive warmth, apparently derived in part from Rogers' earlier formulation of unconditional positive regard, pertained to the deep acceptance of the individual as he was. Genuineness referred to the therapist functioning as himself or herself and without playing any role or attempting to communicate any feelings which he or she was not actually experiencing. The therapist had to be perceived and experienced by the client as a genuine individual and not as a "phony."

These conditions, viewed as the necessary and sufficient conditions for succesful psychotherapy, were essentially therapist conditions or qualities of the therapist which were discernible in his or her interactions with the client. Nothing was really said about the importance of the client or patient as a variable in the outcome of psychotherapy. Rather, it was assumed that these therapist conditions were of sufficient power to determine the progress of psychotherapy regardless of the type of client. Perhaps no other formulation of psychotherapy has placed such emphasis on the important role of the psychotherapist. To their credit, however, it can be emphasized that the client-centered therapists were not content with mere statements or formulations of the desired therapist conditions. They went beyond this point with attempts to define their concepts in operational terms, to create rating scales that could be used to evaluate tape recordings of actual therapy sessions, and to conduct research investigations relating the therapist conditions to various processes and outcome in psychotherapy. This certainly was an important achievement in psychotherapy, for such research is difficult and tedious. However, it is a way of trying to study therapist qualities as manifested in the actual operations of psychotherapy and relating them to outcome.

Now let us look at some of the results secured by investigations of therapist conditions and outcome in psychotherapy. A description of some of the scales used and the results of several studies were published in the volume by Truax and Carkhuff (1967), and we can refer first to that report. These authors summarized several studies performed by them and related colleagues showing the relationship of the rated therapeutic conditions to various measures of outcome. Although most of the findings appeared to be quite positive, there were also some findings which were both interesting and perplexing. Whereas all three of the therapeutic conditions were postulated as theoretically necessary for positive outcome, in some of the studies one of the conditions, and not always the same one, was either not correlated with outcome or was negatively correlated with the measures of outcome. This immediately raises the interesting question of how a factor which is supposedly required for positive outcome can, in some instances, be of no importance or even of negative importance. Another finding of interest was that, in some studies, two of the therapeutic conditions would show a high intercorrelation but would show either little correlation or a negative correlation with the third therapeutic condition. The high correlation between two of the rated conditions suggests also that they were appraising the same factor rather than different ones.

Truax and Carkhuff (1967) attempted to resolve this unexpected result by taking a somewhat empirical orientation. The findings being what they were, they suggested that when two of the scales were positively related and the third was not, attention should be given only to the former and the latter be disregarded. In other words, "when one of the three conditions is negatively related to the other two in any given sample of therapists, then patient outcome is best predicted by whichever two conditions are most closely related to each other" (p. 91). Although this procedure conceivably might work for practical or predictive purposes, it obviously makes little theoretical sense, particularly when the two conditions selected would vary from situation to situation. Bordin (1970), in a review of the book by Truax and Carkhuff, commented upon the matter in a similar way:

The authors display an astonishing facility for shaping all kinds of seemingly contradictory data to fit their theory. For example, two studies come up with the contradictory results that, in one instance, warmth, in the other instance, genuineness, were negatively related to outcome. The puzzling question of how an aspect of relationships that is thought to contribute to personal growth can in such instances act as though it interferes with growth is brushed aside with the happy thought that, since in both instances the offending ingredient is also negatively related to the other two conditions, "then patient outcome is best predicted by whichever two conditions are most closely related to each other." This facility is matched by the ease with which they seem to stretch their theoretical commitments (p. 79).

Thus one might well have some reservations about the actual meaning of the three postulated therapeutic conditions and their possible relationship to positive outcome in psychotherapy. Additional research by other investigators has also provided additional data which failed to support the claims of the client-centered group. In one study that was conducted with therapists who were largely eclectic or somewhat analytically oriented in terms of orientation, and that utilized the scales published by Truax and Carkhuff (1967), the results were largely negative (Garfield and Bergin, 1971). Although ratings of empathy and warmth were positively inter-correlated (.75), both of these scales were negatively correlated with the ratings of genuineness or congruence ($-.65$ and $-.66$). Here, again, one of the essential conditions was significantly correlated in a negative direction with the other two. Furthermore, when the ratings of the three therapist conditions were correlated with a wide variety of outcome measures, including client, therapist, and supervisor ratings of change, as well as pre and post differences on several scales of the MMPI, not one reached an acceptable level of significance. The findings consistently failed to show any relationship between ratings of therapist conditions and measures of outcome.

The negative results reported above have been followed by other similar results (Beutler et al., 1973; Kurtz and Grummon, 1972; Mullen and Abeles, 1971; Sloane et al., 1975), and the earlier promise of these therapeutic conditions has, unfortunately, not received the anticipated support. Mitchell, Bozarth, and Krauft (1977) have reviewed this literature and clearly indicated the increase of negative or nonsupporting results in recent years. The earlier studies by Truax and others also have been criticized as weak methodologically (Lambert and De Julio, 1976; Parloff, Waskow, and Wolfe, 1978), and the psychometric qualities of the scales used to appraise the three conditions have been found wanting (Chinsky and Rappaport, 1970; Rappaport & Chinsky, 1972; Truax, 1972). Although at first it was believed that perhaps these scales might apply only to client-centered therapists and that the negative results secured with other types of therapists might be explained on this basis, the more recent studies and reviews do not appear to lend any strong support to this possible explanation.

The issues pertaining to the research on the therapeutic conditions of empathy, warmth, and genuineness are complex and cannot be discussed in greater detail here. Two recently published reviews are recommended to those who care to pursue this matter in greater depth (Mitchell et al., 1977; Parloff et al., 1978). Some relevant conclusions from these reviews, however, can be mentioned here. Mitchell et al. (1977) state that it is "increasingly clear that *the mass of data neither supports nor rejects the overriding influence of such variables as empathy, warmth, and genuineness in all cases. . . . The recent evidence, although equivocal, does seem to suggest that empathy, warmth, and genuineness are related in some way to client change but that their potency and generalizability are not as great as once thought*" (p. 483). Parloff et al. (1978) in their review come to the following conclusion:

It must be concluded that the unqualified claim that "high" levels (absolute or relative) of accurate empathy, warmth, and genuineness (independent of the source of rating or the nature of the instrument) represent the "necessary and sufficient" conditions for effective therapy (independent of the outcome measures or criterion) is not supported (p. 249.)

The above conclusions, although differing somewhat in their emphases, generally tend to dampen the enthusiasm expressed earlier with regard to empathy, warmth, and genuineness as the essential conditions for facilitating therapeutic change. Negative findings and the failure to replicate earlier results which appeared promising are always disappointing, and the failure to substantiate the earlier reports of the client-centered therapists was particularly disappointing for several reasons. One is that the therapist qualities or conditions conceptualized by the client-centered school have been the type of therapist qualities which have also been presumed to be important therapist qualities by therapists of other theoretical persuasions. Although they may at times be stated differently and formulated within somewhat different contexts, such attributes as therapist empathy, warmth, and genuineness would be considered to be desirable and important qualities of all effective therapists. When studies indicate that careful ratings of such qualities do not appear to be significantly related to outcome, some feelings of insecurity and disappointment would be very likely to occur. A second reason is that the earlier work in this area appeared to mark a significant step forward in the attempt to make the abstract, and often ethereal, concepts of psychotherapy operational. The development of rating scales to appraise significant therapist qualities based on actual therapeutic performance, and then relating such measures to outcome, was of potentially great importance. Nevertheless, while later research has failed to lend support to the very promising findings reported earlier, the general approach of carefully trying to define important therapist characteristics, of developing scales to evaluate these characteristics as they are manifested in the actual interactions with a client in therapy, and then relating the measures of these characteristics to outcome in psychotherapy, is a desirable model to follow.

THE THERAPIST AND THE PSYCHOTHERAPEUTIC INTERACTION

We have thus discussed some of the more general views concerning the qualifications and personal prerequisites of the psychotherapist, as well as reviewing some of the research which has been performed in this area. As is true in many other areas of psychology and the social sciences generally, there are many orientations and views within the field of psychotherapy, and many of them have never been investigated systematically. When attempts are made to conduct such investigations, more often than not, a number of prevailing beliefs fail to be substantiated. Although this is not the happiest state of affairs, it is not a unique one in terms of historical development, and one must see it realistically for what it is—a certain stage in the development of any field. Although individuals generally are more comfortable with unchallenged beliefs, and this is also true of therapists and clients alike, one must also keep in mind that science advances when old beliefs are gradually replaced by newer beliefs based on more solid supporting evidence. Nevertheless, individuals are more comfortable with authoritative views and certainty. Hope and faith are powerful human forces and they also play a potentially important role in psychotherapy. However, advances in psychotherapy can only take place if we face up to the difficult task of testing our most cherished beliefs.

The issue mentioned above is of definite importance as far as the present writer is concerned and is not merely idle philosophical musing. It is one which has been evident many times in my own career as a clinical psychologist and as a psychotherapist. It has also concerned me in my role as a teacher of psychotherapy. How does one try to convey information and knowledge concerning the procedures and techniques of psychotherapy and at the same time acquaint the student with the state of validated knowledge in our field, the gaps in our knowledge, and the need to take a somewhat critical stance toward views which have failed to be supported or which still lack empirical verification? This is a very difficult and often frustrating task. If one presents theoretical views or procedures as if they were received from on high or as if they were self-evident truths which do not require any empirical validation, one may inspire a greater sense of well-being and confidence in the student therapist, but is it really

desirable in the long run? Do we want to train smug individuals who believe they have the final word on psychotherapy? Is the "super psychotherapist" as sometimes portrayed in Hollywood movies a desirable model?
On the other hand, an overly critical emphasis on our lack of knowledge
and on the frequent occurrence of negative findings can produce an overly
discouraged or nihilistic attitude that is also undesirable. There is clearly
a difficult dilemma presented here, and one that is not easy to resolve. This
issue, furthermore, is far from being an academic or outdated one. As I
sit in my study in London writing this, I recall a short column in yesterday's
newspaper which alluded to this very issue. It is reproduced here:

SOCIAL WORK ATTACK "Little or no effort"

  Most social work has little or no effect on the people it is supposed to help,
a psychiatrist said at a weekend social services conference.
  Dr. Colin Brewer, of Birmingham University, said at Canterbury that social
workers who did good were cancelled out by those who did harm.
  The social work and psychiatric services had never been busier, but there
was more human misery, depressive illness, and cases of suicide and attempted
suicide.
  Lord Longford said Dr. Brewer was talking dangerous nonsense. "There
would never be any social reform in this country if we first had to wait for the
social scientists to produce statistics to prove it would be beneficial," he said.
(Daily Telegraph, London, September 13, 1976)

  In this newspaper clipping we have the two opposing views presented,
and to some degree they both have merit. Many of the so-called helpful or
therapeutic activities carried on in our own communities may well be ineffective, or even harmful, and there is some evidence in support of this to
which we will refer later. At the same time, it is also true that it is frequently necessary to institute activities before they are fully shown to have
the desired effects. There are many practical situations where action is required and where we must proceed on the basis of whatever knowledge
we have, scant though it may be. In some cases, indecision and delay may
well be fatal. In some cases, also, the task of carefully collecting and
weighing the data may be a long and difficult one, and practical decisions
must be made and action taken before all the findings are in. However,
although it may be necessary to act in such instances, it is also important
to evaluate our actions and decisions so that in the future we may profit
from our past experiences and improve the bases for our future actions.
  The writer has devoted some space to this issue because he believes it
is an important one for most psychotherapists. The psychotherapist functions as a socially sanctioned healer, and while assuming the role and

responsibilities of all healers, he is, in some ways, unique. There are few professions that make more demands on the personality of the participant than that of psychotherapy, and in which the personality characteristics of the individual are considered to be of such prime importance. It is difficult to think of any professional pursuit that requires the kind of intimate and sustained interaction with a client as that which is deemed characteristic of the psychotherapist. The psychotherapist, by the nature of his or her work, is brought into daily and close contact with all varieties of human suffering, and not only must he or she have the necessary personal strength to face and cope with such ills, but the psychotherapist must also have some conviction that his or her efforts are helpful in alleviating the discomforts of the client.

To a certain extent, therefore, as a psychotherapist one must believe in one's self and in one's therapeutic procedures. It is very difficult to persist in tasks one personally believes to be of no value. Not only is it important to have faith or confidence in oneself and one's therapy if one is to continue in one's life's work, but because of the interactions characteristic of psychotherapy, the beliefs or confidence of the psychotherapist may also have an effect on the patient and the patient's progress in therapy. A therapist who radiates confidence in his ability to help patients may inspire confidence in many of them, which in turn may facilitate progress in their therapy. If, of course, the therapist is overly confident and promises too much, this may backfire and have the opposite result, particularly with some patients. On the other hand, if the therapist is overly pessimistic and indicates little confidence in his procedures, the prophecy may be fulfilled or the client may be done with him quickly. From our earlier discussions of client expectations, the reader may recall that many of these can be influenced or manipulated by the therapist in therapy to some degree. The therapist is a significant figure to the client, and the former's personality, moods, and beliefs, as well as the communications influenced by them, can be hypothesized to exert some influence on the client and his progress in therapy.

All of these different aspects of the issue being discussed here appear to be of some significance for the psychotherapist. The psychotherapist needs to be a scientifically responsible and ethical person and must also be able to inspire a reasonable degree of confidence in the client. He should not make unwarranted statements or promises lest he take on the qualities of a quack who makes statements he does not believe, but at the other extreme, it would not be helpful to present the client with a summary of the many negative findings culled from the psychotherapeutic literature. Obviously, some better solution has to be secured and, in general, each psychotherapist tends to resolve it in his own particular way.

My own view on this matter, for what it is worth, goes something like this. In psychotherapy there are many views, clinical beliefs, and folklore, as well as some reasonably supported facts. When a particular view or procedure has received some empirical or research support, we clearly should note this fact. This type of finding has data back of it, and as a consequence, we can have some confidence in it. The degree of confidence is determined by the kind and amount of research which has been produced in support of a particular method or procedure. For example, we can state with a moderate amount of confidence that outcome in psychotherapy generally is little influenced by the sex or age of the client. We could also state, as another illustration, that recent research findings indicate that a relatively small percentage of clients who undergo psychotherapy appear to become worse than when they started psychotherapy, but that the exact percentage and the precise factors responsible are not yet determined with any conclusiveness (Bergin and Lambert, 1978; Lambert, Bergin, and Collins, 1977; Strupp, Hadley, and Gomes-Schwartz, 1977). On some other items, one can only state that "there appears to be a suggestion that" variable A may influence variable B, but further data are needed. The results of various pretraining programs in psychotherapy, to be discussed later, might be used as an illustration for the preceding sentence since both positive and inconclusive results have been secured.

Without going into much detail, it can also be noted that, in other instances, one can only state that a particular view or procedure has never been investigated and, therefore, must be viewed as an hypothesis. Consequently, it must be treated as such and viewed somewhat more critically as a tentative belief in need of confirmation. In other instances, the limited and conflicting data available suggest that one must keep an open mind on the problem and hope that further and more definitive data will be forthcoming. The field of psychotherapy is made up of many different kinds of views and findings. With some we may have a fair degree of confidence, with some we may feel the data point us in one direction, but just slightly, and in others we may have to conclude that in the absence of data we are proceeding on what appear to be reasonable or warranted hypotheses or assumptions. Final answers are simply not available, and we must proceed on what appears to be the soundest path possible. In some instances, we can have confidence that our procedures are based on reasonably sound empirical results. In others, we must trust our own judgment and intelligence, recognizing fully what we are doing and the bases for our decisions. Finally, we must also be ready to modify our views and even our strongly held beliefs when research data appear to challenge them.

There is also a related issue that has sometimes been discussed and debated among psychotherapists of different orientations. This pertains to whether psychotherapy is to be considered as an art or as a science. In one seminar in which I participated, one of the student participants made the comment that the discussion revealed our lack of knowledge on this particular point and that it highlighted the necessity for research on this problem. Two of the supervising psychotherapists in the group responded in a strong emotional fashion that psychotherapy was an art, would always be an art, and would never become a science. Although it would certainly be very difficult to take the stand that psychotherapy as practiced today is a science, there are many dangers inherent in the view that psychotherapy is fundamentally an art, and, therefore, can never be looked at or investigated in anything approaching an objective manner. To see psychotherapy as solely an artistic enterprise, dependent on the intuitions of the psychotherapist, is to completely remove it from any attempts at objective appraisal or from any means of increasing our understanding of the process in order to improve its effectiveness. Rather, we must avail ourselves of all procedures which may offer us a means of increasing the effectiveness of psychotherapy. The scientific model of research has proven its utility in other areas of knowledge and practice and appears to have definite usefulness in the area of psychotherapy. It has contributed greatly to the advances evident in the field of medicine, and should not be banished because of a biased preconceived view. At the same time, it should be recognized that the more classical models of research must be applied intelligently and modified as necessary if they are to lend themselves to useful application. However, this is a research issue which can be postponed for the time being.

ETHICAL AND PROFESSIONAL RESPONSIBILITIES

When the therapist accepts an individual as a client in psychotherapy, he assumes the responsibilities and professional obligations that go with this role. As a member of a recognized profession and as one performing the duties of a sanctioned healer, the psychotherapist is guided by the code of ethics of his or her profession, as well as by society's laws and regulations. Although the various mental health professions may have somewhat different official ethical codes, they are similar in emphasizing the responsibilities that a person has for his or her client. Since these are usually communicated by each of the professions in their training institutions for individuals undergoing training, there is no need to list them here. In general, they tend to emphasize the responsibility of the professional person to represent himself and his therapeutic skills honestly, to refrain from making false claims or promises that he cannot deliver, to accept only those clients whom he legitimately can expect to help, and to refer, to other qualified persons, those cases that fall outside of his field of expertise or which can be handled better elsewhere. The importance of not charging fees that are beyond the client's means or beyond what are regarded as reasonable, of avoiding taking advantage of his role in his relationship with the client, of respecting the confidential nature of the relationship, and of regarding the client's welfare as a primary concern, are also stressed.

As pointed out earlier, because there is no separate profession of psychotherapy, those who practice psychotherapy are usually governed by the ethical codes and practices of their own profession. It might be expected that because of the special relationship and interaction which occurs in psychotherapy, some particular ethical guides have been developed for the psychotherapist. However, this does not appear to have occurred. In part, this may be due to the efficacy of the codes already developed for the members of the respective mental health professions. Although this generally seems to be the case, there are some special features which are of particular concern in the case of psychotherapy.

One problem is that there are individuals who are engaged in counseling or psychotherapeutic activities who are not members of the recognized mental health professions and who may have had little training in psychotherapy. Since there is no legal certification of the title psychotherapist, there is little that can be done in such instances unless the person involved has indicated to his clients that he is a psychologist, physician, or other legally recognized and licensed profession. In this case, there is a possible case for legal action, since the individual is practicing a profession for which he is legally not qualified. In the long run, the main hope for reducing such practice is probably by public education, even though there are problems in defining precisely what psychotherapy is and how it differs from counseling, guidance, communication workshops, self-discovery groups, and the like.

A related problem concerns those members of the recognized mental health professions who engage in psychotherapy, but who have actually received very little formal training in psychotherapy. This problem has its own complexities. For example, a physician is licensed to engage in the practice of medicine. As such he is legally qualified to treat physical and mental illness. There is no special attention paid to psychotherapy per se. A similar situation holds with regard to the certification and licensing of psychologists. In most states, there is a general certification for psychologists which does not specify the particular specialty of the individual psychologist. Some may be industrial psychologists, or educational psychologists, as well as clinical or counseling psychologists. The main injunction in these instances is the ethical code of the profession which provides a guide for the state associations. It is explicitly stated that it is unethical for a psychologist to offer his services in areas where he has not received adequate training. Although a psychologist who engages in the practice of psychotherapy may be brought before the state licensing board or the ethics committee if he is deemed to be unfit for such practice, it is not easy to get such individuals to stop their practice. Ethical committees do not appear overly eager to bring charges against a colleague, the process is a tedious one, and members of the profession are reluctant to give testimony for many reasons. Consequently, it is only the more serious or notorious cases which finally receive some kind of official or legal action.

Although such loopholes currently exist and there are undoubtedly a number of poorly trained or unqualified therapists who are engaged in some form of psychotherapy, the serious student and practitioner of psychotherapy should be aware of his ethical and professional responsibilities, as well as some of the problems he may encounter in his practice. A nonmedical psychotherapist should be sensitive to problems which might be organic in nature and be ready to make the appropriate referral or seek consultation. This is not as simple a matter as it may seem, for somatic complaints may have other than organic etiology and the proper handling of them may be quite important in the progress of psychotherapy. If a psychotherapist constantly refers his clients, he or she may be indicating a lack of adequacy and self-confidence which could affect the client and the eventual outcome of therapy. On the other hand, if the therapist neglects what may be realistic symptoms or interprets them as resistance on the part of the client, he may be failing in his overall responsibility for the welfare of the client. In a similar fashion, a psychiatrist who is organically oriented may rely too heavily on medication, sometimes increasing the dosage instead of fully appraising the psychological nature of the problem and referring the patient for psychotherapy. Clearly all practitioners must be well versed in psychopathology, as well as being capable of sound judgment.

There are a few other aspects which appear particularly relevant to psychotherapy, although they are not, perhaps, the exclusive concern of psychotherapists alone. We have already made reference to the higher frequency of close contact between the psychotherapist and his client than is true in most other professional relationships and to the fact that the client usually brings forth material of a highly personal nature. In a sense, he or she exposes oneself to the psychotherapist and, thus, places oneself in the "therapist's hands." The therapist may also be viewed as a powerful person in whom one places his trust and well-being. As a consequence, the therapist can have significant power or control over such a client. As noted also, the client may develop transference feelings or a strong emotional attachment to the therapist. In such instances, the client may express admiration for the wonderful qualities of the therapist and even bring the therapist gifts. As reported many years ago by Freud, some patients may even express feelings of love for the therapist. This is all very heady stuff, and although psychotherapists may have been instructed to be aware of and to anticipate such behaviors on the part of the client, some may be overly influenced by their own needs to pay much attention to these strictures. To be placed in such a role may be too satisfying and pleasurable for some therapists to resist. Furthermore, the times have changed greatly since Freud's time and, whereas, as a product of 19th century Vienna, he was horrified to receive confessions of love from some of his female patients, such does not always appear to be the case today. Recently, there have been published several accounts of the seduction of female patients by their male therapists, and there apparently are some therapists who have even viewed this as therapeutically desirable (American Psychological Association, 1975; Holroyd and Brodsky, 1977; Kardener, Fuller, and Mensh, 1973). This is perhaps an unusual instance of the all-knowing therapist prescribing what is best for the client and responding with empathy, warmth, and genuineness!

The above, of course, represent some extreme examples of the intimacy which may develop, particularly in more intensive or long-term psychotherapy, as well as the importance of the therapist's own personal needs as they take precedence over those of the client. Obviously, the therapist who lets his own needs become predominant over those of the client is behaving in a manner both unethical and detrimental to the client's welfare. In our own time where there has been an emphasis on openness and strong expressions of affect, as exemplified in the encounter and marathon groups, including nude marathon groups (Mintz, 1971), such incidents may perhaps be more likely. The emphasis among some recent therapeutic orientations on the openness of the therapist, personally, in therapy may also play a role in creating a different type of relationship, one which modifies or diminishes the more traditional professional role of the psychotherapist. Although some such developments appear to be promulgated by sincere and professionally qualified individuals, they also appear to possibly potentiate the likelihood of undesirable effects on the part of the clients

(Lieberman, Yalom, and Miles, 1973; Hartley, Roback, and Abramovitz, 1976).

Although the previous incidents, perhaps, may be the most dramatic, there are other instances where the therapist's needs may appear to take priority over those of the patient's. Because of the nature of the psychotherapeutic enterprise, there may be manifested on the part of both patient and therapist a need to keep the relationship going regardless of purely therapeutic considerations. Many different reasons may exist for this on the part of the therapist. Initially, he may want a new client to continue in therapy because he has many open hours in his schedule and/or he would not like to lose this income. The therapist may also have the conviction that additional therapy is desirable for the patient. In a clinical situation it may also be a matter of personal pride for the therapist to keep his or her patients coming regularly for therapy instead of having them drop out early. Student therapists, in the writer's experience, are particularly involved with their first few clients and will go to great lengths to keep these clients in therapy whether this is desirable or not. They are willing to see them at any time of day or night, and one student was even agreeable to traveling over an hour to see her client regularly at the client's home when the client showed no inclination to return for future appointments. Such therapists are understandably crestfallen when a client fails to show up for a scheduled appointment, and they must be made to see that their therapeutic zeal to help the patient is also a manifestation of their own personal needs, socially desirable though they may appear to be.

The therapist's needs may also enter in other ways to foster the continuation of the patient in therapy. The therapist may secure personal gratification from having an admiring or grateful patient continue in therapy for a long period. It is positive reinforcement for the therapist's ego and makes up for some of the other patients who are less appreciative of the therapist's services. As a consequence, the therapist may keep some patients in therapy for a long period on the basis of a mutual reinforcement schedule, but not in terms of the actual needs of the patient for change. The ostensibly altruistic theme to the effect that the patient "needs me" or needs more therapy may at times actually reflect some needs of the therapist rather than an objective appraisal of the client's need for continued psychotherapy. In clinical practice it can be noted that some therapists appear to keep their patients in therapy for very long periods of time, and this has also been reported in one study (Stieper and Wiener, 1959). The therapists in such instances may state that these patients need long-term therapy or support and that without such therapy many of these patients would have to be hospitalized. However, in an investigation of this problem in one clinic where the therapists were told to terminate their cases of many years duration, no unfortunate consequences ensued (Stieper and Wiener, 1959; Stieper and Wiener, 1965). Nevertheless, long-term psychotherapy has been accorded a positive status in certain circles, and it is not uncommon to hear of therapy lasting 10 to 20 years, and referred to with a certain pride by the therapist (Kelman, 1971). The problem, of course, is deciding in some relatively objective or reasoned manner, whether such long-term therapy is really in the patient's interest or whether it is determined primarily by personal needs of the therapist. In essence, at what point should the patient be freed of his or her dependence on the therapist?

As far as the writer is concerned, the major responsibility for seeing that psychotherapy is carried out with the greatest dispatch and in the most efficient manner resides in the therapist. The client, after all, is relatively uninformed and gullible in such matters and can be very much influenced by the therapist. This is particularly true in the case of certain clients who are rather passive and submissive. In the case of such clients, therapy may also increase their dependency on the therapist and not only will they be willing to continue therapy for a long period, even at some financial sacrifice, but they may then actually resist terminating therapy. In effect, it has become a way of life for them, and it is difficult for them to give it up. Although the client may very much want to prolong therapy, this does not mean that the therapy has actually accomplished positive gains or has been therapeutic for the client. Instead, it has given him a new crutch and lessened his capacity for independent action. Although it might not be entirely fair to view the therapist's behavior in such instances as unethical, it certainly does not represent competent or acceptable professional performance.

The psychotherapist, therefore, has to be alert to a great many considerations in order to carry out his or her duties in the most responsible and effective manner possible. In addition to displaying a sincere interest in the client and in striving to help him overcome his difficulties, the therapist must also try to be as objective and responsible as possible in appraising the client's problems and in conducting his or her therapeutic work. In an area such as psychotherapy, where there are few explicit and objective guidelines concerning what procedures should be followed and how long treatment should take, the professional and ethical responsibility assumed by the therapist is indeed a heavy one. The particular nature of the psychotherapeutic relationship also would appear to require not only qualities of human sensitivity and empathy, but also those of extreme objectivity in which the client's welfare is in truth the main guide for the therapist's activities. Whereas a knowledge of human personality and behavior, including abnormal behavior, and a knowledge of psychotherapeutic theories and techniques are basic requirements for the effective practice of psychotherapy, by themselves they are not sufficient. The therapist's personal qualities, including a real and objective concern for the client, an awareness of his own needs and interactions in therapy, a relatively mature personality which does not require undue personal gratification at the client's expense, and a deep awareness of his ethical and professional obligations, are of decided importance. The psychotherapist must also be aware of the lacks in our knowledge of the psychotherapeutic process, be alert to the research in his field and be ready to modify his views when they fail to receive empirical validation, and, not least of all, be able to live with uncertainty. Thus the list of requisites for being an effective psychotherapist is not a small one.

REFERENCES

American Psychological Association, Committee on Training in Clinical Psychology. Recommended graduate training program in clinical psychology. *American Psychologist*, 1947, *2*, 539–558.

American Psychological Association. Report of the Task Force on sex bias and sex role stereotyping in psychotherapeutic practice. *American Psychologist*, 1975, *30*, 1169–1175.

Bergin, A. E., and Lambert, M. J. The evaluation of therapeutic outcomes. In S. L. Garfield and A. E. Bergin (Eds.), *Handbook of psychotherapy and behavior change*, 2nd ed. New York: Wiley, 1978.

Beutler, L. E., Johnson, D. T., Neville, C. W., Jr., Workman, S. N., and Elkins, D. The A-B therapy-type distinction, accurate empathy, nonpossessive warmth, and therapist genuineness in psychotherapy. *Journal of Abnormal Psychology*, 1973, *82*, 273–277.

Bordin, E. S. Review of C. B. Truax and R. R. Carkhuff, *Toward effective counseling and psychotherapy*. *Community Mental Health Journal*, 1970, *6*, 78–80.

Chinsky, J. M. and Rappaport, J. Brief critique of meaning and reliability of "accurate empathy" ratings. *Psychological Bulletin*, 1970, *73*, 379–382.

Derner, G. F. An interpersonal approach to training in psychotherapy. In N. P. Dellis and H. K. Stone (Eds.), *The training of psychotherapists*. Baton Rouge, La.: Louisiana State University Press, 1960.

Garfield, S. L. and Bergin, A. E. Personal therapy, outcome and some therapist variables. *Psychotherapy: Theory, Research and Practice*, 1971, *8*, 251–253.

Garfield, S. L. and Kurtz, R. Clinical psychologists: A survey of selected attitudes and values. *The Clinical Psychologist*, 1975, *28*, (Spring), 4–7.

Goldschmid, M. L., Stein, D. D., Weissman, N. H., and Sorrels, J. A survey of the training and practices of clinical psychologists. *The Clinical Psychologist*, 1969, *22*, 89–94.

Hartley, D., Roback, H. B., and Abramowitz, S. I. Deterioration effects in encounter groups. *American Psychologist*, 1976, *31*, 247–255.

Henry, W. E., Sims, J. H., and Spray, S. L. *The fifth profession*. San Francisco: Jossey-Bass, 1971.

Holroyd, J. C. and Brodsky, A. M. Psychologists' attitudes and practices regarding erotic and nonerotic physical contact with patients. *American Psychologist*, 1977, *32*, 843–849.

Holt, R. R. (Ed.), *New horizon for psychotherapy*. New York: International Universities Press, 1971.

Holt, R. R. and Luborsky, L. *Personality patterns of psychiatrists: A study in selection techniques*. Vol. 1. New York: Basic Books, 1958.

Kardener, S., Fuller, M., and Mensh, I. A survey of physicians' attitudes and practices regarding erotic and nonerotic contact with patients. *American Journal of Psychiatry*, 1973, *130*, 1077–1081.

Katz, M. M., Lorr, M., and Rubinstein, E. A. Remainer patient attributes and their relation to subsequent improvement in psychotherapy. *Journal of Consulting Psychology*, 1958, *22*, 411–413.

Kelly, E. L. and Fiske, D. W. *The prediction of performance in clinical psychology*. Ann Arbor: University of Michigan Press, 1951.

Kelman, H. *Helping people: Karen Horney's psychoanalytical approach*. New York: Science House, 1971.

Kurtz, R. and Grummon, D. Different approaches to the measurement of therapist empathy and their relationship to therapy outcomes. *Journal of Consulting and Clinical Psychology*, 1972, *39*, 106–116.

Lambert, M. J., Bergin, A., and Collins, J. Therapist-induced deterioration in psychotherapy. In A. Gurman and A. Razin (Eds.), *Effective psychotherapy. A handbook of research*. New York: Pergamon, 1977.

Lambert, M. J. and DeJulio, S. S. *Outcome research in Carkhuff's human resource development training programs: Where is the donut?* Paper presented at the 8th annual meeting of the Society for Psychotherapy Research, San Diego, California, June, 1976.

Lieberman, M. A., Yalom, I. D., and Miles, M. B. *Encounter groups: First facts*. New York: Basic Books, 1973.

Lubin, B. Survey of psychotherapy training and activities of psychologists. *Journal of Clinical Psychology*, 1962, *18*, 252–256.

Mintz, E. E. *Marathon groups: Reality and symbol*. New York: Appleton-Century-Crofts, 1971.

Mitchell, K. M., Bozarth, J. D., and Krauft, C. C. A reappraisal of the therapeutic effectiveness of accurate empathy, nonpossessive warmth, and genuineness. In A. S. Gurman and A. M. Razin (Eds.), *Effective psychotherapy: A handbook of research*. Oxford: Pergamon, 1977.

Mullen, J. and Abeles, N. Relationship of liking, empathy, and therapist's experience to outcome of therapy. *Journal of Counseling Psychology,* 1971, *18,* 39–43.

Parloff, M. B., Waskow, I. E., and Wolfe, B. E. Research on therapist variables in relation to process and outcome. In S. L. Garfield and A. E. Bergin (Eds.), *Handbook of psychotherapy and behavior change,* 2nd ed. New York: Wiley, 1978.

Rachman, A. W. and Kauff, P. F. Directory of postgraduate psychotherapy training facilities. *JSAS Catalog of Selected Documents in Psychology,* 1972, *2,* 116.

Raimy, V. (Ed.), *Training in clinical psychology.* New York: Prentice-Hall, 1950.

Rappaport, J. and Chinsky, J. M. Accurate empathy: confusion of a construct. *Psychological Bulletin,* 1972, *77,* 400–404.

Sloane, R. B., Staples, F. R., Cristol, A. H., Yorkston N. J., and Whipple, K. *Psychotherapy versus behavior therapy.* Cambridge: Harvard University Press, 1975.

Social Work Attack. 'Little or no effect.' *Daily Telegraph* (London), September 13, 1976.

Stieper, D. R. and Wiener, D. N. The problem of interminability in outpatient psychotherapy. *Journal of Consulting Psychology,* 1959, *23,* 237–242.

Stieper, D. R. and Wiener, D. N. *Dimensions of psychotherapy: An experimental and clinical approach.* Chicago: Aldine, 1965.

Strupp, H. H. The effect of the psychotherapist's personal analysis upon his techniques. *Journal of Consulting Psychology,* 1955, *19,* 107–204.

Strupp, H. H., Hadley, S. W., and Gomes-Schwartz, B. *Psychotherapy for better or worse: An analysis of the problem of negative effects.* New York: Jason Aronson, 1977.

Truax, C. B. The meaning and reliability of accurate empathy ratings: A rejoinder. *Psychological Bulletin,* 1972, *77,* 397–399.

Truax, C. B. and Carkhuff, R. R. *Toward effective counseling and psychotherapy.* Chicago: Aldine, 1967.

CHAPTER 5

Specifying the Therapeutic Variables in Psychotherapy

In the previous chapters we have examined some of the earlier developments in psychotherapy, the needs for such services, the kinds of service available, and have also looked at various aspects of the two main participants in psychotherapy, the client and the therapist. In the present chapter we shall try to delineate and discuss those variables which have been deemed important in previous works on psychotherapy and offer some appraisal of their significance. Where possible, an attempt will also be made to emphasize those procedures which appear to be of value to most psychotherapists, regardless of the orientation from which they have been derived. In this chapter, as it were, we will discuss the selected operational concepts and procedures in a somewhat abstract or conceptual manner and then show their application where applicable in later chapters on the psychotherapeutic process.

THE THERAPIST-CLIENT RELATIONSHIP

As we have already noted, most schools of psychotherapy have tended to place some importance on the relationship which develops in psychotherapy. This obviously is very much influenced by the particular therapist and client who make up the relationship and the interactions which take place. All of the various client and therapist variables already discussed may be of importance in specific relationships, for they are the factors that influence the interactions occurring in psychotherapy. As a consequence, we need not make this presentation overly lengthy.

There are certain factors that appear quite evident. The relationship will develop more positively if both parties regard each other with mutual respect and with some positive feelings. If matters are to proceed smoothly at the beginning, the therapist must not deviate too far from the client's expectations about how a therapist conducts his or her business, must manifest a sincere interest in the client, and must inspire some degree of confidence and trust on the part of the client. On the other side of the equation, the client ideally should manifest an interest in psychotherapy, a positive regard for the therapist, and a desire to work hard in a collaborative manner with the therapist. Since many clients will not necessarily come to therapy with such attitudes and characteristics, it would appear then that the therapist has a major responsibility to structure the situation so that a desirable relationship may take place. He should try to appraise the patient as quickly and accurately as possible, and then to respond in an appropriate manner. He should ascertain the client's reasons for seeking therapy and his expectations about therapy and being helped. The therapist should also give the client a clear idea of what psychotherapy is and some estimate of how long it will take. He must also be sensitive to any doubts and uncertainties the client may show so that these may be clarified.

It goes without saying that the therapist must adapt his responses to the particular client being seen. If the client appears to be a difficult or unmotivated case, or if, for any reason, the therapist responds negatively to him, the therapist should seriously decide if therapy is desirable or whether or not he personally should accept the client for psychotherapy. This presents a real issue in psychotherapy which will only be mentioned briefly here. On the one hand, if a therapist feels negatively towards a patient or if he sincerely believes that he cannot help a given patient, then he may be professionally justified in not accepting the patient for treatment. On the other hand, however, it is possible that certain types of disturbed individuals who are seen as undesirable cases will not receive treatment, and only the "good" cases will be accepted. This is a difficult matter to resolve, since there are reasonable arguments for each side and no easy guidelines to follow.

The initial impressions and interactions of the two participants are, thus, of some importance, for if these are quite negative, the relationship may be terminated before it has any chance to develop. However, if the initial session or sessions proceed without difficulty, there is the likelihood of a deeper relationship taking place in the future. How this relationship is structured and interpreted may vary from one orientation to another, but there are characteristics which would appear to be common to most. Like any other relationship that takes place over a period of time, there develops a common bond between the two participants. The scheduled sessions are a regular and important event in the lives of both participants, although they may be especially regarded as such by the client.

As therapy proceeds and as the patient comes to trust and value the psychotherapist, the patient begins to reveal and examine himself more openly, to express his true feelings more readily, and to respond much more to the suggestions, comments, and interpretations of the therapist. The patient, through the understanding manner and support of the therapist, is better able to face negative aspects of self and to be motivated to attempt to change older and self-defeating patterns of behavior. Because of this relationship, the therapist is actually able to exert some influence on the patient, both to have him see behavioral patterns which are maladaptive and also to try out new patterns which the patient may have been reluctant or afraid to try out previously by himself. To a certain extent, because of the relationship which has developed, the therapist may function as an agent of persuasion or reinforcement for the patient. The patient may be willing to attempt changes because of the support provided by the therapist or, in some instances, in order to please the therapist. Although the latter instance may not be viewed too positively by some therapeutic orientations, it may be a more adequate occurrence when viewed from a learning theory orientation. For example, if the client is motivated to try out some behavior which he previously avoided and sees that no negative consequences follow this behavior, he is more likely to continue with this positive behavior. To the extent that the disappearance of the negative behavior occurs and is replaced with behavior that facilitates positive adjustment, the goal of therapy is being realized. This, of course, is predicated on the behavior being maintained by reinforcement in the client's environment outside of therapy.

Whereas some individuals appear to take an almost mystical view of the psychotherapeutic relationship and would react somewhat negatively to the view of the psychotherapist as a human "persuader" or social reinforcement machine, the social influence role of the therapist has been emphasized by dynamically oriented, as well as behaviorally oriented psychotherapists (Frank, 1973; Krasner, 1962; Strupp, 1973). It would seem reasonable to hypothesize that a person with whom one has formed a rather close relationship and whom one regards with trust and respect can exert considerable influence on the other person. To some extent, therefore, a positive relationship in therapy tends to increase the therapist's influence, for better or for worse, on the client in treatment. The relationship also may be seen as increasing the client's suggestibility or willingness to accept the therapist's explanations for past and current events, as well as to try out new behaviors. The therapist, after all, as an expert in problems of human behavior, is trying to help the client, and the client's hopes for improvement largely depend on the therapist's skills. This, coupled with the therapist's interest and regard for the client, helps to explain, in part, the potential influence of the therapist in the therapeutic relationship.

The relationship which develops in psychotherapy thus provides a general background or basis for the influence which the therapist brings to bear on the patient. It also helps to motivate the patient to continue in therapy, to attempt to cooperate with the therapist and, eventually, to try out new behaviors. There are other aspects which derive from the relationship and the regular meetings of the two participants, some of which will be considered separately later. To the extent that the relationship is a positive one, the patient is more inclined to accept the interpretations, explanations, and insights offered or brought out in the therapy sessions. He is also likely to take on the values of the therapist and even, perhaps, to model some of his behaviors upon those of the therapist. To the extent that the therapist is accurate in his or her perceptions and pronouncements and is a worthy model for the patient, all is well and good. If the opposite is the case, then other less desirable outcomes may be secured.

The psychotherapeutic setting also provides the therapist with an opportunity to observe the actual behaviors of the client. Psychotherapy is not mere talk or intellectual discussion of abstract topics and past events. Although the patient may be on his "good behavior" during the early interviews and be rather cautious in what he discusses, as the relationship develops, he is increasingly able to discuss topics of a more personal nature and also more readily displays his feelings and characteristic modes of responding. The therapist not only is provided with the opportunity to observe typical behaviors of the client as he interacts with another person, but he can also point out these behaviors to the client and emphasize their probable impact on other interpersonal interactions which the client may have with other people. The fact that the therapist responds to these behaviors in a dispassionate and understanding manner may also increase the possibility of change.

The relationship that takes place in therapy, therefore, does appear to be a factor of some importance in terms of the potentiality for progress in psychotherapy. If, as already indicated, the relationship is a positive one, the potential for positive outcome would appear to be enhanced. On the contrary, if the relationship is a poor one, then this potentiality would appear to be lessened. The criterion for judging the quality of the relationship is not the comfort, sociability, and enjoyment of the relationship, for such goals can be secured by means of other relationships. Psychotherapy should not be, in Schofield's (1964) terms, "the purchase of friendship." Rather, the criterion has to be the implementation of positive and adaptive changes in the client. The therapist bears the responsibility to see that the potential influences generated by the therapeutic relationship are used toward this end, and, therefore, he must be constantly aware of what is taking place and how the relationship is being utilized by both the client and himself.

INTERPRETATION, INSIGHT, AND UNDERSTANDING

Attention has already been paid to the concepts of interpretation and insight in our previous discussion of psychodynamic therapies. In the present discussion an attempt will be made to consider these and related concepts from a more general point of view.

In the psychoanalytic view, interpretations were offered by the analyst as a means of helping the patient to penetrate below the surface level of awareness and eventually to come to grips with the unconscious forces motivating his behavior. Whether interpretations dealt with the transference reactions to the therapist, the patient's free associations, his dreams, or his behaviors in or out of therapy, they were essentially explanations offered to the patient. There was thus an explicit belief that helping the patient to gain an understanding or insight about his difficulties was an important means of instituting change in the patient. Whereas it was recognized that this process was not a simple one, it was believed that the transference relationship and the understanding provided by the therapist enabled the patient to overcome his natural resistance to such a process and to gradually accept and act on the basis of his new insights. Although understanding appears to be primarily a cognitive process, it was recognized that cognitive or intellectual understanding (insight) alone was not very significant, unless in some way the patient's affects were also involved (Alexander and French, 1946). Be that as it may, the assumption made was that insights were essential for progress in psychotherapy, and in fact, such therapies were frequently referred to as insight-oriented or uncovering therapies as contrasted with so-called supportive therapies.

Although Rogers (1942), in his first book on nondirective therapy, did emphasize the importance of the client's insights in therapy, in his subsequent writings this topic received less formal attention. The client-centered school, for the most part, believes important insights follow changes in the self, rather than the other way around (Rogers, 1951). Other orientations, directly or indirectly, make use of increased client understanding in their therapeutic procedures or theories. In some of the more directive or possibly eclectic orientations, the giving of explanations to the client appears to be one of the techniques utilized (Thorne, 1968). More recently, several therapeutic approaches have appeared that emphasize the distorted perceptions and understandings of the client as the critical factors at the base of the client's difficulties (Beck, 1976; Ellis, 1962). The therapist's task is to get the client to understand his distorted beliefs, and eventually to discard them and to substitute more realistic ones for them. In this process, the therapist essentially points out the client's faulty belief systems and offers him, or helps him to obtain, a new and more appropriate set of beliefs and perceptions. In fact, one form of this type of therapy was first named "Rational Therapy" by Ellis (1962).

It thus appears that insights and interpretations, or the offering of some type of understanding to the client by the therapist, are utilized as therapeutic procedures in some guise by therapists of many different theoretical persuasions. Even the behavior therapists, who pay no formal attention to such dynamically oriented concepts as interpretation and insight, do attempt to provide their patients with some understanding of how their disturbed behavior has occurred and with a rationale for the procedures to be employed in therapy. Furthermore, as mentioned previously, several behaviorally oriented therapists have begun to incorporate cognitive emphases with their behavioral procedures. In all of these instances, then, some attention is paid to providing the client with some information and understanding of his difficulties, how they arose, why they persist, and how they can be changed.

Although, as noted, many of the different approaches to psychotherapy pay some attention to providing the client with an understanding of his/her problems, how they go about this process differs and the insights and understandings provided the client also vary from one orientation to another. At the same time, the different and varied understandings are all presumedly therapeutic in some fashion or other, and this makes for an interesting and also somewhat puzzling situation. How can such different insights or understandings all contribute to positive outcome? In psychoanalysis the patient tends to be given a Freudian view of his difficulties and past development, and the insights he obtains are based on psychoanalytic concepts. Thus the patient may gradually accept the explanation from the therapist that his difficulties are based on earlier Oedipal conflicts which have been repressed. Another individual, seeing an Adlerian therapist, may gradually come to understand that his problems were influenced by his place in the family, his resulting feelings of inferiority, and his compensatory strivings for power. Still another client seeing a rational-emotive therapist might be told that his difficulties are caused by his irrational beliefs about needing to be perfect and to be loved by everyone. Finally, a behavior therapist would inform his client that his current fears are the result of previous conditioning and that, in therapy, he will learn responses which are antagonistic to his current ones and, as a consequence, his fear responses will gradually be inhibited.

In each of the above illustrations the client is provided with an understanding of his problem from the vantage point of the particular therapist he is seeing. Furthermore, in each instance there is some assumption that the explanation provided is both accurate or "true," and that it is helpful to the client. This is a phenomenon which has intrigued the writer for some time and his thinking about it has been greatly clarified and stimulated by the writings of Jerome Frank (1971, 1973). As Frank has formulated it, practically all therapeutic orientations provide their patients with some rationale or belief system to explain their disturbed behavior, and there are clear parallels here with more primitive methods of healing. However, the important point is that the providing of such a belief system appears to be of some therapeutic value to the patient. The fact that the therapist appears to understand the patient's problems and is able to provide this understanding to the patient appears to reduce the latter's anxiety about his problems and to engender hope for alleviating them. When an individual is experiencing discomfort and does not understand what his symptoms signify, what has caused this unhappy state of affairs, or how serious his condition may be, it is reassuring to contact a professional therapist who seems to know what the problem is, what factors are responsible for it, and who also offers a treatment which supposedly can alleviate the patient's situation. In fact, Torrey (1972) in a very interesting and provocative paper has stated that the mere "naming" of the patient's disturbance by the therapist is an important therapeutic factor which is common to most therapies.

On the basis of what has just been presented, it seems reasonable to hypothesize that the *precise* nature of the insights and understandings provided by the therapist are of relatively minor importance. What does appear to be of importance is whether or not the client accepts the rationale or belief system offered by the therapist. If the client finds the explanation proffered by the therapist to be not quite convincing or incomprehensible, then it is likely that he will not accept it and, consequently, the rationale will have little therapeutic effect. However, if he does accept the explanation of the therapist, it is likely that he will find this reassuring, hopeful, and perhaps, helpful. At least doubts, uncertainties, and ambiguity would appear to be partially overcome by such understanding and belief. In the United States, at least, this process, particularly the matter of the acceptance of a particular belief system by specific patients, appears to be illustrated by the shopping around and the seeking of certain kinds of therapy by prospective clients. People read about various therapies in the popular press and in various paperback presentations of these therapies, and they seek out therapists who are identified with the particular orientations these individuals find most acceptable. My office, for example, receives numerous calls asking if we provide this or that kind of therapy, or where a particular type of therapy is available. It may be that certain clients, for whatever reasons, are more prone to be accepting of some beliefs than of others, and the proper matching of therapy and client might be of some value as was indicated earlier. It is also possible that the personality characteristics of client and therapist may be important in how readily the therapeutic rationale is accepted in individual situations. Some clients are more readily influenced than others, whereas some therapists are undoubtedly more influential or persuasive than others. In any event, although many variables may be operative in this process, it seems plausible to infer that the providing of an explanation for the patient's problems, as well as a rationale for the therapy, may have some therapeutic impact on the patient, regardless of the rationale provided.

In discussing this topic with various professional audiences, I have frequently noticed some expressions of discomfort and concern on the faces of some individuals, and have received some critical responses from others. This, perhaps, is understandable. It seems that the implication of what I have presented is not only that some cherished clinical views and theories appear to be without substance, but even more, that the role of the psychotherapist is demeaned. Instead of the therapists' convictions that they are offering explanations to their patients that are theoretically valid, and on which their therapeutic work is apparently based, the therapists are, in effect, told that whatever they tell patients is equally efficacious, as long as the patients will believe it. It is the matter of belief and acceptance on the part of the patient which appears to be the important process, and not the actual content of the material provided by the therapist. Viewed this way, the reactions of many therapists to such a presentation is easily understandable. To accept the possibility that it does not matter what you tell the patient as long as you are convincing and the patient accepts what you tell him would appear to smack of potential quackery and salesmanship.

This is not an easy problem to resolve. Certainly a professional person who works with emotionally disturbed people is usually motivated by both humanitarian and scientific ideals and aspirations, and has an understandable expectation that his professional calling is a dignified and honorable one. He or she has a need, also, to have some conviction in one's theoretical beliefs and methods of practice. What has been said about the importance of the patient's acceptance of the rationale provided him for understanding his difficulties would appear to apply also to the psycho-therapist. Believing in what he does may be important in how he functions professionally. At the same time, the history of medicine is replete with examples of worthless medicines and practices which, in all good faith and with the best of intentions, were administered to large numbers of people in the past. The interesting thing is that many patients also ap-peared to be helped by pharmacologically ineffective medicines, as ac-counts and studies of the placebo response inform us (Shapiro and Morris, 1978).

There are no ready solutions to this problem. My suggestion is that any therapist who, in any manner, respects the scientific tradition has to recog-nize at the outset that our current knowledge of psychotherapy is far from conclusive and that many of our present clinical beliefs and procedures have yet to be confirmed by empirical research. The very fact that we have so many divergent and conflicting theories and procedures is a reflection of this state of affairs. This being the situation, the psychotherapist must strive to keep an open mind concerning developments in psychotherapy and the procedures he or she currently favors. The psychotherapist should be as open with himself about this matter as he would like his patients to be in their psychotherapeutic sessions with him and to frankly admit to himself that much of what he does is based on reasonably appearing hypotheses, and not on empirically verified truths. This may be difficult but it does not necessarily have to create extreme indecision or doubt in the therapist. The therapist's sincerity in desiring to help the patient and his utilization of the best information and procedures currently available should assuage any inner concerns he may have about his procedures, and assure himself that he is practicing in a highly ethical and responsible manner. To expect certainty in any endeavor would appear inappropriate, and the psychotherapist must realize that he deals with many uncertainties. While he must be aware of these uncertainties, he need not burden the client with them since they would only hamper the activities of therapy. He can inform the client of that which the latter needs to know. He can tell the client his own beliefs about therapy in a straightforward and even convincing manner, even stating that a successful outcome cannot be guaranteed. It is the writer's belief that such a presentation, done in a sincere manner, will have as positive an impact as one that admits of no doubts whatsoever.

In the preceding paragraphs we may have appeared to digress some-what from the main topic under discussion, but this appeared to be a neces-sary elaboration. Some related aspects which pertain to the therapist's own feelings about therapy and the interactions in therapy will be discussed more fully later. For now, we can conclude this section by reiterating the points made earlier. In most therapies, various means are utilized to provide the patient with some explanation of his difficulties and some rationale for the therapy which is to take place. In some this is done mainly during the early stages of therapy, whereas in others, usually those therapies which take a long period of time, the process occurs over a period of time and appears to receive a greater emphasis. Regardless, the patient is given some rationale or belief system, and if reasonably acceptable, it appears to play some role in the progress of psychotherapy. How significant this is and how the process works are as yet relatively unexplored issues. Consequently, the importance of insight and understanding in psychotherapy can be viewed primarily as a reasonable hypothesis. It also appears likely that the potential value in therapy of this variable is interrelated with the client's makeup, his need for an explanation, his view of the therapist, and the type of problem presented. Also of importance in this process is the therapist, his prestige, his own personality, his way of communicating to the client, and his perception of the client. Although this process is far from being fully understood, the author strongly believes that it is important to try to give the patient some understanding of his difficulties in a clear and appropriate manner, and to provide him with an understanding of the rationale and procedures of the therapy to be used. It is the impact which this has on the client which has potential significance for psychotherapy, and not necessarily the content of the particular formulation provided.

CATHARSIS, EMOTIONAL EXPRESSION, AND RELEASE

Early in the history of psychotherapy and at irregular intervals since, some attention has been paid to the role of the release of strong affects or pent-up emotion in psychotherapy. Such patterns had been noted by Breuer and Freud (1950), and at first the "cathartic method" was viewed quite positively. However, Freud came to the conclusion that this procedure did not produce any lasting results, and it was gradually replaced by the particular methods he called psychoanalysis. Although catharsis or abreaction has received comparatively little emphasis since that time and, by itself, does not constitute a form of therapy, it sometimes has a value with selected patients who are acutely anxious, indecisive, or have situationally determined feelings of guilt.

Depending upon the individual case, catharsis may be of some value in psychotherapy. In a selected number of cases the individual client may have engaged in some behavior, or gone through some experience which he or she views as very negative or shameful. Because of this the client is reluctant to tell anyone else of his experience and keeps it to himself. However, this produces very acute and discomforting anxiety or guilt which may finally motivate him to seek professional help. In many instances, the client will not even mention this in the initial interview as a reason for seeking therapy, but will give some other reasons which may be related to the precipitating cause or event. However, as the client learns to trust the therapist, he may then recount the disturbing event with considerable affect and, at times, very apparent relief. In some instances, the session in which this occurs may be characterized by very noticeable emotional release and change in the client's outlook on his situation and mark a significant point in therapy. It is in many ways similar to a highly emotional confession of guilt which occurs in other situations, as well as in psychotherapy.

When such emotional release occurs in therapy and appears to be instrumental in the patient's improvement, it is quite noticeable and is capable of making a definite impression on the therapist, even though its occurrence is not very frequent. The writer can recall three instances which come readily to mind. In the most dramatic one, the client was a young man who was highly upset and agitated. He could be heard moving around in the waiting area and pacing restlessly until my office door was opened to admit him. As soon as he was seated, he began an excited and rapid verbal outpouring of his difficulties. Once this was begun, there was no stopping him. At various points in the session I attempted to offer some comments of therapeutic wisdom, but to no avail. The client talked without stopping and with agitated expressions of affect for about an hour, releasing very visibly his pent-up feelings. At the end of this, he gave what appeared to be a tremendous sigh of relief, thanked the therapist profusely, and was off—leaving, it should be added, a somewhat frustrated therapist who wanted to provide the client with several choice therapeutic insights, but was unable to do so. The other cases remembered were less remarkable, but in each instance they involved activities which the individual had not confided to anyone else and which were a source of depressed feelings or guilt to the individual. In each instance, there was noticeable relief on the part of the client in being able to unburden himself of these concerns, sharing them with the therapist, and, as it were, being received in a nonjudgmental, accepting, and understanding manner.

It should be emphasized, perhaps, that in most cases, catharsis or emotional release alone was not necessarily the only therapeutic variable in operation. In some instances, it facilitated the client's perceiving his situation in a more realistic manner and being able to cope more effectively with the situation. In one instance, a certain amount of needed accurate information concerning masturbation was subsequently provided to the client which was both useful and reassuring. However, the emotional release appeared to play a significant part in these clients' subsequent progress in therapy.

Beyond what has already been said, there are no particular cues concerning when catharsis may be a useful component of psychotherapy or how it may best be utilized. I do not believe that the therapist should or can deliberately strive to induce such a response in the client, although this is a personal belief.[1] Rather, the therapist, by his manner and interactions with the client, provides an environment whereby given clients may feel free to reveal what is disturbing them and express their feelings openly. The therapist, perhaps, can be particularly sensitive to this possibility where the patient appears to indicate accute discomfort of relatively recent origin, but at the same time, does not initially relate these feelings to any particular set of events. Once the beginning of the expression of pent-up feelings is evident, the patient can be encouraged to fully express his feelings and affects.

As already discussed, the therapist, in most instances, is an important figure to the client who seeks his help. To the extent that the therapist appears to be an individual who is knowledgeable about psychological problems, has experience in dealing with such problems, and imparts trust and confidence in the patient, the therapist provides a situation where the patient may be freer to disclose the highly personal matters which are disturbing him. As the therapist accepts what the patient says without in any way judging him, and as he encourages him to fully express his feelings and to "get things off his chest," the patient is more likely to confide in the therapist and to ventilate his pent-up feelings. To a certain extent, the patient has found his or her concerns acutely discomforting and would like to confide in someone, but has not been able to confide such matters even to close friends or relatives. They are potentially too threatening. The therapist, as a neutral and understanding healer, provides the patient with a less threatening opportunity for emotional release.

REINFORCEMENT IN PSYCHOTHERAPY

While reinforcement as a therapeutic variable has been mainly emphasized by those learning theorists and behavior therapists who stress the impor-

---

[1] Other therapists including those involved in marathon and related approaches would likely take a different view (See Nichols, 1974).

tance of operant conditioning, it is also a variable which is utilized in various ways, and perhaps less systematically, by other psychotherapists as well. Although the application of operant techniques to various settings and populations has increased markedly in recent years (Kazdin, 1978; Krasner, 1971), it has received little formal attention from most of the more traditionally oriented psychotherapists. However, the principles of reinforcement do appear to be applied in the interactions which take place in psychotherapy.

Basically what is implied here is that the therapist tends to positively reinforce those responses on the part of the patient which he views as desirable, and to not actively reinforce or extinguish those responses which he deems to be undesirable in terms of his therapeutic goals. Depending on the therapist and the situation, the therapist may or may not be aware that he is reinforcing or failing to reinforce a particular client behavior. Those who are stated adherents of operant procedures would, of course, fully utilize operant principles and contingencies of reinforcement in a planned and systematic manner. They would also focus more specifically on target behaviors in order to observe what changes occur. Most readers probably are familiar with some of the work in this area. The well-known ABA design used in many operant studies can be mentioned briefly for illustrative purposes.

First, a baseline (A) of the behaviors to be modified is obtained by recording the frequency of these behaviors over a given period of time. Then, the operant procedures or programs are introduced and the frequency of the targeted behaviors are once again recorded and any changes are noted. If significant changes are noted during the period when the program is in operation (B), the experimental procedures or reinforcements are once again withdrawn for a given period of time (A) similar to the baseline period and the appropriate measures of behavior taken. Generally, the treatment effects diminish and the behaviors revert to their baseline or pretreatment levels. Similar procedures can be used for decreasing undesirable behaviors or increasing specified desired target behaviors. This design allows one to clearly appraise the effects of the particular operant procedures.

There appear to be a number of reasons why many therapists, particularly psychodynamic ones, have shied away from the deliberate use of operant procedures or reinforcement. In the first place, of course, the client's problems have been viewed in a very different manner. Target symptoms are not the specified focus of therapy, nor are procedures used to deal directly with them. Related to this are views that the approach is very superficial and that the client is treated as an object or is manipulated by the therapist—views that are repugnant to many therapists. Furthermore, operant procedures would be seen as limited mainly to changing some behavioral symptoms, but as not applicable to more complicated problems which involve feelings and views of one's self. Implicit also is the view that the therapist should not impose his or her values upon the client or act in a controlling manner. Rather, from this perspective, the client has the responsibility to decide what values he selects and in what directions he shall go. The therapist, consequently, is an agent who merely facilitates the process of growth and self-discovery. The operant conditioner, on the other hand, is someone who decides what behaviors will be modified, sometimes with and sometimes without the consent of the client, and who then controls the therapeutic situation. As viewed from such a frame of reference, the patient is a passive respondent to the stimuli controlled and manipulated by the therapist.

The above view may explain why many therapists are reluctant to deliberately make use of operant procedures. They may even feel more justified in their views by some of the recent criticisms of behavioral programs in institutional settings where issues of the infringement of the rights of incarcerated individuals undergoing such programs have been raised (Kazdin, 1978). However, some of the issues involved, including the more recent one of the right to treatment, go well beyond the matter of operant conditioning alone and would appear to have implications for all forms of treatment. This is obviously a complicated matter and we should not stray too far from our topic for discussion.

While there are many ostensibly important reasons why therapists appear to avoid the conscious use of operant procedures, some of their reasons for doing so do not seem to be particularly valid. Like it or not, the therapist is far from being a value-free individual who is completely neutral on all matters discussed by the patient or with reference to the behaviors exhibited in psychotherapy. The therapist does have a value system and this does tend to get communicated in some fashion to the client (Krasner, 1963; Rosenthal, 1955; Kessel and McBrearty, 1967). To the extent that the therapist prefers one therapeutic orientation in preference to others, he has made a value judgment which gets communicated to the client. The client who has undergone a psychoanalysis is provided with understandings and a view of human personality which clearly reflects the value system of his analyst. Extreme critics of psychoanalytic training or therapy would even call them instances of brainwashing. If the analytic candidate does not accept the values of the training institute, he will be found wanting and perhaps dropped from the program (Szasz, 1960). In the case of the patient who resists psychoanalytic interpretations, he will find that his particular form of resistance is hindering treatment and is costing him a fair amount of money. Obviously, in both instances, submission may be the better part of valor.

Apart from the matter of values, it is also the contention of behavior therapists that many traditional therapists utilize reinforcement and learning principles, but do so in a haphazard, unknowing, and unsystematic fashion. As a consequence, they believe traditional therapists tend to be less efficient therapists and that their therapy requires a much longer time than is true of behavioral therapies. It is also stated that therapists actually reinforce in a positive way the kinds of responses they desire to get from the patient by nodding or verbally signifying acceptance when such responses are forthcoming, and conversely, indicate a negative reaction or disapproval by overt or subtle means when such responses are not made. Thus although they may not be particularly aware of what they are doing or of their impact on the patient, these therapists are actually "shaping" the responses of their patients. Truax (1966), for example, analyzed the recorded excerpt of one of Carl Rogers' published cases and demonstrated that certain client responses were in fact reinforced by positive reactions from Rogers. "These responses could be categorized as responses which were deemed to be desired ones from the client-centered point of view. Furthermore, as the therapist reinforces such client responses by nodding or by saying, 'hmmmm, that's good,' or a similar verbal statement, the likelihood of increasing the occurrence of such responses is enhanced." Murray (1956) also provided a similar analysis of one of Rogers' cases and demonstrated that therapist approval and disapproval functions as positive and negative reinforcement.

It does seem plausible, therefore, that the therapist is capable of influencing the client's behavior. In a general sense, this is an underlying assumption of all psychotherapies, regardless of how they are conceptualized. The important issue is how this process occurs and how it can be used most effectively for the client's welfare.

A related point, made originally by Truax and Carkhuff (1967), is also worth quoting here: "If psychotherapy or counseling is indeed a process of learning and relearning, then the therapeutic process should allow for structuring what is to be learned, rather than depending on what amounts to 'incidental learning,' where the client does not have clearly in mind from the outset what it is he is supposed to learn" (p. 363). The implications of this statement are rather clear. Regardless of one's basic conceptualization of the psychotherapeutic process, it does seem that any changes which take place would involve learning of some kind. It does not have to be the type of learning process described by a particular learning theorist, but it would be very difficult to deny that some type of learning takes place. If in fact this is so, then the therapist should be knowledgeable about this process and utilize it so that learning takes place in the most efficient manner possible.

One obvious implication is that the therapist, first of all, must be aware of his or her potential influence on the client and in what ways he or she does influence the behavior of specific clients. As already indicated, the therapist does influence the client in a number of ways. Besides more directly informing the client of what is expected of him and indicating what is, in essence, desirable client behavior in therapy, the therapist influences the client's behavior during therapy by the way he or she responds to this behavior. Desirable behaviors receive affirmative or rewarding responses from the therapist, whereas responses which are considered to be of an undesirable sort are punished in some fashion or ignored. The therapist may simply indicate approval by such gestures as nodding or smiling, as well as by more overt verbal statements of approval or praise. In a similar manner, responses thought to be retarding of progress in therapy may receive a frown, a show of concern, or an explicit verbal statement of disagreement.

Clearly, the therapist does engage in such behaviors and they do act as reinforcing stimuli for the client. Whereas different clients will respond differently to the communications of the therapist, most of them will be quite sensitive to them. Not only is the therapist in a position of influence for the reasons already described, but the client's progress is perceived by the client as being largely dependent on the therapist and how he responds to the client. Under such circumstances, it is understandable that the client will be responsive to the differential reinforcements of the therapist.

Consequently, not only should the therapist be aware of his role in influencing the client by means of reinforcement, but it would seem desirable for him to use this knowledge to facilitate the desired changes sought by means of psychotherapy. If this proposition appears to be reasonable, it does seem a bit strange that except for the learning theory oriented therapists, a large number of therapists are so reluctant to accept it. However, as we have noted earlier, there are a number of reasons why this is so. Perhaps the basic reason is that such a view implies a conscious and deliberate manipulation of the patient which many humanistically oriented therapists perceive as an anathema. Nevertheless, this can be seen as a failure to come to grips with what appears to be a realistic occurrence in psychotherapy, and one which conceivably explains some of the behavioral processes which take place.

The kind of phenomenon or issue presented here is an important one which has implications for other aspects of psychotherapy. However, because psychotherapists' convictions are strongly held, it is not an easy task to change their views. Some of the possible implications or applications may be even more negatively received, in spite of the fact that they are being implemented with apparent success by some therapists. One such application that appears to be promising is a more direct approach towards attempts to modify the client's behavior in a positive direction by using real life situations in which the behaviors occur, rather than emphasizing in-therapy behaviors per se. Here, also, a very different view is taken from that espoused in most traditional psychotherapies. The more traditional approaches have generally taken what may be termed an indirect approach to modifying the patient's behavior. The belief is that one works with more general organismic variables such as the patient's personality and the underlying causes as the most effective manner of securing behavioral or surface changes. The other view, advanced by the behavioral therapists, is that the most effective way to secure behavioral change is to proceed directly to attempts to change the behavior in question. A view that involves the application of learning principles is obviously much closer to the latter point of view, although it is not necessarily synonymous with it. An attempt at some illustration of what is implied here may be helpful.

Let us suppose that we have a patient who comes to see us because he is painfully shy in social situations and feels particularly inadequate when around members of the opposite sex. We could postulate that these symptoms are the result of various earlier traumatic experiences and, therefore, therapy will consist of explorations and associations to earlier repressed events and the gradual attainment of insight, or, from a different orientation, that by the displaying of empathy, genuineness, and nonpossessive warmth on the part of the therapist, the client will gradually enlarge and integrate his views of self and have his experiences become congruent with the new self system. In either instance the problem behavior and the desired behavior are approached indirectly, and the assumption is made that by means of such a process the desired outcome will be obtained. In a more direct approach, however, more attention would be paid to the situations in which the undesired behavior occurs, the kinds of stimuli which produce this reaction, the kinds of cognitions and feelings the patient has, what the patient does in response to these stimuli, and the like. A plan of therapy might then be developed in which the patient would at first play out some of these situations in therapy, but would be encouraged to gradually participate in selected real life situations. He might be encouraged at first to simply engage in conversation or small talk with females for brief periods and in relatively safe situations. Gradually, as he is positively reinforced in these initial attempts and feels generally more secure, he may be instructed to venture into more demanding or initially more threatening social situations. As these behaviors are successful, the patient may eventually be able to ask a woman for a date, to be at ease, and to interact in a more "normal" and personally satisfying manner. While other interactions with the therapist would also take place, the procedure just described would appear to play a very important part in the therapeutic program and would focus to a great extent on the specific problem, and the behavioral change which is sought in therapy. Although it may not always proceed as smoothly and simply as the preceding illustration would suggest, the emphasis on dealing directly with the behaviors to be modified is quite clear. It also calls attention to another point of potential importance, and that is the emphasis on utilizing the actual life situations of the client as having a more lasting impact or transfer effect than relying exclusively on in-therapy verbal behaviors.

A few other somewhat related comments are worth making here before we conclude our discussion of what appears to be an important but controversial feature of psychotherapy. One aspect concerns what might be termed an organismic-segmental or part-whole emphasis. As pointed out before, the traditional and more indirect approaches appear to believe that the individual as a whole must be worked with or that some dynamic balance of the organism must be changed if any specific parts, subunits, symptoms, or behaviors are to be substantially or "permanently" modified. One proceeds from the whole to the part as it were. The more direct or learning oriented approach deals more specifically with a part or segment, symptom or behavior of the individual, and attempts to modify it more directly. Although the behavior therapists generally are mainly concerned with the problem or desired behavior, they frequently also secure appraisals of subjective states or attitudes of their clients. Such data have indicated that when the desired behavioral changes are achieved, other desirable effects may also accompany such changes (Bandura, 1969). For example, if a person has a fear of leaving his home, his whole style of living is seriously disrupted, as well as his own views of self. If the phobia is overcome, such an individual may also show other changes including increased self-confidence, better relationships with his wife and family, etc. In this instance, therapy aimed at a specific behavior or aspect of the individual appears to have an irradiating effect which spreads out to influence the total organism.

Only a far wiser man than the writer would venture to state which of these two opposite views encompasses more of the truth. My purpose here is to try to make explicit a very fundamental difference between two important views of psychotherapy. My own evaluation, however, would be influenced greatly by the empirical data provided to support each position as well as the overall economy of the therapy. In this regard, the behavioral view appears to have the edge. However, it is important to emphasize that a sound analysis of the client's difficulties should be made before a plan of treatment is formulated and carried out.

Another aspect which is of some significance pertains to the therapist's view of the psychotherapy he is performing and his satisfaction with it. Besides the fact that many psychotherapists take a negative view of being overly directive in therapy and believe that change comes about solely through the client's initiative, there is an additional consideration with regard to the view held of the therapist's role in the more behavioral or learning theory oriented therapy. Several dynamically oriented therapists have told me that most of the behavioral approaches imply a mechanistic view of therapy that does not appeal to them and that this type of therapy can be performed by technicians instead of highly trained psychotherapists. This may be so, but the critical issue really concerns what techniques are most effective in producing the desired changes. If this can be done with properly trained technicians, then this should be considered. However, it does appear that at least a number of therapists choose an approach to therapy which they themselves find personally challenging and rewarding. Although this is often rationalized by the statement that one must engage in that form of psychotherapy which best suits one's personal style, it is shifting the main concern from that of the client's welfare to that of the therapist's. The therapist's personal satisfaction in therapy is a matter to consider, but it should not be the prime consideration.

In any event, it is evident from what has been presented that the therapist does have some influence upon the behavior of the client and that how he or she responds and interacts in the therapy session can reinforce certain client behaviors. Since such a process occurs in therapy, it seems efficacious for the therapist to utilize this knowledge as explicitly as possible in order to facilitate the goals of therapy.

DESENSITIZATION

Another variable that appears to operate in psychotherapy can be termed desensitization. Although this concept has received more systematic attention and formulation more recently in the writing of Joseph Wolpe (1958, 1961), it was also referred to in earlier discussions of psychotherapy (Garfield, 1957; Levine, 1948; Rosenzweig, 1936). Basically, what is referred to here is that as a patient discusses problems which have been troubling him and repeats this concern over time in the accepting climate of the therapeutic session, these problems appear to become less threatening or troublesome. It is as if when one broods over matters and does not bring them out in the open for examination, these preoccupations become very disturbing, and the individual may even appear to magnify their consequences. Unlike the more acute types of discomfort discussed in relation to catharsis, what are referred to here are more like preoccupations, decisions which have to be made, the lack of meeting one's expectations, and the like. Whereas the specific causal events or patient problems in this regard cannot be specified very distinctly, the process of desensitization which may occur in psychotherapy seems somewhat clearer.

What appears to occur is that as the patient begins to discuss the events which have been troubling him, they gradually seem to lose their threatening quality. By bringing matters out in the open and looking at them anew, the troublesome events do not appear to be as troublesome as they were previously. Several different hypotheses have been offered to explain this process. One is that by simply sharing such thoughts and preoccupations with the therapist and bringing them out into the open, they become less personalized and hence less threatening. A related view is that by having to communicate the items which are disturbing, the individual has to be more objective and realistic in appraising his situation. Personalized distortions and magnifications are more readily perceived and thus modified accordingly with the help of the therapist. Furthermore, the repetition of this material in the therapy situation with no negative reactions to this disclosure makes it appear to be less serious than the client perceived it to be earlier. In terms of a learning theory oriented explanation, the client's anxieties about these matters are gradually extinguished as he discusses them in the security of the therapeutic setting and no negative consequences are forthcoming. The fact that the therapist accepts the disclosures of the client without any evident show of surprise or concern may also contribute to this process of desensitization.

The repeated discussion in therapy of material which the client initially experiences as anxiety provoking or distressing thus may lessen its anxiety provoking qualities. Whether the process is one of gradual extinction over time or whether other processes are involved is by no means clear. However, something akin to desensitization does appear to occur with some patients. As is true with many of the possible variables operating in psychotherapy, it may not always appear to be of major importance in all cases. However, it does appear worthy of note by psychotherapists since the usual verbal interactions occurring within the therapeutic relationship allow the process to take place.

In more recent years desensitization has received more specific attention as a result of the formulation developed by Wolpe (1958, 1961,

1973) which deals with reciprocal inhibition and systematic desensitization. In terms of Wolpe's view, what has been described already as the process of desensitization would perhaps be characterized as unsystematic desensitization. According to Wolpe, if one is to dispel anxiety, some competing process has to be utilized—a process which is antagonistic to it. If an individual is relaxed, by definition he cannot be anxious. This is what is meant by reciprocal inhibition. As a consequence, Wolpe utilized relaxation procedures as part of his therapeutic strategy although other counter conditioners or inhibitors of anxiety have also been used with a measure of success.

In working out his overall approach to therapy, Wolpe also developed a procedure which he named "systematic desensitization," and today his approach is usually referred to by this name. The basic objective is to desensitize the patient to the fears or anxieties which have been troubling him. After first giving the patient some training in relaxation procedures in order to develop a response which can "reciprocally inhibit" feelings of anxiety, the therapist and patient jointly prepare a list of the stimuli which arouse anxiety in the patient. The patient is asked to rank these various situations on a theoretical scale of 0 to 100 in terms of their fear arousing values. A hierarchy of such situations is thus arranged from the least disturbing to the one judged to be the most anxiety arousing. When the patient is relaxed, the therapist then asks him to imagine first the situation or scene which is lowest in the hierarchy. If the patient can visualize this scene without any anxiety, the therapist proceeds to the next item in the hierarchy and so on. If the patient signals that he is anxious when he is visualizing a specific item, he is told to discontinue doing so and to once again relax. The procedure is repeated until the patient can gradually move up the hierarchy of items and visualize what was once a very upsetting scene without any undue anxiety. He has thus become desensitized to the stimuli which earlier provoked severe anxiety.

While this procedure is rather different from the more usual psychotherapy sessions referred to in our earlier discussion of desensitization, somewhat similar processes may be involved. Wolpe's approach is obviously a more focused one with a much more explicit emphasis on the process of desensitization. Most other therapists generally have given relatively little emphasis or attention to it. Although there have been a number of criticisms of Wolpe's theoretical formulations, the empirical results secured by means of systematic desensitization have been relatively good, and perhaps represent the clearest demonstration of the process of desensitization (Bandura, 1969; Davison and Wilson, 1973). It would appear that where phobic or related symptoms are the primary complaint, systematic desensitization is a very useful procedure. Where the complaints are less focalized, such a direct procedure may not be necessary and desensitization may take place in interaction with other aspects of therapy.

RELAXATION

Mention was made of relaxation in the preceding section with reference to systematic desensitization. It may be worthwhile at this juncture to say a few more words about it.

Relaxation as a means of alleviating tension and anxiety has been mentioned from time to time in the history of psychological healing. It received attention quite early in relationship to hypnosis and the use of hypnotic procedures in therapy. About 50 years ago, it received attention in the writings of Jacobson (1929) who developed a program of progressive relaxation. Wolpe (1958) adapted some of Jacobson's procedures in developing his techniques of systematic desensitization and brought relaxation much more into the foreground of psychotherapy. As we all know, attempts to utilize relaxation in order to calm people are made in a large number of everyday situations, including those in psychotherapy.

Most psychotherapists have tended to view relaxation and related procedures as very superficial or temporary palliative measures in therapy, and relaxation procedures constitute just one component in Wolpe's therapy. However, Goldfried (1971; Goldfried and Trier, 1974) has recently reported a way of utilizing relaxation as a coping procedure in therapy which appears quite promising.

Goldfried teaches his clients to utilize relaxation as a means of coping with tension and anxiety provoking situations. Instead of relaxation procedures being learned by the client as a means of being able to progress through a hierarchy of fear provoking situations in therapy, the client is instructed to use relaxation procedures outside of therapy when faced with threatening real life events. The client is thus provided with a practical means of coping with future situations, and not only with the initial problems presented or worked with in therapy. This appears to be a very promising procedure which merits further attention and study, for it offers the client a potential method of meeting future problems, and it is not too difficult to master. To the extent that this procedure also increases the client's self-confidence and allows him to expand the situations he can meet, it would appear to have many self-reinforcing qualities as well. Procedures or experiences in therapy that can be utilized by the client in the real world after therapy is completed and that help him in his subsequent development would appear to be of great potential value indeed (Goldfried and Davison, 1976).

INFORMATION IN PSYCHOTHERAPY

Many patients who seek psychotherapeutic help are, among other things, poorly informed or misinformed on a number of topics which are of some importance in their everyday lives. In a number of instances the imparting of the correct information in therapy can be of definite therapeutic value. However, for some reason, the imparting of information has not received a great deal of attention or been accorded much importance in psychotherapy. It would appear that many dynamically oriented psychotherapists, in fact, look with disfavor upon such an activity and generally try to avoid it. It, again, puts the therapist in a nonevocative or directing role which many of them seemingly attempt to avoid. The underlying reason in some instances is that such activities as providing information or offering suggestions, or even giving a direct answer to a question raised by the patient, are perceived by the therapist as constituting supportive psychotherapy. Many of them prefer to engage in an evocative or uncovering type of psychotherapy, which they consider to be a more intensive and desirable type of therapy. In this form of therapy, the emphasis is on the patient's self-explorations and his seeking of solutions, rather than on the therapist's providing him with answers. As a result, therapist behaviors that are seen as reinforcing the opposite type of pattern and that are perceived as placing the therapist in a supportive or directive type of role are viewed as undesirable. It is true that if the therapist helps to structure the situation so that the patient asks questions and the therapist provides answers, the patient will assume that this is the way therapy should be, and other kinds of processes may in effect be discouraged. Nevertheless, if a reasonable question is asked, or the client appears to suffer badly from misinformation, the therapist can facilitate positive movement by providing the correct information. This is particularly true with regard to matters which cause anxiety or guilt, such as sexual activities and negative feelings toward parents. Where the client has a distinct lack of information on a topic which is relevant to his problems, no amount of uncovering therapy will provide him with the necessary information.

As is true with other aspects of psychotherapy, when and under what circumstances the providing of information may be of therapeutic value depends on the client and the particular problem presented. It should be pertinent to the client's problems and not just a topic of conversation or a response to a request for general information. The therapist must be aware of what the giving of information signifies about his role in therapy and the therapeutic relationship generally. However, he should not overreact or studiously avoid the proffering of information when it may be of value. Some individuals are surprisingly so misinformed about such matters as masturbation, for example, that accurate information offered in a matter-of-fact manner can be extremely guilt-reducing and reassuring.

REASSURANCE AND SUPPORT

Another feature of psychotherapy relates to the reassurance and support which the therapist may provide the client during psychotherapy. These aspects of psychotherapy, like some of those which have already been discussed, have been viewed and evaluated differently by psychotherapists of different orientations.

Reassurance is a frequently offered human response to individuals who are worried or troubled. As such, it is not something which is unique to psychotherapy, but a form of attempted encouragement offered by friends, parents, and a variety of professional persons. Its place in psychotherapy, however, has been somewhat controversial. Although several individuals have accorded it a role in what has been termed "supportive" psychotherapy (Enelow, 1977; Thorne, 1950; Wolberg, 1954), analytically oriented therapists have generally tended to view it as a superficial approach to psychotherapy. To the extent that reassurance is viewed as an activity which fosters an acceptance of a situation and thus avoids further self-exploration, it is seen as countering an uncovering type of psychotherapy, and for this reason is viewed as superficial. Client-centered therapists have also tended to view it negatively, since it is usually considered to be a directive form of psychotherapy. However, reassurance is also acknowledged to be an aspect of therapy present in most forms of therapy (Enelow, 1977; Wolberg, 1954).

Reassurance can be manifested in different ways within the psychotherapeutic situation. Merely seeing a psychotherapist who accepts the patient's problem as nothing unusual and indicates that it can be treated, can be quite reassuring for many patients. Thus the manner of the psychotherapist and the way the interview is conducted may convey considerable reassurance and support to some clients. This can be considered a general feature of many psychotherapeutic approaches. That is, without the therapist deliberately attempting to reassure the client, the therapist's manner and communication may be perceived as reassuring. It is important to be aware of this possible influence and not to view reassurance solely as a simple conscious or superficial ploy on the part of the therapist.

The more deliberate use of reassurance on the part of the therapist can be appraised separately. Reassurance would not appear to be a very powerful therapeutic technique, but in certain instances, and with certain kinds of clients, it may be of some value. Where the client is worried about a current problem due to lack of information or misperception, reassurance, along with the necessary information, may prove helpful. This is particularly so where the client anticipates a negative consequence from some impending action which is clearly overemphasized. The reassurance of the therapist, a clearer understanding of what is actually involved, and the actual occurrence of the event without any dire consequences may suffice to handle the problem situation.

On the other hand, reliance on reassurance when matters are more complex will usually not have positive results. If the individual has a long-standing anxiety or concern about a particular matter and has been offered reassurance by others in the past, it is very likely that reassurance offered by a therapist will be ineffective. This is also one reason why many therapists do not view reassurance as a positive therapeutic technique. Obviously, providing reassurance when it is inappropriate will not be a worthwhile procedure and may tend to undermine the client's confidence in the therapist. Like any procedure, it must be used judiciously.

Along with other aspects of psychotherapy, reassurance from the therapist or from the psychotherapeutic situation may provide some feeling of support to the patient who seeks help with his or her personal problems. The fact that one has a potential source of help stimulates feelings of hope and support. The client now has someone to turn to and is not alone in his attempt to cope with his problems. Thus the client may perceive a source of support in the therapist.

EXPECTANCIES AS A THERAPEUTIC VARIABLE

Since the matter of client expectancies has already been discussed in some detail in the chapter on client variables, only a passing reference will be made to it here as a possible variable in psychotherapy.

The point of reference here is that the client's expectancies, both at the beginning and during the early stages of therapy, may influence the outcome of therapy. Consequently, the therapist must not only be aware of the client's expectations, but he or she should attempt also to foster positive and realistic expectations where possible. Other things being equal, and they probably never are, the patient who has a reasonably positive attitude and expectations about therapy may do better in therapy than one who has an overly and unrealistically positive expectancy or one who has a very negative expectancy for being helped. A positive expectancy would appear to increase the potential reinforcing power of the therapist.

MODELING

Another potential variable which has received increased attention more recently is modeling. Particularly through the work of Bandura (1969, 1971; Rosenthal and Bandura, 1978), modeling has become an important behavioral approach with considerable promise for a variety of behavioral disorders.

The basic premise underlying the use of modeling in psychotherapy is that it may be a more effective facilitator of change than strictly verbal means. The particular behaviors desired can be modeled for the client. In this manner, what is to be learned is clearly demonstrated for the client, instead of merely being described verbally.

In the more traditional verbal types of therapy, the therapist may also function as a model for the client, and the client may attempt to imitate some of his characteristic ways of responding. The client may also be influenced by the therapist's orientation and value system. This is particularly likely if the client responds in a very positive way to the therapist and, consequently, tries to emulate him or her in some ways. However, in verbal psychotherapy, this is not usually a planned or explicit procedure on the part of the therapist, and the therapist makes no planned effort to model specific behaviors for the client. What modeling goes on is an indirect or incidental process.

In the behavioral approach to modeling, however, the process is a planned procedure in which the therapist selects designated behaviors to be modeled for the client. The therapist may be the model, or he can have others act in this role. In some instances, films have been devised and used for specific therapeutic and research purposes (Bandura, 1971). Although a good deal of the work in this area, like that of many of the behavioral approaches, has been concerned with phobic behaviors, the use of modeling can be applied to other types of problems as well. Role playing, where the therapist switches roles with the patient and acts out his role, would also appear to utilize modeling as a procedure in therapy.

In the case of an individual who is afraid of dogs, the therapist may make use of a friendly dog and model the approach behavior which he wants the client to adopt eventually. This may be done in a graduated manner so that the client is encouraged to approach closer and closer to the dog, and eventually is able to touch him and to play with him without any unusual fear. Seeing the therapist play with the animal with evident enjoyment, without fear, and without any negative consequences, appears to motivate the client to try to copy the modeled behavior of the therapist or model. More recently, it should be added, guided instructions on the part of the therapist have been found to enhance the value of modeling so that the combination of the two procedures are considered more effective than modeling alone (Rosenthal and Bandura, 1978). Modeling has also been found to be as effective as systematic desensitization in some studies, as well as requiring less time (Bandura, Blanchard, and Ritter, 1969; Erdwins, 1975).

FACING OR CONFRONTING A PROBLEM[2]

Although most of the previous topics in this chapter have received some attention from various psychotherapists, what is to be discussed here has received very little formal or explicit attention. In fact, the writer had some difficulty in selecting a suitable heading or designation for the process to be described. Nevertheless, he does believe it is of some potential importance in facilitating positive change in psychotherapy, and an attempt will be made to describe as clearly as possible what is involved.

It appears that many individuals develop various types of avoidance behaviors rather quickly and then reinforce these behaviors systematically. If an individual experiences intense fear or anxiety when asked to speak in public, he may, thereafter, studiously avoid all occasions where such an occurrence is potentially possible. Or, if a young and shy individual feels rebuffed and embarrassed in certain kinds of social situations, such situations will be consistently avoided. Although the avoidance behavior may be reinforced by protecting the individual from the acute discomfort he may feel in such situations, it also keeps the individual feeling inadequate and upset about his inadequacy. As long as he avoids the situations that are upsetting to him, he will never be able to really overcome his fears and change his behavior. However, if he can be encouraged to enter these situations and to see that the consequences he anticipates are not actually forthcoming, some reduction in fear and an increase in approach behaviors may result.

The above may be reminiscent of getting the young child into the water when he or she displays a great fear of it and wants no part of it. Various techniques have been used by parents in order to effect behavior change in this situation, some effective and some not. However, the hypothesis is that if the individual can be brought to face the fearful stimuli without negative consequences, the fear will rapidly diminish and approach behaviors will be strongly reinforced. It has appeared to the writer that

[2] Since writing this section I have noted that several behavior therapists have referred to the process being described here as "exposure" to the feared stimulus (Gelder et al., 1973; Marks, 1978).

something like this may explain, at least in part, the positive results secured in such therapeutic procedures as systematic desensitization, implosive therapy, and modeling, as well as in some others. For example, in a number of studies where systematic desensitization has been compared with implosion, similar results have been secured with the two procedures even though they differ greatly in their theoretical assumptions (Gelder et al., 1973). Somewhat comparable findings have been reported in some studies comparing modeling and systematic desensitization (Bandura et al., 1969; Erdwins, 1975). It is hypothesized here that what is common in all of these approaches, and what may be the variable of importance is the fact that, in all of them, the client is in some way confronted with the disturbing situation and finds that there are no catastrophic consequences resulting from this.

It thus seems that where it is possible to help the individual to face disturbing situations with a high probability of no negative consequences, a potentially very therapeutic experience in therapy may ensue. The procedures for accomplishing this can vary, depending upon the case and the circumstances. There is still some debate about whether this should be done gradually or whether, as it were, there should be a frontal attack on the problem with the patient actually confronting the feared situation with relatively little delay. Although the evidence is far from clear, the writer prefers the former approach, since, if the more direct confrontation fails, it may actually increase the patient's fearful behavior and present additional problems in therapy (Wolpe, 1973). However, if the client sees that it is possible for him to face a troublesome situation, each time that he is able to do so lessens its threatening qualities, increases his self-confidence in meeting the situation, and very likely contributes to a general increase in his self esteem. Needless to add, visible evidence of improvement also facilitates an increased expectancy of positive outcome in psychothrapy on the part of the client, which is also of some benefit.

TIME AS A THERAPEUTIC VARIABLE

Another potential variable in psychotherapy which does not receive sufficient attention is that of time. It is quite difficult to estimate its role in psychotherapy because it generally is not an isolated or controlled variable. Rather, in the therapeutic situation it interacts with all other possible variables.

In general, when time is alluded to in discussions of psychotherapy, it is in reference to the fact that a certain amount of time is required for the process of psychotherapy to take place and that it cannot be unduly hurried. From the analytic viewpoint, time is required for the development of the transference relationship, to overcome resistances, and to work through and to integrate the various insights secured in psychotherapy. Time is referred to in this sense also when mention is made of long-term or intensive psychotherapy. Time is viewed then as a necessary medium through which other variables are allowed to operate, although not necessarily as a directly influencing variable.

There are, however, some other considerations to appraise. One can conjecture that in some cases an individual who is upset or disturbed may simply get over this discomfort on his own without any therapeutic help whatsoever. He may, for example, by some means of self-appraisal, self-talk, or self-analysis, find his situation less upsetting or his perception of it changed. What seemed very depressing yesterday may seem less so today. Besides the sheer passage of time, if there is such a thing, external events may also intervene to modify the situation. Dim prospects for acceptance into graduate school or the attainment of suitable employment may be radically changed by the receipt of positive news, and one's whole outlook may correspondingly be changed.

Whatever may actually occur or be instrumental in this type of change in the person, it does appear that such occurrences do take place without any formal psychotherapeutic intervention. Such a phenomenon has been recognized and given some attention with regard to two particular matters in the area of psychotherapy. One observation made in the past concerning the matter of improvement in psychotherapy with children is that children, as developing organisms, can be expected to show certain changes as a result of the process of maturation. Thus if a child has certain fears or wets his bed, there is a high likelihood that these symptoms will disappear as he grows older. The passage of time allows certain maturational changes to take place in the normal process of growth and development. Consequently, if a child with such problems had, at a certain stage of development, received psychotherapy, the resulting improvement could be the natural result of maturational processes rather than of psychotherapy.

A similar point has been made with regard to the evaluation of outcome in psychotherapy generally. This view, frequently referred to as spontaneous recovery or remission, and borrowed from medicine, has been particularly espoused by the British psychologist, Eysenck (1952, 1966), and just as strongly criticized by a number of others (Lambert, 1976; Subotnik, 1972). This view is that certain disturbances may have a time limited quality and that after a certain period of time, the individual shows a spontoneous recovery or improvement. It is known that many physical illnesses run a particular course and, except in the more serious ones, the individual in most cases will recover without specific treatment. It is postulated that psychological disorders, such as neurotic disturbances, may exhibit similar characteristics. Consequently, some critics of psychotherapy have stated that much of the improvement judged to be due to psychotherapeutic intervention, is really due to the self-limiting nature of the disorder, and the remission that occurs over time.

My point in raising this matter here is not to debate the issue of the effectiveness of psychotherapy, which will be discussed in a later chapter, but to note the possible significance of time as a potential variable in psychotherapy. On the one hand, the passage of time may allow certain self-regulating or recuperative processes within the individual to take place and, thus, lead to improved adjustment, aided or unaided by psychotherapy. Here the important variables would be organismic ones residing mainly within the person. On the other hand, in some instances the variables of importance would be real life events or environmental stimuli outside of the organism, but ones which exert a positive influence on the individual. These would thus be situational variables, and these could include a variety of events which are capable of influencing the individual in a significant manner. These latter ones could include interactions with other people who may actually function as quasi-therapeutic figures for the person involved, such as, for example, a friend, minister, or supervisor. In these instances, the situation becomes more complicated, for we may have therapeutic variables involved even though the therapeutic agents are not formally identified as such.

There are a couple of points which are worth emphasizing in terms of this discussion. One is that events which go on outside of the therapeutic hour may be of considerable importance as far as changes in the client are concerned. The therapist, after all, sees the client for, at most, only a few hours during the week. At the same time, however, the therapist is inclined to attach very great importance to the influence of these hours. While this may be a valid inference in some cases, it is also important to recognize that the patient is interacting with a number of people in many different situations during the great majority of his waking hours, and some of these may be of great importance for him. Changes ascribed to psychotherapy may actually be the result of factors occurring outside of the therapy sessions. The therapist should attempt to appraise such matters as accurately as possible and to strive to be objective in evaluating what changes occur. However, it is something which usually does not receive adequate attention, even in psychotherapy research. A related point, therefore, is that some of the changes thought to be derived from psychotherapy may actually be brought about by factors outside of psychotherapy, and clearly this is a matter of some significance if we are to appraise adequately the results of psychotherapy. It is for such reasons, among others, that one cannot accept therapists' judgments of outcome as valid measures. It is also possible, as noted previously, that the client is helped by the essentially psychotherapeutic activities of someone who is not the formally designated therapist. In such instances, as Bergin and Lambert (1978) have pointed out, the improvement is due to the psychotherapeutic influence of others, and is not the result of spontaneous remission. However, in such instances, the formal psychotherapy should not be considered as responsible for the changes or outcome secured.

Finally, in terms of the present discussion, proper attention should be paid to the type of client and the problem presented. It seems reasonable to hypothesize that problems that are of recent origin and in which situational factors appear to play an important role, may be more responsive to time and changing situations than other types of problems. If, for example, an individual is having marital difficulties which are very upsetting to him and which appear to be the primary reason for his seeking therapy, the problem might be resolved by factors occurring outside of therapy. Two recent cases which the writer was supervising may illustrate this. In one, a middle-aged woman sought psychotherapeutic help because she had finally become acutely upset and depressed by her husband's decision to divorce her. She felt very much rejected and abandoned. She dominated the therapy sessions with her verbal outpourings, gave the therapist little opportunity to offer any comments, and generally was not considered to be a very good psychotherapy candidate. However, after a few weeks, her husband changed his mind and a reconciliation followed. Although she verbally expressed her thanks for the therapist's help and probably secured some gratification and release from the cathartic outpourings in therapy, the critical factor did seem to be the events that occurred outside of therapy. In another case, a young man was being divorced by his wife to whom he had been married for 10 years. In this instance, the divorce took place while he was in therapy, and the early stages of therapy were concerned with his acceptance of this reality. Although this case was very different from the preceding one, and went on for a longer period of time, outside events again played a very important part in his overall state of adjustment. In this case, the passage of time and the opportunity for the client to discuss his situation in therapy appeared to be of some importance in his overcoming his feelings of personal loss. However, securing a new female friend after the divorce appeared to be a most significant factor in raising his mood, even if this was not always sustained. Thus time may be a factor which allows the hypothesized variables in psychotherapy to exert their influence on the client, but, it may also allow other extraneous variables to exert their influence as well.

THE PLACEBO RESPONSE

The final variable to be discussed in this chapter is the enigmatic placebo response, one of the most interesting and perplexing phenomena in the history of the healing arts. To a large extent, the placebo response has been used to designate unexpected or unexplained therapeutic results. Its most formal definition and use has occurred in the field of pharmacology and in the testing of the effects of various drugs. In essence, the placebo has been an inert pharmacological substance which is made to look like the active drug. In research carried out by means of the double blind method, one group of patients is given the drug and another comparable group is given the placebo. Neither the therapists nor the patients know which pills contain the active medication and which are the placebos. If the rate of improvement is significantly greater with the drug, then the drug is considered to have a definite therapeutic effect. However, if both groups of patients show similar amounts of improvement, then positive response is considered to be a placebo effect, and the drug is judged to be lacking in effectiveness. All responses which cannot be explained on the basis of actual drug effects are thus considered to be placebo responses, that is, due to some unknown and nonpharmacological causes. Such unknown causes have generally been thought to be psychological in nature, and while unknown or unanticipated psychological causes of patient change may be disappointing to the pharmacologist, they are of decided interest to the psychologist.

In a general way, the placebo response has been considered to be a nonspecific response in psychotherapy, that is, one which comes about without direct reference to the planned interventions of the therapist. In the case of a patient who is given a placebo pill and shows a decrease in his symptoms, it has been believed that the mere taking of a pill may have some suggestive therapeutic effects on the patient. The mere appearance of receiving medication from the physician may be sufficient to indicate to the patient that he is receiving treatment and that he should be better as a consequence. It may also convey the idea that his illness is understood, that there is a treatment for it, undue concern may be brushed away, and hope for recovery generated. The therapist's manner and the patient's personality may also contribute to the placebo effect, although the research data are rather conflicting (Shapiro and Morris, 1978). If the therapist is a recognized authority or has an imposing manner, or if he confidently tells the patient that the medication is very effective and will soon rid him of his discomfort, placebo effects may be heightened. In a related fashion, if the patient has a great deal of confidence in the doctor, is very much impressed by him, or is, in other ways, rather suggestive or impressionable, more pronounced placebo effects may be secured. It should be mentioned also, that although positive placebo effects have tended to receive the greatest amount of attention, negative placebo effects have also been obtained.

The placebo response, ubiquitous and enigmatic, has received a fair amount of study and discussion from both pharmacologically and psychologically oriented investigators. Its precise nature is still not fully understood, although it has appeared to play an important role in the history of medical and related therapeutics. An interesting and comprehensive review has been provided by Shapiro and Morris (1978), which most readers should find both informative and provocative. Consequently, no attempt will be made here to even review some of the literature on this topic. We will simply call attention to its implications for psychotherapy.

It can be noted that a number of psychotherapists react quite negatively to the entire concept of the placebo response. With some justification they point out that the concept is vague, and appears to include a variety of causes and effects. Also, whereas many hypotheses have been advanced to explain the presumed placebo effect, systematic studies have not always lent support to these hypotheses. Although all of this is certainly true, the reaction is sometimes overly strong. Such findings are certainly not unusual in the field of psychotherapy, and of course, some of the hypotheses have not been adequately appraised, and some may be without foundation. However, to the extent that a number of studies of the effects of both drugs and psychotherapy have indicated positive changes for groups provided with some form of placebo control, it does appear that some kind of influence process is activated by placebos of various kinds. Even in studies where the drug or the type of psychotherapy evaluated secures significantly better results than the placebo control condition, some positive results tend also to be secured with the latter. The fact that the more sophisticated research projects in psychotherapy have utilized a placebo control also attests to its potential importance in psychotherapy. Many psychotherapists, however, seemingly tend to feel that acknowledging that there is such a phenomenon as the placebo response is somehow a criticism of their work and of psychotherapy in general. To the extent that many drugs, later shown to be ineffective, have initially secured positive results, apparently by means of the placebo response, and that charlatans have also been successful with a variety of questionable procedures which can be viewed as placebos, the negative view on the part of psychotherapists may, perhaps, be understood.

However, there seems to be another aspect of this response to the

placebo effect. My own speculation is that first of all it tends to discon-
firm the therapist's own firmly held beliefs about what produces change in
psychotherapy. Related to this is the possibility that if much of the change
can be attributed to the placebo response, the therapist may have to
acknowledge that many of his efforts and procedures were actually un-
essential, and this, of course, is a difficult thing to accept. If many of the
therapist's cherished views and the apparently complicated and difficult
processes of therapy can even in part be explained by such a simple and
even fraudulent appearing business as the placebo response, then this
negative pattern of response becomes quite comprehensible. However,
such negative responses seem overly defensive (Shapiro and Struening,
1973). They appear similar to the comments offered earlier with reference to the patient's insight and understanding. Nevertheless, if positive
changes occur in psychotherapy which do not appear to be the result of
our planned procedures, it would seem worthwhile for us to investigate
the possible causative factors involved. If the therapist's confidence in his
procedures can be shown to have a positive effect on outcome, the therapist
should act accordingly. We should want to do anything which maximizes
positive outcome and increases the effectiveness of therapy, even if it is not
in line with our preconceived views. It does appear as if the mere arranging
for an appointment with a therapist and having an initial evaluation interview may have therapeutic value (Friedman, 1963). The therapist should
be sensitive to such possible influences and use his awareness of the
phenomena constructively. The placebo response is far from well understood, but there do appear to be some kinds of "nonspecific" responses in
therapy of most varieties which suggest that we should be alert to such
factors in therapy. Hopefully, additional research may help us to understand what this process or processes are.

REFERENCES

Alexander, F. and French, T. M. *Psychoanalytic therapy*. New York: Ronald,
1946.

Bandura, A. *Principles of behavior modification*. New York: Holt, Rinehart,
and Winston, 1969.

Bandura, A. Psychotherapy based upon modeling principles. In A. E. Bergin
and S. L. Garfield (Eds.), *Handbook of psychotherapy and behavior
change*. New York: Wiley, 1971.

Bandura, A., Blanchard, E. B., and Ritter, B. The relative efficacy of desensitization and modeling approaches for inducing behavioral, affective, and
attitudinal changes. *Journal of Personality and Social Psychology*, 1969,
13, 173–199.

Beck, A. T. *Cognitive therapy and the emotional disorders.* New York: International Universities Press, 1976.

Bergin, A. E. and Lambert, M. J. The evaluation of therapeutic outcomes. In S. L. Garfield and A. E. Bergin (Eds.), *Handbook of psychotherapy and behavior change,* 2nd ed. New York: Wiley, 1978.

Davison, G. C. and Wilson, G. T. Processes of fear reduction in systematic desensitization: cognitive and social reinforcement factors in humans. *Behavior Therapy,* 1973, *4,* 1–21.

Ellis, D. *Reason and emotion in psychotherapy.* New York: Lyle Stuart, 1962.

Enelow, A. J. *Elements of psychotherapy.* New York: Oxford University Press, 1977.

Erdwins, C. F. *A comparison of three behavior modification procedures including systematic desensitization and vicarious modeling.* Unpublished Doctoral Dissertation, Washington University, St. Louis, Mo., 1975.

Eysenck, H. J. The effects of psychotherapy: An evaluation. *Journal of Consulting Psychology,* 1952, *16,* 319–324.

Eysenck, H. J. *The effects of psychotherapy.* New York: International Science Press, 1966.

Frank, J. D. Therapeutic factors in psychotherapy. *American Journal of Psychotherapy,* 1971, *25,* 350–361.

Frank, J. D. *Persuasion and healing,* 2nd ed. Baltimore, Md.: The Johns Hopkins Press, 1973.

Freud, S. On the history of the psychoanalytic movement. In *Collected papers, Vol. 1.* London: The Hogarth Press and the Institute of Psychoanalysis, 1950.

Friedman, H. J. Patient-expectancy and symptom reduction. *Archives of General Psychiatry,* 1963, *8,* 61–67.

Garfield, S. L. *Introductory clinical psychology.* New York: Macmillan, 1957.

Gelder, M. G., Bancroft, J. H. J., Gath, D. H., Johnston, D. W., Mathews, A. M., and Shaw, P. M. Specific and non-specific factors in behavior therapy. *The British Journal of Psychiatry,* 1973, *123,* 445–462.

Goldfried, M. R. Systematic desensitization as training in self-control. *Journal of Consulting and Clinical Psychology,* 1971, *37,* 228–234.

Goldfried, M. R. and Davison, G. C. *Clinical behavior therapy.* New York: Holt, Rinehart & Winston, 1976.

Goldfried, M. R. and Trier, C. S. Effectiveness of relaxation as an active coping skill. *Journal of Abnormal Psychology,* 1974, *83,* 348–355.

Jacobson, E. *Progressive relaxation.* Chicago: University of Chicago Press, 1929.

Kazdin, A. E. The application of operant techniques in treatment, rehabilitation, and education. In S. L. Garfield and A. E. Bergin (Eds.), *Handbook of psychotherapy and behavior change,* 2nd ed. New York: Wiley, 1978.

Kessel, P. and McBrearty, J. F. Values and psychotherapy: A review of the literature. *Perceptual and Motor Skills*, 1967, *25*, Monograph Supplement 2-V25.

Krasner, L. The therapist as a social reinforcement machine. In H. H. Strupp and L. Luborsky (Eds.), *Research in psychotherapy*, Vol. 2. Washington, D.C., American Psychological Association, 1962.

Krasner, L. Reinforcement, verbal behavior and psychotherapy. *American Journal of Orthopsychiatry*, 1963, *33*, 601–613.

Krasner, L. The operant approach in behavior therapy. In A. E. Bergin and S. L. Garfield (Eds.), *Handbook of psychotherapy and behavior change*. New York: Wiley, 1971.

Lambert, M. J. Spontaneous remission in adult neurotic disorders: A revision and summary. *Psychological Bulletin*, 1976, *83*, 107–119.

Levine, M. *Psychotherapy in medical practice*. New York: Macmillan, 1948.

Marks, I. Behavioral psychotherapy of adult neurosis. In S. L. Garfield and A. E. Bergin (Eds.), *Handbook of psychotherapy and behavior change*, 2nd ed. New York: Wiley, 1978.

Murray, E. J. A content-analysis method for studying psychotherapy. *Psychological Monographs*, 1956, *70*, (13, Whole No. 420).

Nichols, M. P. Outcome of brief cathartic psychotherapy. *Journal of Consulting and Clinical Psychology*, 1974, *42*, 403–410.

Rogers, C. R. *Counseling and psychotherapy*. Boston: Houghton Mifflin, 1942.

Rogers, C. R. *Client-centered therapy*. Boston: Houghton Mifflin, 1951.

Rosenthal, D. Changes in some moral values following psychotherapy. *Journal of Consulting Psychology*, 1955, *19*, 431–436.

Rosenthal, T. and Bandura, A. Psychological modeling. In S. L. Garfield and A. E. Bergin (Eds.), *Handbook of psychotherapy and behavior change*, 2nd ed. New York: 1978.

Rosenzweig, S. Some implicit common factors in diverse methods of psychotherapy. *American Journal of Orthopsychiatry*, 1936, *6*, 412–415.

Schofield, W. *Psychotherapy, the purchase of friendship*. Inglewood Cliffs, NJ: Prentice-Hall, 1964.

Shapiro, A. K. and Morris, L. A. The placebo effect in medical and psychological therapies. In S. L. Garfield and A. E. Bergin (Eds.), *Handbook of psychotherapy and behavior change*, 2nd ed. New York: Wiley, 1978.

Shapiro, A. K. and Struening, E. L. Defensiveness in the definition of placebo. *Comprehensive Psychiatry*, 1973, *14*, 107–120.

Strupp, H. H. On the basic ingredients of psychotherapy. *Journal of Consulting and Clinical Psychology*, 1973, *41*, 1–8.

Subotnik, L. Spontaneous remission: Fact or artifact? *Psychological Bulletin*, 1972, *77*, 32–48.

Szasz, T. S. Three problems in contemporary psychoanalytic training. *Archives of General Psychiatry*, 1960, *3*, 82–94.

Thorne, F. C. *Principles of personality counseling.* Brandon, Vt: Journal of Clinical Psychology, 1950.

Thorne, F. C. *Psychological case handling.* Vols. One and Two. Brandon, Vt: Clinical Psychology Publishing Company, 1968.

Torrey, E. F. What western psychotherapists can learn from witchdoctors. *American Journal of Orthopsychiatry,* 1972, *42,* 69–76.

Truax, C. B. Reinforcement and nonreinforcement in Rogerian psychotherapy. *Journal of Abnormal Psychology,* 1966, *71,* 1–9.

Truax, C. B. and Carkhuff, R. R. *Toward effective counseling and psychotherapy.* Chicago: Aldine, 1967.

Wolberg, L. R. *The technique of psychotherapy.* New York: Grune and Stratton, 1954.

Wolpe, J. *Psychotherapy by reciprocal inhibition.* Stanford: Stanford University Press, 1958.

Wolpe, J. The systematic desensitization treatment of neuroses. *Journal of Nervous and Mental Disease,* 1961, *132,* 181–203.

Wolpe, J. *The practice of behavior therapy,* 2nd ed. New York: Pergamon Press, 1973.

CHAPTER 6

Common and Specific Factors in Psychotherapy

In the preceding chapter we have examined a number of variables or aspects of psychotherapy which appear to be of some significance in the process of psychotherapy and in its outcome. Some of them have received particular emphasis in certain theoretical approaches to psychotherapy and have been largely identified with those approaches. Although this fact was noted, an attempt was made to look at each of the psychotherapeutic variables in a more generalized manner, lifting them, as it were, from their theoretical bed. If they seemed of potential value in psychotherapy, they were discussed and in some cases defined or explained by the author in a manner which may have differed significantly from the way they are viewed typically within a particular orientation. This is in line with the eclectic orientation attempted in this volume. A somewhat comparable attempt will be undertaken in the present chapter which is designed to supplement the previous one.

The views to be presented here have intrigued me for many years as I have studied and thought about the different approaches to psychotherapy. While the emphasis in psychotherapy appeared to be on the presentation of different theoretical and procedural systems of psychotherapy, I was impressed with the potentially common threads which seemed to run through diverse systems and by the fact that therapists in practice behaved in ways which were not specified by their theoretical orientations. Earlier publications which influenced my thinking were those by Rosenzweig (1936), Levine (1948), Heine (1953), and Rosenthal and Frank (1956). All of these suggested the possibility of at least some common elements occurring in diverse forms of psychotherapy, and I subsequently made reference to several common factors in psychotherapy in an earlier textbook on clinical psychology (Garfield, 1957). Jerome Frank and his colleagues also referred to such phenomena as "nonspecific" factors in psychotherapy (Frank, 1973; Stone, Imber, and Frank, 1966), since they were not specific to any particular form of therapy, and this term has been used more recently to refer to therapeutic effects not directly due to the specified treatment procedures. However, more recently, Frank (1971) has discussed common and specific factors in psychotherapy, and his presentation has further influenced my own thoughts on this topic.

A basic hypothesis to be advanced in this chapter is that despite many apparent differences in theoretical orientations and procedures, many of the divergent schools of psychotherapy rely on essentially common factors for securing some of the changes that are believed to occur in their respective psychotherapeutic endeavors. Although each of the schools may emphasize specific factors or processes considered to be unique to their particular form of psychotherapy, an examination of what may actually be occurring allows for a somewhat different interpretation. This was exemplified in our previous discussion of the role of insight and understanding in psychotherapy. Although the different orientations in psychotherapy may provide different types of understanding, it is not these specific insights which appear to be of some potential value in psychotherapy, but rather, the provision of some rationale for explaining the patient's problem which may be the important variable. Thus it is not necessarily the precise explanation offered by a particular school that is potentially therapeutic, but the more general process of giving the patient some kind of understanding of what is troubling him and his acceptance of this explanation.

To the extent that all approaches claim to be successful in alleviating the problems of the patients seeking their help, it seems plausible to assume that there may be variables or processes common to most approaches which are the operative ones instead of the more specific ones advanced by the separate approaches. Although this view is offered as a hypothetical one, it is one which appears to have some plausibility, is congruent with at least some research findings on outcome in psychotherapy (Gelder et al., 1973; Sloane et al., 1975; Luborsky, Singer, and Luborsky, 1975), and is one which is worth considering in more detail.

A somewhat similar view of the psychotherapeutic process was also presented by Lennard and Bernstein (1960) in their analysis of psychotherapy as a social system. One of the conclusions drawn from their study was the following:

First we saw that despite major differences in the outlook and the behavior of each therapist and each patient, there are major similarities among therapist-patient pairs in terms of the way the interaction unfolds longitudinally. This finding raises many questions for those who tend to stress differences between therapists in their theoretical orientation and who overemphasize the importance of the "school" to which a therapist belongs as the determinant for what transpires during therapy. It could be claimed that specific acts (techniques) occurring in one kind of therapy and not in another are the significant factors in the "cure" of the patient. From this point of view, it is the "differences" in therapy which count. However, we are inclined to disagree that this is wholly true. If emotional illness is the result of long and continued faulty interaction from childhood on between the patient and a wide variety of his role partners, then it is hard to see how one or another circumscribed aspect of therapist behavior could provide the necessary restorative experience. We believe that the most important contribution of therapy lies in the experience, in the total and recurrent pattern of patient and therapist interaction, extending over an enduring period. The enormous amount of similarity in the therapeutic systems suggests to us that what is shared by different therapist-patient pairs may be at least as therapeutic as that which is unique. (pp. 193–194)

In more recent years there has been increased attention paid to the potential importance of common or nonspecific factors in psychotherapy (Frank, 1971, 1973; Garfield, 1973; McCardel and Murray, 1974; Patterson, 1967, 1969; Staples et al., 1975; Strupp, 1970; Torrey, 1972). In addition, behavior therapists have become more concerned with the influence of expectancy and placebo effects on outcome in systematic desensitization (Brown, 1973; Kazdin and Wilcoxon, 1976; McReynolds et al., 1973) and others have suggested that common variables may be operative in hypnosis and behavior therapy (Spanos, Moor, and Barber, 1973).

In a recent review of research on psychotherapy with children, Barrett, Hampe, and Miller (1978) offer an interesting observation based on their own research:

It would seem redundant to state that reciprocal inhibition therapy and play therapy are two different techniques. To a large extent, though, the activities conducted under these two names are quite similar, so much so that in our own research we found it possible and profitable to describe a generic set of procedures that we found ourselves using no matter which kind of treatment we were using. Moreover, these common procedures probably accounted for the fact that we obtained no differential treatment effect. One treatment *was* the other. Therefore, it appears to us that the first step is that of discovering and describing those procedures that are common to nearly all child treatments and assessing their impact. Once the impact of these procedures is known, we can determine whether those maneuvers that are exclusive to one type of therapy add anything beyond the "G" variable. (p. 431)

Rosenthal and Bandura (1978) also comment about common features in discussing various symbolic procedures in behavioral therapies:

Similar information and meaningful inferences can be drawn from many permutations of input. Hence, it is not surprising if symbolic modeling produces much the same results as related guidance techniques bearing other labels like systematic desensitization, role playing, and flooding. Nominal format differences may prompt contrasting brand names that emphasize superficial distinctions but obscure commonalities. Ordinarily, all such methods share a number of important treatment features which overlap substantially in form, organization, substance, and functional consequences.

Thus there has been a greater recognition and acknowledgment of possible common factors operating within the various forms of psychotherapy, although most proponents of the different approaches to psychotherapy continue to emphasize the unique values of their own approach.

It is also worth emphasizing that the view of common factors advanced here is by no means judged to account for all of the possible variables operating in psychotherapy. There may be more specific variables as well, and ones which may be particularly important in working with certain types of problems. An attempt will also be made to discuss some of these. However, let us now proceed to consider the matter of possible common factors in psychotherapy.

COMMON FACTORS IN PSYCHOTHERAPY

Having advanced the proposition that there may be common factors operating among the various psychotherapies, let us begin by looking at what seem to be the more obvious similarities among them. All psychotherapy begins when an individual experiences a degree of discomfort or difficulty which finally motivates him or her to consult a therapist. Thus all of the psychotherapies have in common a disturbed individual who seeks help. They also utilize a therapist who has been designated as such and who is perceived generally as a socially sanctioned healer. The mere fact of seeking help and receiving the therapist's assurance that he will undertake to help him is also of some potential significance. The fact that the patient is doing something constructive about his difficulties and has engaged the services of an expert who appears to understand his problems may generate considerable hope in the patient that his situation may change for the better. The matter of generating hope in the patient, as Frank (1973) has pointed out, may be an initially important factor in facilitating change, and it is a process which appears to occur in most of the psychotherapies.

Most of the psychotherapies also utilize a verbal means of communication and interaction between the therapist and client, but since it is what is communicated and how the communications are made which appear to be important, nothing more need be said here about the verbal means of communication per se. However, in all therapies the client is afforded an opportunity to tell the therapist about his problems, to confide personal matters, and generally to unburden himself of those things which have been troubling and perplexing him. The therapist, in most instances, will manifest an attentive interest in what the client has to tell him and may also ask some questions or ask the client to elaborate upon some of the matters being discussed. At certain times the therapist may indicate his interest and professional concern by nodding his head, by reflecting on some of the client's statements and feelings, and by noting down some of the client's statements. Such responses of the therapist may indicate to the client that the therapist understands his problems, that he has encountered such problems before, and that there is indeed some hope or possibility of change for him. Such common features of psychotherapy may indeed have some therapeutic effect on the client. Besides generating a more optimistic outlook on the part of the client, they may also signify an important turning point in the patient's current life situation. He is not facing, alone, some unknown difficulty about which he knows little and is apprehensive, but he now has the understanding support of someone who has agreed to help him in overcoming his difficulties. To the extent, also, that most of the psychotherapies provide the client with regularly scheduled appointments, the client has the assurance of knowing that he will see his therapist at a fixed time and can look forward to such meetings. There is thus a promise of continued support and help.

Some of the other common variables which may be operating in psychotherapy have already been discussed in the previous chapter and can be merely mentioned in brief form here. In most of the psychotherapies, the client develops a relationship with the therapist. Whereas the importance of the relationship may be stressed in some forms of psychotherapy and receive little formal emphasis in others, the fact that a relationship does form and take place in therapy seems quite evident. It is true that the type of relationship which occurs may be influenced by the particular type of therapy, but again there appear to be features which are common to most. In any good relationship there will be some mutual respect and regard for the other person, and this would appear to hold also for the relationship which occurs in psychotherapy, regardless of the type of therapy offered. The "good" therapist in any variety of psychotherapy would also be expected to show those qualities which have been considered as desirable and as facilitating the therapeutic process, whether the therapist be a client-centered, cognitive, behaviorally oriented, or analytically oriented therapist. Since, perhaps, this may not appear readily apparent to some readers, it may be worthwhile to elaborate a bit on it here.

There have been a few studies of the therapy behavior of some well known psychotherapists in which the differing styles of these therapists were clearly apparent and were in conformity with the tenets of the different schools they represented. In one interesting experiment, the same client was interviewed by Carl Rogers, the late Fritz Perls, and Albert Ellis, representing the client-centered, gestalt therapy and rational-emotive approaches respectively (Zimmer and Cowles, 1972). The therapy behaviors of each of these well-known therapeutic leaders was what one would have anticipated from knowing their work. They operated on the bases of different premises, their personality styles were distinctively different, they appeared to influence the client in different ways, and they actually functioned in a different manner. For example, an analysis of the transcribed interviews showed very marked differences in therapist verbal behavior, particularly between Ellis and Rogers. In the case of Rogers, he was less directive and authoritative, more reflective, and the majority of the verbal utterances made during the session were made by the client. In contrast, Ellis performed in a much more directive and authoritative manner, and dominated the session in terms of verbal output. Other differences could also be noted, but these will suffice.

One might, on the basis of what has just been presented, question the previous assertion about common factors in the therapeutic relationship and ask what these therapists had in common. First of all, in spite of their differences, each of the therapists was an acknowledged authority and leader of a particular school of psychotherapy. To this extent, they all had some potential influence on the expectancies of the client. Second, each of them had strong convictions about the utility and validity of their own form of therapy, an attribute which may have been communicated to the client and have had some effect on her. Finally, although the client did perceive each of the therapists differently and had different reactions to them, she did mention both positive and negative features of her interactions with all three of them. Unfortunately, since this was a filmed demonstration, and not a study of regular therapy, no conclusions can be offered concerning the relative effectiveness of the three therapists with their different approaches, or as to what components of the different therapies were the most important in their effect on the client. However, to the extent that the client did respond positively to certain attributes of the three therapist-therapy combinations, there was, again, a common feature in all three. The client saw all three as helpful, even though they were different and functioned in different ways. One could argue that each of the different therapists was utilizing a different but equally effective therapeutic procedure, or one could state that in spite of the apparent differences, the client responded to whatever procedures the therapists offered as long as she viewed them as being a means of helping her. Neither view, of course, can be supported or rejected on the basis of this particular example.

Another source of support for the view concerning common factors comes from the very interesting study reported by Sloane and his collaborators (Sloane et al., 1975). In this study, three very well-known and experienced behavior therapists were compared with a comparable group of psychoanalytically oriented therapists. Each therapist saw ten patients over a four month period of therapy and thirty patients were used as a wait list control group. Although the control group also showed some significant gains on selected measures of outcome, on the whole, both therapy groups showed significantly greater change on ratings of primary symptoms. However, the two therapy groups did not differ significantly from each other. Although the two groups of therapists followed the characteristic procedures of their respective orientations and were clearly differentiated in this regard—as appraised by sample recordings of actual therapy sessions—they secured essentially similar overall outcomes in their psychotherapeutic work. Although this, in itself, is a most interesting finding, there were some others that were even more surprising.

A tape recording of the fifth interview for all the therapists was analyzed in terms of several of the therapeutic conditions specified by the client-centered therapists. In this analysis, five therapist-offered conditions were rated. The behavior therapists showed significantly *higher* levels of depth of interpersonal contact, accurate empathy, and therapist self-congruence (genuineness), but there were no differences between the two groups of therapists on unconditional positive regard and depth of interpersonal exploration. The authors of this report found these findings to be quite surprising: "in view of the fact that behavior therapy has been at times characterized as a rather impersonal process with little regard for the patient as a human being in contrast to the close empathic relationship of psychotherapy. However, both groups of therapists showed high levels of these variables" (Sloane et al., 1975, pp. 148–149).

These results of the study by Sloane et al. (1975) are of particular interest for our present discussion. Not only did the two very different forms of therapy secure quite comparable results in terms of outcome, but the behavior therapists also exhibited high levels of positive therapist qualities in their therapy—even though such matters receive practically no formal emphasis in presentations of their approach to therapy. In other words, although behavior therapists place little emphasis on the therapeutic relationship as a significant variable in psychotherapy, in their actual work with clients they appear to develop as good relationships as are secured by therapists of other orientations in which considerable emphasis is placed on the therapeutic relationship.

There were also some other findings of interest in the study by Sloane et al. (1975) which are worth quoting here:

The successful patients in both therapies placed primary importance on more or less the same items. The following items were each termed 'extremely important' or 'very important' by at least 70 percent of successful patients in both groups:

1. The personality of your doctor.
2. His helping you to understand your problem.
3. Encouraging you gradually to practice facing the things that bother you.
4. Being able to talk to an understanding person.
5. Helping you to understand yourself.

In addition, at least 70 percent of the successful psychotherapy patients rated as extremely or very important:

1. Encouraging you to shoulder your own responsibilities by restoring confidence in yourself.
2. The skill of your therapist.
3. His confidence that you would improve. (pp. 206–207)

These views of the patients are particularly intriguing in light of the postulated theoretical premises of the therapies studied. As Sloane and his collaborators pointed out:

Nearly all these items can be classified as 'encouragement, advice, or reassurance', factors common to both behavior therapy and psychotherapy. None of the items regarded as very important by the majority of either group of patients describes techniques specific to one therapy. . . . Most noticeable is the great overlap between the two groups, suggesting that, at least from the patient's point of view, the effectiveness of treatment was due to factors common to both therapies rather than to any particular theoretical orientation or techniques. (p. 207)

All in all, as these investigators themselves point out, the findings of this study do appear to support the view that there are common factors operating in both behavioral therapy and psychoanalytically oriented therapy which are of potential significance as far as outcome is concerned.

Somewhat comparable results were reported in an earlier study by Ryan and Gizynski (1971). They interviewed fourteen patients who had received behavioral therapy, most of whom had shown definite improvement in therapy. While there are some defects in this study, the results are of interest: "The patients felt, and the authors would agree, that the most universally helpful elements of their experience were the therapists' calm, sympathetic listening, support and approval, advice and 'faith.' " (p. 8)

Other investigators have reported somewhat similar findings. Heine (1953), for example, in studying patients treated by Adlerian, client-centered, and psychoanalytically oriented therapists found that they exhibited similar patterns of change. Also, patients who showed similar changes tended to report similar factors as responsible for the changes. Feifel and Eells (1963) reported that the patients they studied stressed the personal qualities of the therapist and the opportunity to discuss their problems as variables of importance, whereas therapists emphasized their therapeutic techniques in this regard.

Thus it is conceivable that many differently designated psychotherapies use many similar procedures or interactions which have an influence on the client, although they are either not emphasized or not attended to in the formal account of the therapy. Furthermore, these conceptually neglected variables may actually be of some importance in whatever outcomes are secured. What is really needed is research that goes beyond any particular orientation and that will examine other possible variables (common ones) that may be therapeutic. Too many therapists appear to be locked in by their particular orientation. It is extremely important to go beyond the postulated variables being studied and to study the behavior of the therapist and his interactions with the client or patient. As Davidson and Seidman (1974) have remarked in a recent review: "important variables have been selected a priori and any others systematically left out of investigative efforts. There is no real sense of an effort toward discovery, rather only the application of a conceptually closed paradigm to a new content area." (p. 1008)

We can be even briefer in discussing the next few variables which may be common to most of the psychotherapies since they have been discussed in more detail previously. The matter of insight and understanding has been alluded to several times already and should by now be a familiar topic. The only point to be made now is that the variety of rationales and explanations offered to the client by the different schools of therapy is a fascinating area for study in its own right. The significant aspect which is common to all of the orientations is the importance of the client's acceptance of the rationale provided him. Although one may question philosophically the value of adhering to a false set of beliefs, there is little question that having some belief system allows the individual to order and explain his experiences, thus providing him with some semblance of security. Whereas the individual has hitherto been unable to understand certain aspects of himself and, thereby, to be very anxious about this, the rationale provided by the therapist is not only reassuring by explaining such matters to him, but to a certain extent, it may also allow him to interpret and explain future events. Thus the rationale or understandings provided in psychotherapy may also function as a coping mechanism for the individual. As long as it seems meaningful to the individual, it has some utility regardless of what it is.

Catharsis and release would also appear to occur in most of the verbal psychotherapies, and to the extent that such a process is not deliberately sought or induced by the therapist, it may even occur as an unexpected or distracting event in therapy. In one description of a case receiving behavior therapy, the client insisted on talking about a particular event to the therapist and not following the particular instructions for that session. The therapist, however, allowed the client to express himself, and there was considerable emotional release which was followed by significant forward movement in the therapy. Desensitization, similarly, would appear to occur in many different kinds of therapy where the client is given the opportunity to examine certain problems repeatedly. As already mentioned, even if desensitization is not formally recognized as a process or specific attention paid to it, some desensitization may take place.

Another aspect of psychotherapy which appears to be common to most approaches but which has not been stressed particularly is that the therapist has the opportunity to observe and react to the characteristic behaviors of the client. Although some therapists do appear to become overly involved with the mere verbal content of the client or his expression of feeling, many do pay attention to the behavior the client exhibits in the therapy session. To the extent that this is done, there is some communality among the different approaches on what may be dealt with, even if different interpretations of the behavior are offered. If the client is habitually late to therapy, is always sarcastic in his comments to the therapist, continually asks the therapist what he should do, or, worst of all, is behind in paying his fees, to the extent that these behaviors are commented upon and discussed by the therapist, a common procedure is being used. Furthermore, dealing with the actual current behaviors of the client may be more effective than mere verbal discussions of a more abstract nature.

The client may also receive reassurance and support from the therapist, directly or indirectly, which encourages him to try out new behaviors. To the extent that some of his attempts along these lines are successful, the client is reinforced in his efforts to change. Whether this reassurance and encouragement is provided by the empathic communications of the therapist, by the insights secured in therapy, by the direct encouragement of the therapist, or by specific instructions or exercises provided by the therapist, the common feature in all is that the client is motivated to attempt new behaviors which he or she previously avoided.

A related feature of most therapies is that they all in various ways attempt to modify the patient's perception of himself and his world. In most successful psychotherapy, a key feature is the patient's change or reorganization of his perceptual reality. Although this may actually be more a result of successful therapy than a therapeutic variable per se, it is still worth noting here. It would seem that the recent emphases on cognitive approaches in therapy are very much linked to attempts to modify the perceptions of the client (Rosenthal and Bandura, 1978). In spite of different emphases, many of the different forms of psychotherapy actually try to change the perceptions of the client.

It does seem, therefore, that in spite of apparent differences in the theories and methods of the various approaches to psychotherapy, there may be a number of common factors which are operative in most of them. Furthermore, it appears also that these factors may in fact play an important role in producing some of the positive changes which are presumed to take place in psychotherapy. If this actually is the case, then it may be beneficial to pay more attention to these common factors than to rely exclusively on the separate theoretical formulations provided by the different schools of psychotherapy. These latter formulations, as it were, are somewhat incorrect or imprecise, and although they provide a rationale for carrying out psychotherapy, they carry a certain amount of unnecessary excess baggage. The situation is somewhat analogous to the one described by Charles Lamb in his classic essay, "A Dissertation on Roast Pig". In this amusing essay, Lamb describes how an accidental fire burned down the cottage of the swineherd, Ho-ti, in ancient China and everything was burned, including the pigs. Until now, people had eaten raw pork, but Ho-ti and his son accidentally tasted the roasted pig and discovered that it was vastly more delicious than raw pig. After this, Ho-ti built and subsequently burned down other cottages so that he could continue to enjoy roast pig. This practice was observed by others and, consequently, Ho-ti and his son were brought to trial, and the obnoxious roast pig was presented as evidence in court. The members of the jury touched the burnt meat and brought their burnt fingers automatically to their lips, thus tasting the delicious roast pig. To the surprise of all, the verdict of "Not Guilty" followed.

Lamb continues his delightful description of this historic event as follows:

The judge, who was a shrewd fellow, winked at the manifest iniquity of the decision: And when the court was dismissed, went privily and bought up all the pigs that could be had for love or money. In a few days his lordship's townhouse was observed to be on fire. The thing took wing, and now there was nothing to be seen but fire in every direction. Fuel and pigs grew enormously dear all over the district. The insurance offices one and all shut up shop. People built slighter and slighter every day, until it was feared that the very science of architecture would in no long time be lost to the world. Thus this custom of firing houses continued, till in process of time, says my manuscript, a sage arose, like our Locke, who made a discovery that the flesh of swine, or indeed of any other animal, might be cooked (burnt, as they called it) without the necessity of consuming a whole house to dress it. Then first began the rude form of a gridiron. Roasting by the string or spit came in a century or two later, I forget in whose dynasty. By such slow degrees, concludes the manuscript, do the most useful, and seemingly the most obvious, arts make their way among mankind. . . . (Lamb, 1935, p. 110)

While roast pig appears to be much more desirable than raw pig, it is very inefficient to secure roast pig by burning your house down. If we can produce some better conceptualizations of the variables which appear to be important in successful psychotherapy, then it is also likely that our procedures would become more effective and efficient. It is also likely that the great proliferation of therapeutic approaches would gradually diminish.

SPECIFIC FACTORS IN PSYCHOTHERAPY

Just as there may be common factors in psychotherapy that operate in most of the psychotherapies, so may there be some specific factors or procedures which are of particular value in treating specific kinds of clinical problems. In essence, there are certain characteristics of most psychotherapies which represent common factors generally present in a psychotherapeutic endeavor, but in addition some of the psychotherapeutic approaches utilize some procedures which are distinctive and which may be particularly useful for specific disorders. The general hypothesis that follows is that an effective therapy would utilize the basic common factors already discussed in a more rational manner than they are now employed, plus some specific procedures selected for the particular case at hand. Thus instead of utilizing one general approach for all patients regardless of what type of problems they present, there would be a greater attention to the use of selective procedures for the individual patient. This, obviously, would appear to call for some significant changes in the way psychotherapists are trained, and in the way they carry on their psychotherapeutic work. It would signify a more systematic and eclectic approach to psychotherapy in general, something which may not be easily forthcoming. Although it does appear as if a majority of psychotherapists actually function as eclectics (Garfield and Kurtz, 1977), their eclecticism in many instances differs from the formulation presented here.

Although many or most of the therapeutic approaches may actually secure whatever positive outcomes they claim to secure by essentially relying on common psychotherapeutic factors, some of the approaches appear to have particular value for certain kinds of problems. This seems to be the case with regard to some types of behavior therapy, although it may partially be due to the fact that behavior therapists are particularly likely to carry out research investigations and report their results.

A considerable amount of the research reported by behavior therapists has been concerned with a variety of phobic behaviors ranging from the now popular fear of snakes to fears of enclosed spaces, fear of open spaces, fears of speaking in front of a group, and a variety of other social phobias. Such behavioral procedures as systematic desensitization, implosion, and modeling have to a significant extent been developed or utilized for overcoming phobic behaviors. Some critics of behavioral approaches have even stated that these approaches are limited and apply only to phobic disorders, an accusation that Wolpe (1964) has vigorously denied. Be that as it may, behavioral techniques have generally appeared to be quite effective with patients with phobic disorders, regardless of the precise procedures used or the theoretical premise followed.

Consequently, if a given client consults a psychotherapist because of phobic symptoms or if the latter appear to be important in his reasons for seeking help, it would seem wise to utilize a behavioral approach. Speaking in a very general way, procedures taken from systematic desensitization and modeling would appear to be the easiest and most effective ones to use. They could also be combined or integrated for certain cases, particularly where in vivo procedures could be used. More systematic descriptions of these and other behavioral procedures are available elsewhere (Bandura, 1969; Wolpe, 1973; Wolpe and Lazarus, 1966), and no attempt to present such procedures will be made here. It is possible that some specific procedures may prove to be more effective with certain kinds of phobias than others, but the reported work in this area is too conflicting to provide an accurate guide at present (Gelder et al., 1973; Kazdin and Wilson, 1978). It should also be pointed out that although these different behavioral approaches themselves utilize some of the common therapeutic factors mentioned previously, they do appear to have some specific values as well. More than most other approaches, they deal directly with the client's problem and quickly help him or her to engage in behaviors which confront the disturbing stimuli. Because of this, as well as the relative speed with which they produce change, they would appear to be the treatment of choice for such problems.

Before going on to another illustration, it would be well to elaborate somewhat on what has just been said and to offer some comments which apply to psychotherapy generally. In some instances the client does in fact appear to have a focal or specific problem such as a specific phobia, and in these cases a straight behavioral approach may be effective and sufficient. However, in other cases, the problems may be more complex, and some other overall procedure or strategy may be more effectively employed. Here, the important consideration is the proper appraisal of the client and his problem, so that the most appropriate therapeutic plan can be devised. The proper diagnosis and evaluation of the client has been emphasized by many psychotherapists of different orientations, but it has not really led to uniquely different procedures being applied to the different cases. In the present approach, the matter of adequate assessment of the client's problem is of the utmost importance, since it should determine the kinds of procedures selected for use with the individual case. Since theoretically here the therapist is committed or willing to use a larger array of procedures than is typically the case of a psychotherapist who follows only one particular approach, he must have some basis for deciding what procedures will be used in each case. Furthermore, the evaluation of the client's problem is not limited to the initial interview with the client at the start of therapy, but is a continuous process throughout therapy. Not only may the client present new problems later in therapy that she was reluctant to discuss at the beginning, but the extent of the problem may not be as clear initially, and the therapist may be in a better position to evaluate it once the process is underway. This, of course, may necessitate some change in the procedures being used. An example may illustrate what is involved here.

A young businessman consulted the writer about some sexual difficulties. After some discussion, it appeared that he was being troubled currently by premature ejaculation. In the next session or so he discussed this particular problem in some detail and it appeared that a straightforward behavioral approach similar to one described by Wolpe (1973; Wolpe and Lazarus, 1966) might suffice for this client. However, as the sessions continued, it became clear that what the client was describing was something which had occurred many years in the past and which he brooded over and presented as something recent. What subsequently became clearer was a general inadequacy in approaching women and in establishing relations with them. This seemed much more fundamental than the past occurrence of premature ejaculation, and consequently, this became a focus of therapy. His current activities were discussed and he was encouraged to make appropriate approach behaviors to the women with whom he had contact. As these proved to be successful, his interactions became more realistic and satisfying. He also brought up some difficulties he had in dealing with his father. In addition to allowing him to ventilate some of his negative feelings towards his father, and to change some of his perceptions concerning this relationship, we discussed some possible explanations of why these distorted perceptions had occurred and continued. The client also participated in some role-playing sessions prior to going out of town to visit his parents. A successful visit on this occasion was also of therapeutic value in reinforcing changes secured earlier, confirming perceptual and verbal changes with changed behavior. Shortly thereafter, therapy was terminated with the feeling on the part of both participants that some positive changes had occurred. What appeared to be of primary importance in this therapeutic intervention was an increase in the client's self-efficacy (Bandura, 1977).

Not all cases, obviously, turn out as well as this one, and everyone should be justifiably skeptical of clinical reports of supposedly successful cases of treatment. Not only is a case report filtered through the mind of the individual who reports it, and thus is essentially lacking in any objective controls, but the passing of time also seems to endow almost any case treated in the past with unusual therapeutic virtue. However, it was selected for illustrative purposes and some less successful cases also come to mind. Somewhat different results were secured in another case where the writer attempted to limit his procedures to systematic desensitization primarily because the client presented quite specific problems which had not responded to more traditional therapy with a previous therapist. For a variety of reasons which need not be discussed here, the therapist wanted to circumscribe his approach in this case and see if some of the client's extreme fears would respond to desensitization. Although some fears did in fact decrease noticeably, a major one did not. In this instance, either the procedures chosen or the time devoted to the therapeutic effort were not adequate, and the treatment was relatively unsuccessful. However, let us return to our discussion of possible specific factors in psychotherapy.

Although some of the behavioral procedures for dealing with phobias perhaps provide the best examples of specific therapeutic factors or procedures, some others can also be suggested. One of the important contributions from the behavioral camp has been to clarify problems which appear to result from deficits within the individual, as contrasted with other types of disorders where the individual has the necessary skills or behaviors in his repertoire but is prevented from utilizing them because of fears and avoidance behaviors. In the latter case, deconditioning the client or substituting approach behaviors for avoident ones may be sufficient to allow the individual to function effectively. However, where the individual is deficient in certain behaviors, merely getting him to overcome his fears or engage in approach behaviors is frequently not sufficient. The individual may have to be taught new social skills which he has not acquired previously, but which may play a role in his problems. A simple example comes to mind. A young man complains that he is depressed at his lack of social success with women. "When they see me coming, they turn away." Some of this is easily comprehensible. The individual is extremely unattractive, untidy, in fact, dirty, and a very marked bodily odor is evident when he gets close to you. One could, of course, treat all these as surface symptoms and of little real importance, but the fact remains that the individual would be offensive to many, if not most people. He may also be quite unaware of why people avoid him. The most direct approach, and one which seems quite sensible, is to work with the client on understanding his obvious deficiencies and learning how to make a more attractive appearance. He could be told to bathe more frequently, to wear clean clothes, etc. This may not require a very sophisticated knowledge of psychotherapy, but it might lead to some positive changes. The individual might also be helped in attaining social skills which may help him in meeting others and in his social interactions generally. Similar examples could be provided (Goldfried and Davison, 1976; Leitenberg, 1976), but this may be sufficient.

A somewhat related area pertains to what has been termed assertiveness training by behavior therapists. These rather forthright procedures have been used by behavior therapists where the client has had significant problems in being able to express himself or to assert himself in certain situations. The procedures have included relaxation, systematic desensitization, behavioral rehearsal, modeling, and practical exercises in real life (Wolpe and Lazarus, 1966). The overall approach, training in assertiveness, is included here as an example of a specific factor or treatment package in psychotherapy because it has been developed with a particular problem, that is, lack of assertiveness.

There are a number of other clinical problems that would also appear to be dealt with rather successfully and efficiently by use of behavioral techniques, including fear of public speaking, enuresis, school phobias, and other specific behavioral disturbances. Thus where a specific behavioral problem is at issue, it would appear desirable for the therapist to consider devising a therapeutic program which would utilize appropriate behavioral techniques for handling the problem (Goldfried and Davison, 1976; Rimm and Masters, 1974). In the case of children with behavioral disturbance where the role of the parent appears to be of decided importance, work with the parents along behavioral lines would also appear to be of value. Since children are very much under the influence of the parents, and the latter tend to be significant reinforcing agents for their children, an approach of this type should be more effective than the traditional one to one therapy frequently offered in the past. The family interactions should be observed and the parents dealt with directly. They can also be used as therapeutic agents in the overall therapeutic program (Patterson, 1971).

Whereas many behavioral techniques would thus appear to have value in the modification of specific types of behavioral problems, there are a number of other types of problems which do not appear to lend themselves as readily to behavioral techniques alone. In fact, there are many types of disturbances for which the effective treatment is not at all clear. In some cases there is a diffuseness of complaints or symptomatology which appears to pervade the entire personality and for which an analysis of specific behavioral difficulties does not appear to be a feasible or fruitful approach. Some of the more existential writings have referred to an overall feeling of alienation on the part of many people, some of whom seek out psychotherapy (May, 1958). In some instances, there is a pervasive feeling of discontent, listlessness, and lack of direction, which is not quite the same thing as what is characterized as clinical depression. There is a lack of harmony with one's environment and a questioning of one's values. Some have even referred to the "existential neuroses" of our time. It would appear that at least some of these categories of disturbances may be related to identity crises and conflicts that occur during adolescence, as well as in later life when individuals become more introspective, take stock of their lives, and question their values and current goals. Whatever the case, these do appear to be problems that involve personal values and concerns and that have been manifested particularly among middle class individuals and those in colleges and universities.

Although these types of problems may be difficult to categorize, one general characteristic appears to be a self-searching process in which the individual seeks to come to grips with himself and his life situation, and which tends to produce some dissatisfaction and discomfort. In a sense, the individual appears to be seeking a personal philosophy of life or a frame of reference for ordering his life style. Although perhaps most of us go through such a process during our adolescence and early adulthood and work out our own solutions, a number seem to have difficulties and seek some sort of counseling or therapeutic help. What seems to be required in these instances is an opportunity for the individual to give expression to his discontents and confusions to some sympathetic listener who may help him to clarify some of his philosophical problems, and to try to secure some more integrated and acceptable outlook on life. For such individuals, it may be necessary to provide a moderate period of time during which the individual is provided a setting in which he can try to clarify the conflicts and issues which are causing him inner turmoil, and attempt to work out some resolution which will be adaptive for him. To the extent that we could designate what is being described here as a somewhat specific type of problem which could be handled with a particular approach to therapy, we would be indicating a specific type of therapy (or factor), even though the entire description is on the speculative side and empirical confirmation is not at hand.

Another possible example of a specific type of therapeutic approach or factor is what has been referred to as crisis intervention or crisis psychotherapy (Ewing, 1978; Jacobson, 1965; Harris, Kalis and Freeman, 1963; Butcher and Maudel, 1976). Such therapies have developed out of attempts to apply theories of crisis to individuals undergoing specific current crisis situations. Thus they are aimed at specific types of problems and tend to be more structured brief forms of psychotherapeutic intervention.

These crisis oriented forms of therapy may vary in some respects, but they share a common emphasis on the current crisis as a focus of therapy, on the coping mechanisms of the individual, and on attempts to restore the individual to his/her previous level of adjustment as quickly as possible. The therapy tends to be more structured, to have a specific focus, to be brief, and to require a more active stance on the part of the therapist. Another emphasis is that the client should be seen as soon as possible after a crisis is experienced in order to prevent the individual's symptoms of difficulty from becoming more fixed.

A brief form of crisis or emergency therapy would appear to be of specific value in obvious crisis situations where the person is acutely upset, experiencing discomfort, or where there is some threat to the person's life or to others.

Although this presentation is of necessity quite crude and sketchy, the overall outline or rationale is clear. There are certain features of psychotherapy as currently practiced that appear to be common to most of the different forms of psychotherapy and that appear to be responsible for some of the changes which are reported to take place in psychotherapy. Although these common factors have received some attention from serious students of the psychotherapeutic process over the past forty years, they have generally received little emphasis because of the tendency for different schools of psychotherapy to promulgate and emphasize their own theoretical schemes and practices. However, it does appear that some common therapeutic factors do exist and that it would be more parsimonious and constructive to view the psychotherapeutic process with these factors in mind.

At the same time, but perhaps less well developed and delineated outside of the behavior therapies, there are also some therapeutic approaches and procedures which appear to be particularly well suited for treating certain specific types of problems. For this reason, some of them have been identified as specific factors in psychotherapy. For most psychotherapeutic endeavors, many of the common factors described would be utilized as basic variables in the psychotherapeutic process. In many instances, also, some selected specific factors would be utilized as well. However, in some cases, while common factors would also play a part in the psychotherapy, particular attention would be focused on the specific techniques or factors which appear to be particularly suitable for the individual problems presented.

As some readers may have already recognized, the approach being advanced here has many similarities to the scheme produced by the British psychologist, Charles Spearman, for viewing intelligence. In this writer's opinion, it has been a fruitful conception for the understanding and appraisal of intellectual functioning, and it appears to also hold some potential utility for a better understanding of the psychotherapeutic process. As presented here, it is admittedly very crude and unsystematic, but, at the same time, it appears worthy of consideration. The future goal of helping to make psychotherapy a more efficient and effective process would appear to lie in a clearer recognition of the fact that different procedures are required for different kinds of problems and that one approach cannot be all things to all men and women. Although there are common features among individuals who seek help, and there are also common factors which appear to be of value in psychotherapy generally, there are also specific factors which need to be understood and applied in different kinds of cases. A better knowledge of the common and specific factors in psychotherapy should be of value in securing more effective outcomes in our therapeutic endeavors.

REFERENCES

Bandura, A. *Principles of behavior modification.* New York: Holt, Rinehart and Winston, 1969.

Bandura, A. Self-efficacy: Towards a unifying theory of behavioral change. *Psychological Review,* 1977, *84,* 191–215.

Barrett, C. L., Hampe, I. E., and Miller, L. Research on psychotherapy with children. In S. L. Garfield and A. E. Bergin (Eds.), *Handbook of psychotherapy and behavior change,* 2nd ed. New York: Wiley, 1978.

Brown, H. A. Role of expectancy manipulation in systematic desensitization. *Journal of Consulting and Clinical Psychology,* 1973, *41,* 405–411.

Butcher, J. N. and Maudal, G. R. Crisis intervention. In I. B. Weiner (Ed.), *Clinical methods in psychology.* New York: Wiley, 1976.

Davidson, W. S. and Seidman, E. Studies of behavior modification and juvenile delinquency: A review, methodological critique, and social perspective. *Psychological Bulletin,* 1974, *81,* 998–1011.

Ewing, C. P. *Crisis intervention as psychotherapy.* New York: Oxford University Press, 1978.

Feifel, H. and Eells, J. Patients and therapists assess the same psychotherapy. *Journal of Consulting Psychology,* 1963, *27,* 310–318.

Frank, J. D. Therapeutic factors in psychotherapy. *American Journal of Psychotherapy,* 1971, *XXV,* 350–361.

Frank, J. D. *Persuasion and healing,* 2nd ed. Baltimore: The John Hopkins Press, 1973.

Garfield, S. L. *Introductory clinical psychology.* New York: Macmillan, 1957.

Garfield, S. L. Basic ingredients or common factors in psychotherapy? *Journal of Consulting and Clinical Psychology,* 1973, *41,* 9–12.

Garfield, S. L. and Kurtz, R. A study of eclectic views. *Journal of Consulting and Clinical Psychology,* 1977, *45,* 78–83.

Gelder, M. G., Bancroft, J. H. J., Gath, D. H., Johnston, D. W., Mathews, A. M., and Shaw, P. M. Specific and nonspecific factors in behavior therapy. *The British Journal of Psychiatry,* 1973, *123,* 445–462.

Goldfried, M. R. and Davison, G. C. *Clinical behavior therapy.* New York: Holt, Rinehart & Winston, 1976.

Harris, M. R., Kalis, B., and Freeman, E. Precipitating stress: An approach to brief therapy. *American Journal of Psychotherapy,* 1963, *17,* 465–471.

Heine, R. W. A comparison of patients' reports on psychotherapeutic experience with psychoanalytic, nondirective and Adlerian therapists. *American Journal of Psychotherapy,* 1953, 7, 16–23.

Jacobson, G. Crisis theory and treatment strategy: some sociocultural and psychodynamic considerations. *Journal of Nervous and Mental Disease,* 1965, *141,* 209–218.

Kazdin, A. E. and Wilcoxon, L. A. Systematic desensitization and nonspecific treatment effects: A methodological evaluation. *Psychological Bulletin,* 1976, *83,* 729–758.

Kazdin, A. E. and Wilson, G. T. *Evaluation of behavior therapy: Issues, evidence, and research strategies.* Cambridge, Mass.: Ballinger, 1978.

Leitenberg, H. (Ed.), *Handbook of behavior modification and behavior therapy*. Englewood Cliffs, NJ: Prentice-Hall, 1976.

Lennard, H. L. and Bernstein, A. *The anatomy of psychotherapy: Systems of communication and expectation*. New York: Columbia University Press, 1960.

Levine, M. *Psychotherapy in medical practice*. New York: Macmillan, 1948.

Luborsky, L., Singer, B., and Luborsky, L. Comparative studies of psychotherapies. *Archives of General Psychiatry*, 1975, *32*, 995–1008.

May, R. The origins and significance of the existential movement in psychology. In R. May, E. Angel, and H. F. Ellenberger (Eds.), *Existence*. New York: Basic Books, 1958, pp. 191–213.

McCardel, J. and Murray, E. J. Nonspecific factors in weekend encounter groups. *Journal of Consulting and Clinical Psychology*, 1974, *42*, 337–345.

McReynolds, W. T., Barnes, A. R., Brooks, S., and Rehagen, N. J. The role of attention-placebo influences in the efficacy of systematic desensitization. *Journal of Consulting and Clinical Psychology*, 1973, *41*, 86–92.

Patterson, C. H. Divergence and convergence in psychotherapy. *American Journal of Psychotherapy*, 1967, *21*, 4–17.

Patterson, C. H. Some notes on behavior theory, behavior therapy, and behavioral counseling. *The Counseling Psychologist*, 1969, *1*, 44–56.

Patterson, G. R. Behavioral intervention procedures in the classroom and in the home. In A. E. Bergin and S. L. Garfield (Eds.), *Handbook of psychotherapy and behavior change*. New York: Wiley, 1971.

Rimm, D. C. and Masters, J. C. *Behavior therapy*. New York: Academic Press, 1974.

Rosenthal, D. and Frank, J. D. Psychotherapy and the placebo effect. *Psychological Bulletin*, 1956, *53*, 294–302.

Rosenthal, T. and Bandura, A. Psychological modeling. In S. L. Garfield and A. E. Bergin (Eds.), *Handbook of psychotherapy and behavior change*, 2nd ed. New York: Wiley, 1978.

Rosenzweig, S. Some implicit common factors in diverse methods of psychotherapy. *American Journal of Orthopsychiatry*, 1936, *6*, 412–415.

Ryan, V. and Gizynski, M. Behavior therapy in retrospect: Patients' feelings about their behavior therapists. *Journal of Consulting and Clinical Psychology*, 1971, *37*, 1–9.

Sloane, R. B., Staples, F. R., Cristol, A. H., Yorkston, N. J., and Whipple, K. *Psychotherapy versus behavior therapy*. Cambridge: Harvard University Press, 1975.

Spanos, N. P., Moor, W., and Barber, T. X. Hypnosis and behavior therapy: Common denominators. *American Journal of Clinical Hypnosis*, 1973, *16*, 45–64.

Staples, F. R., Sloane, R. B., Whipple, K., Cristol, A. H., and Yorkston, N. J. Difference between behavior therapists and psychotherapists. *Archives of General Psychiatry*, 1975, *32*, 1517–1522.

Stone, A. R., Imber, S. D., and Frank, J. D. The role of nonspecific factors in short-term psychotherapy. *Australian Journal of Psychology*, 1966, *18*, 210–217.

Strupp, H. H. Specific vs. nonspecific factors in psychotherapy and the problem of control. *Archives of General Psychiatry*, 1970, *23*, 393–401.

Torrey, E. F. What western psychotherapists can learn from witchdoctors. *American Journal of Orthopsychiatry*, 1972, *42*, 69–76.

Wolpe, J. Behavior therapy in complex neurotic states. *The British Journal of Psychiatry*, 1964, *110*, 28–34.

Wolpe, J. *The practice of behavior therapy*, 2nd ed. New York: Pergamon Press, 1973.

Wolpe, J. and Lazarus, A. A. *Behavior therapy techniques*. Oxford: Pergamon Press, 1966.

Zimmer, J. M. and Cowles, K. Content analysis using fortran: Applied to interviews conducted by C. Rogers, F. Perls, and A. Ellis. *Counseling Psychology*, 1972, *19*, 161–166.

CHAPTER 7

The Psychotherapeutic Process—I

Thus far we have looked at the participants in the psychotherapeutic process and at some of the postulated variables and factors presumed to be operating in this process. To a certain extent, this has been a somewhat segmented or abstract presentation that, however, seems necessary before one attempts a more functional description of the psychotherapeutic process itself. A description of what the process entails or, what is a desirable psychotherapeutic process, will be attempted in the present chapter. Hopefully, what has gone before will form some basis for a better understanding of the process to be described.

INITIATING PSYCHOTHERAPY

As already noted, most psychotherapy takes place because an individual, after experiencing some discomfort or dissatisfaction, decides that his discomfort will not disappear by itself and seeks some type of help for it. Depending on his situation, he may discuss the matter with his wife or with a friend who has previously received psychotherapy, or he may consult his family physician. Eventually, he may be directed to a particular clinic or to a particular therapist. In such instances, the potential client appears to take the initiative, himself, for seeking therapeutic help. In other instances, the individual may come to the clinic or the psychotherapist only after some urging or pressure from other individuals or agencies. Parents frequently are urged to seek treatment for their children by school officials when their children are viewed as problems in the schools. In some instances, one marital partner may threaten divorce if the spouse does not seek professional help; in other cases a judge may require psychotherapy as a condition of probation; and in some instances, a family on welfare will decide finally to accede to the request of their social worker that they seek help at a nearby clinic.

154

Although all of the cases just alluded to may appear to be in need of some kind of treatment and may make an appearance at the therapist's office, their reasons for seeking treatment are obviously different and their motivation and interest in treatment are also different. It is important to be aware of such differences and to try to ascertain the patient's reasons for seeking help, as well as why he seeks such help at this particular time. The therapist should have a reasonably clear idea of why the patient is seeking treatment now so that he understands the circumstances which have motivated the patient to take this action. There is little sense in playing games or going through certain motions if it seems clear that the patient is really not interested in seeking help or in being helped, but is merely acceding to outside pressures. It is best to get this clarified in the opening session and face whatever the reality of the situation is.

Another important matter to clarify in the initial session is what the client views as his problem or disturbance. A serious attempt should be made to clarify just what the client would like to see changed in order that both participants agree on the explicit goals of therapy. If the client's complaints are vague or unclear, the therapist should help clarify them so that he or she has a clear understanding of what the client seeks in therapy. Not infrequently the client may present a variety of complaints which in some ways may resemble a long shopping list. To give an implicit acceptance of all of these as matters that will be resolved in therapy does not appear to be a good procedure. Rather, it is worthwhile for the therapist to ask the client which of the problems he considers to be the most important or troublesome so that they might focus on them. Even though the nature of the client's main problems may change later in therapy, it is desirable that the issues or problems be stated as clearly as possible and that they be understood by both parties at the start of therapy. Although some therapists appear to favor a procedure which allows the client to verbalize freely with little intrusion from the therapist, this approach is deficient if the therapist does not fully understand what the client is saying to him. I have found that beginning therapists in particular are sometimes hesitant to stop the client at a certain point and frankly admit that they do not understand the point the client is trying to make. Particularly in the initial interview, the therapist needs to be aware of what the client is saying about his problems and what he conceives the goals for therapy are. If the therapist does not have an accurate idea of what it is that requires modification or change, it is not likely that he will be able to devise the most effective therapeutic approach. Also, if the client is asked to indicate the relative importance of the problems he presents, the therapist has a better understanding of what is most disturbing to the client and how the priorities of treatment can be arranged.

Besides having the client give some account of why he is seeking therapy at this time, the therapist may want to secure other related information. Generally, the therapist will want to know when the client's difficulties started or began to be viewed as a problem by him. It may be worthwhile also to find out if the client's difficulties are related to particular situations or people. If the client's current living or family situation appears to play a role in his current problems, it would be prudent to explore this in more detail as well.

The setting in which the psychotherapist works will also influence, to some degree, how he interacts with the client and what information or clarification is sought. If it is a clinical setting in which the patient is first seen by an intake worker, then a certain amount of background information concerning the patient and his problems will be secured. It is unnecessary for the therapist to essentially repeat this information gathering process. Rather, the therapist can simply ask the patient to tell him, in the patient's own words, what he sees as the main problems. Unless there are ambiguities in the report of the intake worker or there are certain areas that the therapist would like to have elaborated, the therapist can focus more directly on matters pertaining to therapy. If the therapist is conducting the initial interview then more attention would be devoted to the areas mentioned previously. However, I, personally, do not believe it is essential to get a traditional type of social case history, unless there are particular problems presented. If the patient's complaints appear bizarre or there is a possible question of serious pathology, then the necessary inquiries and appraisals should be made. Otherwise, I would secure only the information which seems necessary for evaluating the client's problems and planning a possible approach to therapy. In other words, the focus is on psychotherapy.

The initial session, therefore, provides the client with the opportunity to present and discuss his problems with the therapist, as well as allowing the therapist to clarify these matters and to make some appraisal of the client. It is well for the therapist also at this time to ascertain the client's expectations about psychotherapy, both about matters pertaining to outcome and also about how therapy takes place. Just as there should be clarification about what problems will be tackled in therapy, there should also be a clarification about what will occur in the sessions ahead. As was emphasized in a previous chapter, the client and the therapist may have quite divergent expectations about psychotherapy and it is important that these be clarified and discussed at the initial session (Garfield and Wolpin, 1963). It seems to be particularly desirable to find out what the client's expectations are so that the therapist can respond in as appropriate a manner as possible. As a general rule, it is wise not to take anything for granted, but to be as explicit as possible. In this way, few false assumptions will be made. It is quite easy to assume with certain clients that they are knowledgeable about certain matters, only to discover that one's assumptions were incorrect. The writer, for example, recalls an incident in which he was seeing an intelligent and well educated woman for the first interview and, on the basis of some of her remarks, assumed that she anticipated therapy would continue for a long period. Because his own appraisal of her problems indicated that matters could be handled in about 10 to 12 interviews, the client was informed that although she might have other expectations, the therapist believed that therapy would require only 10 to 12 sessions. The woman was, in fact, quite startled by this statement of the therapist and responded that she had only counted on about five sessions! The moral of this incident is that it is always wise to test assumptions wherever possible.

In the initial interview, therefore, the therapist should ascertain the patient's expectations about psychotherapy and attempt to orient the patient to what will take place in the light of the information he has secured. He must be careful to appraise the patient's reactions to what he has told him so as to bring out any feelings of disappointment and the like. An attempt should be made to clarify and work through these feelings in order to see if there is a viable basis for therapy. It is the author's personal conviction that therapy should proceed from a basis of clear understanding and agreement between the two participants. If the patient has reservations about what the therapist has informed him about therapy, it is best to try to bring these out in the open in the hope of resolving them. On the other hand, if the patient had expectations concerning a particular kind of therapy which the therapist does not provide, it is best to acknowledge this at the start, and perhaps, have the patient seek help elsewhere. Even this, however, should be done in a sympathetic and understanding manner, so that the individual does not feel "put down."

After the patient's problems and expectations have been clarified, the therapist should provide him with some brief understanding of how therapy will proceed, how long it may be expected to take, what will be expected of the patient, and similar matters. Thus the patient will be informed as to what awaits him in the future and points of difference can be resolved. If the therapist is undecided about the future course of therapy or if there is some discrepancy between his and the patient's estimate of how many sessions are required, it may be desirable to compromise by agreeing on a trial period over a specified number of sessions. Increasingly, I have found this type of approach to be a useful one, providing one does this in a decidedly honest manner, and that it is not actually a means of seducing one into long term psychotherapy. In essence, one can state that while 15 to 20 sessions may be required, the therapist is not completely sure about this, but that a more precise appraisal will be possible after four or five sessions, at which time both parties can reappraise the situation and come to some new agreement. Freud, himself, encountered situations where he deemed it wise to undertake what he termed a trial analysis, and this seems to be an appropriate procedure in a certain number of cases.

In addition to the above matters, other matters of a more practical nature also have to be settled at the time of the initial interview. These include such things as the fee for the sessions, how they will be paid, the time for scheduling regular interviews in the future, the importance of being on time for appointments, and the like. The patient should also be given an opportunity toward the end of the session for asking questions about any of the matters which had been discussed previously and, perhaps, what his reaction has been to these matters. The therapist should also be observing the patient throughout the interview to note characteristic mannerisms and patterns of behavior and how he responds to the particular topics discussed. Sometimes the patient may verbally assent to something, but his facial features and bodily gestures may indicate a more negative response. Depending on the situation and what is discussed, the therapist may simply note this and file it away mentally, or may indicate to the patient that while he said "yes," he didn't seem really confident about his assurance. In this way, the issue can be explored further. The therapist's observations of the patient, along with the verbal material communicated, allow him to reach some judgment about the patient, to formulate some predictions about the course of therapy, and to reach a decision concerning the acceptance of the patient for therapy. If the therapist has serious reservations about being able to help the patient or if for whatever reason he does not want to work with him, he should face this straightforwardly and inform the patient in an appropriate manner. If at all possible, he should suggest several other alternative sources of help which the patient might be able to contact.

The client, of course, also attempts to size up the therapist during the initial interview. Whatever fantasies the client may have had about what kind of person the therapist might be are now confronted with reality. If the discrepancies are too great, the patient conceivably may be disappointed and drop out of therapy. However, this does not appear to be a very significant problem in terms of the general appearance of the therapist per se. Of more importance is the impression created by the therapist in terms of what he tells the client about therapy, how he attends to the client's account of his problem, and how he generally responds to the client's concerns. If he communicates sincerity, interest, and competence, the client in most instances will respond favorably, will adjust his expectations accordingly, will generate a more hopeful attitude toward the future, and will look forward to cooperating with the therapist in their mutual therapeutic endeavor.

Thus, the initial interview and the initial phase of therapy are of definite importance for setting the proper stage for what is to take place subsequently. If this is carried out well, the process of psychotherapy should develop without unusual difficulties. However, if this is not done, and if ambiguities and misunderstandings are not resolved early in therapy, then there is a greater likelihood of premature termination and perhaps a slower rate or lack of progress altogether. The initial interview, or interviews if this seems necessary, should clarify the client's questions and expectations concerning therapy, and should result in some sort of mutual agreement between therapist and client at the end of the session or sessions. In fact, at the very end of the session, it is worthwhile for the therapist to summarize this mutual agreement and understanding.

Before proceeding to the next aspect of the psychotherapeutic process, it may be well to emphasize one point which the writer believes is of some importance for all psychotherapists and would-be psychotherapists. This is to never make the mistake of accepting what the patient tells you as the actual truth of what has occurred. This statement is frequently received very negatively by my students, so I had better hasten to explain what I mean by this statement. Essentially, what the patient tells the therapist about his experiences are his perceptions of events and his perceptions of others. Although it is very important for the therapist to understand how the patient views the world about him, it also is essential that he remember that these are perceptions and not necessarily the true reality of the situation. It is essential that the therapist keep this in mind, for the two are not necessarily the same; if the therapist does not differentiate them, he could conceivably reinforce patient attributes which are not desirable. In more extreme cases, such as severe paranoid disorders and the like, this distinction is more readily apparent and there is no problem in distinguishing between the patient's perceptions, which are clearly distorted, and the actual stimuli and environmental events to which he reacts. However, in the large majority of cases seen in outpatient psychotherapy, the matter is much less apparent. When the patient describes his employer, or his wife, or any particular event, the therapist has only the patient's description for what has occurred. In essence, the patient presents his side of the story and usually we have no other account of the events depicted. It should be kept in mind, therefore, that we are getting just the patient's view of whatever he is recounting to us, and that while this is the base from which we work, we must not assume that what the patient tells us always has some external validity. These accounts or reports of the patient represent his perceptions, influenced also by what he is willing to recount to us at a particular time. If, as sometimes happens, the therapist does have occasion to talk to the patient's spouse, he may be quite surprised at receiving a very different account of the events previously described by the patient. In fact, the therapist may have difficulty in recognizing the spouse that he sees from the description previously provided by the patient. In some instances, these discrepancies are quite dramatic indeed.

Since the preceding account may appear to be very obvious, unnecessary, or, contrarywise, implying that the writer believes all patients are liars, it seems worthwhile to elaborate and illustrate what has been said. If we saw a patient who told us that he was being followed by strange creatures from Mars who were spying on him, we most likely would not accept this account as an accurate one. In trying to understand the patient, however, we would want him to tell us all that he could about these strange experiences, and we would attend to his verbalizations with interest and no apparent disbelief. However, if we saw a man or a woman as a patient who described his or her respective spouse as cold, unaffectionate, and lacking in understanding, we are less inclined to remind ourselves that we are dealing with the perceptual report of the patient and not with the "true facts" of the case. The important thing is that the therapist should strive to be an objective observer and participant in the process of psychotherapy. While he should try to understand why the patient sees things as he does, and should also be able to empathize with him, he does not have to give up his objective view of the situation. The therapist must not get caught up in the patient's perception of his situation and lose the objectivity required for helping the patient reorganize his own perceptions in order to function more adaptively. The therapist's personal response to the patient is also a factor of some importance in this regard. If he responds in a very positive manner to the patient and identifies with him, he is more inclined to accept the patient's views as correct views, and to be very sympathetic and empathetic, but also, perhaps, to lose objectivity. Surprisingly, if the therapist responds negatively to the patient, he or she is more likely not to accept the reports of the patient as being accurate. In this instance, the patient by his own behavior indicates to the therapist how he may influence others to react negatively to him. However, the therapist has to be aware of his feelings in such cases and to not let such feelings interfere with the handling of the case. Besides the loss of objectivity, the communication of negative feelings, as distinguished from pointing out the consequences of the patient's behavior, may have a detrimental effect on the therapeutic relationship and subsequent progress.

A few actual clinical examples may illustrate what has been described above. One client, with whom the writer worked for several years, described his wife early in therapy as slovenly, unattractive, stupid, culturally illiterate, and lacking in understanding, to state matters briefly. Toward the end of therapy, the wife had somehow become attractive, intelligent, and considerate. Since the therapist never had the opportunity of meeting the client's wife, he could, of course, form no accurate picture of her or decide which, if any, of the client's descriptions were accurate. He could only conclude that in both instances he was dealing with the client's perceptions of his wife, and that it was these perceptions with which realistically he had to respond.

The writer also recalls many clinical staff conferences in which professional colleagues gave reports to the effect that a patient had a domineering mother, a rejecting father, or a shrewish wife. When he inquired if the clinical worker had seen the mother, father, or wife, the invariable answer was: "No, this is how the patient described them." The description of a person by another may differ quite significantly from how that particular person is actually perceived by others, but somehow this difference is frequently overlooked. Thinking back, the writer can also recall an experience early in his career which made him sensitive to the issue being discussed here. One psychiatric colleague in an outpatient clinic for veterans would frequently expound on his cases in the intervals between appointments. This colleague, who gave the impression of being quite involved with his cases, appeared to make a recurrent comment about many of them. This was something like: "Oh, this patient really has a bitch of a wife." After a number of such instances, I asked him one day if he had, in fact, seen the wife in question. His response was that he had not, but the type of wife the patient had was clear from what the patient had told him. I was intrigued by this, since most of my patients did not seem to be married to "bitches." Being also very much influenced by psychodynamic views at that time, I made inquiries concerning my colleague's wife, since I thought this might be influencing his own perception of his patient's accounts, but from all I could gather, he was happily married and had a good relationship with his wife.

The final illustration that seems worth mentioning occurred in an outpatient staff meeting and was a rather unusual one. A husband and wife had come to the clinic because they were having serious difficulties. Each was seen separately for an intake interview by two different psychiatric residents, and the staff meeting was held to consider the two applications for treatment. As it happened, the resident who had seen the husband presented his case first. In brief, his account was that the husband was trying valiantly to support his family and keep them going. However, this was a difficult task, for in spite of his working at two jobs, his wife was so completely inadequate. Although he brought in enough money, she was a poor manager of the household and could not run it efficiently. Besides squandering money, she did not take proper care of either the house or their two young children. When the husband came home, the house was a disorganized mess, there was no supper ready for him, and the children were usually dirty and hungry. This will serve as a brief synopsis of the resident's report of the husband. The response by the clinic staff was one of great sympathy and desire to help this poor unfortunate and mistreated person. Consequently, there was a unanimous decision that he be accepted for psychotherapy, the greatest recognition that the staff could accord him. It was now the turn of the second resident to give his report on the wife, and it seemed as if both the facts of the case and the outcome were easily predictable. However, we were in for a surprise. The resident seemed somewhat perplexed and at first wanted to check to be sure that the right cases were being discussed. When this was confirmed, he began his presentation. According to his account, based on the interview with the wife, the wife was having a most difficult time trying to take care of her children properly and to maintain some semblance of adjustment. Her husband was frequently out of work, did not give her sufficient money with which to clothe and feed the children, would frequently go on alcoholic binges when he had money, and was physically abusive to both her and the children. If her mother had not given her money from time to time, she and the children would actually have had to go hungry on many occasions. When the presentation was finished, there was somewhat of a hush and then some rather angry reactions toward the husband. The sympathies of the staff had swung entirely away from the husband toward the wife, and there was a strongly negative view expressed with regard to the husband. As a result, it was decided to offer the wife psychotherapy, and to change the previous unanimous decision to accept the husband for psychotherapy. He was now considered unsuitable for psychotherapy. It was as if the husband had deceived the staff and, consequently, was being punished. Although there were many interesting aspects of this staff conference, the point of interest for the present discussion is that the entire staff was very much swayed by, and based their professional decisions on, reports of the perceptions of the parties involved, and were not at all aware of or concerned about matters of fact or truth. In essence, they accepted the wife's version as the true one, without in any way seeing that both reports were similarly unsubstantiated. No further comments need be offered.

THE DEVELOPING RELATIONSHIP AND EARLY PROBLEMS IN PSYCHOTHERAPY

As therapy proceeds, there is initially a continuing process of appraisal on the part of both participants as they begin to form some sort of relationship. If the initial interviews have clarified the nature of the problems to be dealt with, the client's expectations about psychotherapy and the procedures to be followed, there should be a clear basis for the development of a mutual working relationship in therapy. In the subsequent early interviews, each participant has a chance to test out his earlier impressions of the other and to see if matters are proceeding as each might have anticipated. If the subsequent impressions on the part of the client are not perceived as meeting his expectations or needs, he may express his dissatisfaction or he may show his displeasure in other ways. He may cancel appointments, he may ask about the use of medication, he may inquire if there are any quicker ways to be helped, and he may fail to keep appointments and drop out of therapy. Obviously, if the therapist notes any cues which suggest dissatisfaction with therapy, it would be well to try to bring the topic up for discussion and clarification.

Although the writer does not subscribe to Freud's notion of psychic determinism, he does believe that the therapist should be an astute observer of the client's behavior in the therapy situation and that he should be sensitive to any communications from the client which appear to be relevant for or pertain to the therapy process or interaction. Even though the therapist initially has done his best to ascertain the client's expectations about therapy, and has appeared to reach a mutual understanding with the client of what is to follow, some clients may still entertain somewhat distorted and wishful hopes for therapy which are not being fulfilled. Consequently, the therapist always has to be alert to the explicit and implicit communications from the client, and particularly when these pertain to the process of psychotherapy, itself, the therapist should attempt to bring out and clarify the client's possible dissatisfactions. If a client should make some passing reference to an aspect of the current therapy and then go on to discuss some other topic, it would be well for the therapist to go back to this reference and try to ascertain what the client really meant by that particular statement. Sometimes, comments with a negative implication for therapy are rather disturbing to the therapist, and if the client goes ahead to discuss other matters, the therapist may remain silent. However, this does not appear to be a wise procedure, particularly at the early stages of therapy. Beginning therapists appear to find this an awkward topic to deal with and defend themselves against it by stating that they did not want to interrupt the client's flow of communication. Nevertheless, in such instances, the client's possible dissatisfaction or doubts about therapy are not explored, and a matter of importance for the relationship is left unresolved.

The early periods of therapy following the initial interviews are also those in which the roles of the participants become clarified. After the initial interview or so in which the therapist plays a prominent role in structuring what takes place, the therapist in most therapies, with the possible exception of behavior therapy, will allow the patient to determine the content of what is to be discussed. At this stage of therapy, the patient should be encouraged to talk freely and to ventilate whatever feelings he or she may need to express. This seems desirable for several reasons. As indicated earlier, there may be matters which the patient did not feel free to discuss with the therapist initially. However, as the patient begins to feel more secure and to place his trust in the therapist, he may begin to divulge more intimate and troublesome matters. Providing an atmosphere in which the patient feels free to share his concerns with the therapist also may facilitate some emotional release or catharsis, as well as contributing to a process of desensitization. The opportunity to bring up new concerns may also change the focus or goals of therapy in a more realistic manner as far as the patient's real problems are concerned. Finally, such structuring of the roles in therapy helps to signify the important role of the patient in determining what is to be discussed, as well as reinforcing the fact that no matter how troublesome the topic, the therapist is sympathetic, willing to listen, but does not function as a moralistic judge of the patient's behavior. It also indicates the role of the therapist as a listener and reflector of feelings, which seems important at this stage of therapy, and deemphasizes the role of the therapist as someone who will necessarily provide direct answers and instructions. The role of the therapist may change as the need for such change occurs, depending on the requirements of the individual case. However, during the early stages of therapy, the opportunity for client expression appears worth fostering and reinforcing.

At this stage of therapy where the relationship is being formed, it is important that the therapist be perceived in a positive way by the client. If the therapist is perceived in this fashion, his potential impact on the client is more likely to be of some consequence. The various processes already referred to in terms of hope, optimism, and motivation to change are more likely to become operative. Consequently, it is important for the therapist to convey interest, respect, warmth, competence, and genuineness in his interactions with the client. This, of course, should not be a staged performance, for most clients are able to detect insincerity on the part of the therapist and, on the whole, such behavior tends to have a negative rather than a positive effect. If for any reason the therapist believes she cannot work effectively with a particular client, she should try to analyze the possible reasons for this, and if necessary, refer the client elsewhere.

As therapy proceeds at this stage, each of the participants is able to form a clearer picture of the other and to anticipate certain expected behaviors on the part of the other. The client, for example, may get a better idea of what is expected of him and the kind of person that the therapist is. He will also observe what kind of material the therapist seems interested in, and what kinds seem not to be received so well. Depending on the type of personality he has, he may try to respond in ways he believes will please the therapist, or he may become antagonized by the way the therapist is conducting the therapy and is responding to him. Thus some clients may tend to agree with everything the therapist says, while others will take the opposite stance. Interpretations of any kind, no matter how bizarre, will be accepted by some clients, while others will tend to reject even rather mild statements of inferred criticism. The range of client reactions to the behavior and pronouncements of the therapist may be expected to vary widely, and they will influence not only what type of relationship develops, but the progress of therapy as well. The therapist, as a consequence, must be an astute observer of the client's behavior and constantly be alert as to how the client is responding in the session. Just as the client begins to form some picture of the therapist, a similar process takes place with regard to the therapist. With each additional session he has another opportunity to see how the client responds to his various interactions and to perceive some of the client's characteristic patterns of behavior. As these become clearer in therapy, he is in a better position to evaluate the impact of his behaviors on the client and also to anticipate how the client will respond to various verbal interventions.

As the therapist secures a better understanding of the kind of person the patient is, he can adapt his particular approach or pattern of interaction accordingly. It should be emphasized that the therapist generally has several sources of information which allow him to form some hypotheses about the patient. The patient has certain kinds of complaints and he also gives the therapist some account of how these problems developed. In recounting this, the patient generally provides some information about his current life situation, and how he sees the world around him. In addition, how the patient tells his story and how he presents it to the therapist is also quite informative. Does he merely give a sketchy outline of past events, does he leave out references to important people in his life situation, does he have to be prompted to recall or include certain information, does he imply that his current difficulties are primarily the fault of someone else, or does he believe that there must be some organic or physical cause for his difficulties?

The style of the patient's communication may tell us as much or more than the content per se. Most important, however, is the opportunity the therapist has to observe the behavior of the patient as he participates in the therapy situation. To paraphrase an old Chinese proverb, "One behavior is worth a thousand words," and although outwardly psychotherapy consists largely of verbal behavior, there are other kinds of behaviors and behavioral cues manifested in the psychotherapeutic situation. Actually, the patient will display in the therapy situation many of his characteristic patterns of behavior, and it is exceedingly important that the therapist understand this and respond appropriately to such cues. The patient may be extremely deferential and obsequious, he may be overly demanding and critical, he may bestow lavish praise on the therapist, he may be anxious and tense throughout the interview, or he may have difficulties talking about a particular topic. The patient may also ask very personal questions of the therapist, may attempt to treat him as a personal friend or professional colleague, or constantly ask when is he going to get better. In other instances the patient may give somewhat more indirect personal cues, but ones which, nevertheless, the therapist should note and respond to as he believes necessary. For example, if after a few sessions the patient should ask the therapist how long he has been practicing or how many patients actually have been helped by his procedures, the query should not be regarded as polite conversation or as a simple request for information. Such a communication would appear to express doubts about the effectiveness of the therapist's approach and the likelihood of the patient's being helped. Since this has very important implications for the patient's attitudes and expectations about therapy and for the developing relationship, it would be important for the therapist to bring out the patient's implied concerns and to attempt to clarify them if at all possible.

The behaviors and related cues which the patient exhibits in therapy are thus very important communications and sources of data for the therapist. Obviously, then, the therapist has to be attentive to them and to respond to them in some appropriate manner if therapy is to progress satisfactorily. If, for example, the patient's praise of the therapist is really too lavish and out of proportion to what has been accomplished, it would appear desirable for the therapist to point this out to the patient, painful though this may be for many therapists. If the therapist is going to try to change the distorted perceptions and maladaptive behaviors of the patient, then it is best to deal with them as they actually occur in the therapeutic situation. Here is an opportunity to deal with actual behaviors as they occur in a real life situation. To the present writer, this provides a much better chance to try to modify patient perceptions and behaviors than merely talking about past events or events which the patient recounts, but to which the therapist has not been a participant-observer. The behaviors which occur in therapy are actual behaviors which take place in the "here and now" between the two participants, and thus they should not be easily discounted or dismissed. Assuming, of course, that the therapist is an objective observer, the behaviors which occur in therapy and which are discussed constitute a part of the reality of the patient and therapist. They are not fantasies or constructions of the therapist, but can be pointed out and, as it were, documented by the therapist. One does not have to present any theoretical interpretations which may be misunderstood or rejected by the patient. The latter, of course, may be reluctant to face up to the implications of his behavior, but he cannot easily deny that he has behaved in a particular way. And, if this behavior is characteristic of him, he will provide other instances of it.

On the other hand, if the behavior displayed by the patient is quite clear, it is very difficult for the patient to deny or disavow it. The writer, for example, recalls an initial interview with a young man. After a certain amount of discussion, the patient mentioned an additional problem with which he would like to be helped. The patient then stated he would like to be helped to become more assertive in his interactions with others. This took the writer completely by surprise, since in terms of the patient's overt behavior, assertiveness would have been the last thing he would have considered to be a problem for this young man. This questioning view about assertiveness as a problem was expressed by the writer and references made to the patient's behavior thus far in the interview. After very little discussion, the patient smiled, said he understood what the therapist was referring to, and that he agreed with him.

While some therapists may believe that the writer's behavior in this instance was too confrontative in nature at this beginning phase of therapy, it was the writer's view that the patient's behavior was very clear, that it was important at the outset to try to clarify the goals of therapy, and that by this straightforward approach the therapist was indicating that therapy was to be concerned with problems that needed help, and not anything that the patient merely might mention. Since the patient was actually quite assertive in this interview, it seemed important and potentially therapeutic to point out the realities that were taking place right at the outset and not to accommodate any distortion or attempted controls on the part of the patient. Although the writer is both a biased observer and reporter in this instance, his behavior in this instance did appear to have a positive influence on the therapy which followed.

There are a few additional points that the writer would like to make in this regard. I do not believe that it is necessary or desirable to bring in the concept of transference in dealing with the manifested behaviors of the client. Whether the client developed such behavioral patterns when he was a child in response to his parents is beside the point, and although explaining it to him in this way may be satisfying to the therapist as a means of demonstrating his knowledge of personality theory, it will not necessarily change the client's behavior. In fact, in some instances where such an etiology is inferred by the therapist, it may be denied by the patient and followed by considerable debate until the patient overcomes his "resistance" and accepts the interpretation. Telling the patient that he is responding to the therapist as he has previously responded to his father is not of any critical importance at this point in therapy. The important fact is that the patient is responding in a particular fashion to the therapist right now and, to the extent that this type of behavior is both characteristic of the patient and has negative consequences, it is important that the patient be aware of his behavior and try to modify it. The negative consequences of the current behavior and the need for change are the essence of the matter.

Another aspect which should be kept in mind is that the therapist should avoid having a preconceived and fixed view of both the client's problems and of his handling of the case. Although, as indicated earlier, it is desirable to have as clear goals for therapy as possible and to formulate some plan for therapy, the therapist should be ready to modify his own perceptions and formulations as required by the continued contacts with the clients. What seemed very clear initially may seem less clear as therapy progresses, and other problems may also come to the fore. Certain behavioral patters which were not very evident at the beginning of therapy may become visible as the patient becomes more involved in therapy or as he feels more secure in his relationship with the therapist. The writer also feels strongly that preconceived notions of the "dynamics" of a case based on the initial complaints of the client should not be held too rigidly and/or forced down the client's throat. Rather, they should be seen as possible hypotheses which may be confirmed or rejected by subsequent events in therapy. In fact, the model of the scientific approach of having hypotheses which are viewed as working hypotheses only, and which require subsequent confirmation if they are to be retained, is a good one for all psycho-therapists to follow.

The early stages of psychotherapy are thus important for a number of reasons. They allow the therapist additional opportunities to appraise the patient and to observe characteristic patterns of behavior. As the therapist gets to know the patient better, he is better able to plan and adjust his therapeutic procedures accordingly, and, eventually, to take a more direc-tive role in therapy if this seems indicated. During this period, furthermore, the therapist has to be particularly alert to any possible communications from the patient concerning therapy or the therapist, so that any misper-ceptions or negative reactions can be clarified. It is in the very early stages of therapy that such a problem as continuation in therapy is most critical, and the therapist has to be alert to any cues from the patient which may indicate dissatisfaction or disappointment. Such feelings and attitudes on the part of the patient also impede the development of a positive relation-ship with the therapist which appears to be of some importance both for continuation, and for subsequent progress in therapy. The therapist, how-ever, should not attempt to keep the patient in therapy by making unreal-istic promises or by catering to any demands of the patient, regardless of their therapeutic implications. Although such behaviors on the part of the therapist conceivably may keep the patient in therapy for awhile, in the long run they are self-defeating and not in the best interests of the patient.

During this period the therapist also has to be attentive to such possible problems as the client's being late for appointments, the cancellation of appointments, and of even greater significance, the failure to show up for a scheduled appointment. The therapist should not ignore such behaviors but should comment on them, and if the client does not volunteer an answer, a further query should be made. Reasonable explanations for being late or for cancellations should be accepted without any further comment from the therapist. The fact that the therapist notices and comments on such behavior is sufficient to indicate that it is of some importance in therapy. However, if such behavior occurs again, then it may have to be discussed in greater detail and its negative implications for therapy pointed out to the client. Failure to keep an appointment without notifying the therapist appears to be a more serious matter and would appear so even to the client. Consequently, this is something which has to be discussed with the client, and an attempt must be made to ascertain the reasons for such behavior. It is quite important that the therapist, in such instances, clearly differentiates his role from that of a parent or authority figure who has caught someone in a misdeed and is considering possible punishment. The therapist's concern has to be in terms of the implication of the client's behavior for psychotherapy. He is not questioning the client because he has misbehaved or is being impolite and inconsiderate. While the latter implications are certainly there, the focus should be in terms of what this signifies for psychotherapy, and what reasons there may be for possibly avoiding the therapeutic session. The therapist, obviously, must not act in a punitive fashion and must clearly communicate that the concern is a therapeutic one. It is understandable that the therapist may be upset at such behavior for in a real sense it is a negation of his therapeutic efforts, but again, he has to strive for objectivity and reflect this in his concern for the therapeutic relationship. The usual matters of politeness and social etiquette do not apply in this situation.

If a pattern of cancelling or missing appointments develops early in therapy, it is usually a clear sign that therapy is not progressing satisfactorily, and in most instances the therapist should not allow such a situation to continue indefinitely. This is sometimes a particular problem in the case of practicum students or psychiatric residents who may have only a few cases in therapy as part of their practical training and who are understandably very reluctant to lose any of their precious cases. However, it is best to learn proper procedures at the start and to face the reality of what is taking place.

Missing appointments would appear to reflect a lack of desire to continue in therapy or some dissatisfaction with the way therapy is going. It is likely that the client may have already communicated some such feelings in subtle ways which may have been overlooked by the therapist. It may be useful, therefore, when such a pattern occurs, that the therapist reflect on his therapy notes and recollections of previous sessions to see if he can discover any possible indications for this behavior which may have been overlooked previously, and to formulate some possible hypotheses for the client's behavior. In discussing the matter with the client, the therapist should be alert for any possible indication of dissatisfaction which the client may not want to verbalize openly. The therapist then should try to construct some formulation or conclusion about the client and attempt to resolve the situation as constructively as possible. If, in fact, the therapist feels there are valid external reasons for the cancellation or missing of appointments, the relationship can proceed on a more clearly understood basis in which both parties have discussed a mutual problem and have secured some resolution of it. However, if the discussion of the problem shows that the client has considerable misgivings about therapy or is continuing on an erratic basis because of pressure from others, a serious discussion about whether it is feasible to continue should be undertaken. This should be conducted in a manner which allows the client to make a decision to withdraw from therapy, if he is so inclined, without any feelings of guilt or of letting the therapist down. If necessary, the therapist himself should make the suggestion for terminating therapy at this point and also inform the client that if he should later feel otherwise and want to resume therapy, the therapist would be happy to see him. It appears better to terminate a problematic therapy in this joint fashion than to have therapy terminated by the client's failure to appear for repeated appointments. Although there does not appear to be any research on this matter, self-terminated cases may be less likely to return for help in the future.

Finally, if a client misses two successive appointments without notifying the therapist, it is probably best to acknowledge this obvious lack of interest in continuing psychotherapy. A letter can be sent to the client stating that in view of his missing the last two scheduled appointments, the therapist assumes he is not interested in continuing therapy at this time. Consequently, the case is officially being closed. However, the letter can also state that the client may apply for therapy in the future if he so desires.

The preceding pages, hopefully, provide the reader with some understanding of what is involved in the relatively early stages of psychotherapy, and of the therapist's role and responsibilities in this undertaking. It is also a worthwhile procedure for the therapist early in therapy to clearly state the client's problems as the client sees them, the therapist's own formulations on this matter, and his goals and plans for therapy. By writing these down in his notes, the therapist not only clarifies these matters for himself by having to formulate them as clearly as possible, but he also has a record of them to which he can readily refer. As a later stage, he may have reason to add, subtract, or in other ways to change his original plans. However, the original complaints which have brought the client into therapy should be a main focus both in guiding therapy and in evaluating the subsequent outcome. If a client seeks out therapy because he is afraid to leave his house, and at the end of therapy it is noted that the client now gets along better with his wife at home but is still afraid to leave his house, one cannot view the therapy as really being successful. Noting down clearly at the outset what changes are sought is thus a guide to therapy and a basis for evaluating the effectiveness of the therapy.

The writer also recommends that the psychotherapist make certain predictions in writing about the future course of psychotherapy with each client, and then put them away until the case is terminated. In this way the therapist can check the accuracy of his formulations and predictions, and perhaps even improve and modify some of his views of the psychotherapeutic process. This can be quite a sobering experience for the therapist as the writer can attest. For example, I once noted down my prediction that a given patient was too somatically preoccupied to be a motivated and involved patient in psychotherapy, and would drop out of therapy before the eighth interview. As it turned out, he stayed in therapy with me for almost four years and never missed an interview. I also learned a fair amount from this case. I have also learned that many of my predictions are not supported by what later occurs in psychotherapy, and this has also influenced me in modifying some of my views over the years. The more specific and concrete the prediction one makes, the easier it is to support or reject it, and conversely, certain predictions about the dynamics of the case cannot be verified or rejected unless the predictions are translated into some kind of behavioral or operational terms. There is one possible danger, perhaps, in making such predictions, in that a therapist might try to make his predictions come true, a self-fulfilling prophecy as it were. However, this does not appear too likely, and a therapist who would deceive himself in this fashion would probably deceive himself in others as well.

CONTINUING PSYCHOTHERAPY AND ADAPTING TO CLIENT INDIVIDUALITY

As therapy progresses beyond the beginning stages, the role or activity level of the therapist may change as he tries to deal with the client's difficulties. As described earlier, during the early interviews the therapist may be quite reflective of the client's feelings, as well as encouraging the client to express himself as fully as possible. However, depending on the client and the nature of the problem persented, the therapist may become more active in certain ways. It may be at least partially correct to say that whereas common therapeutic factors dominate the early interviews, as therapy proceeds more specific factors are called into play. The relative emphasis of these two groups of factors, as well as when specific factors may be emphasized particularly, will vary of course with the individual client. In some instances more specific procedures may be employed quite early, say the third interview or so, whereas in others, they may not come to be employed for several more interviews. It should also be remembered that what may be regarded as specific factors or approaches may also have a more general effect. If the therapist, for example, initiates the procedure of systematic desensitization, he is not only using a specific procedure for a specific type of problem, but by the very fact of directly doing something in a concrete manner for the client, he may also be generating hope and fostering confidence in the therapist.

In contrast to some traditional approaches to psychotherapy where there is a greater emphasis on a central dynamic conflict whose solution is expected to have a generalized radiation effect, and thus to influence a variety of more specific behaviors, the eclectic approach expounded here calls for a more diversified use of procedures, depending upon the types of problems presented. As a corollary of this, the role of the therapist is also different and, again, depends on the requirements of the case. To the extent that the therapist may want to employ several rather specific procedures as therapy progresses, his role will change into a more directive and specific one. Any procedure which is deemed potentially useful may be used, and if a particular approach does not appear to be effective, a different one can be tried. This does appear to differ from such approaches as client-centered therapy or psychoanalysis. In psychoanalysis, for example, a major emphasis would be on free association and interpretation as the procedures for all cases, and while the analyst might be more verbally active as therapy progresses, the same procedures would be followed throughout. In client-centered therapy, the emphasis is placed on the necessary and sufficient conditions of therapist empathy, warmth, and genuineness, and the therapist's role would be consistent throughout therapy. In the current approach, however, the therapist is seen as playing a more active role as the therapeutic relationship is developing and as therapy proceeds.

The therapist, in this approach, has to have a clear conception of what the goals of therapy are in each case so that appropriate procedures and techniques can be devised and applied. To this extent, the eclectic therapist has much in common with most behavior therapists who also use a similar approach in appraising their clients and devising a therapeutic program which seems suitable for them. However, as has already been stated, the orientation is different and an eclectic therapist does not limit himself to just behavioral approaches. There is much more emphasis on the therapeutic relationship and on the common factors in psychotherapy. However, in any given case, if the problem appeared to be quite specific and readily treated by means of a behavioral procedure primarily, then such a procedure could be used.

Let us now, however, discuss a bit more specifically what may occur as psychotherapy continues beyond the beginning stages. The client has had an opportunity to disclose the matters which are disturbing him and the changes he would like to see take place, he has had some opportunity for release of feelings, and he has had an opportunity to appraise the therapist and form some sort of relationship or "therapeutic alliance." The therapist, on his part, has been able to form a clearer picture of the client as an individual, has noted characteristic patterns of behavior, has become alert to possible difficulties in therapy, and has begun to plan his procedures for the therapy which is to follow. He has a potentially wide array of techniques and procedures which he can use, and he has to select those which he believes will be useful. The only strictures are that the procedures do appear applicable to the case in hand, and that the therapist be reasonably informed and proficient in their use.

Perhaps an example or two will be of help in order to illustrate what has been described. Let us take the case of a young man who calls in for an appointment because he would like some help with his personal problems. During the interview he appears despondent and unhappy about his current situation. He is in his mid 20's, is working, and is living at home with his parents. Besides his parents, there are no others living with him at home. He has recently broken off with the "only girl friend" he has ever had. At first he mainly verbalizes his feelings of being unhappy and discouraged. Although he feels that life should treat him better than it has, his discontent seems to be of rather recent origin. As the initial session proceeds and he is given an opportunity to present his problems, a few things appear to be reasonably clear. He expresses some dissatisfaction about still living at home with his parents and being treated as if he were still a young boy. Nevertheless, although he has thought of moving out on his own, he has never put his thoughts into action. He gives the impression of being a somewhat shy person who is also not very assertive. The main reason, however, for his current despondency appears to be the break-up of the relationship with his girl friend, which was of some significance to him. He feels rather strongly rejected and discarded over this matter, and it seems to have had a pervasive influence on how he views both himself and his current situation.

Although this individual is somewhat deferential and submissive with regard to the therapist, he also gives the impression of being interested in therapy and in trying to do something about improving his state of affairs. He has had no difficulties on his job and is willing to pay a moderate fee in line with his income. It was the therapist's impression that this young man was a reasonable candidate for psychotherapy and that arrangements could be made for future interviews. The individual did not appear to be seriously depressed; rather, his despondency seemed to be situational and very much related to his rupture with his girl friend, which stirred up feelings of personal inadequacy as well as depression. Consequently, the therapist attempted to present some summary or formulation of what had been presented as a tentative basis of agreement with the suggestion that these might become more specific during the next interview. It was stated that the patient was currently despondent with his present life but that the loss of the girl friend appeared to be the event which largely accounted for his feelings. Therefore, this relationship would have to be explored in more detail. It also seemed that he was quite ambivalent about his home situation and this would also have to be evaluated. Finally, it appeared also that he lacked confidence more generally in his interpersonal relations, and felt he wasn't able to assert himself in some situations where such behaviors would have been beneficial. These were then set up as three problem areas that the patient felt were important and that we would attempt to work with in therapy. In answer to the patient's question about how long therapy would take, the therapist informed him that while one could not always give a precise answer, it did seem that approximately 10 to 15 sessions might be sufficient. The patient was also informed that we would be better able to judge this matter after four or five sessions. Since the patient had no particular expectations about what would take place in therapy, but was willing to do "whatever was requested," little time was spent on this matter.

Because the initial interview is of particular importance, it has been presented in greater detail than the remainder of the therapy in this illustrative case. The rest of this account will, of necessity, have to be more condensed. In the second interview, the patient was encouraged to go into more detail about the problem areas designated previously, and to express his feelings as fully as possible. This he did reasonably well, devoting most of the time to describing his relationship with his former girl friend. During this session the patient was the active participant and did most of the talking. The therapist primarily responded by reflecting the patient's feelings, emphasizing an occasional point made by the patient, and occasionally asking a question for purposes of clarification. From the therapist's standpoint, at least, the session went well and the patient was involved with his retelling of his experiences. At the third interview the patient appeared to be noticeably less despondent and during the interview appeared to be organizing his own perceptions and understanding of what had taken place. This was noted and verbally reinforced by the therapist. Some of the patient's difficulties in his relationship with his former girl friend also became clearer during this interview, and attention was drawn to them by the therapist in a noncritical but questioning manner, e.g., "Do you think that perhaps some of the difficulties you are describing were due to the fact that you always asked your girl friend to make the decisions, and that she felt you should make them?" Thus in this interview, the therapist became more active in suggesting possible characteristic behaviors of the patient which might account for some of his difficulties. At the same time, he demonstrated close interest in the patient and what he was saying, as well as reinforcing the patient's attempts to examine his patterns of behavior in the past and to see how his behaviors contributed to the problems encountered. Some attention to increased awareness and understanding were thus important components of this session.

In the next few interviews, the patient's lack of assertiveness became highlighted even more as he began to discuss his problems at home. Attention was paid to his desire to be independent, but also that, at the same time, he enjoyed having his mother take care of certain of his needs. Certain references were also made to his somewhat similar behavior in therapy. Although the patient was cooperating very well in therapy, and was motivated to try and change his behavior, he not only tended to be very respectful of the therapist, but also very careful not to disagree with him, even when he might not fully agree with him. Thus apart from discussing characteristic behaviors of the patient, an attempt was made to illustrate what was being discussed with reference to the behaviors manifested in the therapy sessions. This seemed to make an impression on the patient, and he verbalized the need for becoming assertive. As a result two specific procedures were used. He was encouraged to be aware of his lack of assertiveness in his interactions with others and to clearly label the situations where more assertive behaviors would have been more beneficial. Along with this, he was encouraged to try to assert himself in these situations. In addition, some role playing or behavioral rehearsals were attempted in the therapy situation. Desirable behaviors were verbally reinforced by the therapist. Gradually, the patient became more assertive in the therapy situation and apparently, from his verbal reports, more assertive outside the therapy situation.

The above excerpt should suffice to give one at least some brief illustration of how the therapist may proceed in working with a client, and how different emphases and procedures may be employed at different stages as psychotherapy progresses. Different cases would, of course, require a somewhat different approach although the general pattern might be quite similar in broad outline. The important features are that the therapist provide a climate which is potentially therapeutic in terms of the hypothesized common factors in psychotherapy and which facilitates the patient's own motivation for change, and then selects specific procedures in terms of the patient's particular problems. If the hope for improvement generated in the beginning stages of therapy is accompanied by some tangible signs of progress, then the patient is thereby reinforced in his efforts for change and progress is enhanced. The early stages of psychotherapy, therefore, are of vital importance in the therapeutic process, and early indications of progress frequently are prognostic indicators of ultimate outcome (Marks, Gelder and Bancroft, 1970; Mathews et al., 1974).

Before concluding this section, it may be well to add a few additional comments about some other problems which the therapist should be alerted to during the first few interviews. As a general rule, the therapist should take the responsibility for the direction in which therapy should move. Consequently, he should be sensitive to patient behaviors in therapy that somehow seem to be opposite to the agreed upon goals of therapy, or that appear to be headed in directions which he believes are undesirable. Since the behaviors and interactions which occur in the early interviews may well set a pattern for later ones, it is important that the therapist intervene constructively in order to try to set therapy on an appropriate course. If, for example, the patient avoids talking about the problems for which he or she seeks therapy, it is appropriate for the therapist to point this out and to explore with the patient the possible reasons for this. Similarly, if a patient has been asked to engage in some behaviors outside of therapy, to practice relaxation at home, or to role play a particular situation, and obviously fails to do so, this has to be faced openly and its implications discussed. This, of course, has to be done in a manner which is not overly critical of the patient or which makes him defensive. However, it should be done, and it can be presented as something directly related to the mutually agreed upon goals of therapy.

What has just been presented is not meant to imply that if no progress occurs it is the patient's fault. Although this may sometimes be the case, it is also too frequently used as a rationalization by the therapist. What is being stressed here is that the therapist has the responsibility for trying to keep therapy on a goal-directed course. If the patient is beginning to show behaviors or patterns which appear to block proper progress, then the therapist has to take the initiative in correcting the situation. In some instances, if the therapist's attempts appear to be unsuccessful, then a more direct confrontation as to the patient's real desire to change and the desirability of continuing therapy should be faced. It seems better to face this situation early in therapy than to allow the therapy to drift aimlessly and eventually to be terminated on an unhappy note. The writer very vividly recalls one patient who talked incessantly about all kinds of topics but avoided those of more direct concern. I made several unsuccessful attempts to intervene, but then allowed the patient to continue in this matter, hoping that the situation would change. No real progress was made, however, and therapy was finally discontinued with dissatisfaction on the part of both participants. In this instance, the therapist was not forceful enough in trying to restructure what was occurring in therapy, and he allowed the early pattern to persist. It is possible that I may not have been successful even if I had confronted the patient more forcefully, but at least, I would have forced the issue more clearly into the open. In any event, the therapist should try to gauge the way therapy is proceeding in the early states and modify his or her approach accordingly.

REFERENCES

Garfield, S. L. and Wolpin, M. Expectations regarding psychotherapy. *Journal of Nervous and Mental Disease,* 1963, *137,* 353–362.

Marks, I. M., Gelder, M. G., and Bancroft, J. H. J. Sexual deviants two years after aversion. *British Journal of Psychiatry,* 1970, *117,* 173–185.

Mathews, A. M., Johnston, S. W., Shaw, P. M., and Gelder, M. G. Process variables and the prediction of outcome in behavior therapy. *British Journal of Psychiatry,* 1974, *125,* 256–264.

CHAPTER 8

The Psychotherapeutic Process—II

Whereas the focus at the beginning of therapy is on gaining a clearer picture of the client and his problems, on allowing the client an opportunity to express himself as fully as possible, on developing a tentative plan for the therapy, and on gradually selecting more specific procedures in terms of the problems presented, as therapy continues, the therapist has to consider additional aspects. As a continuing process, he should be appraising how therapy is proceeding and what progress is being made. Are matters going along in line with the expectations the therapist has, or do there appear to be some unexplained problems or lack of progress? Without being overly compulsive about the situation, the therapist should keep an eye on the overall pattern and progress of therapy. If all has gone quite well in the beginning stages of therapy, unusual problems may not be forthcoming, but it is best for the therapist not to become complacent. Sometimes, a marked improvement in the client early in therapy may be the result of some situational factors which may be of a temporary nature. When the external situation changes, the client's progress may also be interrupted and in fact show a downward dip. As in all problems encountered in psychotherapy, the therapist has to appraise the situation as adequately as possible, and to utilize this appraisal to modify his approach in therapy if this seems necessary. If new problems should crop up as therapy proceeds, then again, the therapist has to evaluate what is taking place and react accordingly.

THE INTERMEDIATE STAGES OF THERAPY

It is not possible to describe all of the various interactions which may occur as therapy continues, nor can one provide concise guides for appraising progress during the ensuing stages of psychotherapy. If the published results of outcome in psychotherapy are taken at face value, the best prediction seems to be that about two-thirds of those who continue in psychotherapy will show some improvement, or state that they are somewhat better than they were at the beginning of therapy (Bergin, 1971; Eysenck, 1952, 1966). Although there are a number of issues and problems connected with the very difficult task of evaluating outcome in psychotherapy, we can postpone any discussion of these matters until a later time. For the present, let us accept the proposition that not all clients will improve as a result of psychotherapy and that perhaps a third or so may fall into this category. This at least gives the therapist some sort of reference point for having his own expectations about therapy be somewhat realistic, although it seems quite reasonable to assume that some therapists may be more successful than others—an assumption that most psychotherapists appear to hold in the belief that they are part of the former group. One can at least keep this average figure in mind as a matter of expectancy.

In addition to the possible *rate* of anticipated improvement, one should also consider the *amount* of improvement that might be expected. Obviously, this matter would be expected to be influenced by a number of factors pertaining to the individual case. More severe types of psychopathology would be considered more difficult to treat and perhaps to have a poorer prognosis for therapeutic gain. Other factors which have also been mentioned are the chronicity of the disorder, the duration of the problem, the situational elements involved, the client's personality resources, and his motivation for treatment. Thus to be realistic, any prognosis would have to be based on some kind of adequate appraisal of the client. However, granting this, one can again have recourse to research findings as one means of securing some general level of reasonable expectation about degree of improvement. This also is a complicated matter, which we will gloss over for the present and simply look at the results reported in typical investigations. To go into such problems here would divert us from the focus of our present discussion. What results have been reported suggest that maximum improvement or total "recovery" is secured in a small percentage of cases, noticeable improvement is secured in a large percentage of cases, smaller amounts of improvement in perhaps a smaller percentage of cases, and in a relatively small percentage of cases, the client becomes worse (Avnet, 1965; Bergin and Lambert, 1978; Meltzoff and Kornreich, 1970; Strupp, Hadley, and Gomes-Schwartz, 1977). Without debating these data further and accepting them as tentative facts, the therapist has to realize that in most instances the client may still have some complaints or difficulties which have not been fully resolved at the time therapy is terminated.

Whereas the preceding view and the reasons for it may not be very happily received by therapists and would-be therapists, it is the writer's view, as already emphasized throughout this volume, that the therapist has to be, or should strive to be, an objective observer, and should be informed about the research in his or her field. Supporting data for the view presented will be presented in a later chapter, but a few examples can be provided here. In research studies which use such descriptive terms as "recovered" to indicate restoration to maximum level of functioning or the complete disappearance of all symptoms, the percentage of patients who rate themselves in this way rarely exceeds 15 percent (Avnet, 1965). In a related fashion, where numerical ratings of outcome are used, the percentage of patients who receive the top rating is also around 10 percent or so, and the mean rating of all patients is clearly below this figure (Sloane et al., 1975). In some reports, also, which report statistically significant gains as a result of therapy, the test scores used to appraise outcome still indicate significant pathology at the end of therapy (Levis and Carrera, 1967). Such findings, then, have to be considered by the therapist as a background for his own expectations and appraisal of the therapy he is conducting.

As indicated earlier, however, the therapist should attempt to evaluate the progress of therapy with each individual case as therapy proceeds and not just at the end of therapy. If therapy does not appear to be progressing satisfactorily, then the therapist should try to see what is causing the impasse and what can be done to modify the situation so that a more fruitful course is followed. In exploring the situation, the therapist may consider possible events in the client's current life situation, certain features of the client which may not have been correctly evaluated previously, possible deficiencies in the techniques or procedures employed, or possible factors in the relationship influenced by how the therapist is being perceived by the client. Unfortunately, there are no simple instructions that a therapist can follow in such instances, and in some cases, he may not be able to fully ascertain what is blocking the progress in therapy or be able to rectify the situation. Sometimes the cues which are provided may not be overly clear, or the therapist may be unwilling to recognize them. For example, in one case that the writer was supervising, the client asked a question about therapy at the end of the session and was told to bring it up at the next session because her time was up. The question referred to how therapy was going to bring about change. Although the therapist was told to be alerted to this type of query, he made no reference to it in the next session when the client also failed to bring it up. In the following interview, the client again made a similar reference toward the end of the session and the matter was again postponed. In this instance, therapy was not progressing very well, and one of the possible reasons was that the client had some resentment toward the therapist for not giving her certain information and ignoring her requests. The therapist was not very eager to face her implied criticisms and, consequently, let several opportunities for clarifying matters go by the board. When he finally brought up the matter at the subsequent interview, the client was able to express her feelings as well as expectations about the therapist, the therapist acknowledged his failure to respond adequately to her queries, and a clearer focus of what was to follow was derived. This did seem to facilitate progress.

Sometimes, a given patient may indicate several problems which either are related or appear to be of some significance to him. Depending on the situation, some may be handled concurrently, or the therapist may decide to concentrate first on the one problem which appears most important, or which appears most remediable. As therapy continues, it may be important to reevaluate the original plan and, in some cases, to reorder the priorities originally established. For example, in one case the client had mentioned being overweight as a very disturbing problem and as being related to her feeling depressed and sleeping a great deal. Since the therapist inferred that her low self-esteem was probably related to her overweight condition, and that attention to this problem might help the former condition, as well as providing a specific program which the client could follow early in therapy, he suggested that the client get a notebook and record all that she ate and the times for doing so. The client agreed to this, but subsequent events changed the importance of following this procedure. A more important problem was disclosed in the subsequent interview, and although the client did keep an account of her eating habits, she was obviously more concerned with other matters, and this was relegated to a minor role. The therapist decided not to make any issue of this matter, and the major emphasis was placed on the more significant problem. As this began to show decided improvement, the client herself announced that she had decided to follow a diet and declared, with some satisfaction, that she had already lost seven pounds. In this instance the therapist thought it beneficial to modify his plans as new material was presented by the client, and to allow the client not to follow through on an agreed upon plan. If the situation had been one in which more significance were attached to the program of weight loss, the therapist's behavior might have been different. However, in general, when a client does not appear to be following through on something which has been set up and mutually agreed upon, it is wise not to force the issue immediately, but to wait and see if some possible reasons for this may be ascertained. At a later point, one may have a better understanding of the client's behavior and thus be better able to deal with it. Although it is desirable for the therapist to have some plan and hypotheses to guide his therapeutic approach, the therapist also has to be flexible and be able to modify the therapeutic plan if circumstances indicate that this is necessary.

Throughout therapy, therefore, the therapist constantly has to monitor and evaluate how therapy is going and to see if there appear to be any difficulties which require attention or a modification of approach.

EVALUATING THE PSYCHOTHERAPEUTIC INTERACTION

Another point worth mentioning here pertains to the therapist's perceptions and feelings as he works with a given patient in psychotherapy. Although psychotherapy may appear to be a glamorous occupation to many people in which the therapist seemingly penetrates the deepest layers of the human psyche and does marvelous wonders for suffering humanity, in real life it does not appear to be quite so glamorous. Psychotherapy, like many other professional occupations, can be very demanding and sometimes even a very tedious and frustrating undertaking. What is sometimes depicted in popular accounts of psychotherapy does not necessarily correspond to the actual interactions that occur, or to the discussions of what has transpired in therapy sessions. Miraculous cures are hard to come by, and anyone who has listened to countless tapes of therapy sessions for either teaching or research purposes can tell you that not many of them are particularly exciting. This, of course, may be somewhat different for the therapist who is personally involved with the case at hand than for the observer, but even so, various factors will influence the therapist's perceptions of the case and his responses to it.

By the very nature of things, the therapist will perceive different patients in different ways, and the demands of each of them will also vary. The therapist as a person will also respond differently to different patients, regardless of the professional aspects of the case. Some patients convey respect and admiration for the therapist, some are very likable and attractive individuals in their own right, and some seem to take to therapy very well, responding with definite and discernible progress. In such cases, therapy is likely to be a pleasurable undertaking for both parties, and the therapist may secure understandable gratification from his work. These kinds of patients make therapy seem worthwhile and provide the intermittent reinforcement necessary for keeping the whole enterprise going, even if other factors might also play a role in the patient's improvement.

Anyone who has worked as a psychotherapist who has observed positive changes take place and has received the grateful thanks of patients or their relatives, knows how gratifying and reinforcing such experiences are. However, such experiences, unfortunately, may not necessarily constitute a majority of the experiences that most therapists have, and to fail to acknowledge this is to place one's head in the sands. Except in the case of very prestigious clinics or therapists, who can afford to be very selective in the patients they accept for treatment, most therapists will tend, over time, to see a variety of patients who vary widely on almost any aspect of personality and psychopathology. A number of these will be considered as difficult or trying cases by most criteria, or as unmotivated or poor candidates for psychotherapy; yet, they also need help and need to be seen by some helping individual.

If a psychotherapist had complete freedom in selecting the cases with which he would like to work, it is conceivable that for purely selfish reasons he would select only those cases that he likes, finds personally gratifying, or with whom he feels there is a high probability of success. Things being what they are, this is not possible in most situations. Therapists need a reasonably full case load to earn the kind of income they feel entitled to, and clinic case loads also have to be maintained. Besides these matters, there is, of course, the fact that there are many people with serious psychological problems who are in need of help, and mental health workers have been trained and designated to provide this service for society. In fact, if the situation should change drastically and the demand for services diminish, there would be other types of problems that these professions would have to face. Be that as it may, most therapists tend to have a heterogeneous group of patients, although there are differences, as noted earlier, in the clientele of different clinics and therapists. As a consequence, most therapists can be expected to have some patients who appear to be particular problems for them. Generally, the difficulties will become more apparent as therapy progresses and as certain of them are brought into sharper focus. Before discussing this problem further, let us make a few additional observations about the perceptions and feelings of the therapist as he interacts with his patients in the therapeutic situation.

As indicated in the preceding paragraph, psychotherapy is a serious and demanding undertaking. This holds for the client as well as for the therapist, but it is the therapist who has the ultimate responsibility for seeing that therapy moves along and that some progress is made. The therapist, by the very nature of his role, takes on a significant responsibility when he accepts someone as a psychotherapy client. He also has to give a lot of himself in this undertaking since psychotherapy involves a constant interaction with another person. The interaction is also a somewhat unique one in that the focus is on the other individual's personal difficulties and problems. The psychotherapist is thus privy to human suffering and to private confidential matters of some importance to the client. Furthermore, he must be very attentive during the therapy session, not only to the content of the material the client relates to him, but to the behaviors of the client as well, and be ready to offer appropriate responses when indicated. Thus the therapist must be in an alert state during the session. If the therapist has a reasonable number of patients, it should be apparent that his work does demand considerable attention and effort on his part. It is conceivable, too, that the therapist may be affected by how the therapy with a particular client is going, by his remaining store of energy during the latter part of his day, by pressures from his own personal and professional life, and by specific kinds of problems which may take place from time to time.

In terms of what has just been described, it is important that the therapist not only be able to understand the communications and behaviors of the client, but that he also be aware of his own perceptions and reactions to the client and the possible factors influencing them. Certain kinds of clients may influence the therapist in certain ways, even though the therapist seemingly strives for objectivity in his dealings with the patient. The therapist, for example, may respond in a somewhat deferential manner to a "very important client" and be more reluctant to confront this client than he would another client, even when this would appear to be required. He may also be too hesitant in dealing with a client who holds the threat of a suicidal attempt over him, or conversely, he may try to demonstrate his therapeutic competence by being too confrontative with a very disturbed individual who is unable to cope with such confrontations. He may see some clients as overly demanding and thus not respond to some demands which are essentially reasonable. The therapist also may not be always aware that he looks forward to certain appointments with clients, and with some apprehension to others. This is to say that the therapist, in spite of his erudition and skill, is still human and he, too, must be aware that his judgments and evaluations of clients are based on his perceptions, which at times may be somewhat biased by factors occurring in therapy or outside of therapy.

Once therapy is underway, the kinds of problems mentioned previously, as well as others, may make their appearance, depending upon the particular case and the type of relationship established. Consequently, when the therapist is aware of a problem in therapy he must not only evaluate possible client factors but also, his own possible contribution to what is taking place. Far too frequently in psychotherapy, the blame for the impasse or the failure in psychotherapy tends to be placed on the client. The client was overly defensive, was resistive to psychotherapy, or was poorly motivated—these are the kinds of comments one hears not infrequently at case conferences or discussions of psychotherapy. One gets the impression that it is the client's fault when things do not go well in therapy. Although this may certainly be the case in some instances, it is not always so. It does, however, appear to make the therapist and his or her colleagues feel better about the poor outcome secured. In one case conference that the writer attended, a report of a therapy interview was presented concerning a case in which no real progress had been obtained after some 30 interviews. The therapist in his presentation was highly critical of his client and very frustrated in regard to his interactions with his client. This client was not accepting any of the therapist's psychodynamic interpretations and was seemingly blocking all of the therapist's attempts to help him. To the writer, it seemed as if a real impasse had been reached much earlier in therapy, that the client was obviously dissatisfied with the lack of any progress, and that the frustrated therapist was openly hostile to the client for his lack of progress. The participating staff members, however, tended to place most of the responsibility for lack of progress upon the client, and the clinic director even apologized to the therapist for assigning him such a poor case. In this particular case, some of the difficulties were apparent much earlier and should have been responded to at that time. The therapist should also have been more aware of his own perceptions and feelings about the client, and should have tried to modify his approach to the client instead of persisting in what appeared to be a fruitless procedure.

When a patient demonstrates or persists in certain behaviors which the therapist believes are undesirable and as interfering with the therapeutic process, the therapist would be wise to try to ascertain the possible reasons for such behaviors. Is this behavior characteristic of the patient usually, or is the patient responding in part to influences occurring in therapy as a result of the therapist's behavior? That is to say, if a patient begins to be overly critical of the therapist because he does not understand what is going on in therapy or because he does not see any visible progress, is this behavior simply a manifestation of the patient's essential negativism and tendency to criticize, or is there some justification for the client's criticism? If the therapist is able to appraise both how he has been perceiving the client in his interactions with him, as well as how the client may perceive what is occurring in therapy, he may be better able to understand why the client is reacting in this negative and critical manner. He is then in a much better position to evaluate the current problem, to clarify it with the patient, and, hopefully, to do something to rectify it.

There are no specific rules that can be laid down for the intermediate or later stages of psychotherapy beyond the more general ones already discussed. Sensitivity, objectivity, and constant scrutiny and appraisal of what is occurring in therapy would appear to be required of the psychotherapist. He has to be aware of his own role and influence as they may affect the patient, and he must avoid placing undue blame on the patient when therapy is not progressing as he would like it to progress. He must also be very much aware of any feelings he has toward specific clients, particularly as these may affect his professional objectivity and handling of the case. For example, does the therapist reach a decision to increase the frequency of interviews for one patient and decrease the frequency for another patient for "valid" therapeutic reasons, or for some other reasons. Similarly, does he go out of his way to change the appointment schedule for one patient but steadfastly refuse to do so for another patient. Constant vigilance would appear to be required for good therapeutic management as well as for liberty.

CONSISTENCY AND FLEXIBILITY IN THERAPY

Above all, it would seem that the therapist has to be reasonably flexible as therapy proceeds. This should not be interpreted to mean that the therapist simply flies by the seat of his free associations or intuitions. The therapist should have some hypotheses to guide him and some tentative plan for therapy. However, as already emphasized, he has to be ready to test his hypotheses as time goes on and be willing to modify them in the light of new observations and information. Particularly when things are not going well or when problems arise, it would be desirable to evaluate the situation in therapy, to seek the reasons for this, and to modify one's plans accordingly. Furthermore, even if one is convinced that his interpretation of events is absolutely correct, it does not seem wise to persist in the face of consistent difficulties and lack of progress. A search for other explanations may be worthwhile. Again, it should be stressed that what is being referred to here does not signify a shifting from pillar to post on the part of the therapist, or a lack of some unified approach to the patient. Rather, the therapist should not adhere to a rigid formulation, derived either from theory or from his inferences about the patient, and persist in trying to ram this down the patient's throat. A too rigid adherence to some theoretical view about the patient's dynamics or focal problem can lead to frustration on the part of both therapist and client, and produce no meaningful change in the patient. The patient, if she is docile enough, may eventually agree with the therapist's formulations, but no particular positive change in the patient necessarily will be forthcoming. In other instances, the patient may well decide that he is wasting his time and money, and leave therapy.

One other point should be mentioned here and this pertains to the consistency of the therapist's role in psychotherapy. Since the writer has stated that the therapist's role at various stages of therapy should vary in terms of activity and related matters, this may be seen as contradicting some views of therapy where consistency in the therapist's role is advocated. Client-centered therapy, for example, delineates a consistent role for the therapist in terms of providing maximum amounts of empathy, warmth, and genuineness, and in avoiding making suggestions or being, in any way, directive in therapy. Other viewpoints in therapy also believe that inconsistency in the therapist's role leads to confusion, or even to an impairment of the therapeutic endeavor. This is particularly true in those therapies which emphasize the importance of the patient's role as an active one in psychotherapy, and believe that it is not desirable for the therapist to behave in a way which will interfere with the patient's responsibility for securing change. Related to this is the feeling that sudden changes in the therapist's activity or role in therapy may be confusing to the patient since he has adapted to a certain style of the therapist, and if the latter suddenly behaves in a very different manner, the patient may be uncertain as to what has produced this change and as to what is now going to take place in therapy.

Although the above points are not without some merit, on the whole, the writer has come to take a somewhat different view. It is true that in any relationship the individuals involved gradually form some consistent picture of each other and build up certain expectations concerning the behavior of the other person. When there is an occasion where the anticipated behaviors are not forthcoming, or where very different behaviors are manifested, the individuals involved may be rather surprised. However, such unanticipated change or surprise is not always a negative matter, for on some occasions the surprise may be a very positive one, indeed. Whereas consistency is an important characteristic in many interactions, its value has to be appraised in the light of the specific situation. Too much consistency can be viewed as rigidity and, of course, too little consistency may lead to chaos. There are certain matters in which the therapist has to be reasonably consistent, and others in which overtly his role may be superficially inconsistent or changeable. In such matters as expressing interest in trying to help the client overcome his difficulties and in being a person the client can trust, it seems important for the therapist to behave consistently. To do otherwise, would appear to seriously and negatively influence the client's hopes for improvement and the collaborative relationship deemed desirable for progress in therapy. Even in this matter, however, the therapist should be honest in how he views the situation, for if the client detects a lack of sincerity, his trust in the therapist will suffer and influence his attitudes toward the therapist and therapy as well. However, in other aspects, a change in the therapist's role to becoming more active and instituting certain procedures which appear to be desirable, are inconsistent only in a strict behavioral sense. Such changes are not capricious ones, but ones which are taken in terms of a certain plan of therapy, and a suitable explanation can and should be provided to the client. From this point of view, what takes place is not a drastic change in the therapist's role, but instead represents a planned stage in therapy. It can be noted, too, that Alexander and French (1946) also advocated changing roles for the therapist depending on the client's problem, but their emphasis differed from that which is presented here.

How changes in therapeutic procedures are instituted in psychotherapy has to be considered and planned in terms of the individual patient, his particular problems, and the personality of the patient. In some instances, therapy can proceed in a very quick and efficient manner. Usually, the patient in such cases is well integrated, the presented problems are reasonably clear and specific, and the indicated procedures can be followed with good effect. In other cases, however, the situation may be very different. There may be a multiplicity of complaints, some of them may be rather vague or diffuse, and the individual appears to be quite inadequate in many respects. In such cases, considerably more time may have to be spent in initial explorations, in trying to delineate the problems more specifically, and in a more general evaluation of the patient. If there appear to be features of the patient's personality and behavior which are central to his difficulties or which may constitute problems in therapy, then these may require special attention early in therapy or throughout therapy. If a patient, for example, is overly critical of everyone he discusses in the initial interviews, the therapist would do well to keep this in mind. If this is indeed a general characteristic of the patient, the therapist should at least entertain the hypothesis that the patient will, at some point, become overly critical of him, and he should be prepared to deal with it as the occasion requires. Depending on the particular case and the stated goals of therapy, this behavior may be handled lightly, or it may become an important focus of therapy even though it was not mentioned as a problem initially by the patient. In a somewhat similar fashion, a patient who appears overly servile and dependent has to be responded to in a manner appropriate to his personality, as well as to his stated problems. In such cases the therapist has to be alert to the problem of not fostering or reinforcing the patient's dependent behavior. If he decides to institute certain procedures, he should attempt to involve the patient in discussing what procedures seem desirable and discuss also possible procedures for helping the patient become more independent and assertive.

From what has been described, it should be evident that the therapist has to be a very alert and active participant in the therapeutic process. He has to appraise his clients as accurately as possible, devise some initial plans for therapy, be able to modify his plans when this seems indicated, and to monitor the process of therapy as it takes place. To be maximally effective, the therapist has to be flexible and to utilize whatever procedures seem potentially useful for the given case. He should not sit back and place all the responsibility on the client, nor should he follow the same approach with every client.

THE LATER STAGES OF PSYCHOTHERAPY

At some point or other, therapy begins to enter its final period and considerations about possible termination may begin to emerge. How this is handled will be determined in large part by how therapy was structured at the beginning and whether any specific time limits were set initially. In the latter case, there is usually a more specific termination point which acts as a very concrete guide for both participants, and may have a significant influence on how psychotherapy progresses. Although it appears that time-limited therapy is not utilized by the majority of therapists, it has some special features which are worth mentioning. To begin with, time-limited therapy provides the client with a clear idea of how long therapy will take. The particular time limits are decided by the therapist or are a matter of clinic policy, and may vary from setting to setting. A number of clinics appear to offer a brief type of time-limited therapy, which takes from 6 to 10 interviews (Harris, Kalis, and Freeman, 1964). This may constitute a general procedure for all patients, or it may be utilized only for selected cases; for example, those who are facing a particular crisis situation or those who are felt to be unsuitable for longer term therapy (Butcher and Koss, 1978). In one clinic, for example, all patients are seen initially for seven therapy sessions, and the intake process has been streamlined so that the patient is able to begin therapy without some of the usual delays which occur in many clinical settings (Levanthal and Weinberger, 1975). Those patients who are judged to have made sufficient progress are terminated at the end of the seventh session. Those who are considered to require further treatment may then be continued in therapy or referred elsewhere. This actually seems like a very sensible procedure since approximately two-thirds of the cases appear to be sufficiently improved to be discharged after the seventh interview.

The setting of a time limit for psychotherapy not only removes some of the ambiguity surrounding the length of treatment, but it also appears to set a goal for the client. Several advocates of time-limited therapy have stressed this aspect (Rank, 1936; Shlien, 1957; Taft, 1933). The patient and therapist are provided with a finite period in which to secure whatever progress they hope to secure. It may thus act as a motivating variable in therapy, and to the extent that a specific amount of time is indicated, it may also foster greater hope and confidence in the therapy as contrasted with a statement by the therapist that he cannot give the patient a precise indication as to length, but that therapy might take a long time. The relative brevity of therapy may also generate a positive and hopeful attitude on the part of the patient. Several studies have indicated that time-limited therapy is actually as effective as, or more effective than, unlimited psychotherapy (Gurman and Kniskern, 1978; Luborsky, Singer, and Luborsky, 1975; Shlien, Mosak, and Dreikurs, 1962; Muench, 1965). Even if comparable results are secured for the two types of therapy, the fact that time-limited therapy is seemingly more efficient in terms of the time required would appear to make it a desirable type of therapy. There are, however, a number of views on this matter, and we shall not discuss it further here.

Where no clear time limit has been set in psychotherapy, it is likely that the client will raise some question about possible termination if the therapist does not do so himself. If the question is raised, the therapist should respond to this query, and if he has not anticipated the matter of termination, or if it comes long before any previously stated termination date, it should be explored with the client. As stated earlier, any question or comment which pertains directly to therapy should be responded to immediately, but a question about possible termination is particularly important. The client's reasons for bringing this matter up, even in a passing fashion, should be ascertained by the therapist and the matter fully discussed. Such a communication from the client indicates that he has been thinking about termination, and the therapist needs to find out why this is so.

In a number of instances, the client's comment or query about the possible cessation of therapy may signify that he feels he is getting along quite well and that he, himself, has been thinking that therapy should be approaching its end. If the therapist has also been in the process of reaching a similar conclusion, then the matter of termination should be discussed and a mutual agreement on it secured. In such an instance, the client, as it were, has anticipated the thinking of the therapist, and the matter can be resolved with little difficulty. However, if the matter of termination seems to be premature or to possibly indicate something else, then the therapist has a very different issue to confront, and he needs to discover what is motivating this particular response on the part of the client.

There conceivably may be a number of different reasons why the patient may, at a certain point in therapy, ask the therapist about how much longer therapy will last. If the patient has never been given any clear idea about this, it seems to be a reasonable question. Most individuals like to have some idea of how long a particular activity will take, and most organized activities have a clearly stated or generally recognized time limit. University programs are considered to be 4-year programs, mortgages are given for a specified period of time, football games have one hour of playing time, etc. Furthermore, most people do not tolerate ambiguity very well. Thus if the patient has not really been given an adequate indication of when therapy might be completed, this can be discussed and some suitable answer provided. If a patient's query about any matter seems reasonable, it is the writer's view that it should be judged and responded to in this fashion, and that it need not necessarily be viewed as a dynamically motivated resistance to therapy. On the other hand, if this is not the case, then the matter must be handled differently.

In some instances, the patient may indeed raise some question about the termination of therapy before any such consideration would be presumed to be appropriate. If, in fact, this occurs relatively early in therapy and there has been very little movement or change thus far, it would appear to be a rather unusual and unexpected query, and thus in need of an explanation. The therapist in such a situation would have to be quite forthright in stating that he is rather puzzled by this question and wonders why the patient has raised it. If this move on the part of the patient masks a more direct concern about lack of progress or any other concerns about therapy, it is desirable to bring the matter out and try to clarify it. Sometimes the patient may have misunderstood or misinterpreted an earlier statement of the therapist, and the issue can be clarified without much difficulty. In some instances, the patient may have had certain expectancies about therapy which were never clearly verbalized, and, therefore, an opportunity can be provided for clarifying these views of the patient. There may, of course, be many different reasons why the patient makes such a comment, and these can only be ascertained by suitable inquiry on the part of the therapist. If the patient's query does imply an impatience with lack of progress, then it is an issue of some importance.

Does the therapist perceive the situation in the same way as the patient does? If not, why not? If the therapist believes that therapy is progressing satisfactorily, and the patient has the opposite perception, then it would appear that the therapist has not been very effective in understanding the patient's perceptions and communications with regard to therapy. In such an instance, it is imperative that the therapist try to ascertain the reasons for this unhappy state of affairs and why he has been insensitive to the real feelings of the patient. If this can be cleared up, then therapy may be able to continue on a better understood and sounder basis. If not, it will remain as a problem, but at least if it is discussed, the therapist may be more aware of it, and the patient may have a more specific idea of how long therapy may be expected to take and what kinds of progress may be anticipated. Obviously, if the patient is very dissatisfied, he may be inclined to terminate therapy, either by informing the therapist of his decision or by simply failing to return for subsequent appointments. In these instances, the therapist has to accept the decision of the patient, but perhaps he/she may learn something from the experience and be in a better position to handle such problems in the future.

It sometimes happens in psychotherapy that the patient actually progresses much more rapidly than was originally anticipated. The patient's problems diminish noticeably, his/her situation looks brighter, and in general, life seems worth living again. Sometimes the unexpected improvements can be explained by the therapist. For example, the problems of the patient may have been influenced primarily by a specific crisis in the patient's life which has been largely overcome, or there has been a significant change in the patient's life situation which has, along with therapy, contributed to a real change in the patient's functioning. In other instances, the possible reasons for the patient's rapid and unexpected improvement are not at all clear, and this may mystify the therapist. It is interesting that such unanticipated progress has been viewed by some dynamically oriented therapists as a rather negative development in psychotherapy instead of as an unanticipated happy occurrence. Such therapists have labelled this type of phenomenon as an escape or "flight into health," and have tended to view it as a serious form of resistance (Menninger, 1958). The reasoning here is that if the patient claims he is well, there would then appear to be no further reason for continuing therapy; thus the patient is able to remove himself from the self-analysis and confrontation which further therapy implies. Consequently, such therapists are not very pleased when a patient of theirs states that he is over his difficulties, is getting along very well, and sees no need for any further therapy. Whereas this would appear to be a perfectly rational view for most people, it is not so regarded by this group of therapists. They would make some attempts to interpret the patient's behavior as an attempt to flee from therapy. They may point out that many of the real sources of his difficulties have not been uncovered, that he is fore-going an opportunity to really come to grips with his problems, and that while his current symptoms may have appeared to clear up, this is ex-pected to be a temporary phenomenon. Furthermore, even if the patient's symptoms do not return, he can anticipate the appearance of other symp-toms, since the causes of the symptoms have not been brought to light.

Although the matter of a flight into health has received some attention in the publications of analytically oriented clinicians, the writer is un-aware of any attempt to study this problem in any systematic manner. Admittedly, the incidence of this phenomenon is unknown and probably quite infrequent. Consequently, it would be a somewhat difficult problem to investigate. Nevertheless, in the absence of any real empirical studies, we have to be aware of the fact that we are dealing with theoretical in-ferences and hypothetical constructs. The writer's views are no better in this regard, and the reader is hereby alerted to this fact. However, it does appear that more than one view can be taken to interpret or explain a given phenomenon and, that in the absence of any compelling evidence in support of one particular point of view, one should have an open mind and entertain more than one hypothesis.

It is likely that there may be some instances of patient behaviors which could reasonably be interpreted as flights into health. This, however, should not be taken to mean that all rapid or unanticipated improvements in patients undergoing psychotherapy are, therefore, to be considered cases which fall into this category. This would appear to be utterly unfounded and a clear instance of how a particular theoretical view may be blindly adhered to by a therapist with the resulting attempt made to push this interpretation and have it accepted by the patient. Too much of this kind of therapy appears to occur, unfortunately. Once the therapist has made an interpretation derived from his theoretical position, this interpretation is regarded as "the truth" by the therapist, as well as by some of his like-minded colleagues, and the attempt is made to force this view or "insight" onto the patient. Any nonacceptance on the part of the patient is then viewed as resistance. What is exemplified here is a rigid adherence to one hypothesis and a failure to entertain other hypotheses. However, having made this criticism, let me continue with the present topic.

It would appear possible to examine each case in which there is an un-expected report of improvement by the patient and to evaluate it in the light of whatever facts are available and whatever inferences are reasonable. If it actually does appear to the therapist that there is really no noticeable improvement in the patient, but the latter claims that there is and believes there is no further need for therapy, then the therapist should respond in some appropriate manner. In this instance, the patient may indeed be communicating a desire to leave therapy, and it would be worthwhile for the therapist to try to discover the reasons for this behavior on the part of the patient. Does the latter find therapy threatening, is he disappointed in the therapist, has he been encouraged by someone else to seek another kind of therapy or a different therapist, or exactly what accounts for his apparent reason for stating he is well and wants to end his therapy? Although the therapist should try to ascertain the possible motives for the patient's decision, and then to try to deal with these in a constructive manner, it does not appear wise for him to argue with the patient or try to convince him that he is making a bad mistake in running away from therapy. This only may make it more difficult for the patient to be honest in his dealings with the therapist and, also, more difficult for him to resume a relationship with the therapist in the future if there were a need to do so. If no resolution is possible, it seems best to accept the inevitable, to wish the patient well, and to offer him the opportunity to contact you in the future if he should ever feel the need to do so.

However, if after considering the patient's reasons for bringing therapy to an end, the therapist feels that the patient's case has merit, he should then acknowledge this and go ahead to discuss an early termination. If this is brought up early in the interview, it may be that this can be the last interview if this seems warranted. Otherwise, a mutually agreed on date in the future can be set for the terminal meeting. I see nothing wrong in such a procedure if the patient does appear to be functioning better and if he clearly indicates that he is satisfied with the way things are going. The therapist, if he believes it is feasible, can go over the list of the patient's initial presenting complaints and ask the patient how these affect him currently. However, if the patient indicates that they are under control and do not constitute real problems for him presently, it seems best to accept the possibility that the patient may actually be better and that further therapy is not required.

Psychotherapy at present is far from being completely understood, and as a consequence, in the same way that we may encounter problems that were not anticipated earlier in therapy, it is conceivable that occasionally we will encounter some positive developments which are quite unexpected. This has occasionally been the writer's experience, and it would seem likely that other therapists may have had similar experiences. The fact that we may be unable to predict such occurrences or to fully account for them is an indication that our knowledge of the psychotherapeutic process is far from complete.

Consequently, when a client shows some improvement and asks questions about when therapy is going to terminate, it seems worthwhile to discuss this matter fully, and if termination seems reasonable, to consider an early end to therapy. If the therapist does not respond favorably to such a comment, he should evaluate very thoroughly why he responds as he does. There are undoubtedly reasons why he is reluctant to have the client terminate, and these may be quite varied. Among them are that the therapist, himself, has become overly involved with the client, that he resents the client's reaching such a decision before he has, that he has set goals that the client has not reached, or even that cases are scarce and he would like to keep his clients for a longer period of time.

Rosenbaum (1964) in a thoughtful paper has also discussed this problem. Among other things, he emphasizes the importance of the therapist's attitudes towards therapy and how they may influence decisions concerning early termination from therapy. "If the therapist believes that hours spent in therapy and weeks spent in personal growth change are necessarily proportional, he may encourage the patient to remain in treatment after the patient is capable of consolidating his gains on his own. These considerations include, for young therapists in private practice, the simple need to make a living." (p. 507)

Therapists in training are particularly likely to become involved with their cases and to resist possible termination, even when the case is a difficult one with many problems. In one instance, for example, where a number of difficulties had been encountered in therapy, and progress was somewhat limited, the client inquired about when the therapist thought they would be ending therapy. This was done somewhat indirectly and as the client, after a pause, made an additional comment, the therapist did not respond to the previous query. Instructed to do so in the next session and to explore what the client's feelings were on this matter, the therapist did refer back to the client's previous query concerning when therapy might end. In response, the client stated that she had been able to handle the problems for which she sought therapy and thought this might be a reasonable time to think about termination. The therapist, however, did not respond favorably or really directly to this view, but indicated that there should be further discussion. In effect, the therapist was reluctant to let go of his client, even though it seemed feasible to discuss termination at this point. Although there was room for further improvement, the fact that the client felt well enough to broach the topic of ending therapy, and that, on the basis of what had already taken place, the therapist was in no position to promise further change, a decision to terminate therapy was eminently reasonable. After this interview, the client missed a number of appointments, the interviews that followed were rather unproductive, and therapy was eventually terminated. It might have been better to have listened to the client and to have agreed on a mutual decision to terminate therapy. As Rosenbaum (1964) remarked: "The therapist should let the patient define mental health, improvement, or relief in his own terms." (p. 507)

As a general policy, it seems wise to be attentive to the statements and communications of the patient, and to accord greater weight to them than to one's own theoretical views, heretical though this may sound. If, during what the therapist may regard as the early or middle stage of therapy, a patient indicates that he is sufficiently improved to want to terminate therapy, the therapist should modify his views and accept the possibility that termination is a reasonable decision. Nothing is really lost and much may be gained by such a decision. If the patient is able to function adequately, it is better for him to leave therapy and function independently. If the decision is premature, the patient can always return for additional sessions. On the other hand, to indicate to the patient that you do not agree with his own self-appraisal is to diminish his self-esteem, possibly increase his own concerns about himself, and even to affect the relationship in therapy.

PLANNING FOR TERMINATION IN PSYCHOTHERAPY

We have already anticipated the matter of termination by discussing the matter of unanticipated improvement and earlier than expected termination. However, in the majority of cases such a desirable problem will generally not arise. Consequently, it becomes important during the final stages of therapy for the therapist to gauge the client's progress, to anticipate a possible time for termination, and to discuss this with the client in terms of reaching some mutual agreement on the matter.

The particular problems of termination will vary with the type of client, the length of therapy, the type of therapy, and with the kind of relationship which has developed in therapy. A very dependent client, as might be anticipated, has more difficulty in separating from therapy and in severing his relationship with the therapist than do less dependent clients. Consequently, for such a reason, as well as others, the therapist should avoid behaviors which tend to foster the client's dependency on him. Where the client appears to be quite a dependent individual, a discussion as to a time for future termination should be instituted as soon as possible. This allows the client to prepare for it as best he can, and his possible concerns about leaving therapy and being on his own can be dealt with during the later stages of therapy. Time-limited therapy has the advantage of fixing a definite time for termination at the beginning of therapy, but this is not always a procedure with many therapists and is not always possible. Consequently, the therapist has to be alert to signs of improvement and indications as to possible terminal dates for therapy.

One's goals for therapy will also influence one's estimate of the time required for therapy and its eventual termination. As psychotherapy is currently practiced, there is a wide range in the time therapy is expected to last. Analysts and analytically oriented psychotherapists at one end of the scale tend to think in terms of years as their units of time, whereas most behavior therapists and those who practice time-limited or brief therapy, at the other end of the scale, think in terms of weeks. It is interesting in this connection to note that a period of therapy lasting a year is regarded by some as a long period of therapy, but is regarded by others as brief psychotherapy (Sifneos, 1965). Generally, long-term therapy which lasts several years is reputed to have a goal of personality reconstruction, whereas the briefer therapies aim at treating the patient's presenting complaints or resolving current conflicts. No attempt will be made here to discuss the matter of therapeutic goals, except to point out that it theoretically and practically influences the length of therapy and presents somewhat different problems with regard to termination.

Where therapy takes a long time, it would appear that, regardless of theoretical assumptions, the patient becomes more dependent and attached to the therapist and the therapy. As a result, termination becomes more of a problem and more time is spent on it in therapy. In brief therapy, where more specific goals are attained in a relatively short period of time, the possible problems of termination are quite less and little time need be spent on them. The patient's personality also interacts with the length and type of therapy so that in some instances a more intensive relationship is developed in therapy, and it cannot easily be dissolved or terminated.

For the reasons just mentioned, the matter of termination has received more theoretical and clinical discussion in the dynamically oriented and long-term psychotherapies than it has in most of the other forms of psychotherapy (Freud, 1950; Glenn, 1971; Weiner, 1975; Wolberg, 1954). In fact, termination is not viewed as a particular problem or topic of importance in the briefer therapies, and it appears plausible, therefore, that the length of therapy is a critical variable in creating the problem. Theoretical notions of separation also play a role in the matter of termination in the psychodynamic therapies (Glenn, 1971).

Putting aside differences among the different therapeutic approaches for the moment, let us look more generally at the possible clues the therapist may receive which suggest that termination should be considered. The most obvious one is that the patient's complaints have disappeared. If the patient recounts evidence of continuous progress, then the therapist clearly has to consider termination in the near future and bring the matter up for discussion. If the patient agrees readily to an early end to therapy or even mentions that he had been wondering about this, too, a definite date can be agreed upon and therapy terminated forthwith, as already mentioned in the preceding section. In the present instance, however, the improvement is more in line with the therapist's expectations and termination is the final step in what has been occurring in therapy.

In some cases, the client, while showing some improvement, does not communicate it as clearly as in the previous case. However, the client seems to have relatively little of importance to talk about and seems preoccupied in a positive way with his current life activities. When the therapist pursues this further, it does appear that while all of the client's problems have not been resolved, he is functioning quite well and feels optimistic about his future situation. In other words, the client does not feel he has any significant problems and believes he can handle those he has. When the matter of possible termination is mentioned, such a client may make the comment that he has also thought about this and that essentially therapy has served its purpose.

The groups of cases mentioned above present no problems with reference to termination. There are other cases, however, which do. Some of these are the dependent type of person referred to earlier, whereas with others, therapy has not always progressed in a uniform or clear manner. With very dependent individuals, even in cases of noticeable improvement, it is important that therapy not be prolonged unnecessarily and that the patient be alerted and reminded of termination as early as possible. Although such patients may at times be overtly laudatory of the therapist, he should, as much as possible, avoid behaviors that reinforce the dependency patterns of the patient. Clues about such matters will be apparent early in therapy so that the therapist should be able to anticipate probable problems and plan some strategy for dealing with them. If possible, some time indication should be given at the beginning of therapy, and the frequency of interviews should also be set with such possible problems in mind. If reasonable progress appears to be in the making, the therapist should mention some probable date for termination to the patient so that this reality can begin to be faced as soon as possible. Also, if after the mention of termination, the patient seems to be very fearful or apprehensive about termination, it is sometimes a good procedure to gradually reduce the frequency of visits so that the patient's attachment to therapy is diminished and he is able to see that he can function adequately without the support of the therapeutic relationship.

A case illustration may be useful here. Many years back, when the writer was more involved with long-term therapy than he is at present, he worked with a very dependent individual who had a variety of somatic and interpersonal complaints. The patient was seen on a weekly basis, and after several months he asked if he could be seen more than once a week. When asked why he thought this was necessary, he said that he thought it might facilitate therapy and increase the rate of improvement. Although the therapist attempted to reflect the patient's concerns about therapy and the desire for more rapid improvement, he stated that he did not believe it wise or necessary to increase the frequency of the interviews. It might make the patient too dependent on the therapist, and time was an important factor in therapy anyway. The patient reluctantly had to accept this, although he mentioned it once again a short time later. Over a period of two and a half years, during which his dependency was alluded to, as well as other more important aspects, the patient eventually showed definite improvements. When the topic of termination was brought up, the patient expressed clear concern and wanted matters delayed. After some discussion, the therapist offered a plan of decreasing visits to facilitate the termination process. The next appointment would be in two weeks, the following one in three weeks, the one after that in one month, the next in two months, and the final session three months later. The patient agreed to give this plan a try and it worked out successfully. In this case, it was believed worthwhile to stagger the visits with increasing time intervals so the patient could adapt more readily to leaving therapy. The patient's personality, plus the length of therapy, were both factors in making termination a problem in this instance.

In general, it seems like a good procedure to make some reference to a possible or indicated termination date some time before the time occurs. In some instances, this will merely be a reference to the tentative date mentioned as a possibility in the beginning interviews. As such, it is a reminder to the patient that therapy is not an endless process and that a finite number of sessions remain. It conceivably may also act as a possible motivation for the patient to apply himself conscientiously to making the most of his remaining sessions. If no particular time indication has been given at the beginning of therapy, it may be worthwhile at a certain stage later to discuss with the patient how he is progressing. This will allow for some exchange as to how therapy is moving, and in the light of this, some possible statement of what remains to be done and the necessary time for this. In this way, the matter of termination is approached in a reasonable manner and the idea of a natural termination point for therapy is communicated. Such a discussion also allows the patient to clarify his or her remaining goals for therapy and perhaps to indicate a shorter remaining period than that mentioned by the therapist. If this is agreed on, both the remaining goals and the termination point become more specific, and therapy can proceed to its end with a clearer understanding by both participants. If, on the other hand, the patient feels that either little progress has been secured or that he/she would like to spend more time on a particular problem, these matters can also be discussed and their validity or utility evaluated. The instance of lack of progress is a more complicated one generally and needs to be appraised very carefully. If the patient's complaints appear justified and the therapist has no ready solutions at hand, this should be discussed quite openly and frankly. The alternatives available should be indicated and the patient allowed to make a decision, including termination, if this is one of the alternatives. In the case of a request for additional sessions, the therapist should also evaluate this request. If it seems reasonable and specific problems are mentioned which are within the scope of therapy, a new tentative termination date can then be set. If, however, the request appears to reflect concerns about leaving therapy, these concerns should be brought to the fore, and perhaps a staggered plan of appointments or similar plan should be proposed.

Whereas some proponents of long-term psychotherapy believe that termination is a potential traumatic event for a large number of patients, involving separation anxiety, this does not appear to be a particular problem for most patients. Since most of the psychotherapy is in fact brief therapy, as noted in an earlier chapter, termination is not a particular problem and the therapist does not have to spend any real time on it. However, as noted before, it is worthwhile to make a clear reference to termination several weeks before the anticipated time. In most instances, the client will acknowledge this and that is all that is required. If, however, there is some other reaction to this information, the therapist can proceed to clarify it with the client. It also seems worthwhile to refer to the terminal interview once again in the interview which precedes it. Termination can be a problem, however, when the therapist without any warning whatsoever tells the client that the current interview will be the last one. Even where therapy has been in existence for only a brief period of time, such an announcement can have a very negative effect on the client. He is just beginning to know the therapist and to place some trust in him, when suddenly the rug is yanked out from under him. In the case of patients who have been in therapy with the therapist for some time, the sudden announcement that therapy is to be terminated today or that the therapist is leaving and the patient is being transferred to another therapist can be quite devastating. It is for such reasons that it is always best to anticipate possible termination and to share this with the patient. The sudden and unexpected departure of the therapist is a negative experience for the patient and should be avoided as distinctly irresponsible and unprofessional behavior, yet the writer can recall a few actual instances of such behavior. In one case, the patient had been seeing his therapist for about a year and a half when the therapist announced that this was his last session with the patient since he was leaving the clinic and going into private practice. Clearly, if this kind of handling could have been avoided, it would have been better for all parties involved. This case was transferred to the writer, and it required a fair amount of time for the patient to fully release the hostility he had for his previous treatment and to trust his new therapist. It should be remembered that most individuals who seek out some form of psychotherapeutic help usually have feelings of low self-esteem, and of not being highly regarded by others. A sudden notice of the therapist's termination or of the patient's transfer to a different therapist is not only very poor professional practice, but it can be viewed as another rejection by the patient with accompanying negative effects.

There is one other topic that also needs to be discussed before we conclude the present chapter. This has to do with decisions about possible termination when inadequate progress has resulted. Whereas termination would appear to be a natural consideration where progress has been obtained, decisions as to termination when little or no progress has been obtained is a more problematic and difficult issue to resolve. Nevertheless, it is one which has to be faced in a certain number of cases.

In spite of the best of intentions on the part of the therapist, there are instances where the client and his problems appear resistant to change. The reasons may be diverse and frequently may not be understood. In some cases the fault may appear to lie with the client. He may give the impression of lacking suitable motivation for change or his particular patterns of behavior may seem to be so deeply ingrained that there is little response to the various procedures attempted by the therapist. In other instances, the home and family situation of the client may be so utterly poor and overwhelming that whatever therapy is attempted seems woefully weak by comparison. Thus, in a certain number of cases, client or related variables may seemingly be the possible reason for lack of progress. As already mentioned, it is not infrequent that the blame for lack of therapeutic progress is placed on the client, and in some instances, this may be justified. Some presentations of psychotherapy have in fact emphasized the suitability of the client as a necessary condition for progress in therapy (Strupp, 1973).

In a certain percentage of psychotherapy failures, the cause would appear to be the lack of skill on the part of the therapist or the use of inappropriate or ineffective techniques. The therapist may be lacking in the necessary requisites or skills, and he may handle the case in a poor and inappropriate fashion. There are numerous examples which could be given here, and some have already been presented in previous sections. The therapist may have misjudged the strengths of the patient, he may have been too passive in his approach, he may have been too critical of the patient, and he may have failed to use more appropriate techniques. Whatever the reason, there are many instances where the main cause of lack of progress appears to be therapist variables, and although many therapists may be unable to see the errors in their own work, they are able to see the inadequacies in the work of other therapists.

It is also likely that in some cases the lack of progress is caused mainly by a poor fit between therapist and patient, or interaction variables. The styles and expectancies of the two participants may be too discrepant, or the particular approach used by a therapist may be poorly suited to a given patient. This type of problem has been increasingly recognized in recent years although we have not advanced very far in our practical procedures for coping with it (Kiesler, 1971). Ideally, the type of therapist, and the type of treatment, would be selected in terms of the specific client and his problems. This appears to be a desirable goal, but in practice, the patient is referred to a therapist by someone he knows, or in a clinic setting, to the therapist who has an opening in his schedule. The kind of treatment approach selected will depend on the theoretical preference of the available therapist. As a consequence of this situation, the interaction of a particular therapist and patient pair may not be that which is most desirable, and progress may be less than satisfactory.

For the reasons just mentioned, it is conceivable that therapy does not proceed in a positive manner, and after a certain period of time the lack of progress becomes quite apparent. This is clearly a problem situation which the therapist must evaluate carefully in order to ascertain what factors may be responsible. It is not good practice to allow therapy to drift aimlessly and the therapist has the responsibility for trying to rectify the situation. If he does perceive some possible reasons for the lack of progress, he can then react accordingly. In some instances, he may have been incorrect in his appraisal of the patient or misjudged the severity of his problems. The procedures he is using may be inappropriate or inadequate, and will need to be replaced by others. If the therapist feels that he does not fully understand the lack of progress secured, it may be worthwhile to discuss this openly with the patient and to find out his views. If there do not appear to be any answers or solutions to the problem at hand, it seems desirable to discuss the matter of possible termination with the patient. In essence, the therapist's communication would go something like this: In spite of the best intentions of both parties, the patient has shown little improvement over a reasonable period of time. The therapist has examined the situation and tried to discover the possible reasons for this, but without success. He has tried a different procedure and discussed the matter with the patient in the hope of being more successful. However, little progress has been secured and this should be faced openly and realistically, even though it is, of course, disappointing to both therapist and patient. Consequently, the therapist believes he should discuss with the patient the feasibility of continuing therapy. If the patient agrees that termination seems to be reasonable, this should then be agreed upon.

It can also be stated that the patient can see how he gets along without therapy, that he might continue on his own with some procedures which appear to be worth continuing, and that he could arrange for an occasional visit in the future if he believes this would be helpful. If the patient should ask about other sources of possible therapeutic help, the therapist should accommodate him by providing several names of clinics or therapists. On the other hand, if the patient should indicate that, in spite of any real progress, he would like to continue with the therapist in psychotherapy, the therapist should explore the patient's feelings about this and then, perhaps, agree to continue seeing the patient for a fixed number of interviews in order to see if any change will occur. The number of additional interviews should be relatively brief, and the ultimate decision about termination should be made when these interviews have been completed.

The above statements have been rather categorical in nature for the purpose of illustrating what might actually occur in a hypothetical case. What is actually done will have to be determined by the therapist in terms of his best judgment and appraisal of the particular case. What is being stressed here is that the therapist should constantly be evaluating the progress of his psychotherapy and modifying his approach as the situation appears to demand. Furthermore, if after a reasonable period of time, therapy shows little sign of progress and the therapist is unable to rectify the situation or to institute a new approach with some probability of success, then the therapist has the responsibility to consider terminating the patient's therapy. Some therapists may take exception to this view and believe that it is the mark of a frustrated therapist who, in essence, is rejecting his patient and turning him out into the cold. This, of course, may be the case in some instances, but it should not confuse the point being made here, nor should it be a rationalization for keeping a patient in therapy for unnecessarily long periods of time when there is no visible sign of progress. Although there has been very little research on this problem, it does appear that some therapists are very reluctant to let their patients terminate therapy regardless of progress or lack of progress, and one hears of people being in therapy for 20 years or more. This seems, to the writer, to be a rather deplorable type of situation in which the dependency of the patient on the therapist has been reinforced to an astonishing degree. One must really feel important if another human being cannot exist without him. In one clinic, for example, it was discovered that some patients had been in psychotherapy for a very long period of time. When the matter was investigated further, it was found that a small number of therapists accounted for most of these patients. When the clinic administrators decided that it was desirable to close the cases, the therapists in question stated that these patients had been kept out of the hospital for many years, and that to terminate their psychotherapy would lead to their hospitalization. However, the patients were discharged and a follow-up study made of them (Stieper and Wiener, 1959, 1965). Their rate of hospitalization and relapse was no different from that of any comparable group of patients and most of them continued to function without their therapy and without requiring hospitalization.

No one, of course, likes to acknowledge failure in any undertaking of importance. However, unless one is successful 100 percent of the time, and the probabilities of this are very slight, one has to acknowledge some failures in his activities from time to time. The athlete is not always successful, the surgeon is not always successful, and neither is the psychotherapist always successful. Consequently, it is best to face reality directly and not to take refuge in various belief systems or rationalizations. When a patient does not show satisfactory progress, one can do what he can to rectify the situation, but if this is not successful, the facts must be faced and the idea of termination entertained. It is the writer's contention that, in the long run, this is the fairest and most justified way to treat one's patient. Hopefully, such instances will include only a small portion of those patients with whom the therapist attempts to work in psychotherapy. In the majority of instances, the matter of termination will be a natural culmination of the therapeutic process in which the patient has secured some positive gains.

REFERENCES

Alexander, F. and French, T. M. *Psychoanalytic therapy*. New York: Ronald, 1946.

Avnet, H. H. How effective is short-term therapy? In L. R. Wolberg (Ed.), *Short-term psychotherapy*. New York: Grune & Stratton, 1965.

Bergin, A. E. The evaluation of therapeutic outcome. In A. E. Bergin and S. L. Garfield (Eds.), *Handbook of psychotherapy and behavior change: An empirical analysis*. New York: Wiley, 1971.

Bergin, A. E. and Lambert, M. J. The evaluation of therapeutic outcomes. In S. L. Garfield and A. E. Bergin (Eds.), *Handbook of psychotherapy and behavior change*, 2nd ed. New York: Wiley, 1978.

Butcher, J. N. and Koss, M. P. Research on brief and crisis-oriented therapies. In S. L. Garfield and A. E. Bergin (Eds.), *Handbook of psychotherapy and behavior change*, 2nd ed. New York: Wiley, 1978.

Eysenck, H. J. The effects of psychotherapy: An evaluation. *Journal of Consulting Psychology*, 1952, *16*, 319–324.

Eysenck, H. J. *The effects of psychotherapy*. New York: International Science Press, 1966.

Freud, S. Analysis terminable and interminable. In *Collected Papers, Vol. V*. London: Hogarth Press and the Institute of Psychoanalysis, 1950, pp. 316–357.

Glenn, M. L. Separation anxiety: When the therapist leaves the patient. *American Journal of Psychotherapy*, 1971, *25*, 437–446.

Gurman, A. S. and Kniskern, D. P. Research on marital and family therapy. In S. L. Garfield and A. E. Bergin (Eds.), *Handbook of psychotherapy and behavior change*, 2nd ed. New York: Wiley, 1978.

Harris, M. R., Kalis, B. L., and Freeman, E. H. An approach to short-term psychotherapy. *Mind*, 1964, *2*, 198–206.

Kiesler, D. J. Experimental design in psychotherapy research. In A. E. Bergin and S. L. Garfield (Eds.), *Handbook of psychotherapy and behavior change*. New York: Wiley, 1971.

Levanthal, T. and Weinberger, G. Evaluation of a large-scale brief therapy for children. *American Journal of Orthopsychiatry*, 1975, *45*, 119–133.

Levis, D. J. and Carrera, R. N. Effects of ten hours of implosive therapy in the treatment of outpatients: A preliminary report. *Journal of Abnormal Psychology*, 1967, *72*, 504–508.

Luborsky, L., Singer, B., and Luborsky, L. Comparative studies of psychotherapies. *Archives of General Psychiatry* 1975, *32*, 995–1008.

Meltzoff, J. and Kornreich, M. *Research in psychotherapy.* New York: Atherton Press, 1970.

Menninger, K. *Theory of psychoanalytic technique.* New York: Basic Books, 1958.

Muench, G. A. An investigation of the efficacy of time-limited psychotherapy. *Journal of Counseling Psychology,* 1965, *12,* 294–299.

Rank, O. *Will therapy.* New York: Knopf, 1936.

Rosenbaum, C. P. Events of early therapy and brief therapy. *Archives of General Psychiatry,* 1964, *10,* 506–512.

Shlien, J. M. Time-limited psychotherapy: An experimental investigation of practical values and theoretical implications. *Journal of Counseling Psychology,* 1957, *4,* 318–323.

Shlien, J. M., Mosak, H. H., and Dreikurs, R. Effect of time limits: A comparison of two psychotherapies. *Journal of Counseling Psychology,* 1962, *9,* 31–34.

Sifneos, P. E. Seven-years experience with short-term dynamic psychotherapy. *Proceedings of the 6th International Congress of Psychotherapy.* Selected Lectures, London, 1964, pp. 127–135. Basel/New York: S. Karger, 1965.

Sloane, R. B., Staples, F. R., Cristol, A. H., Yorkston, N. J., and Whipple, K. *Psychotherapy versus behavior therapy.* Cambridge: Harvard University Press, 1975.

Stieper, D. R. and Wiener, D. N. The problem of interminability in outpatient psychotherapy. *Journal of Consulting Psychology,* 1959, *23,* 237–242.

Stieper, D. R. and Wiener, D. N. *Dimensions of psychotherapy: An experimental and clinical approach.* Chicago: Aldine, 1965.

Strupp, H. On the basic ingredients of psychotherapy. *Journal of Consulting and Clinical Psychology,* 1973, *41,* 1–8.

Strupp, H. H., Hadley, S. W., and Gomes-Schwartz, B. *Psychotherapy for better or worse: An analysis of the problem of negative effects.* New York: Jason Aronson, 1977.

Taft, J. *Dynamics of therapy in a controlled relationship.* New York: Macmillan, 1933.

Weiner, I. B. *Principles of psychotherapy.* New York: Wiley, 1975.

Wolberg, L. R. *The technique of psychotherapy.* New York: Grune & Stratton, 1954.

CHAPTER 9

Cognitions, Affects, and Behaviors

Psychotherapy, as we have seen, relies largely on verbal communications and interactions between therapist and client. The initial phase of psychotherapy usually consists of the client's verbal recounting of his difficulties, his reasons for seeking therapy, and some of his past history. Similarly, what the therapist understands about the problems to be worked with in therapy and their antecedents are based on the verbal information provided by the client. Furthermore, much of what subsequently takes place in psychotherapy consists of verbal interactions between the two participants throughout therapy. Even behavior therapy, which has a somewhat different focus, still makes considerable use of verbal instructions and communications. To a great extent, therefore, and particularly in the more traditional forms of therapy, psychotherapy has been largely a verbal therapy. In fact, it has been referred to as "the talking therapy."

Since language and verbal communication have been viewed as the distinguishing feature which most clearly differentiates the human species from the other animal forms, it is perhaps not surprising that verbal communication plays such a large role in man's life and that forms of verbal therapy have been developed for dealing with certain types of problems which are found so frequently among the human animal. Nevertheless, since many of these problems deal with other than purely verbal or cognitive problems, one may wonder how it is that verbal means of therapy can be used to overcome some problems which appear to be largely emotional or behavioral in their external manifestations. Such an attitude is sometimes found in some individuals referred for psychotherapeutic treatment who honestly ask, "How can just talking help me?" This is particularly true in those cases in which there are also somatic complaints which have been diagnosed as "psychosomatic" in origin. On proper reflection, the question raised does not appear unreasonable and does seem to require some sort of suitable answer, but one to which many psychotherapists have given relatively little thought.

It is of interest to mention, also, that many therapists in training have a rather difficult time in providing a suitable answer to their client's query as to how psychotherapy is going to bring about a change in their condition. After some hesitation and verbal fumbling on their part at this unexpected question, the usual response is to the effect that the client will have an opportunity to understand his problems, to talk about them, and in some instances, to also express his feelings. These types of responses to the client's questions are interesting in several ways. The first is that beginning therapists are rather taken back by such questions and have no ready answers. Generally, they have such a positive attitude toward psychotherapy, themselves, that they seem surprised that anyone except possibly a critical professor would even raise such questions. A second aspect that can be noted is that their answers are usually quite general and lacking in specificity. Sometimes, too, besides being vague, their answers will be couched in abstract or technical terms which may tend to mystify the client sufficiently so that he does not pursue the matter any further. Finally, when stripped of their excess verbiage, the answers most frequently state that understanding or insight will produce change. If an occasional client pursues matters further and asks how understanding can change his particular behavior, no adequate answer is usually forthcoming.

The preceding description of what sometimes takes place in early therapy sessions is not meant to highlight the inadequacies of beginning psychotherapists, for the writer has had the same experiences, but to emphasize an important issue in psychotherapy which has not received adequate attention. The issue of how purely or primarily verbal or cognitive therapies can produce significant changes in human behavior and adjustment appears to be an important and central one for the field of psychotherapy, and one which deserves serious consideration. Because of this, it has been deemed desirable to discuss this problem specifically in the present chapter and to see what tentative conclusions can be derived.

TRADITIONAL AND RECENT EMPHASES ON COGNITIONS IN PSYCHOTHERAPY

Although Freud at first experimented with hypnotic procedures and paid particular attention to cathartic release by the patient (Freud, 1950a), he eventually gave up these methods (Freud, 1950b). Some of the reasons given for this were that not all patients could be hypnotized and that the cathartic methods did not appear to produce lasting results. The patients tended to relapse later or to develop substitute symptoms. Freud gradually came to develop the method he termed psychoanalysis, which, to a great extent, emphasized the recall of forgotten (repressed) traumatic experiences and the attainment of insight and understanding into the development of the patient's problems. The premise was that the recall of forgotten material and the understanding of why the patient behaved as he did, or developed the symptoms he exhibited, would lead to the discarding of the symptoms and the attainment of a better level of adjustment. Although emotional reactions to therapy and to the analyst also received some emphasis, even their resolution was primarily by verbal and cognitive means. The verbal associations of the patient and the cognitive interpretations offered by the therapist were viewed as the main techniques of therapy and were also the procedures by which such emotional or affective phenomena as resistance and transference were overcome. For these reasons it seems fair to say that although some attention was paid to the emotions and behaviors of the patient in therapy, the primary emphasis in terms of affecting the desired changes in the patient was largely a cognitive one. Freud himself made a statement to the effect that while the voice of the intellect was gentle or soft, it was persistent and ultimately reached the patient.

Nevertheless, as far as the writer is concerned, the process of how cognitions could or did lead to changes in behavior and affects was never very clearly elucidated. The process of "working through" in psychoanalysis, which appears to deal with the patient's acceptance of insights and their consolidation has never been a clearly detailed process; rather, it has appeared to me as a dimly perceived process of persuasion on the part of the analyst. As such, it remains unclear as to how noncognitive changes are actually secured. Perhaps because of the emphasis on understanding and cognition in psychoanalytically oriented psychotherapy, there has always been an emphasis on selecting educated, intelligent, and highly verbal patients. For similar reasons, educated intellectual individuals may conceivably be more attracted to such cognitively oriented therapies than they are to other types of therapy. Even if these suppositions are correct, however, the question remains of how cognitive procedures or cognitions can produce behavioral change. This is not to deny that they may not do so, but mainly to raise the issue of how this may be accomplished.

Although what appears to be largely a cognitive approach was followed by the analysts, they also were aware of possible limitations of this approach. In several places one finds references to the effect that intellectual insight alone was not adequate for securing significant improvement in therapy (Alexander, 1963; Alexander and French, 1946). What is referred to here is the observation that a patient might have secured what appeared to be profound insights into his problems and their causes, and could also verbalize them adequately, but still manifest his original symptoms and have secured no improvement even after years of therapy. The phenomenon must have occurred with sufficient frequency to have received the attention and discussion it did. Clearly, and correctly, it was viewed as a serious problem in analytical therapy. This matter has also received some attention from critics of psychoanalysis who have offered the rather jeering remark that after years of analysis the patient still has his symptoms, but now he understands why he has them.

Although it is not possible to draw any definite conclusions from the comments just made, they do point up what seems like an important and, as yet, not fully understood problem in psychotherapy. Some people may appear to profit from the verbal-cognitive interactions which occur in psychotherapy, but some apparently do not. Furthermore, we do not really understand either why some respond favorably to such interventions and some do not, or what is actually involved in this process. Are there some cognitive procedures that are applied effectively in the favorable cases of outcome, or is the type of problem or type of client the variable of importance here? No precise answer can be given here, although it would appear that both of the possible answers suggested are at least partially correct or tenable. However, it is also tenable to consider that other factors may have played a role in therapy that did not receive as much explicit recognition or emphasis as the more cognitive variables emphasized in the particular theoretical view of therapy utilized. As already discussed in the chapter on common factors in psychotherapy, influences may occur in therapy which are not officially recognized or acknowledged in terms of the tenets of a particular school of psychotherapy.

Although insight-oriented therapy has appeared to rely on a cognitive approach in seeking to effect change in psychotherapy, such therapy was a long-term procedure in which insights were to be secured gradually as the relationship in therapy developed, and as repressed material slowly reached the patient's awareness. In more recent years, some newer cognitive therapies have appeared which deal more directly with cognitions, are relatively brief, and which are based on different theoretical views of personality disturbance. One of these is what is now called Rational-Emotive Therapy or R.E.T., developed by Albert Ellis (1962). Ellis, after becoming dissatisfied with psychoanalysis, gradually worked out his approach which stressed that the client's maladjustments were largely due to distorted or unrealistic perceptions and cognitions. Since these cognitions of the client appeared to be causing the client's difficulties, Ellis believed that it was best to work with them directly and to help the client replace them with more realistic beliefs and expectations. Because of this emphasis, his therapy was first called Rational Therapy. Later, he pointed out that cognitions were intimately related to emotions and that emotional disorders could be caused by unrealistic or distorted cognitions. As a result, he renamed his therapy R.E.T.

Ellis also came to the view that many unhappy and disturbed individuals had common distorted views and beliefs which were at the basis of their discontents. These included the beliefs that they should be universally loved, that they had to be admired by everyone, that they had to be successful in every activity, and the like. As a result, many such unrealistic expectations could be anticipated, and the therapist could deal with them directly and expediently. No time had to be wasted in trying to explore hypothetical unconcious conflicts or dealing with transference reactions. The therapist's role was an active and confrontative one in which the false beliefs of the client were exposed and constantly pointed out and demonstrated. In this approach to therapy, therefore, cognitions were explicitly recognized as factors of central importance in affecting therapeutic change. The distorted beliefs were identified, the patient was directly confronted with them as the causes of his difficulties, and he was persuaded to give them up and to replace them with more realistic views. Cognitions were also recognized as influencing emotions. Although patients were also directed to engage in certain behaviors and activities outside of therapy, this feature has not received as much theoretical emphasis as have the more purely cognitive aspects.

Since the appearance of R.E.T. on the therapeutic scene, there have been other forms of therapy appearing with a strong emphasis on cognitive factors as variables for affecting change. One such example is the cognitive therapy developed by Aaron T. Beck (1976). Originally an outgrowth of his work with depressed patients, Beck has extended his views to include therapeutic work with other types of disorders. Although Beck's approach has a number of similarities with that of R.E.T., it also has some unique features which need not be spelled out here. In addition, Beck appears to place more stress on combining some behavioral techniques with his cognitive approach, although the major emphasis is clearly on cognitive factors and he does, in fact, call his therapy a cognitive therapy.

Another recent development which was briefly alluded to in an earlier chapter is what is now being referred to as cognitive behavior therapy. This movement was facilitated by the work of Bandura (1969) whose influential book stressed the importance of symbolic mediating processes in behavior modification. As the name implies, this development has been one in which attempts have been made to combine some cognitive features of therapy with either standard or modified behavior therapy procedures.

Some of the individuals prominent in this development have been Gold-fried (1971 and 1974; Goldfried, Decenteceo, and Weinberg 1974); Mahoney (1974; Mahoney and Arnkoff 1978); and Meichenbaum (1977). Meichenbaum, for example, has reported some research studies in which a combination of R.E.T. and systematic desensitization was purportedly more effective than systematic desensitization alone in treating such conditions as fear of public speaking and examination anxiety (Meichenbaum, 1972; Meichenbaum, Gilmore, and Fedoravicious, 1971). Although these studies have certain inadequacies, the results secured are not the point of emphasis here. Rather, the important fact is that several behaviorally oriented therapists have come to recognize cognitive variables as being of some importance in their therapeutic work and have made some attempts to include such variables in combination with their behavioral procedures. This, in a way, compliments the use of behavioral procedures by the more cognitively oriented therapists. These developments appear to offer some convergence of theory and techniques, and, hopefully also, to offer some promise for the development of more effective therapeutic procedures.

The more recent developments of cognitive therapies differ in important ways from the more traditional use of cognitive techniques in dynamically oriented psychotherapies. The rationale for the emphasis on cognitive variables is much clearer and more direct, there is much less emphasis on relationship variables and on the dynamics of unconscious conflicts, there is more exclusive attention to the present realities of the client, and generally, the period of treatment appears considerably reduced. The latter item is of great practical importance if the lengthier types of therapy cannot be shown either to be more effective or to be better suited for certain types of problems. The more recent developments also appear to emphasize more distinctly the particular role that cognitive variables may play in modifying emotional and behavioral disorders. However, the particular views presented by the proponents of this orientation are still at a rather crude level of development and do not appear to be fully adequate in explaining how cognitive factors make for change in other aspects of human functioning. Some of them also appear to be at least partially contaminated by the use of noncognitive variables without explicit theoretical recognition of the influence of such variables in their therapeutic rationale. However, in recognizing the possible importance of cognitive variables and in explicitly trying to combine other types of variables such as behavioral ones with more purely cognitive ones, the cognitive therapists are attempting to develop more effective therapeutic techniques—and this is all to the good. We shall return to a discussion of this latter matter further on in the present chapter.

AFFECTIVE EMPHASES IN PSYCHOTHERAPY

Whereas most traditional psychotherapies pay at least some lip service to the importance of emotional or affective factors in the genesis of personality disturbance, as well as in therapy, affective aspects have not received much explicit attention in terms of therapeutic techniques—that is, how affective features are used to influence the process of psychotherapy. Many therapists, to be sure, have been aware of the importance of emotional expression and release in therapy and have been aware that something is amiss when the therapy sessions have been devoid of emotional expression on the part of the client. However, such matters have not received the explicit attention or the emphasis given to cognitive variables in the uncovering and dynamic therapies or the cognitive therapies, or to the emphasis on behavioral variables provided by the behavior therapists. At times, confrontations have been instituted with clients in order to arouse emotional reactions, and a number of therapists have been aware of the potential values of emotional release and catharsis, but, again, these aspects of therapy have not been accorded very much importance in the various therapeutic approaches. Some analysts have also referred to a process of emotional reeducation as a feature of their therapy, but descriptions of how this process is presumed to operate are far from clear (Alexander and French, 1946; Wolberg, 1954).

Thus while there has been some recognition of the importance of emotions and of affective change in psychotherapy, the procedures for inducing such change have not been very clear and the main emphasis appears to have been placed on other types of variables. This, sometimes, has been noted as a possible weakness in some of the psychotherapies which have tended to be overly intellectual in content or overly behavioral in procedure. Yet disturbed emotional states, including the rather painful experiences of anxiety, apprehension, and depression, have been the most distinguishing and identifiable features of the so-called neurotic disorders which have been the focus of most of the various forms of psychotherapy.

In part, perhaps, because of this deficiency in many of the psychotherapeutic approaches, some new modalities of psychotherapy or quasi therapy have appeared with noticeable frequency in recent years. The encounter movement and the marathon groups are noticeable examples of this trend. These approaches appear to place great emphasis on the free and full expression of feelings and emotions. Openness and frankness in all interactions are stressed, and except for physical violence, no holds are barred in the scheduled sessions. One of the aims of the encounter movement would appear to be to remove all or most of the individual's acquired inhibitions. Various games and techniques are used in order to foster strong emotional expression including that of having the participants shed all of their clothing and participate in so-called "nude marathons" (Mintz, 1971). If many of the other therapeutic approaches seem to neglect the expression of emotions and the release of affect, some of the encounter and marathon groups may appear to emphasize them with a vengeance! The social pressures of the group may also be utilized to force emotional expression and disclosure from some of the more recalcitrant members of the group, and in some of the encounter groups the leader may quite overtly challenge members who are not thought to be sufficiently involved or self-revealing (Lieberman, Yalom, and Miles, 1973).

If these types of encounter groups and related developments may be seen as attempts to emphasize an important aspect of the human condition, which has not received sufficient emphasis in the more conventional forms of psychotherapy, it seems likely that their approach has overcompensated for the apparent lack of attention to emotional factors and is too one-sided. Although emotional factors play an important role in the individual's overall adjustment to his life situation, they do not constitute the essence or totality of human existence. To emphasize openness and free expression of emotions and feelings at the expense of intellectual, behavioral, and other aspects of the individual's functioning is to single out and stress one component at the expense of the others. Furthermore, in a comprehensive study of encounter groups, those groups which did not provide adequate cognitive explanations or rationales to their participants were judged as less satisfactory than those which did (Lieberman et al., 1973).

Not only are these approaches potentially one-sided in their emphasis, but some of them include aspects that have potentially serious negative consequences, at least for some of the individuals who seek out participation in these types of groups. Apart from such considerations as the selection of suitable candidates for encounter groups and the professional qualifications of the group leader, which are important in themselves, some of the features of at least some of the more demanding types of encounter groups may be very upsetting to some individuals and, in some instances, the latter may become "casualties" of the encounter group. In the well conducted large scale study of a variety of encounter groups by Lieberman et al. (1973), in which rather stringent criteria were set up for judging casualties resulting from the encounter experience, nine percent of the participants were considered to fall into this category. Because the encounter group leaders knew they were being observed and because 25 of the 104 casualty suspects could not be reached by phone, Lieberman et al.

(1973) believe that the incidence of casualties secured is a conservative estimate. The types of psychological casualties included psychotic decompensation, depression, and anxiety symptoms. "Others suffered some disruption of their self-system: they felt empty, self-negating, inadequate, shameful, unacceptable, more discouraged about ever growing or changing" (Yalom and Lieberman, 1971). Although other reports of encounter groups have usually not been as negative, the studies reported have generally contained a number of methodological weaknesses (Hartley, Roback, and Abramowitz, 1976).

Another point to consider is that the intensity of the experience sought in the encounter or marathon group may be simply too much for some of the participants to handle adequately. Although a considered focus on their emotional life may be potentially worthwhile, the rapidity of the developments within the group may go beyond their level of tolerance. In effect, some group members are forced to participate and disclose at a rate that is actually beyond their capacity or tolerance level. Whereas individual therapy is geared more to the ostensible needs of the individual client, the encounter group process is geared to the group. Those who are not prepared to participate in this process as well as the majority may thus suffer negative consequences.

Apart from the matter of possible casualties, which may result from some encounter group experiences, the results of this type of activity on an overall basis are open to question. Although some individuals regard their encounter and marathon experiences quite positively, there is a fair amount of evidence which suggests that the gains secured from this experience frequently are temporary and disappear with time (Bednar and Kaul, 1978; Jones and Medvene, 1975; Lieberman et al., 1973; Treppa and Fricke, 1972). As a result, some observers have tended to view such group endeavors as being comparable to a religious revival meeting or other type of group gathering, where a high degree of emotional excitement is whipped up, but whose lasting effect is minimal for most participants. Whereas the type of emotional expression and release may be similar to that described earlier for catharsis, the setting is very different, and because of the external pressures brought upon the individual for open emotional display, the two processes may not be identical. Even if they were, catharsis or release in other forms of psychotherapy would be viewed as merely one feature of therapy and generally would not receive the emphasis that such expression receives in encounter groups.

Although there appear to be limitations and some possible dangers in the emphasis on emotional expression and openness given by those involved with encounter groups, for such aspects have to be viewed within a broader context of human functioning and maladjustment, nevertheless, emotional variables are of potential importance for the psychotherapeutic process. To the extent that the encounter movement has focused attention on these aspects of therapy, albeit to an exaggerated degree, they may have some positive impact on correcting some neglected features of psychotherapy. The excesses of some of the adherents of this movement, however, have tended to make at least a fair number of therapists respond rather negatively to their activities. Nevertheless, this should not make us lose sight of the positive implications of some of the features of this and related movements.

THE BEHAVIORAL EMPHASIS IN PSYCHOTHERAPY

As already noted, the development of behavior therapy has been a decidedly vigorous and important recent development in psychotherapy. Arising from a more rigorous tradition and background in psychology and being quite critical of earlier approaches, particularly the psychodynamic ones, which emphasized unconscious motivation and inferred hypothetical personality constructs, the behavior therapists have placed their emphasis on observable behavior. From this point of view, it is the individual's maladaptive behavior which is causing the individual to experience difficulties and which has to be modified if he/she is to function more adequately. Consequently, it is behavioral change which is sought, and this can be handled directly without having to go back into the client's early childhood or to deal with inferred conflicts and related matters. Furthermore, the process is more efficient since one deals directly with the problem at hand, and changes in the client's behavior can be appraised objectively. There is also a strong emphasis on the importance of objective empirical evaluation of the therapy that is carried out.

The behavior therapy movement, at first rather slow in getting started, has progressed vigorously in the last 15 years or so, and in many ways has been somewhat of a revolution within psychotherapy. Some psychotherapists, in fact, view behavior therapy as distinct and outside of the field of psychotherapy. This, however, is a somewhat unrealistic point of view, for behavior therapy appears to have had a significant impact upon psychotherapy generally.

Apart from the research emphasis and the accompanying stress on the objective assessment of outcome in therapy, an emphasis of some importance in this field, the behavior therapists have accorded behavior the significant place in psychotherapy which it merits. Even if one does not wholly agree with a behavioristic point of view, one cannot argue convincingly against the important goal of behavioral change as a desirable outcome in psychotherapy. Furthermore, if behavioral change is a desired goal in many cases, it is also perfectly reasonable to consider procedures which deal directly with the behaviors in question.

Although analytically oriented therapists may agree that behavioral change is desirable, they, for the most part, would disagree with the rationale and procedures for securing such change. Many of them might also take the view that the behavioral approach is too narrow, treats the client in an overly mechanistic manner, and deals only with the surface aspects or symptoms of the client's problems (Glover, 1959; Weitzman, 1967; Yates, 1970). As a result, behavioral therapy tends to be regarded by such therapists as a superficial type of treatment in which the causes of the client's problems are not dealt with, and as a consequence, if the symptoms do disappear, substitute symptoms can be expected to make their appearance at a later date. The only adequate answer to this difference in point of view is to carry out some adequate research studies in which the two different therapeutic approaches are compared in a systematic fashion with comparable subjects randomly assigned and with adequate follow up study. Since a definitive study of this type, to the author's knowledge, has not yet been reported, we will have to base our tentative conclusions on what research is available and on logic and common sense, perilous though these might be.

Whereas the doctrine of ascertaining the cause of a person's disturbance in order to fully treat the disturbance effectively has a definite appeal and also some merit, it is important to consider whether this is universally necessary. Although it is true that similar appearing symptoms may have different causes and, consequently, might require different kinds of treatment, one may not always be able to discover the actual cause, nor is it necessary to go over all of the possible past events in a person's life which theoretically might pertain to the development of the symptom in order to treat it. Diagnostic evaluation is important in deciding what the problems are and in formulating a treatment program. However, once this is done, then the most direct and efficient, or less dangerous, form of treatment should be used. Although the analogy with medicine may be useful in some contexts, it is not necessarily applicable in all. Many of the psychological disorders are not the equivalent of medical illnesses, particularly where the etiology and treatment of specific medical illnesses are relatively well understood and specific treatments are available. As far as the writer is concerned, we have sometimes taken the wrong models from medicine and overlooked some more appropriate ones. To use an analogy, it has appeared as if in psychotherapy in the past, recourse was usually made to drastic surgery (intensive long-term psychotherapy) instead of trying simpler measures first. If some palliative measures are successful in ameliorating certain kinds of disturbances, why not use them, at least in a first attempt at treatment, instead of resorting to serious long-term treatments?

In any event, there is no good reason to fail to consider a therapeutic approach that deals directly with the behavior one wants to change, and which appears to offer promising results. Furthermore, concerns about the emergence of substitute symptoms when the original symptom has been rather successfully dealt with do not appear to be justified. An impressive number of studies have been reported in which follow-up data do not give any significant indications of substitute symptoms appearing after behavior therapy has been completed (Baker, 1969; Nolan, Mattis, and Holliday, 1970; Paul, 1967; Ullman and Krasner, 1965; Wolpe, 1961). This concern, therefore, does not appear to be a valid one and should be discarded. Rather, the focus should be on what treatments are most effective and *efficient* with what kinds of problems, and on the designing of treatment approaches or techniques which are best suited for handling specific kinds of problems.

It seems reasonable that in a sizable number of cases problems in behavior are the source of difficulty and behavior change is an important or even primary goal. Consequently, attention has to be paid to procedures which may produce behavioral change, even if they seem to be somewhat simplistic or mechanistic. After all, it is the client's welfare which is the primary concern of the therapist, and not his own personal preference or activities. Furthermore, the emphasis on behavior is a salutory one which in many ways had been neglected in psychotherapy previously. Where behavior disorders specifically are a major referral problem, behavioral procedures and clear attention to behavioral considerations would appear called for in most instances. In those instances in which new skills or patterns are required for more effective functioning, it does not appear to be sufficient to discover why the individual has failed to acquire normal social skills or to help him to express his feelings about his lack of such skills. He must be helped to learn the new required behavior patterns and to be able to apply them to the socially relevant situations. Such a procedure clearly involves principles of learning and behavior, even though personal attitudes, beliefs and feelings may also be related to the behaviors in question.

To the extent, therefore, that previous psychotherapies have tended to emphasize feelings and cognitions, the emphasis on behavior provided by the behavior therapists can be seen as a much needed corrective emphasis. Even though behavior therapy may not be the cure-all and end-all for psychotherapy that some of its staunch advocates proclaim it to be, it will have made a significant contribution to the field if the behavior of the individual is accorded its proper importance. At the same time, it can be stated again that, except in certain cases, to focus exclusively on only one aspect of human functioning is to neglect other aspects which are also of critical importance. Some awareness of this, as we have noted, has already been evident in the development of so-called cognitive behavior therapy. Whereas this appears to be a potentially worthwhile development, it also may be somewhat incomplete or limited in not giving attention also to other aspects of the individual's adjustment. Since the person is a cognitive, feeling, as well as behaving organism, theoretical as well as practical considerations would indicate that the person should be viewed in terms of all his or her attributes, and not just one. In the section which follows, some preliminary attempt will be made to sketch out some possible implications of this view.

THE PLACE OF COGNITIONS, AFFECTS, AND BEHAVIORS IN PSYCHOTHERAPY

As we have seen, the various approaches to psychotherapy and behavior change appear to have emphasized a particular channel of change or aspect of human experience in their overall psychotherapeutic approach. Some seem to place great emphasis on cognitive means of promoting change, some on the release of feelings and openness, whereas others focus primarily on a behavioral approach. Although the various groups of therapeutic approaches differ in these ways in terms of their theoretical orientations and therapeutic procedures, they, nevertheless, all claim to be successful forms of psychotherapy. Thus in spite of what appear to be significant differences between these different types of therapy, they all claim to be successful and have their own body of staunch followers. At the same time, as the preceding discussion has attempted to indicate, each of these emphases would appear to neglect or underplay significant aspects of human functioning. Clearly, this is a matter which requires further consideration.

If one can reasonably hypothesize that all aspects of human personality and behavior are of potential importance in most attempts to secure positive change by means of psychotherapy, then several subsidiary hypotheses also appear tenable as preliminary attempts to explain the current situation in psychotherapy. One hypothesis, already presented previously, is that the stated theoretical views of the different schools of psychotherapy are really not the "true" explanations of the changes reportedly secured in psychotherapy. Rather, the results may be due to common factors in all or most of the psychotherapies which are not explicitly recognized in the theoretical views presented. This hypothesis would also allow us to consider two related corollaries. One is that in varying degrees the different types of psychotherapy may actually utilize psychotherapeutic variables which do not receive much formal emphasis in their presentations of therapy. For example, behavior therapists may establish close emotional relationships with their patients, as suggested by the research of Sloane et al. (1975), and they may also provide opportunity for emotional release. In addition, they utilize cognitions in giving the patient a rationale for therapy, as well as for understanding how his/her symptoms may have developed. Thus although the formal emphasis is on behavior, these other aspects may also play a role in the therapy and in the type of outcome secured. Similar examples could be provided for the other approaches, but are not necessary here. Another corollary of our hypothesis is that certain individuals whose problems are mainly of a behavioral, cognitive, or affective type, or who respond best to an approach featuring one of these emphases, may secure better results with one approach than another. To the extent, however, that each approach receives a somewhat random group of patients, the overall results become somewhat similar for most of the different psychotherapeutic approaches. These, it should be made clear, are simply hypotheses and speculations, but are interesting nevertheless, and are not in conflict with existing research findings.

A final hypothesis to be entertained here is that to the extent that most of the psychotherapies tend to stress their particular emphasis and related procedures, their therapeutic effectiveness is less than the maximum effectiveness possible. By failing to utilize all the significant channels of human interaction and influence, each of the psychotherapies is less powerful than it might be and has variable degrees of effectiveness depending upon the type of case being seen. To become more effective, a psychotherapeutic approach would have to pay more systematic attention to all important aspects of human functioning—cognitive, affective, and behavioral. In a related fashion, more specific approaches could be developed for particular kinds of problems in which the major emphasis was placed on those aspects which seemed most important. For example, in overcoming specific fears or in attempting to develop necessary social skills, a major emphasis would be placed on behavioral procedures. However, cognitive and emotional aspects would not be neglected. In other instances, affective aspects or cognitive ones might be emphasized to a greater extent. The approach used would be tailored to the individual case so far as possible, drawing on all relevant procedures, and being cognizant of human personality and behavior.

It is the writer's belief that in practically all the therapies that are relatively successful, what actually occurs is not necessarily what is described by the formal theories and procedures of a particular school. Many other processes may be involved, but these go on incidentally and without any clear or acknowledged recognition of what may actually have occurred. Although the formal description of a particular therapeutic approach may in essence focus on one part of the elephant and serve to identify that approach, operationally what actually takes place may include other parts of the elephant as well. This, however, may be done erratically and without any clear recognition of the totality of the processes involved. Consequently, our therapeutic procedures in many respects may be less efficient, and less successful than they might be if we were to enlarge our understanding of the variables that are important in the therapeutic process and develop our procedures accordingly. In order to accomplish this goal, we shall eventually have to give up our segmental and partisan approaches to psychotherapy, and to recognize clearly that progress can only be made if we give proper attention to the totality of human functioning. Man and woman are organisms in which cognitions, emotions, and behaviors are interrelated and integrated aspects of their being and, although particular aspects may be pronounced in certain types of psychopathology, an effective approach to psychotherapy has to be aware of this interrelationship and be able to utilize this awareness constructively. It appears likely that many of the psychotherapies have developed in an attempt to compensate for apparent deficiencies in existing approaches. However, in this process, they have tended to stress, in their own approach, deficiencies perceived in others, and in so doing, have neglected some of the potential positive features of the approaches they have attempted to rectify. Nevertheless, in the final analysis, psychotherapy is best viewed as a complex cognitive, affective, and behavioral learning process.

REFERENCES

Alexander, F. The dynamics of psychotherapy in the light of learning theory. *American Journal of Psychiatry,* 1963, *120,* 441–449.

Alexander, F. and French, T. M. *Psychoanalytic therapy.* New York: Ronald, 1946.

Baker, B. L. Symptom treatment and symptom substitution in enuresis. *Journal of Abnormal Psychology,* 1969, *74,* 42–49.

Bandura, A. *Principles of behavior modification.* New York: Holt, Rinehart and Winston, 1969.

Beck, A. T. *Cognitive therapy and the emotional disorders.* New York: International Universities Press, 1976.

Bednar, R. L. and Kaul, T. J. Experiential group research: Current perspectives. In S. L. Garfield and A. E. Bergin (Eds.), *Handbook of Psychotherapy and Behavior Change,* 2nd ed. New York: Wiley, 1978.

Ellis, A. *Reason and emotion in psychotherapy.* New York: Lyle Stuart, 1962.

Freud, S. On hysterical mechanisms. In *Collected Papers,* Vol. I. London: The Hogarth Press and the Institute of Psychoanalysis, 1950a.

Freud, S. On the history of the psychoanalytic movement. In *Collected Papers,* Vol. I. London: The Hogarth Press and the Institute of Psychoanalysis, 1950b.

Glover, E. Critical notice of Wolpe's "Psychotherapy by reciprocal inhibition." *British Journal of Medical Psychology,* 1959, *32,* 68–74.

Goldfried, M. R. Systematic desensitization as training in self-control. *Journal of Consulting and Clinical Psychology,* 1971, *37,* 228–234.

Goldfried, M. R., Decenteceo, E. T., and Weinberg, L. Systematic rational restructuring as a self-control technique. *Behavior Therapy,* 1974, *5,* 247–254.

Hartley, D., Roback, H. B., and Abramowitz, S. I. Deterioration effects in encounter groups. *American Psychologist,* 1976, *31,* 247–255.

Jones, D. and Medvene, A. Self-actualization effects of a marathon growth group. *Journal of Counseling Psychology,* 1975, *22,* 39–43.

Lieberman, M. A., Yalom, I. D., and Miles, M. B. *Encounter groups: First facts.* New York: Basic Books, 1973.

Mahoney, M. J. *Cognition and behavior modification.* Cambridge, Mass.: Ballinger Publishing Company, 1974.

Mahoney, M. J. and Arnkoff, D. B. Cognitive and self-control therapies. In S. L. Garfield and A. E. Bergin (Eds.), *Handbook of psychotherapy and behavior change,* 2nd ed. New York: Wiley, 1978.

Meichenbaum, D. Cognitive modification of test anxious college students. *Journal of Consulting and Clinical Psychology,* 1972, *39,* 370–380.

Meichenbaum, D. (Ed.), *Cognitive behavior modification: An integrative approach.* New York: Plenum, 1977.

Meichenbaum, D. J., Gilmore, J. B., and Fedoravicius, A. Group insight versus group desensitization in treating speech anxiety. *Journal of Consulting and Clinical Psychology,* 1971, *36,* 410–421.

Mintz, E. E. *Marathon groups: Reality and symbol.* New York: Appleton-Century-Crofts, 1971.

Nolan, J. D., Mattis, P. R., and Holliday, W. C. Long-term effects of behavior therapy: A 12-month follow-up. *Journal of Abnormal Psychology,* 1970, *76,* 88–92.

Paul, G. L. Insight versus desensitization in psychotherapy two years after termination. *Journal of Consulting Psychology,* 1967, *31,* 333–348.

Sloane, R. B., Staples, F. R., Cristol, A. H., Yorkston, N. J., and Whipple, K. *Psychotherapy versus behavior therapy.* Cambridge: Harvard University Press, 1975.

Treppa, J. A. and Fricke, L. Effects of a marathon experience. *Journal of Counseling Psychology,* 1972, *19,* 466–467.

Ullman, L. P. and Krasner, L. *Case studies in behavior modification.* New York: Holt, Rinehart and Winston, 1965.

Weitzman, B. Behavior therapy and psychotherapy. *Psychological Review,* 1967, *74,* 300–317.

Wolberg, L. R. *The technique of psychotherapy.* New York: Grune and Stratton, 1954.

Wolpe, J. The systematic desensitization treatment of neuroses. *Journal of Nervous and Mental Disease,* 1961, *132,* 189–203.

Yalom, I. D. and Lieberman, M. A. A study of encounter group casualties. *Archives of General Psychiatry,* 1971, *25,* 16–30.

Yates, A. J. *Behavior therapy.* New York: Wiley, 1970.

CHAPTER 10

Making Psychotherapy More Specific

Most psychotherapies, as we have noted, have for the most part tended to be general or universal psychotherapies. That is, a somewhat uniform procedure has been used or followed with practically all patients, and the overall rationale has been similar. There has also been a somewhat comparable phenomenon in research on psychotherapy that has been called the "uniformity myth" by Kiesler (1966, 1971). What Kiesler has called attention to is the apparent assumption in much of the psychotherapy research that patients, therapists, and outcome variables are uniformly comparable, and thus are lumped together in the research studies.

A number of individuals recently have called attention to this problem, with the result that there is a growing awareness of the need for looking at the specific individual requirements of each case seeking psychotherapeutic help (Berzins, 1977; Strupp and Bergin, 1969). In other words, what kind of therapy or therapist is best suited for a particular patient with a particular set of problems? Since individual needs vary, it seems reasonable to believe that treatment requirements should vary also. It is also conceivable that with well over 100 different kinds of psychotherapy, each type of therapy may be best suited for a particular kind of clinical problem. If this were in fact so, then we could refer patients with certain types of problems to the specific type of psychotherapy that was especially effective with this kind of problem. Some cases would be referred for Gestalt therapy, some for psychoanalysis, some for Adlerian individual psychotherapy, some for transactional analysis, some for rational-emotive therapy, some for client-centered therapy, some for Jungian therapy, some for Sullivanian interpersonal therapy, and so on. Unfortunately, none of these have either made a claim to be unusually effective in handling a particular kind of problem, or have presented any evidence to make such a belief tenable. Rather, they appear to be general or universal psychotherapies, good for whatever ails the patient.

In the past, on the basis of my experience in several different clinical settings, the choice of the type of psychotherapy to be offered a given client was limited to two—either supportive or uncovering psychotherapy. Supportive therapy was usually considered for those who were judged deficient in personality resources, motivation, or other positive assets, whereas uncovering or reconstructive therapy was considered the treatment of choice for those clients with better personal resources. Beyond this gross, and sometimes overlapping dichotomy, there were no other alternatives. Thus there was really little specification of therapy for the great heterogeneity of clients seeking help for their individual problems.

Of all the different psychotherapeutic approaches currently plying their wares in the therapeutic market place, the behavior therapists appear to have made the most progress in attempting to devise procedures to fit the problems of the individual client. This is an important contribution, even if the procedures currently used may not be totally effective in all instances. At least the behavior therapists do have a variety of procedures and attempts are made to select those which appear useful in the given instance and to map out a program of therapy. This, in many ways, resembles what seems to be a desirable model for psychotherapy more generally.

It would appear also that more attention will have to be paid to improving our diagnostic systems and procedures. This is an important but complex matter which has presented numerous difficulties in the past and which has yet to be adequately resolved. The official nomenclature and classification system of the American Psychiatric Association or that of the World Health Organization, which are the two best known and most widely used diagnostic schemes, do not appear to be adequate for the purposes of psychotherapy. Other systems are also similarly inadequate. However, until a suitable scheme is forthcoming, psychotherapists essentially will have to function as best they can in the light of the current realities. We shall have to make as careful appraisals as possible of the client's presenting complaints and their history, and consider these as the initial focus for therapy, recognizing that we may have to modify our plans and procedures as therapy progresses. We will also have to consider the person who has the complaints, how he presents them, his current life situation, his interpersonal skills and deficits, as well as his expectations about therapy. The author, unfortunately, has no ready solutions or set procedures for coping with this problem. He is merely calling the attention of the reader to its existence, and to point to some possible ways of trying to handle it at a clinical level.

Nevertheless, in spite of our conceptual and practical difficulties with regard to client diagnosis and evaluation, some progress can be made if the psychotherapist will broaden his therapeutic outlook and lessen his partisan adherence to just one theoretical approach. Although this type of statement may be seen as a backward step in which theoretical clarity and consistency are given up for a muddled eclecticism, at this stage of our knowledge of psychotherapy it seems like a worthwhile step, and one that is actually occurring with many psychotherapists. As mentioned previously, a recent survey does indicate that a majority of clinical psychologists in the United States identify themselves as eclectics and do attempt to utilize procedures from various theoretical approaches (Garfield and Kurtz, 1976, 1977). This also may be taken as one indication of the dissatisfaction many psychotherapists have found in simply following one system of psychotherapy. If one is to develop a suitable therapeutic plan for a particular client, he/she most likely will have to broaden his or her orientation and procedures.

SPECIFICITY AS EXEMPLIFIED IN BEHAVIOR THERAPY

Within the limits of their approach, behavior therapists have shown a positive tendency to try to fit their procedures to the presenting problems of the client. They have, for example, distinguished between behavioral deficits and behavioral excesses as one broad type of differentiation and have developed different procedures for handling these two categories of problems. Behavior therapists first try to specify the behaviors that either are to be diminished as problem or undesirable behaviors, or that are to be shaped or increased as the desired behaviors. The particular program of reinforcement or punishment will be developed for the individual case. Attention is paid to the reinforcement history of the individual so that potentially effective reinforcers can be selected for use in the behavior change program. Furthermore, the program will generally be monitored to check on its effectiveness, and appropriate changes will be made if this seems necessary. Attempts are also made to analyze complex behaviors, to separate them where necessary into their most important component parts, and to devise separate procedures for these specific components of the problem behaviors.

Although the specific procedures which make up systematic desensitization have by now become somewhat routinized, nevertheless, in most instances the particular fear hierarchy is developed in terms of the individual client. The attention to specific problems has also led a number of behavior therapists to attempt to deal with a great variety of clinical problems and to develop programs and techniques for dealing with them. Although these individuals have had a certain theoretical framework, they have not limited themselves to a particular group of techniques. They have analyzed a problem situation and then selected or devised techniques which appeared potentially useful for dealing with the problem at hand. In the relatively recent past, they have attempted to devise procedures for improving the ward behavior or specific behaviors of chronic psychotic patients, autistic children, delinquents, criminals, school phobics, persons with learning disabilities, and a variety of others (Kazdin, 1978; Marks, 1978; Ross, 1978; Yates, 1975). What is being emphasized as desirable here is the close attention and analysis paid to the problem and to the particular procedures devised or used. These are specific programs for specific problems. Furthermore, the behavior therapist will usually not limit himself or herself to just one type of behavioral technique, but will use as many as are deemed useful for securing the desired changes.

Perhaps at this point it may be well to present a summary of one case treated by behavior therapists which is a dramatic and pointed illustration of how specific procedures were devised to save a child's life. In this instance, a young infant of about 9 months of age was hospitalized because of severe and continuous vomiting resulting in a serious loss in weight which threatened the infant's life (Lang and Melamed, 1969). The infant had been hospitalized on three previous occasions because of this condition. A variety of diagnostic tests had been done and a number of treatments tried, but with no apparent success. As a result, the physicians involved in the case consulted the psychology department.

Although the infant had attained a weight of seventeen pounds at the age of six months, at the time Lang and Melamed were consulted, he weighed only twelve pounds, he was in a seriously critical condition, and was being fed through a nasogastric pump.

The infant was first observed by the psychologists for two days during and after normal feeding periods. Most of the food was regurgitated within ten minutes of each feeding. In order to obtain a clearer picture of the patterning of the infant's response, electromyograph (EMG) activity was monitored at three sites—on the underside of the chin, the upper chest at the base of the throat, and straddling the esophagus. In this way a precise picture of the patterning of the infant's muscular responses associated with vomiting could be ascertained, and the schedule for aversive conditioning worked out accordingly. "The authors were concerned with eliminating the inappropriate vomiting, without causing any fundamental disturbance in the feeding behavior of the child" (Lang and Melamed, 1969, p. 4). It was fortunate that the child did not vomit during feeding, and that sucking behavior, which usually preceded the vomiting, could be distinguished on the EMG.

After this two-day observation and monitoring period, aversive conditioning procedures were instituted. As soon as vomiting occurred, a brief but repeated shock was administered and was continued until the vomiting response was terminated. Based on the observation of a nurse and the confirmation by the EMG, shock was administered "at the first sign of reverse peristalsis," and a tone was presented coincident with each shock presentation. After only two sessions, shock was rarely required. By the sixth session, the infant did not exhibit any vomiting during the testing procedures. He was then discharged from the hospital six days after the final conditioning trial. At this time the infant's level of activity had increased, a steady gain in weight was evident, and the infant showed more interest and response to his environment. One month after being discharged from the hospital, he was eating well, he looked healthy, and his weight was up to 21 pounds. One year after treatment, the child continued to be healthy and alert.

As is apparent, this was a very serious intervention on the part of these behaviorally oriented psychologists. The child's physical state was precarious, all previous attempts at trying to alleviate the child's vomiting and to help him retain his nourishment had failed, and the psychologists were brought into the case at what appeared to be the last possible moment. Because the situation was a critical one, whatever was to be done had to be done very quickly. The therapeutic procedures devised by Lang and Melamed under these very unusual and trying conditions turned out to be highly effective and the child's life was saved. Furthermore, as indicated, followup investigations after the treatment was concluded indicated that the child's health and development subsequently were quite normal. This case is a very clear demonstration of a specific treatment plan developed by very creative therapists to deal with a very specific and serious clinical problem. These therapists did not rely on a traditional procedure which they were in the habit of using with all of their cases, but used their wisdom and ingenuity to devise procedures appropriate for the problem which was presented to them. Furthermore, it also illustrates how one case can very convincingly provide evidence of the effectiveness of the therapeutic procedures used without even having recourse to a control group!

Besides the very dramatic illustration of the specificity of effective therapeutic intervention provided by Lang and Melamed (1969), there are many other illustrations in the behavior therapy literature that could also be offered (Eysenck, 1960; Ullman & Krasner, 1965). Many of these are much less striking in terms of the kind of problem dealt with, but they also illustrate the matter of specificity of therapy which is the focus of the present discussion. Although there is a great variety in the types of cases reported, one other illustration can be presented briefly.

One early case report was published by Ayllon (1963) in which a therapy program was devised for a hospitalized woman of 47 years of age who had a diagnosis of schizophrenia. The staff had been unable to modify three problem behaviors manifested by this patient in the hospital. These behaviors were stealing food, hoarding ward towels, and wearing excessive clothing. With regard to the latter problem, for example, the patient would put on several pairs of stockings, a half-dozen dresses, sweaters, and additional items.

The therapeutic program was devised to modify each of these specific behaviors. The patient weighed 250 pounds and was dangerously overweight. She did not follow a prescribed diet and stole food from the dining room counter as well as from other patients. Consequently, the patient was seated alone in the dining room and whenever she approached a different table or attempted to pick up extra food, she was removed from the dining room. In 2 weeks the pattern of stealing food was eliminated. Also, since extra food was no longer obtainable, the patient mainly ate the diet prescribed for her. At the end of 14 months with this regimen, her weight had stabilized at 180 pounds.

A different procedure, stimulus satiation, was followed to decrease the patient's hoarding behavior. The patient usually hoarded from 19 to 29 towels in her room and seemed successful in replacing the towels removed by the nursing staff. The removal of towels was discontinued and a program of stimulus satiation instituted. At different times during the day when the patient was in her room, a nurse came in and gave her a towel without comment. During the first week, the patient was given an average of seven towels daily. By the third week, the average daily rate was increased to 60. By the time the number of towels kept by the patient in her room reached 625, she began taking some of them out. At that point, no more towels were given to her. During the next year, the mean number of towels found in her room was only 1.5 per week, clearly a significant decrease. The following account reflects the change which occurred in the patient's attitude and behavior:

During the first few weeks of satiation, the patient was observed patting her cheeks with a few towels, apparently enjoying them. Later, the patient was observed spending much of her time folding and stacking the approximately 600 towels in her room. A variety of remarks were made by the patient regarding receipt of towels. All verbal statements made by the patient were recorded by the nurse. The following represent typical remarks made during this experiment. First week: As the nurse entered the patient's room carrying a towel, the patient would smile and say, "Oh, you found it for me, thank you." Second week: When the number of towels given to the patient increased rapidly, she told the nurses, "Don't give me no more towels. I've got enough."

Third week: "Take the towels away . . . I can't sit here all night and fold towels." Fourth and fifth weeks: "Get these dirty towels out of here." Sixth week: After she had started taking the towels out of her room, she remarked to the nurse, "I can't drag any more of these towels, I just can't do it." (Ayllon, 1963, p. 57)

The third and final therapeutic strategy dealt with the excessive clothing and other items worn by the patient. Food reinforcement was used in an attempt to modify this behavioral pattern. The patient was allowed a specific weight allowance beyond her body weight. When her total weight exceeded this, the patient was told she weighed too much and had to miss a meal. By manipulating the weight allowance over a period of time, the weight of the patient's clothes was reduced from twenty-five to three pounds. At the end of treatment, the patient wore what was considered a normal amount of clothing.

Although this case illustrates the planning and arrangement of specific treatments for specific problem behaviors, it can be mentioned also that other changes occurred concomitantly with the specific changes sought. As the patient began to dress in a normal manner, she became less seclusive and began to participate in the social events of the hospital. At this time also, her parents visited her and took her home for a visit—the first time this occurred during the patient's nine years of hospitalization.

Although this latter case may not be viewed as impressive or as challenging as the case of the child treated by Lang and Melamed, it, nevertheless, illustrates how specific therapeutic programs were developed to handle the specific problems of the individual case. In a similar way various types of treatment procedures have been developed for a variety of clinical problems and complaints by behavioral therapists. They have developed behavioral treatments for specific fears, overeating, smoking, hyperactivity, anti-social aggressive behaviors, lack of assertiveness, autistic behavior, enuresis and the like (Garfield & Bergin, 1978). Not all of these therapeutic procedures are necessarily or totally effective, but all of them reveal an inventiveness on the part of those involved for devising procedures for coping with very specific types of problems. This has been a distinctive attribute of behavior therapy which has not been matched by any form of psychotherapy, and one which, to some extent, could be emulated by other approaches.

As a further illustration of this work we can mention briefly some of the differing kinds of therapy procedures which have been developed for some specific kinds of commonly occurring problems.

Behavioral approaches were first developed with reference to a variety of phobic behaviors. Reciprocal inhibition, or systematic desensitization, based on a counter conditioning theory, was one of the first groups of techniques to receive clinical recognition. With the passage of time, other procedures such as flooding, modeling, and guided participation were also developed. All of these procedures had in common the arrangement of specific therapeutic steps for overcoming specific fears of particular individuals, and they generally involved exposure to the fear provoking stimulus.

With the relative success of such behavioral approaches, a variety of other procedures have been developed in recent years for overcoming a number of different problems. For example, response prevention and bringing patients into contact with the stimuli that triggered compulsive rituals has been relatively effective in reducing ritualistic behaviors (Marks, 1978). The treatment of sexual disorders, influenced by the work of Masters and Johnson (1970), has involved procedures for reducing anxiety, the training of sexual skills, the modification of attitudes towards sexual activity, and the like. Specific procedures are used also for such different problems as premature ejaculation, erectile failures, ejaculatory failures, and anorgasmia (LoPiccolo, 1975). Operant procedures also have been developed and applied to a variety of problematic behaviors ranging from delusional speech and social withdrawal to such behaviors as hyperactivity, academic performance, and anti-social activities (Kazdin, 1978). Practically all of these programs emphasize a careful study of the behaviors to be modified, the conditions which appear to be sustaining these behaviors, the institution of procedures for changing the behaviors, and methods for carefully monitoring the effects of the therapeutic procedures. Thus the focus tends to be on the analysis of the individual case and the adapting of procedures to meet the requirements of the case at hand. In the case of unassertive behavior, for example, the procedures found helpful include the changing of beliefs about oneself and the expectations concerning others, role-playing, modeling, and practice in real life situations. In cases of obesity, a treatment package may include adhering to a prescribed caloric intake, eating at only certain times and at certain places, recording all food eaten and the time this was done, regular recording of one's weight, positive reinforcement for weight loss, and the like. Thus procedures and treatment packages have been developed for specific problems, and although these have not always been successful, they augur well for future therapeutic developments.

AN ECLECTIC APPROACH TO SPECIFICITY IN PSYCHOTHERAPY

Although the preceding sections may appear to reflect a particular bias on the part of the writer in favor of behavior therapy, this is not really the case, nor is an advocacy of behavior therapy a goal of this chapter. Rather, it is the author's conviction that one has to have an open mind on all matters and to evaluate a particular view in terms of its apparent adequacy and on the basis of the evidence presented in support of that view. In terms of the behavior therapists, one has to admit quite frankly that they have been a very enterprising and inventive group of therapists who have tackled a variety of difficult problems with enthusiasm and resourcefulness. In fact, they have devoted attention to very difficult clinical problems which most of us in the field of psychotherapy have preferred to ignore or avoid because they seemed hopeless, that is, chronic schizophrenia, childhood autism, etc. One cannot help but admire this kind of professional activity. Also, as has already been stressed, the attempts to devise specific treatments for specific problems appears to be a most desirable attribute. Besides these features, the behavior therapists deserve recognition for their attempts to evaluate their results in a systematic fashion and to report their findings in the published literature. These all deserve positive recognition and acknowledgment. However, although an open-minded and conscientious psychotherapist would want to be acquainted with the developments occurring in behavior therapy and to utilize some of its techniques and procedures, he need not limit himself solely to behavioral techniques. Instead, he may pay more attention than the behaviorists to the possible common factors in psychotherapy and to other aspects as well.

To a certain extent, an eclectic approach to the use of specific procedures in psychotherapy has already been discussed in the previous chapter on common and specific aspects of psychotherapy. However, for the sake of completeness, we can add some further comments. A basic consideration is that the therapist evaluate the client and his problems as adequately as possible, and then to have very clear and explicit goals for therapy. The more concretely and specifically the goals can be stated, the more readily a program of therapy can be devised for the particular client. The therapist may also have to consider the priority of goals and what procedures should be used in the early stages of therapy. The particular constellation of factors in any given case will tend to determine what or how many procedures should be instituted initially. In some cases, the therapist may want to delay the instituting of certain therapeutic procedures because, in spite of the client's statements, the problems mentioned do not appear to be of prime importance. In other cases, the therapist may decide for various reasons that it is desirable to start a program of say, relaxation or systematic desensitization immediately. It may be in the latter case that a particular fear is judged to be a very critical problem, or that while the problem is not of the highest importance, it is worthwhile to do something concrete which may have relatively quick results in order to increase the client's overall feeling of adequacy and hopefulness of change. In any event, clarifying and specifying the goals of therapy, and then deciding on what particular approach and procedures might be feasible, would constitute the initial phase of therapy. The eclectic therapist would be differentiated from most therapists who adhere to one approach by the attempt at greater specification of goals and procedures, and by his willingness to use specific procedures from any orientation, including behavioral ones, if they seem appropriate to the case at hand. He would be differentiated from the behavior therapist by his greater attention to common, cognitive, and affective variables in therapy, and by his willingness to use other techniques besides strictly behavioral ones.

Although the eclectic therapist would appear to have the advantage of having a broader orientation to psychotherapy and potential access to a wider variety of therapeutic techniques and procedures than his school-oriented colleagues, it must also be acknowledged that his path is less clearly illuminated. There is some personal comfort for the therapist in believing in and adhering to a given theoretical system. He can follow certain stated procedures and explain certain phenomena in terms of his theoretical system. This is of no little importance, for over and over again the writer has been impressed with the fervor with which some adherents of particular viewpoints cling to, or espouse, their specific orientation. Not infrequently, such individuals are unable to shift their views and to accept the emphases of other viewpoints, even in the face of supporting evidence. Just as patients appear to get some therapeutic benefit from the naming or explaining of their problem by the therapist, so do many therapists get some personal benefit from the specific structure and explanations provided by their theoretical system. A unified theoretical view thus does have this benefit for the psychotherapist. The eclectic therapist, however, has much less of this kind of support, and this is something of a disadvantage. However, he or she can make use of any technique which appears to be therapeutically worthwhile and, potentially, can provide the most flexible approach to psychotherapy. For the time being, the eclectic therapist will have to place a considerable amount of his or her confidence in empirical results and tenable hypotheses, instead of in a unified and developed theory of psychotherapy. However, this seems to be a defensible and justifiable stance in the light of our present knowledge and theoretical development in the field of psychotherapy.

Although the absence of a unifying and guiding theory has its drawbacks and does not allow the individual to proceed with the kind of assurance and direction that such a theory provides, it also does have some features which currently may be seen as positive. It does not provide a false sense of security and certainty which sometimes characterize those who believe they have discovered the truth and have the utmost faith in their procedures. An awareness of one's limitations and of the gaps in our current knowledge, is in the long run a positive thing, even though it may make for uncertainties and even discomfort on certain occasions. It is better to see the situation for what it really is than to have what may be an incorrect or biased orientation. By the very nature of things, the eclectic psychotherapist has to be open to all reasonable developments in psychotherapy which appear to have some potential merit. There are no procedures which are automatically excluded because they run counter to his theoretical orientation. Rather, procedures that are not supported by empirical studies can be discarded because they have been found wanting, instead of because they are not congruent with his theory. This means that the eclectic psychotherapist is interested in evaluating his work and in the results reported by other therapists and investigators. Without such evaluation, no real progress in psychotherapy can be made, and it is in the interests of the field and the people we serve that everyone try to participate and contribute to such appraisals.

The eclectic approach to psychotherapy also allows the therapist to pay appropriate attention to the individual requirements of the clients for therapy and to select those specific, as well as general, procedures that the specific case requires. In fact, such an approach necessitates specificity, not only in terms of the individuality of the client, but in the understanding that any single approach to therapy is not the best approach for all clients. The therapist has to be selective in his choice of procedures and be able to devise a plan of therapy which utilizes whatever specific procedures seem warranted.

There are a few other aspects which can also be mentioned before we leave the present topic. One is that it appears important for the therapist to keep a proper perspective on whole-part relationships when working with any client. By this is meant that the significance of any particular problem of the client has to be viewed and understood in terms of its particular importance for the individual as a whole. The same holds for the use of any specific treatment procedure. A corollary of this is that the therapist has to be alert to the impact that any particular feature of therapy has on the client, to evaluate the situation accurately, and to be able to modify his approach accordingly. Perhaps some examples will be useful in illustrating what is meant here.

Whereas one has to begin with the patient's complaints as the initial starting point for psychotherapy, two patients who appear to give comparable reasons for seeking therapy may not be precisely the same. Let us take two individuals who verbalize a fear of flying or that they are socially inadequate. In one case, the fear of flying, for example, may be the main or sole complaint, whereas in the second case, it may be just one of many. Even if the therapist should decide on the use of a procedure such as systematic desensitization (S.D.), he might handle the two cases quite differently. In the one instance, S.D. may suffice as the main therapeutic approach, and therapy could last for only a short time. There would appear to be little need for any other interventions. However, in the hypothetical second case, progress might be slow, and there would appear to be a need for other interventions as well. More opportunity might be allowed for the patient to discuss feelings of inadequacy, some need for assertive training might be indicated, and perhaps even the need to involve the spouse in the therapy. Thus the two therapeutic programs would gradually evolve quite differently. In some instances, a specific type of therapy for a particular problem, if successful, can have a more generalized and important effect upon the patient. A patient who has overcome his fear of flying, for example, may also show an increase in overall self-esteem and confidence. In another case, this may not occur, the results may be more focalized and limited, and other attempts will have to be made to secure these additional outcomes. Conversely, in some cases, more general improvement in such aspects as self-confidence and positive self-image may allow the patient to progress more rapidly on specific problems.

The therapist has to be sensitive to whatever clues are manifested by the patient so that emphases and procedures can be flexibly modified. The writer recalls one case he supervised where initially there appeared to be one central complaint, fear of driving in traffic. The case appeared to be ideally suited for S.D. and the therapist attempted to follow this procedure. This patient, however, appeared very anxious and fearful when in the clinic, and this should have provided some awareness to the therapist that what might be involved here was not a simple case of a specific phobia. The patient, furthermore, was very fearful of closing her eyes as part of the training in relaxation. The therapist, although partially aware and concerned about this, did not adequately evaluate the situation and only slight gains were achieved by means of S.D. In this case, no adequate assessment was made of other aspects of the case and, consequently, the attempt to push through with one approach was relatively unsuccessful.

In summary then, an eclectic approach places responsibility on the therapist to make an adequate appraisal of the client and his problems, and to work out some plan for therapy which seems initially appropriate for the particular client. The therapist selects those procedures that, on the basis of empirical evidence, seem to be most effective for the specific problems presented by the client. In the absence of research data, the therapist has to rely on his own clinical experience and evaluations, or on his best clinical judgment, realizing that he should evaluate his work as therapy proceeds. Once therapy is under way, the therapist should monitor the client's progress and make whatever modifications seem to be necessary in order to facilitate positive movement in therapy.

REFERENCES

Ayllon, T. Intensive treatment of psychotic behavior by stimulus satiation and food reinforcement. *Behavioral Research and Therapy*, 1963, *1*, 53–61.

Berzins, J. I. Therapist-patient matching. In A. S. Gurman and A. M. Razin (Eds.), *Effective psychotherapy. A handbook of research.* Oxford: Pergamon Press, 1977. Pp. 222–251.

Eysenck, H. (Ed.), *Behavior therapy and the neuroses.* Oxford: Pergamon, 1960.

Garfield, S. L. and Bergin, A. E. (Eds.), *Handbook of psychotherapy and behavior change, 2nd ed.* New York: Wiley, 1978.

Garfield, S. L. and Kurtz, R. Clinical psychologists in the 1970s. *American Psychologist*, 1976, *31*, 1–9.

Garfield, S. L. and Kurtz, R. A study of eclectic views. *Journal of Consulting and Clinical Psychology*, 1977, *45*, 78–83.

Kazdin, A. E. The application of operant techniques in treatment, rehabilitation, and education. In S. L. Garfield and A. E. Bergin (Eds.), *Handbook of psychotherapy and behavior change*, 2nd ed. New York: Wiley, 1978.

Kiesler, D. J. Some myths of psychotherapy research and the search for a paradigm. *Psychological Bulletin*, 1966, *65*, 110–136.

Kiesler, D. J. Experimental design in psychotherapy research. In A. E. Bergin and S. L. Garfield (Eds.), *Handbook of psychotherapy and behavior change.* New York: Wiley, 1971.

Lang, P. J. and Melamed, B. G. Case report: Avoidance conditioning therapy of an infant with chronic ruminative vomiting. *Journal of Abnormal Psychology*, 1969, *74*, 1–8.

LoPiccolo, J. Direct treatment of sexual dysfunction. In J. Money and H. Musaph (Eds.), *Handbook of Sexology.* Amsterdam: ASP Biological and Medical Press, B. V., 1975.

Marks, I. Behavioral psychotherapy of adult neurosis. In S. L. Garfield and A. E. Bergin (Eds.), *Handbook of psychotherapy and behavior change,* 2nd ed. New York: Wiley, 1978.

Masters, W. H. and Johnson, V. *Human sexual inadequacy.* Boston: Little, Brown & Company, 1970.

Ross, A. O. Behavior therapy with children. In S. L. Garfield and A. E. Bergin (Eds.), *Handbook of psychotherapy and behavior change,* 2nd ed. New York: Wiley, 1978.

Strupp, H. H. and Bergin, A. E. Some empirical and conceptual bases for coordinated research in psychotherapy: A critical review of issues, trends, and evidence. *International Journal of Psychiatry,* 1969, *7,* 18–90.

Ullman, L. P. and Krasner, L. *Case studies in behavior modification.* New York: Holt, Rinehart and Winston, 1965.

Yates, A. J. *Theory and practice in behavior therapy.* New York: Wiley, 1975.

CHAPTER 11

Research in Psychotherapy

Thus far in this book, our main attention has been devoted to trying to understand the psychotherapeutic process and the kinds of procedures which may be used in trying to secure changes in clients by means of psychotherapy. Although references have been made in each chapter to numerous research findings, and the importance of research in psychotherapy has been emphasized, no specific attention has been given to research as a topic in its own right. The present chapter, therefore, will be devoted to a discussion of this important aspect of psychotherapy. Our concern here will be on some basic general features of research in this area rather than on the technicalities of research design per se.

Scientific research has contributed greatly to the expansion of knowledge and to a marked increase in our material well-being. Although no one would seriously deny the value of such research, there are some who would argue that science and scientific procedures are applicable only to certain kinds of problems and pursuits. The methods of science have clearly paved the way for significant advances in the physical sciences, and to a lesser extent perhaps, in the biological sciences. However, according to some observers, when we get into the social sciences and particularly to the problems of human adjustment and the human psyche, these methods are inappropriate and unsuitable. Furthermore, a number of psychotherapists believe that psychotherapy as practiced is an art and that it involves such difficult to grasp human qualities as intuition and sensitivity, which are beyond the methods of science. Although there is some truth to those assertions, they appear to be overly extreme and, in some instances, reflect biases against the attempt to utilize more exact and empirical procedures for appraising the processes of psychotherapy.

Although psychotherapy is indeed a complicated process, there is no good reason that attempts to investigate it cannot be undertaken. Admittedly, some of the methods used in the more exact and quantitative sciences may not be completely applicable to research in psychotherapy. However, this does not in any way imply that appropriate procedures cannot be developed and applied to the area of psychotherapy. Furthermore, considerable research has been carried out, and we are now in a much better position to plan research which is meaningful and clinically relevant.

The need for research in the area of psychotherapy is quite evident. As already mentioned, we have a situation where there are already over 100 different schools or types of psychotherapy, these approaches differ enormously in their theories and procedures, and yet all appear to lay claim to being the most effective type of psychotherapy. In addition, adherents of one psychotherapeutic approach appear highly critical of opposing approaches. When such a bewildering state of affairs exists, one can only hypothesize that the available facts and research data must be minimal and that considerable work needs to be done to bring some order into this rather chaotic state of affairs. Later, in the next chapter, we will attempt some survey and appraisal of the existing research data on the effectiveness of some types of psychotherapy. However, before doing so, it seems desirable to familiarize ourselves with some of the basic considerations pertaining to research in the area of psychotherapy.

BASIC CONSIDERATIONS IN PSYCHOTHERAPY RESEARCH

If research in psychotherapy is to be of any real value, it will have to pay attention to the basic canons of research design, as well as taking into consideration the unique characteristics and requirements of the psychotherapeutic situation. When one examines the latter, it seems clear that attention will have to be devoted to the variables which are deemed important to the psychotherapeutic process, as well as to any possible influencing or contaminating variables which might influence this process. That is, we must consider all of the variables which presumably may influence the course of therapy, but we must *not* overlook extra-therapy variables which might play some role in influencing outcome.

The basic variables hypothesized to be important in psychotherapy can be categorized in a number of ways, but in general they derive their reputed significance from one or the other participant in psychotherapy and in the possible interaction effects between these two. Thus we can speak of client or patient variables as one class of variables which have obvious importance for outcome in psychotherapy, and a previous chapter dealt in some detail with this group of variables. Included here were such client variables or attributes as age, sex, educational level, social class status, degree of disturbance, type of disturbance, expectations about therapy, motivation, suggestibility, and the like. Conceivably, any aspect of the client that could influence outcome in psychotherapy would be a variable of importance with reference to research. Furthermore, since client variables presumably affect the possible outcome of psychotherapy, they are of critical importance for two types of research investigations. One is comparative studies of the relative effectiveness of two or more types of psychotherapy. If two very different groups of clients are assigned to different types of therapy respectively, we will not be able to draw any valid conclusions concerning the relative effectiveness of the two types of therapy. Any differences obtained could be due to differences in the two samples of clients, and not to the differences in the therapies. Also, if no differences are secured, one cannot rule out the possibility that client differences in the two samples have influenced the outcome obtained, and that other results might have been secured if the samples of clients were matched or comparable in most important respects. Consequently, in comparative studies of outcome the research investigator has to make some effort to insure the comparability of his groups of subjects and to guard against bias in the selection of subjects. He can do this by matching subjects on essential attributes before assigning them to the respective treatment or control groups, or by insuring complete randomization in the allocation of subjects to the treatment groups. Such procedures are a means of reducing possible bias or selectivity in assigning clients to the different types of treatment and to increase the probability that whatever differences are secured can be presumed to be the result of the independent or manipulated variable, that is, the type of treatment.

Client or patient variables obviously are also the central variables in research that attempts to discover what patient attributes may be predictive of outcome in psychotherapy, or more specifically, what kind of patients or clinical problems will respond best to specific kinds of treatment. This is clearly a potentially important kind of research in psychotherapy and reflects the more recent emphasis on trying to discover what types of interventions may be most effective with particular kinds of problems (Kiesler, 1971; Strupp and Bergin, 1969).

Client variables are thus variables of basic importance in research in psychotherapy, and inadequate attention to such variables has undoubtedly contributed to some of the conflicting findings reported in the literature. Another consideration here is that in considering client variables in psychotherapy research, the investigator should pay adequate attention to those variables that are of some potential significance, not just to those which are easily appraised and secured. For example, in trying to select two comparable groups of subjects, the investigator may try to equate them on variables on which he has information but which may not be crucial ones, and fail to pay attention to variables which are of greater importance. Thus he may equate his group on the basis of age, sex, and marital status, but not on the degree of disturbance, willingness to undergo treatment, and similar variables. To the extent that the former group of attributes may not be critical ones for the study being undertaken, the matching of groups is really a sort of window dressing that actually does not handle the problem adequately.

The critical problems in evaluating client variables are the selection of the variables that presumably are related significantly to outcome and, also, the adequate appraisal of these variables. One of the serious problems here is that so many of the client variables hypothesized to be of potential significance for psychotherapy are not couched in operational terms. They tend to be personality variables or other hypothesized constructs which are poorly defined, are viewed in different ways by different therapists, and which are difficult to measure or evaluate. A concept conceivably may pertain potentially to an attribute of possible importance, but if it cannot be operationalized in some way or adequately appraised, it will have little actual value since it cannot be reliably evaluated. Thus such constructs as ego strength, motivation for therapy, anxiety, and the like, present real problems for research. Different measures of the same construct frequently show modest or low correlations with each other, and one is not really sure what each is actually measuring. In the final analysis, our methods of appraising the variables we are interested in investigating have to be reliable and valid ones. If they are not, then the research investigation is seriously weakened. To the extent that many of the research investigations conducted by behavior therapists have utilized behavioral criteria of outcome which have some degree of reliability and validity, their research is not as much influenced by this type of problem. However, to the extent that other client variables may also be involved in influencing outcome, such considerations pertain to behavioral therapies as well.

Another problem that needs some mention concerns whether the results secured in any investigation can be generalized, and patient variables are also of importance in this regard. Any research investigation of psychotherapy utilizes a finite number of clients or subjects. The number and type of clients studied are of some importance for the kinds of conclusions and generalizations to be drawn from the particular study. If the number of clients is relatively small, one has to be particularly cautious in drawing conclusions since sample size affects reliability. The type of sample also has to be considered. If one has a very mixed group of patients, the results may not be applicable to many other patient populations, or if the sample is very selective, the results again may be limited only to a comparable group of patients and not apply to others. A great deal of the earlier research in psychotherapy was carried on with mixed or heterogeneous samples of subjects from a particular clinic or hospital setting with the implication that the results were meaningful for all other clinical and hospital settings, an inference that was frequently found wanting. Usually, such samples covered the psychiatric waterfront with the traditional exclusion of brain damaged and mentally retarded patients. Since not all clinical settings secured the same kind of patients in exactly the same kind of mix, comparabilitly of results was hampered. A better strategy is probably to try to do research on more specified patient samples who have a somewhat similar type of problem. In this way variability in research samples will be lessened, and perhaps more reliable results can be secured.

There is one other aspect of this problem which has also received some attention and discussion. This also pertains to the matter of the ability to generalize results and refers primarily to research studies carried out with college student volunteers. Although some of these studies have been clearly referred to as analogue studies, that is, experimental demonstrations of operations presumed to be analogous to those occurring in actual psychotherapy (Heller, 1971), others have not made such a distinction and have treated their studies as studies of psychotherapy. A number of studies of behavior therapy, in particular, have been carried out with student volunteers, although client-centered research, as well as others, have also used college student subjects. The issue here is, are college student volunteers who are recruited for such research studies by means of advertising or for the meeting of course requirements to be considered comparable to patients who seek out treatment for supposedly comparable complaints? (Marks, 1978) If the two groups of subjects are in fact different, are the results of the one applicable to the other? Unless the results secured with students or other types of volunteers are cross-validated on some sample of actual patients with comparable complaints, the results are probably best viewed as preliminary and tentative, for it is not uncommon for more negative results to be secured with clinical patients. It is a perfectly reasonable procedure to try out new techniques on student volunteers in a more controlled laboratory type of setting, but before these results can be considered to have wider application, they would have to be cross-validated on a clinically appropriate sample. Otherwise, one would be safest in generalizing the results obtained only to a like sample of student volunteers. In all research, however, the greater the specificity of the client variables appraised, the greater the probability of securing reliable results.

Besides the variables ascribed to the client, the possible variables associated with the therapist are also important in psychotherapy research. Those that have tended to receive the most emphasis have been personal attributes of the therapist and his length of experience in psychotherapy. As was noted in a previous chapter, whereas many desirable personal qualities have been deemed important for the psychotherapist, comparatively little research has been conducted on such variables, and of the research that has been done, much of it has produced conflicting and disappointing results (Parloff, Waskow, and Wolfe, 1978). Although a few studies have shown some relationship between the experience of the therapist and outcome, the overall results are relatively modest at best and leave a large amount of the variance unaccounted for (Auerbach and Johnson, 1977). Predictive research on clinical psychologists and psychiatrists in training have also been rather disappointing (Holt and Luborsky, 1958; Kelly and Fiske, 1951).

The most promising research on therapist attributes appeared to be the research conducted by the client-centered therapists on the fundamental variables of empathy, warmth, and genuineness. As reported in the volume by Truax and Carkhuff (1967), it did appear as if some basically important therapist attributes, long recognized and emphasized by clinicians, had been carefully defined and operationalized by means of reasonably well constructed rating scales of taped therapist performance in actual therapeutic interaction. The writer, in reviewing this important work, was very much excited by the potential contribution of this research (Garfield, 1968). However, subsequent research and appraisal has failed to support this earlier promise. The reliability of the scales used for appraising these therapist variables has been called into question (Chinsky and Rappaport, 1970), and other research, as noted earlier, has failed to fully support the claim that these therapist offered conditions are correlated positively with outcome in psychotherapy (Garfield and Bergin, 1971; Lambert, DeJulio, and Stein, 1978; Mitchell, Bozart, and Krauft, 1977; Parloff, Waskow, and Wolfe, 1978).

Thus although it seems most likely that the qualities of the therapist are of some importance in psychotherapy, and this is a view held by most clinicians, the research to identify these qualities has as yet not produced any truly definitive findings. That certain therapist attributes or styles are of potential importance in the progress of psychotherapy is suggested from the findings of several studies. In the study of encounter groups by

Lieberman, Yalom, and Miles (1973), for example, some therapist behaviors appeared to be related to the number of casualties produced. In some other studies of self-reports by patients who had received psychotherapy, there are also suggestions that certain personal qualities of the therapist were regarded as important by these patients (Feifel and Eells, 1963; Sloane et al., 1975; Strupp, Fox, and Lessler, 1969). However, these results, based as they are on post-therapy or retrospective reports of patients, provide only limited data on therapist variables. Nevertheless, they do suggest possible leads that may be important in research on psychotherapy. Certainly it does not seem at all prudent to overlook the potential influence of the therapist on the process and outcome of psychotherapy and to make no attempt to study such influence systematically. In this regard, it is interesting to note the analysis of individual studies of psychotherapy reporting negative effects provided by Strupp, Hadley, and Gomes-Schwartz (1977). Only a very few of these studies evaluated or mentioned possible therapist attributes. Where potential correlates of negative effects of psychotherapy were listed, they most frequently referred to *patient variables,* and not to therapist variables. This is clearly a one-sided emphasis which needs correction.

Consequently, although our techniques and rationales for appraising therapist variables are limited and leave much to be desired, any systematic research will have to make some attempt at studying potential variables of this type. Otherwise, we continue the uniformity myth that all therapists are equal and interchangeable, and we will have to settle for "average" results. Comparable studies of diagnosticians have shown that there is tremendous variability in the accuracy of different clinicians (Chambers and Hamlin, 1957; Holtzman and Sells, 1954). Although the average of a group of clinicians shows them to be little better than chance in their diagnostic acumen, some clinicians are decidedly accurate, whereas others seem to be completely off the mark. Similar studies of psychotherapists would be extremely helpful, particularly if some intensive studies were then pursued to study those who were most effective so that knowledge of the attributes which contribute to desired outcome could be ascertained.

One other point that has been commented on by some research critics can also be mentioned. A fair number of studies of psychotherapy have tended to use psychotherapists in training. Such individuals tend to be more readily available, or more easily induced to participate in research investigations. To the extent that these individuals are not yet fully trained and proficient psychotherapists, how much confidence can we place in the results secured and how far can we generalize from the findings obtained?

If training and experience make some difference in the quality of the psychotherapy performed, then it would seem most prudent to generalize only to situations where comparable therapists are employed. If one is conducting research on the possible effectiveness of psychotherapy, it seems reasonable to use experienced and capable therapists. On the other hand, to the extent that a significant percentage of clients in clinical settings are being serviced by therapists in training, research on the effectiveness of such therapy can be considered of possible practical value. The kinds of generalizations made would, of course, differ for the two different situations.

In addition to considering therapist and client variables, ideally, research should also consider the possible interaction between these two sets of variables. Since one therapist may conceivably be more effective with certain kinds of clients and some clients may work better in therapy with certain types of therapists than others, attention should be paid to these possible interaction effects. This obviously calls for a more complex research design and is at least partially the reason that few studies of this kind have been attempted. However, in spite of its difficulties, attention will have to be paid to problems of this kind, and such matters will have to be considered in appraising the possible variables influencing outcome in psychotherapy (Berzins, 1977).

A final note of importance in psychotherapy research concerns outcome variables and the methods of evaluating outcome. This aspect of research has received a relatively large amount of attention, in contrast to some other aspects of research in psychotherapy, and, consequently, there are some reasonable guidelines for research.

The outcome of psychotherapy refers to the changes that are secured by means of the therapeutic intervention. The type of outcome indicates the effectiveness of the therapy. As a consequence, criteria of outcome are of decided importance for both research and practice in psychotherapy. Research in psychotherapy which is not intimately linked with criteria of outcome is ultimately of limited value, and the importance of any research on the effectiveness of psychotherapy would also be very much influenced by the quality of the criteria of outcome used. Let us, therefore, first examine some of the criteria of outcome which have been used in such research.

Probably the most frequently used criterion of outcome in psychotherapy generally has been the judgment of improvement provided by the therapist. Because the therapist is available and can offer some judgment concerning the outcome of psychotherapy, such evaluations can be readily secured, and this most likely accounts for the frequency with which this type of evaluation has been used. As a result, various types of rating scales have been used in research to ascertain the therapist's evaluation of outcome. In defense of this procedure, it is usually stated that the therapist is the one who has been most intimately involved with the patient and is in the best position to make a first-hand appraisal of outcome. Although this statement is at least partially correct and appears to have some face validity, there are some limitations in relying on therapists' judgments as the sole or primary criterion of outcome. In the first place, the therapist is not a completely objective observer or rater. To the extent that he has been an involved participant in the psychotherapy being evaluated, he cannot be presumed to make a completely unbiased evaluation, no matter how well he knows the patient. In addition, different therapists may judge their effectiveness in idiosyncratic ways. Some may be overly optimistic, while others may be too severe in their judgments. One also cannot adequately evaluate the reliability of their ratings. Finally, to the extent that therapists' ratings are global ratings of outcome or improvement that are made at the end of therapy, there are further inadequacies or limitations in the utility of the ratings made. One is that the therapist has to compare the client's condition at the end of therapy to what it supposedly was when the client began therapy. Not only may the therapist's recollection be faulty, but the overall level of the client's integration and adjustment may tend to influence the therapist's evaluation accordingly (Mintz, 1972). That is, a client who was only mildly disturbed to begin with may be seen as very much improved at the end of therapy, because he is functioning at a relatively high level at the end of therapy, even though the changes secured are modest. Also, global rating scales of improvement may be poorly defined and lacking in terms of clear operational definitions of the categories used. For these reasons, therapists' ratings of outcome leave much to be desired and cannot be relied upon as a sole criterion of outcome.

The ratings of outcome by patients who have undergone psychotherapy have also been frequently used as one of the criteria of outcome, and they appear to have somewhat similar limitations as measures of outcome as the ratings secured from therapists. The patient should be in a good position to evaluate what changes he or she has undergone, but, again, there are problems of subjectivity, perception, attitudes toward the therapist, and the need also to justify one's expenditure of time and money. Nevertheless, because the patient is a central participant in psychotherapy, and is usually agreeable to providing some ratings, such evaluations have been widely used.

In a number of studies both therapist and client ratings have been secured, and the findings are interesting. Although the total percentage of those judged to be improved is similar in the two sets of ratings secured, the correlation between the two sets of ratings tends to be rather modest. In one study, for example, where such ratings were obtained, both sets of ratings indicated that about 70 percent of the clients were considered to be "improved". However, the correlation between the ratings was .44 (Garfield, Prager, and Bergin, 1971). Other studies have reported even lower correlations. In the study by Sloane et al. (1975), a correlation of .21 was secured between the ratings of patients and therapists, whereas a nonsignificant correlation of .10 was reported for these two sets of ratings by Horenstein, Houston, and Holmes (1973). Somewhat similar findings were also reported by Ryan and Gizynski (1971). With such low agreement between the ratings of the two groups of participants in psychotherapy, the value and meaningfulness of these criteria of outcome are open to some doubt.

Besides these kinds of outcome ratings, the ratings of supervisors, significant others, and independent judges have also been used in psychotherapy research. Although supervisors' ratings may also be open to similar kinds of criticism as those already mentioned in the case of therapists, particularly where they rely on the therapist's report of what has occurred in therapy, in at least one study their ratings were less positive than those provided by either the therapists or the clients (Garfield, Prager, and Bergin, 1971). The ratings by such significant others as parents, spouses, close friends, and employers, would also appear to be of potential value in evaluating psychotherapy. However, similar problems seem to be evident with the use of such ratings as well. The ratings of parents of children with specific behavioral problems were reported to be overly positive as compared with other criteria in two well controlled studies (Patterson 1971). Ratings by employers or work supervisors might be of value in some cases, but securing such data could be viewed as an invasion of the client's privacy and as a threat to the confidentiality of the therapeutic contacts. Certainly, many clients might not want their employers to know that they had received psychotherapy. On the other hand, ratings made by independent trained observers on the basis of interviews or tapes of therapy sessions can be checked for reliability and be of some utility in appraising outcome. Among all the various ratings obtainable, they would at least appear to be the ones open to the least subjective bias. The fact that therapists and clients perceive outcome somewhat differently in a sizeable number of cases is an interesting finding which is worthy of further investigation in its own right.

Besides ratings and judgments of overall outcome which suffer from the fact that they tend to be made mainly at the end of therapy, other types of ratings can be secured which are potentially of greater value. Instead of a global judgment of improvement, attention can be focused on specific complaints or problems presented at the intake or initial session with the patient, and which can be evaluated again at the end of therapy without reference to the initial ratings. These have several advantages. They deal with more specific problems and behaviors instead of a global measure of improvement, and they are based on judgments or ratings which are made at the same time the specific behaviors or complaints are evaluated.

In addition to ratings, a variety of psychological tests and questionnaires have also been used to appraise outcome in psychotherapy. Obviously, such estimates of progress in therapy are no better than the tests upon which they are based. To the extent that well standardized tests are used, comparisons between comparable studies are possible if the tests are appropriate to the outcomes sought by means of therapy. If the tests used are lacking in validity or are otherwise inappropriate for the types of outcome to be anticipated, then such instruments probably will provide very little useful data.

The use of tests thus does not provide any simple or ready-made solutions for evaluating outcome in psychotherapy. The tests must have some demonstrated reliability and validity for the particular variables they are supposed to measure, and the hypothesized variables must also be directly relevant for the desired therapeutic outcome. It is a relatively easy matter to use a popular test or battery of tests, but the tests should be appropriate to the types of problems presented by the client. Many so-called general tests of personality may not be the most appropriate instruments to use unless an overall personality change is the goal of therapy. Within limits, the changes sought by means of therapy should determine the kinds of measures used.

One of the problems evident in psychotherapy research is the wide variety of tests and questionnaires used in such research. This has led to real difficulties in comparing and evaluating the results of different studies. Tests that purport to measure the same or similar variables frequently show disappointingly low correspondence between them. As a result it has been extremely difficult to draw definitive conclusions from the diverse and conflicting results secured. If comparability of results are to be obtained, it would be desirable to have research investigators utilize the same standardized tests. However, this would only be feasible if comparable groups of patients with similar treatment goals were being studied. Since patients may have variable problems, standard tests may not be completely applicable, and other outcome measures would also have to be used.

Still another type of outcome criterion used is a measure of the actual behavioral change sought by means of psychotherapy. This type of measure of outcome has understandably been utilized most frequently by behavior therapists. Since they tend to focus their work on behavior and to conceptualize the patient's problems in behavioral terms, it follows naturally that evaluation of outcome would be primarily concerned with behavioral change. There are several positive features of this type of emphasis. Behavioral change is important in most cases and should be included in most appraisals of outcome. This has not been the case in a large number of instances, and has been a weakness in previous research. Furthermore, behavior is observable and thus can be appraised in a reasonably objective manner. Although behavioral measures are obviously of more importance in some disorders than in others, and can be more easily appraised in some cases than in others, attempts should be made to utilize behavioral measures wherever possible.

The behavior therapists have devised a number of research designs and procedures which have been used successfully in a variety of research studies. Among these are the ABAB design for single cases, the measurement of approach behaviors in the case of phobic disturbances, developing hierarchies of desirable behaviors, measuring generalization and transfer of designated behaviors, and more complicated designs. Many of these can be adapted in various ways for use in evaluating outcome in psychotherapy.

Recently, Strupp and Hadley (1977) have offered some suggestions concerning the evaluation of outcome that deserve mention in the context of our present discussion. They have discussed the lack of congruence among different appraisals of outcome, but instead of questioning the value of such evaluations on this basis, have stated that each evaluation perspective is of some importance. For example, although patients and therapists may evaluate the outcome of therapy differently, they are evaluating it from different perspectives or vantage points, and both perspectives need to be considered in evaluating outcome. They also believe that other perspectives should also be considered. Consequently, they have offered what they term a tripartite scheme of evaluation. In essence, three vantage points for evaluation of therapy are suggested: society, the individual client, and that of the mental health professional. Society is concerned with social roles and mores, and thus the focus here would be on the observation of behavior in terms of social expectations and criteria. From the individual client's viewpoint, the important criteria of outcome would involve subjective perceptions and feelings of self-esteem and well-being. The criteria of professional mental health personnel would depend on observations of behavior, psychological tests, and clinical judgments as mediated by some theoretical view of personality structure and overall personal functioning and integration. Although there is some overlap among these criteria, they do represent somewhat different vantage points and frames of reference.

Although the scheme proposed by Strupp and Hadley points up one important aspect of the problems encountered in appraising therapeutic outcome, it does not provide a complete solution to these problems. If the three modes of evaluation are discrepant, what kinds of judgment concerning the effectiveness of psychotherapy can be made? Are all three types of evaluations to be considered as valid? According to Strupp and Hadley, a truly adequate and comprehensive appraisal is possible only if the three types of data are evaluated and integrated, but who will perform the integration? Presumably, an independent and objective fourth party would be called for. However, if this person is a professional mental health worker, one component of the tripartite arrangement may appear to be over-weighted. In any event, the tripartite scheme of evaluation is an interesting one that does call into question the limitations of relying on a single source for data on outcome. Research that attempted to investigate, systematically, the bases for the differences among different sources of outcome evaluation would appear to be of potential worth.

There are thus a number of basic considerations pertaining to the client, to the therapist, and to the criteria of outcome which have to be considered in research on outcome in psychotherapy. Deficiencies in any aspect will of necessity affect the value of the results secured. Consequently, the serious student of psychotherapy must not only try to keep abreast of the research which is done in his field, but he must also be able to evaluate the merits and limitations of the research studies that he reads. This stricture holds for all aspects of psychotherapy research, and not just those that have been discussed thus far.

CONTROLLED AND UNCONTROLLED RESEARCH

In addition to variation in the variables already mentioned, research in the area of psychotherapy has demonstrated diversity in other aspects as well. Some reports of research have tended to be rather well designed and controlled studies that are modelled after the more traditional experiment in scientific research. The dependent variables, or outcome criteria, are clearly specified and the independent variables, or therapeutic conditions, are manipulated in a clearly designated manner. However, the laboratory experiment is only one type of research model, and because it is a very difficult one to follow in most clinical situations, many other types of research studies have been carried out in the field of psychotherapy.

One of the most common types of reports on outcome in psychotherapy is a simple evaluative report on a certain number of patients who have received treatment in a clinical setting over a given period of time. In some instances, the report is of a retrospective study of a sample of patients who have been treated in the past, and the investigator simply goes through the closed case files in the clinic and tabulates the final evaluations or comments noted in the files by the various therapists who have treated the patients in the period studied. As shown in one such investigation, such reports have many deficiencies (Garfield and Kurz, 1952). Among other things, many records tend to be incomplete, some of the information is inadequate, there is considerable variability among therapists in how they evaluate outcome and in how they record it, and the outcome is based on the therapist's global judgment made at the end of therapy. In the study referred to above, a large number of therapists did not provide any final appraisal of outcome, and in those cases where evaluations were recorded in the case files, a variety of descriptions and terminology was used so that it was extremely difficult to equate these judgments. Consequently, although such an investigation may be of some value to the clinical facility in showing a need for more systematic appraisal, it is of little value in telling us anything about the effectiveness of psychotherapy.

In other instances, somewhat better prospective clinical investigations have been carried out in that the study has been designed in advance, and patients, as well as therapists, may be asked for evaluations of outcome based on rating scales devised for the study. Although this type of study has certain improvements over the previous one, it, too, has limitations. The judgments of outcome tend to be global and poorly defined, and, usually, the information about client variables also leaves a great deal to be desired. Because of this, some investigators have attempted to improve this particular approach to research by adding more objective and comprehensive measures of outcome, usually some standard tests and questionnaires. This type of research, although an improvement again, still allows us only very limited kinds of conclusions. It may tell us something about the rate of estimated improvement in a group of usually heterogeneous clients who have undergone psychotherapy with a particular sample of therapists in a specific clinical setting at a given time. If these results are generally seen as positive, they may be viewed as affirming the effectiveness of the psychotherapy being carried out in that clinical setting, or even of the effectiveness of psychotherapy more generally. However, such conclusions are basically not tenable in the absence of some sort of control group. Without adequate controls, one cannot draw any cause and effect relationships with any reasonable degree of confidence.

The matter of adequately controlled studies is an important one in all research, and is certainly so in the case of research on psychotherapy. If one is to draw certain inferences or conclusions about the effect of one variable on another, one must be able to control all other variables which may be operating in the situation at hand and which could also have some influence on the second or dependent variable. For example, if someone is studying the effect of noise level on performance but fails to control for other variables such as temperature which might also influence performance, the results which are secured may be contaminated by the influence of the uncontrolled variable. In the case of the study of outcome in psychotherapy mentioned earlier, we may have an observable effect, that is, 68 percent of the patients who received psychotherapy are judged to have shown some improvement. However, we cannot convincingly state that this result is due to psychotherapy unless we have ruled out the possibility that other factors may also have played a role in the improvement secured. One of the more obvious considerations here is what would have occurred if this same group of patients had not secured psychotherapy but had simply been left alone. Over a similar period of time, would they also have shown a comparable percentage of improvement or would the percentage of improvement have been less or more? Unless we have data on this question or have some other reasonable basis for making judgments, we are unable to provide any adequate answer to this type of question. Consequently, our ability to draw conclusions about the effectiveness of therapy is thereby limited. The matter of controlling for possible extraneous influences on psychotherapeutic outcome is thus of some significance, and it is for such reasons that a control group is most desirable in research evaluating outcome.

For the reasons just mentioned, research in psychotherapy has increasingly made use of some type of control group. One obvious kind is to have an untreated control group—that is, a group of clients that is considered to be comparable to the group receiving psychotherapy, but that is given no treatment. Both groups receive the same evaluation procedures, and whatever differences are secured are presumed to be due to the effects of treatment. Although this procedure seems to be an adequate one, it is not always easy to carry it out, and there are also some possible limitations in its use. If the therapy being evaluated takes a long period of time, it is extremely difficult to secure and retain a control group which is somehow kept away from receiving psychotherapeutic help. Clearly, there are ethical as well as practical considerations involved, for no ethical practitioner would want to withhold therapy for a long period from patients who are seriously disturbed and in need of treatment. Where the length of treatment is relatively short, this is not as serious a problem.

In addition, there are also difficulties in getting a control group that is comparable to the treatment group or in securing randomly selected groups for the research investigation. If a large number of the initially selected control group patients refuse to wait, and seek treatment elsewhere, it is not always possible to replace them in kind, and such attrition raises questions about the representativeness of those patients who are content to wait for treatment and constitute the control group.

In spite of the problems, the no-treatment control group has been used in several research studies on psychotherapy. It was used in some of the earlier studies carried out by Rogers and his co-workers (Rogers and Dymond, 1954), and quite recently in the important study by Sloane et al. (1975). These studies were carried out with outpatients with whom such a research design would appear to be more difficult than it would be with inpatients whose lives are essentially controlled by the institution. Essentially, what was used has been called a waiting list or wait-list control group. When patients are seen initially, they are told there is a waiting list for assignment to therapy but that they will be called as soon as an opening occurs, and they are promised that they will be given therapy. In the study by Sloane et al. (1975), the patients were told that they would definitely be assigned to therapy within four months at the latest since this was the period of therapy evaluated.

Whereas a no-treatment or waiting list control group adds considerably to the value of a study attempting to appraise outcome in psychotherapy, this type of research design has also been criticized by some as not being completely satisfactory (Paul, 1967). Here, however, the criticism stems from a different source and is concerned more with the variables which are presumed to be of significance in affecting change. For example, if a research study indicates that significantly greater changes are secured by means of psychotherapy than is the case with no treatment, are the results really attributable to the stated psychotherapeutic procedures or are they attributable to some other possible variables? Could it be that instead of the hypothesized variables in psychotherapy producing the change secured, it is simply having an opportunity to talk to someone that is responsible for the obtained improvement? This point of view appears to derive largely from work in the area of pharmacology on the so-called placebo effect (Shapiro and Morris, 1978). In testing drugs it has been found that some individuals will respond positively to any type of medication or pill, even if it contains ingredients which are physiologically inert. That is, the mere taking of a pill seems to have a therapeutic effect, regardless of what the pill contains. Thus in research on new drugs, the experimental drug is usually compared with a placebo that resembles it in appearance and also tastes as much as possible like it. If similar results are secured from the two pills, even if they are very positive, the effects of the experimental medication are judged to be due to the placebo effect rather than to the specific medication. Only if the "real" drug produces a decidedly superior result as compared with the placebo will it be judged to be an effective pharmacological agent.

As a result of such work, several investigators in the area of psychotherapy have deemed it important to utilize what has been termed an "attention-placebo" control group, as well as some type of no-treatment control group (Paul, 1967). This type of research design clearly seems capable of providing more worthwhile and definitive information than the others already discussed. If the psychotherapy treatment group secures better results than any of the control groups, the results are more impressive in indicating that it is the psychotherapy which appears responsible for the changes secured. If, however, the group receiving psychotherapy shows greater change than a no-treatment control group, but does not differ from the attention-placebo group, one may then hypothesize that the changes secured by means of psychotherapy are essentially placebo effects which could be secured by other kinds of interpersonal interactions.

One of the difficulties in using an attention-placebo group beyond possible ethical considerations, and the extra effort involved in utilizing an extra control group, is in making the attention-placebo procedures believable and realistic. In order to have an effective control group of this kind, the rationale and procedures devised for the research investigation must have credibility, but at the same time must not utilize procedures which are part of the psychotherapy being investigated. It is not always easy to design such procedures and the investigator has to be quite creative in this regard. The control group has to be an effective or valid one, or it does not serve adequately the function which it was set up to serve. In evaluating the significance of research studies it is important, therefore, that the particular types of control groups be scrutinized carefully to see if, in fact, they fulfill the conditions ascribed to them.

There would appear to be little question that well designed and controlled studies can contribute much more valuable information to our knowledge of psychotherapy than can uncontrolled studies. Research which is worth doing is worth doing well. However, there are many other kinds of research that are not primarily involved with the effectiveness of psychotherapy and that do not necessarily require the use of complicated control groups. Among these are studies of prognosis in psychotherapy, the matching of therapist and patient, premature termination, the significance of structure or therapist activity in therapy, and the like. Each of these types of studies has different concerns, but the matter of a controlled study in terms of controlling significant variables is just as important here as in the use of control groups in the study of outcome. No matter what one is studying, one needs to control for the influence of chance or extraneous variables if he or she is interested in how a specific variable or variables affect some criterion variable. If there is no control over such influences, it is difficult to conclude that a particular cause is responsible for the results secured. It is only when we can draw conclusions with at least some degree of confidence that we can advance our knowledge.

STATISTICAL AND CLINICAL CONSIDERATIONS

Another matter worth discussing here pertains to various statistical and clinical considerations regarding the significance of the results obtained through research. Since there are many individuals who are considerably more knowledgeable and informed about the intricacies of research design and statistical analysis than the present author (Gottman, 1978; Kiesler, 1971), no attempt will be made to discuss such matters. Rather, some points of importance for the psychotherapist who follows the literature in his field will be discussed.

Statistics and statistical analyses are important aids in research. They help us to understand the data and results that have been obtained in research investigations, and they allow us to make various comparisons between different sets of results. Thus they have many uses in research, and it would be difficult to carry out most types of research without the use of appropriate statistics. There is one area, however, in which their value is sometimes misinterpreted or incorrectly appraised. This has to do with various statistical measures used to determine the significance of the findings secured in a particular study. For example, if two groups of subjects are compared statistically after treatment on the basis of the differences secured, a test of significance is used and the results are reported as reaching a certain level of significance. In contemporary research the .05 and .01 levels of statistical significance are commonly used. When a finding is reported to be significant at the .05 level, this denotes that the result obtained could have been secured by chance about five percent of the time. Thus the interpretation is made that because a chance occurrence of this type is very unlikely, the results are considered to be significant—that is, not due to chance. This is the value of such statistical tests of significance, for they allow you to make some judgment about the possibility that the findings obtained are simply chance fluctuations. The size of the groups, their variability, and the actual differences obtained will all influence the resulting level of significance. However, such measures only tell you part of what may be important to the professional clinician. They tell one about *statistical* significance, but not about *clinical* significance.

If an investigator has large samples of subjects, a small difference may actually turn out to be statistically significant, that is, not due to chance. However, the difference may be so small that it is of little practical value. It may suffice for a doctoral dissertation or for possible publication, but be inadequate for clinical purposes. In order to make a decision or judgment for practical purposes, other kinds of criteria have to be employed. Basically, the issue is not merely whether a finding is statistically significant, but also how much of the variance between the variables studied is accounted for by the findings secured. For example, let us assume that we are comparing two types of treatments and that treatment A is found to be significantly better statistically than treatment B. When we go beyond the test of significance and examine the actual results obtained, however, we discover that the patients receiving treatment B show a slight decrease in status, whereas those receiving treatment A have improved a small amount. Although the difference between the two groups is statistically significant, the actual gains shown by the patients receiving treatment A is so small that it appears to be of relatively little clinical value. Or, it may be that upon examining the results carefully, we note that only 15 percent of the patients receiving treatment A actually show what might be termed significant clinical improvement and it is this small group which appears to account for the significant findings secured. Although this latter finding might be important in terms of seeking out possible predictive variables for positive response to treatment A, the overall findings would tend to indicate that this treatment has only limited value for most patients.

Some actual reports in the literature can also be cited to illustrate the point made previously. In one study that examined possible correlates of premature termination from psychotherapy, it was found that age was significantly related to such early termination (Sullivan, Miller and Smelser, 1958). However, the age difference between the terminators and remainers was only two years, and it would be very difficult to apply this finding in any constructive way. In other words, the actual difference is so small that it is of little clinical utility. In another study evaluating the effectiveness of implosive therapy, a significant degree of improvement was reported (Levis and Carrera, 1967). However, an analysis of the scores on the MMPI, one of the criteria used, raises some question about the extent or clinical significance of the improvement secured. Although the mean score on the schizophrenia scale was reduced by nine points in the desired direction, from a mean of 83.5 to a mean of 74.1, the final score obtained is still considered to be indicative of serious pathology. Although one would have to admit that these patients were quite seriously disturbed at the beginning of therapy, their status at the end of therapy still revealed an important degree of pathology, even though there was a statistically significant degree of improvement. Clinical judgments of improvement would also appear to be important in deciding how significant this degree of improvement really is.

Thus statistical significance, although an important and necessary requirement in research on psychotherapy, is not necessarily sufficient in reaching clinical judgments about the effectiveness of particular approaches and procedures in psychotherapy. One must also examine the data provided by the investigator in order to appraise the extent of the changes secured. For this reason it is important that the research report contain adequate and sufficient data in order that the reader can evaluate and interpret the findings presented. The presentation of data is extremely important, and this is an obvious advantage that systematically reported research has over narrative accounts or clinical reports. The investigations that have been discussed above did present sufficient data so that the reader could evaluate critically the research reported.

It should be clear that the author is not criticizing the use of statistics in research on psychotherapy, since statistical procedures are essential research tools and provide us with significant information. What is being discussed and evaluated here is the meaning of statistically significant results as compared with the possible clinical significance of the results secured. Like any other tools, statistics may be inappropriately applied and misused. However, they make a valuable contribution when used intelligently and appropriately. It is the author's practice to disregard findings which lack statistical significance even though a number of investigators sometimes try to make much of "trends" in their findings which have failed to reach an acceptable level of significance, but which appear to be in the desired direction. In other words, statistical significance is a necessary but not necessarily sufficient condition for judging the practical significance of a set of research results. One must also determine how much of the variance is accounted for by the particular findings at hand before one can make a more reasoned judgment. For example, the correlation between height and intelligence has usually been reported as being somewhere in the neighborhood of .15. Large samples of subjects have been studied, and the finding is significant statistically and thus a reliable one. If future large scale samples are tested one can expect that the results will not vary too much from .15. However, this finding accounts for only about two percent of the variance, and thus, height is not considered a very good predictor of intelligence.

It is unfortunate, perhaps in part because of the pressure from journals to conserve space, that sometimes essential data for evaluating the results of a study are not included in the published report. However, in most cases it is possible to make some appraisal of the data presented and to reach at least some tentative conclusions about the utility of the research reported.

Mean or average scores are not always informative and one should scan the distribution of scores if they are available, as well as the percentage of cases which attain certain scores or levels of improvement. In this way, the reader may get a better and more concrete picture of what has taken place. Two groups with comparable means may have very different distributions, and this finding may be of some value. For example, in one instance practically all of the patients may show modest gains, whereas in another instance, a certain number may show very large gains although the majority of the patients show little or no gain at all. In the latter instance, it is possible that the particular approach may be very effective with certain kinds of patients, or that a small number of therapists were particularly effective and accounted for most of the overall change that was secured.

Consequently, further analyses of the research data may be quite useful in expanding our understanding of the phenomena we are studying. One impression, for example, that the writer has had of many reports on outcome in psychotherapy is that the number of clients who are judged to be maximally improved are a relatively small number of those who are treated. If a five-point scale is used for judging improvement, either the mean improvement for the group of clients being studied is well below the top value of five, or, if the percentage of patients receiving the various ratings are provided, the number at the top is small. Although the overall findings are statistically significant and may also be of some significance practically, this type of finding suggests that psychotherapy as currently practiced is not yet a very powerful treatment for most patients. In the study by Sloane et al. (1975) results like these were actually obtained. The therapy groups began treatment with an average symptoms rating of three (moderate severity) on a scale ranging from zero (absent) to four (severe). At the end of therapy, their symptoms were rated as being between one (trivial) and two (mild). The results secured tend to be more within the mild or moderate range of improvement, and suggest that considerable progress is necessary before our procedures will attain the kind of effectiveness and power that we would like them to have.

SOME GENERAL OBSERVATIONS ON RESEARCH IN PSYCHOTHERAPY

As the reader is undoubtedly aware, the author, in spite of a critical view of much of the research in psychotherapy, has a strong bias favoring research and a strong belief in its importance for advancing the state of knowledge in this field. In clinical work, generally, but especially in psychotherapy, there is still too much deference toward individuals with status and reputation, as well as toward those who speak with authority and conviction. People appear to be interested and swayed by those who make glowing promises or who claim to have the key to the promised land. It seems as if it is sufficient merely to be told that a particular approach is very effective. Rarely are research data requested to support a particular claim or pronouncement. Apparently psychotherapists, like other lesser humans, also believe what they want to believe, rather than manifesting a desire for evidence. Although such a state of affairs is perhaps understandable, it is also lamentable, for the majority of psychotherapists have received some scientific and research training. This type of training may be utilized for certain activities or in certain situations, but it seems to go out of the window where psychotherapy is concerned. Students, perhaps, can be forgiven their transgressions, since they are so eager to learn the mysteries and techniques of psychotherapy that it seems somehow inappropriate, or a sign of ingratitude, to display a questioning or critical attitude. However, fully trained individuals who persist in such behavior may have to be viewed as placing personal needs above the needs for evaluating and improving the level of therapeutic efficacy.

I would like to propose the view that every professional psychotherapist has some responsibility to contribute in some way to the advancement of our knowledge of the field. For some practitioners this may take the form of participating as a therapist in some kind of clinical or research investigation or in contributing some of his work with patients to a broader cooperative research project. Clearly not everyone is capable of devising or directing a research project on psychotherapy. This involves a great deal of time and expertise. However, most psychotherapists can contribute in various ways. Another simple procedure is to try to objectify one's own work and to make one's own case files more systematic. Instead of just writing some narrative notes in the file, the psychotherapist could at least use a simple rating scale and strive to make as objective ratings as possible at the beginning and end of therapy. If it serves no other purpose, it may at least help the therapist to be more concerned with the outcomes he or she secures in psychotherapy, and with the need for evaluation. More systematic record keeping may also allow the psychotherapist to be more readily able to profit from his/her past experience with certain types of cases and to formulate hypotheses which might later be tested by means of more systematic investigation. Furthermore, if individual clinicians get into the habit of trying to be more objective and systematic in the evaluation of their own work, they are more likely to be agreeable to participating in a research project carried out in their own center or elsewhere.

It is certainly understandable that many psychotherapists are reluctant to carry out research or to participate in research projects carried out by others (Bednar and Shapiro, 1970). There is a natural concern about exposing oneself to others, and there also appears to be some suspicion of researchers on the part of clinicians. It is as if the latter believe that the former are out to expose or discredit their work. It is also true that the demands placed upon clinicians to fill out forms or to adhere to certain research protocols are sometimes time-consuming and difficult, and there is no particular reward for the person who cooperates. In fact, he may conceivably be shown up to be an ineffective therapist! For such reasons, it is understandable that many practicing therapists may not be particularly eager to participate in research projects.

There are also some other reasons given by therapists for not participating in research investigations which do not appear as valid as the reasons given above. Some believe that the extra demands placed on the patient for taking tests or completing forms interferes with the process of psychotherapy. Some therapists have even been opposed to taping their therapy sessions for reasons such as this. However, in many instances such complaints do not appear to be fully justified, but, instead, reflect either a defensiveness on the part of the therapist or a negative view of research. A large number of studies have been carried out without any apparent negative effects on the patient, and tape recordings of therapy sessions are standard procedures in many training and clinical centers. In fact, even video taping of families appears to have no real interfering effect on the interactions which occur between the family members.

If research is to take place in a clinical setting, it is important that the research investigators consider the demands they are making on the clinical staff and the potential threat they constitute, and plan accordingly. They should meet with those who are being asked to participate and give them some general understanding of the proposed project and its importance for the field of psychotherapy. Although certain aspects of the research may have to remain secret in order not to bias the results to be obtained, some general orientation to the project and its overall rationale should be provided. It is desirable that discussions be held with the staff so that ambiguities can be clarified and their own doubts and misgivings be explored and answered. It is also worthwhile to ask them for suggestions so that they feel more like professional collaborators instead of people who are being used or exploited. It is also extremely important to emphasize and to guarantee the complete confidentiality of the project so that the work of any individual staff member remains completely anonymous, and even to withhold the identity of the clinic if this seems to be reasonable. It is also a sound procedure to provide the participants with a report of the overall results secured, since they can be presumed to have more than a passing interest in these results, and they deserve such personal consideration.

It is indeed unfortunate that a large number of professional psychotherapists have a rather negative view of the value of research on psychotherapy. There are some who adhere strongly to the view that psychotherapy is a distinctly personal affair and that the research is a contrived and quantitative affair which can never get at the essence of the process and, consequently, is of little value. Such individuals are not swayed or influenced in any manner by research data and, perhaps, research will have no effect on their work as psychotherapists. Most psychotherapists, however, would probably not fall into this category. A number of these, nevertheless, would state that much of the research which has been done is of little direct value or relevance for them. There is some justification for this view since a number of studies have used college students or volunteers as subjects, administered very artificial or brief periods of therapy with students in training as therapists, and have used certain measures of outcome that may not be of direct clinical concern. To the extent that these limitations do exist, the criticisms made of research are justified. However, such criticisms do not apply to all research studies, nor should the implication be drawn that all research is useless or inconsequential. Recent reviews of research provide evidence of the utility of research findings, as well as indicating the lacks in our current knowledge (Garfield and Bergin, 1978; Gurman and Razin, 1977).

Many psychotherapists also appear to overreact to the possible difficulties of doing research and, consequently, come to feel that research is too complicated for them. Research is for the "experts" to carry out and not for clinicians. Again, although there is some truth to this assertion, it, too, is overdrawn. Research tends to be conceptualized in terms of an over idealized image of scientific or laboratory research with complicated statistical designs. Whereas such research represents one type of research, it is not the only one. Certainly, clinical psychologists and many psychiatrists and social workers have received enough training in research procedures to engage in at least some type of clinical research. It is very important to recognize that there are many types and levels of research possible, and that they may serve different purposes. Certain kinds of research or systematic data collection, for example, may be of real practical value for a specific clinical setting or may provide a basis for more refined research investigations. In the writer's opinion, most clinics are potential sources of data, and more systematic procedures for securing and recording data would allow for many types of clinical research investigations. Such types of information as actuarial data on the patients seen, the number of sessions missed, the average length of treatment, average time on the waiting list, the relationship of certain variables to early termination or to measures of outcome, patterns of performance of individual therapists, and many more could be secured in most clinical settings with the proper planning, interest and just a little extra effort. Furthermore, although many of these types of analyses may not be seen as conclusive research, or as work which merits publication, they can provide information which is of real value to the clinical facility in appraising the work of the center and in identifying problems that have not received adequate attention previously.

The type of clinical research just referred to may also be a step toward considering and planning a more rigorous type of investigation which might have implications beyond the particular setting involved. For example, if an analysis of accumulated data revealed a possible relationship between time on the waiting list and the refusal of psychotherapy, a study could be planned and initiated in which new patients were randomly assigned either to the waiting list or to immediate therapy, and the results analyzed. This would be a more definitive test of the hypothesis in question. Other comparable kinds of studies might also be undertaken, depending on the types of data secured or the particular interests of certain members of the staff. Such research should be seen as a regular and important part of the clinic's functions, for in the long run, such investigations may help in the identification of clinical problems and in the improvement of clinical services and procedures.

Research, then, should not be viewed as some esoteric or ethereal activity that is engaged in by others and that is far removed from the realities of professional existence. On the contrary, it can be of potentially great practical value and can definitely be carried out in most clinical settings. It need not and should not necessarily be divorced from ongoing clinical activities. In fact, the more directly research is performed on clinical problems of a practical nature, the more directly relevant may be the results secured by means of research investigation. Instead of being a luxury, so to speak, research can be viewed as a means of making practice more effective and efficient. All clinicians have a responsibility to at least play some role in research which may contribute either to the enhancement or improvement of the clinical activities in which they are engaged, or in the eventual advancement of our understanding of psychotherapy. Research and the evaluation of clinical services are a practical necessity if we are to move beyond the existing state of practice and to make our procedures more effective.

There are thus many aspects to research in psychotherapy and many kinds of research which can be done. Even single cases can be evaluated in a systematic manner and offer leads and information of potential value (Lazarus and Davison, 1971; Leitenberg, 1973; Shapiro, 1966). Some research can be done in a relatively straightforward and simple manner while other types may have to be carried out with complex designs and statistical analyses. At the same time, for reasons already discussed, not all research is of equal value. The psychotherapist must be able to evaluate critically the research reports he scrutinizes and when he is in doubt concerning certain procedures or results, he should consult with others who may be more knowledgeable about such matters. When planning a research project, it may be wise to get expert consultation. However, when discussing such matters with so-called experts, the clinical investigator should be sure that he understands what is being suggested and not let his project become so modified that it is no longer the project he was interested in doing. With proper discussion, the final project should be a better worked out plan for investigating the problem which he is interested in pursuing. As is true of other endeavors, what is worth doing is worth doing well, and poor research will only provide poor answers.

REFERENCES

Auerbach, A. H. and Johnson, M. Research on the therapist's level of experience. In A. S. Gurman and A. M. Razin (Eds.), *Effective psychotherapy: A handbook of research.* Oxford: Pergamon Press, 1977.

Bednar, R. L. and Shapiro, J. G. Professional research commitment: A symptom or a syndrome. *Journal of Consulting and Clinical Psychology,* 1970, *34,* 323–326.

Berzins, J. I. Therapist-patient matching. In A. S. Gurman and A. M. Razin (Eds.), *Effective psychotherapy. A handbook of research.* Oxford: Pergamon Press, 1977, pp. 222–251.

Chambers, G. S. and Hamlin, R. The validity of judgments based on "blind" Rorschach records. *Journal of Consulting Psychology,* 1957, *21,* 105–109.

Chinsky, J. M. and Rappaport, J. Brief critique of meaning and reliability of "accurate empathy" ratings. *Psychological Bulletin,* 1970, *73,* 379–382.

Feifel, H. and Eells, J. Patients and therapists assess the same psychotherapy. *Journal of Consulting Psychology,* 1963, *27,* 310–318.

Garfield, S. L. Review of Truax, C. B. and Carkhuff, R. R. Toward effective counseling and psychotherapy: Training and practice. In *Contemporary Psychology,* 1968, *13,* 464–465.

Garfield, S. L. and Bergin, A. E. Therapeutic conditions and outcome. *Journal of Abnormal Psychology,* 1971, *77,* 108–114.

Garfield, S. L. and Bergin, A. E. (Eds.), *Handbook of psychotherapy and behavior change,* 2nd ed. New York: Wiley, 1978.

Garfield, S. L. and Kurz, M. Evaluation of treatment and related procedures in 1216 cases referred to a mental hygiene clinic. *Psychiatric Quarterly,* 1952, *26,* 414–424.

Garfield, S. L., Prager, R. A., and Bergin, A. E. Evaluating outcome in psychotherapy: A hardy perennial. *Journal of Consulting and Clinical Psychology,* 1971, *37,* 320–322.

Gottman, J. and Markman, H. J. Experimental designs in psychotherapy research. In S. L. Garfield and A. E. Bergin (Eds.), *Handbook of psychotherapy and behavior change*, 2nd ed. New York: Wiley, 1978.

Gurman, A. S. and Razin, A. M. (Eds.), *Effective psychotherapy: A handbook of research.* Oxford: Pergamon, 1977.

Heller, K. Laboratory interview research as analogue to treatment. In A. E. Bergin and S. L. Garfield (Eds.), *Handbook of psychotherapy and behavior change.* New York: Wiley, 1971.

Holt, R. R. and Luborsky, L. *Personality patterns of psychiatrists: A study in selection techniques,* Vol. 1. New York: Basic Books, 1958.

Holtzman, W. H. and Sells, S. B. Prediction of flying ability by clinical analysis of test protocols. *Journal of Abnormal and Social Psychology,* 1954, *49,* 485–490.

Horenstein, D., Houston, B., and Holmes, D. Clients', therapists', and judges' evaluations of psychotherapy. *Journal of Counseling Psychology,* 1973, *20,* 149–153.

Kelly, E. L. and Fiske, D. W. *The prediction of performance in clinical psychology.* Ann Arbor: University of Michigan Press, 1951.

Kiesler, D. J. Experimental designs in psychotherapy research. In A. E. Bergin and S. L. Garfield (Eds.), *Handbook of psychotherapy and behavior change.* New York: Wiley, 1971.

Lambert, M. J., DeJulio, S. S., and Stein, D. M. Therapist interpersonal skills: Process, outcome, methodological considerations, and recommendations for future research. *Psychological Bulletin,* 1978, *85,* 467–489.

Lazarus, A. A. and Davison, G. C. Clinical innovation in research and practice. In A. E. Bergin and S. L. Garfield (Eds.), *Handbook of psychotherapy and behavior change.* New York: Wiley, 1971.

Leitenberg, H. The use of single case methodology in psychotherapy research. *Journal of Abnormal Psychology,* 1973, *82,* 87–101.

Levis, D. J. and Carrera, R. Effects of ten hours of implosive therapy in the treatment of outpatients: A preliminary report. *Journal of Abnormal Psychology,* 1967, *72,* 504–508.

Lieberman, M. A., Yalom, I. D., and Miles, M. B. *Encounter groups: First facts.* New York: Basic Books, 1973.

Marks, I. Behavioral psychotherapy of adult neurosis. In S. L. Garfield and A. E. Bergin (Eds.), *Handbook of psychotherapy and behavior change,* 2nd ed. New York: Wiley, 1978.

Mintz, J. What is "success" in psychotherapy? *Journal of Abnormal Psychology,* 1972, *80,* 11–19.

Mitchell, K. M., Bozarth, J. D., and Krauft, C. C. A reappraisal of the therapeutic effectiveness of accurate empathy, nonpossessive warmth, and genuineness. In A. S. Gurman and A. M. Razin (Eds.), *Effective psychotherapy: A handbook of research.* Oxford: Pergamon, 1977.

Parloff, M. B., Waskow, I. E., and Wolfe, B. E. Research on therapist variables in relation to process and outcome. In S. L. Garfield and A. E. Bergin (Eds.), *Handbook of psychotherapy and behavior change*, 2nd ed. New York: Wiley, 1978.

Patterson, G. R. Behavioral intervention procedures in the classroom and in the home. In A. E. Bergin and S. L. Garfield (Eds.), *Handbook of psychotherapy and behavior change*. New York: Wiley, 1971.

Paul, G. L. *Insight versus desensitization in psychotherapy*. Stanford, CA: Stanford University Press, 1966.

Paul, G. L. Insight versus desensitization in psychotherapy two years after termination. *Journal of Consulting Psychology*, 1967, *31*, 333–348.

Rogers, C. R. and Dymond, R. F. *Psychotherapy and personality change*. Chicago: University of Chicago Press, 1954.

Ryan, V. and Gizynski, M. Behavior therapy in retrospect: Patients' feelings about their behavior therapists. *Journal of Consulting and Clinical Psychology*, 1971, *37*, 1–9.

Shapiro, A. K. and Morris, L. A. The placebo effect in medical and psychological therapies. In S. L. Garfield and A. E. Bergin (Eds.), *Handbook of psychotherapy and behavior change, 2nd ed*. New York: Wiley, 1978.

Shapiro, M. B. The single case in clinical-psychological research. *Journal of Genetic Psychology*, 1966, *74*, 3–23.

Sloane, R. B., Staples, F. R., Cristol, A. H., Yorkston, N. J., and Whipple, K. *Psychotherapy versus behavior therapy*. Cambridge: Harvard University Press, 1975.

Strupp, H. H. and Bergin, A. E. Some empirical and conceptual bases for coordinated research in psychotherapy: A critical review of issues, trends, and evidence. *International Journal of Psychiatry*, 1969, *7*, 18–90.

Strupp, H. H., Fox, R. E., and Lessler, K. *Patients view their psychotherapy*. Baltimore: Johns Hopkins Press, 1969.

Strupp, H. H. and Hadley, S. W. A tripartite model of mental health and therapeutic outcomes: With special reference to negative effects in psychotherapy. *American Psychologist*, 1977, *32*, 187–196.

Strupp, H. H., Hadley, S. W., and Gomes-Schwartz, B. *Psychotherapy for better or worse. The problem of negative effects*. New York: Jason Aronson, 1977.

Sullivan, P. L., Miller, C., and Smelser, W. Factors in length of stay and progress in psychotherapy. *Journal of Consulting Psychology*, 1958, *22*, 1–9.

Truax, C. B. and Carkhuff, R. R. *Toward effective counseling and psychotherapy*. Chicago: Aldine, 1967.

CHAPTER 12

Evaluating the Effectiveness of Psychotherapy

Now that we have discussed the many different features of psychotherapy and the problems of carrying out research investigations of psychotherapy, it is appropriate to review some of the work which has been done to evaluate the effectiveness of psychotherapy. Although a sizeable amount of work has been done and many types of results have been reported in the literature, this topic has generated considerable controversy and still remains a controversial issue. Perhaps, in the light of our previous discussions concerning the complexities of research on psychotherapy, this kind of situation will not come as a complete surprise to the reader. In any event, no work on psychotherapy can be regarded as completed without some attention to the important issue concerning the effectiveness of psychotherapy, or the various psychotherapies. Several rather comprehensive reviews of this literature are available elsewhere, and the author will not attempt to duplicate these efforts (Bergin, 1971; Bergin and Lambert, 1978; Eysenck, 1966; Luborsky, Singer, and Luborsky, 1975; Meltzoff and Kornreich, 1970). Rather, we shall examine some of the general findings and offer some appraisal of them.

The adequacy of psychotherapeutic treatment is obviously of critical importance, for all of the different types of psychotherapy are based on the premise that they are effective, and in fact, are more effective than competing forms of psychotherapy. The writer cannot recall any school of psychotherapy which has proclaimed that it is ineffective. However, although practically all schools have claimed effectiveness for their particular approach, very few have made any serious attempts to carry out systematic research investigations appraising the effectiveness of their psychotherapy. This, indeed, has always been a curious phenomenon as far as the present writer is concerned. People are apparently willing to accept the claims of others, or to believe without demanding any type of evidence or proof to

267

substantiate the various claims made. This, as noted previously, is an amazing occurrence when one considers that most professionally trained psychotherapists have received training in the sciences and in accepted procedures of research. Clearly, decisions as to the therapeutic approach one follows appears to be made on bases other than empirical evidence. Personal beliefs, individual experiences, identification with a charismatic leader, and something approaching religious conversion may all conceivably play a role in this regard. Whatever is involved, one can expect that discussions concerning the effectiveness of psychotherapy, or of particular therapeutic approaches, may entail emotional factors as well as logical or evidential ones. In any event, let us look at some of the results that have been published on outcome in psychotherapy, keeping in mind the kinds of problems encountered in this research.

Although there were earlier published summaries of studies of outcome in psychotherapy, the one that received wide attention and stirred up a considerable amount of controversy was that published by the British psychologist, Hans Eysenck, in 1952. This article by Eysenck attempted to summarize a number of studies, including reports of psychoanalysis and of more "eclectic" types of psychotherapy, as well as reports of what he considered were two control groups that had not received formal psychotherapy. He also reanalyzed some of the data in the studies he reviewed and presented his own modified summary of these results. In essence, Eysenck reported that the results of psychoanalysis were less favorable than those secured by other forms of psychotherapy and that both sets of results were no better, if as good, as those secured by the two control groups. Eysenck also added fuel to the fire by stating that in view of the ineffectiveness of psychotherapy, training in this activity should not be included in training programs for clinical psychologists.

On the basis of the data summarized and interpreted by Eysenck, the proportion of cases judged to be improved by means of psychoanalysis ranged from 39 to 67 percent. The percentage reported to be improved for the "eclectic" psychotherapies ranged from 44 to 77 percent. These results were based on an analysis of five studies of psychoanalysis and nineteen studies of so-called eclectic psychotherapies. If the patients who terminated psychoanalytic treatment before it was judged to be completed are excluded from the calculations, the percentage of improved cases increases to an average of 66 percent, which is similar to the average of the eclectic cases. This average improvement rate, however, did not exceed the results obtained from the so-called control groups.

As might be anticipated, this publication of Eysenck's' caused a considerable uproar among psychotherapists and drew forth a number of critical rejoinders (DeCharms, Levy, and Wertheimer, 1954; Luborsky,

1954; Rosenzweig, 1954). There were a number of critical points made by these critics and others that clearly had merit. These included the following: the evaluations of outcome in the different studies were made by therapists with different goals and orientations, the patient populations were not always comparable, Eysenck had manipulated and made his own interpretation of some of the reported findings, and the control groups used by Eysenck were open to serious question since they were not really untreated control groups. One control group consisted of hospitalized "neurotics" who supposedly had not received formal psychotherapy (Landis, 1938), whereas the other group consisted of 500 patients treated by general practitioners as a result of "disability claims due to psycho-neurosis" (Denker, 1946). For such reasons, Eysenck's conclusions did not impress many psychotherapists, although they did constitute a challenge to them to provide better data in support of the view that psychotherapy is effective.

Undaunted by such criticisms, Eysenck (1961) extended his evaluations of psychotherapy with an analysis of additional studies and devoted greater attention to the results of more recent studies which used control groups. His conclusions this time were even somewhat stronger than those presented earlier, although he did have a kind word for behavior therapy. "With the single exception of the psychotherapeutic methods based on learning theory, results of published research with military and civilian neurotics, and with both adults and children, suggest that the thera-peutic effects of psychotherapy are small or nonexistent, and do not, in any demonstrable way, add to the nonspecific effects of routine medical treat-ment, or to such events as occur in the patients' everyday experience" (Eysenck, 1961, p. 720).

This evaluation was updated and published in the *International Journal of Psychiatry,* along with comments from a number of knowledgeable people in the field who represented diverse views (Eysenck, 1965, 1966). Again, there were a number of critical comments from psychoanalysts and psychotherapists who presented the view that Eysenck had overstated and biased his case, although several of the reviewers agreed that Eysenck's presentation had merit. Although it sometimes appears as if Eysenck was singlehandedly taking on the field of psychotherapy, there was no obvious and conclusive resolution of the debate. In fairness to Eysenck, it did appear as if he had marshalled a large amount of research data to support his contentions, that he had posed a significant challenge to the proponents of psychotherapy, and that he was putting his critics on the defensive. Al-though some of his analyses and conclusions could be fairly contested, in a real sense he was forcing his psychotherapeutic opponents to present data to support their views.

The next really significant response to Eysenck's appraisal came from Bergin's (1971) extensive review of the outcome literature, although the volume by Meltzoff and Kornreich (1970) also contained an extensive review of outcome studies and reached more positive conclusions than those secured by Eysenck. Bergin, among other things, decided to reappraise the earlier studies upon which Eysenck's 1952 article was based, and which were also included in his later critical reviews. A critical problem mentioned by Bergin was that of interpreting the various categories of improvement used in the different studies. One point of controversy, for example, was interpreting the categories of "improved" or "slightly improved" in the report of the Berlin Psychoanalytic Institute. While Eysenck decided, in his tabulation of results, to place one group of patients falling into his "slightly improved" group into the "unimproved" group for purposes of analysis, Bergin, after reading the original investigator's description for this category, decided to place such patients into the "improved" group. As a consequence, Bergin obtained a much higher rate of improvement in these studies than did Eysenck.

Although Bergin emphasized the ambiguities in the Berlin report, he felt that his subjective interpretations of these reults were as defensible as those of Eysenck. In his analysis of the 19 studies of eclectic therapy, however, Bergin's appraisal of outcome was very similar to that of Eysenck— 65 percent improvement as compared to 64 percent. It was primarily in the interpretation of the results of psychoanalysis that there was a marked divergence. However, Bergin also took exception to the high spontaneous remission rate posited by Eysenck. On the basis of an analysis of several studies, he found the median spontaneous remission rate to be around 30 percent. The average improvement rate of 65 percent for the eclectic psychotherapies was thus considerably above the spontaneous remission rate, although Bergin interpreted the overall effects of psychotherapy to be modest ones.

Obviously, it is very difficult to draw any definite conclusions from these results if they are open to such widely different interpretations. The writer's own view is that we are better off to pass over them and draw whatever conclusions we can from more definitive studies. This whole controversy, however, does illustrate some of the problems encountered in trying to evaluate outcome when gross categories of improvement based on therapists' judgment are used as the criteria of outcome.

A few further comments are in order before we proceed to discuss other findings on outcome in psychotherapy. As pointed out in the previous chapter, the results of outcome studies are influenced by the type of criteria used. In most of the earlier studies upon which Eysenck based his first report, the criteria were judgments of improvement, usually provided by the therapist. Such studies are questionable on that basis alone. Furthermore, there is no indication of the reliability or validity of such judgments, and in most of these early studies, no control groups were used. Consequently, although controversies based on such data may be exciting for some individuals, they provide no basis for drawing conclusions. We must look to other types of studies.

A few individuals have attempted to review only studies that appear to meet certain minimum criteria of research acceptability and to base their conclusions on such data, whereas others have tried to rate studies in terms of acceptability and to give more weight or credence to those studies with the fewest deficiencies. This seems like a reasonable procedure, even if different reviewers might vary in their evaluation of some studies. Certainly not all studies are of equal merit, and it does not appear to be a wise procedure to group together findings from studies which vary greatly in their efficacy.

The conclusions from several recent reviews (Bergin, 1971; Bergin and Lambert, 1978; Meltzoff and Kornreich, 1970) tend to be somewhat more positive than those offered by Eysenck. These generally state that psychotherapy, on an overall basis, has a modestly positive effect. Although psychotherapy does not presently appear to be a very powerful treatment, it does appear to produce some degree of positive change beyond what might be anticipated from the passing of time alone or no treatment at all. Also, some research indicates that psychotherapy may secure improvement in social effectiveness more quickly than the mere passage of time (Bergin, 1971; Frank, 1974). Although this seems to be a fair conclusion to be drawn from the research data currently available, and provides some support for practitioners and devotees of psychotherapy, it requires some elaboration. This type of conclusion is based on published accounts of research, and is an amalgamation of various types of studies and therapies. How well it would apply to a particular clinic or to a particular therapist is open to question. In addition, not all of the various psychotherapies are represented in the studies from which such a conclusion is drawn. In fact, *most* of the different forms of psychotherapy are *not* represented, since either their practitioners have not contributed at all to the available research literature or the studies published by them do not meet acceptable criteria for being included in a grouping of the relatively well-designed and controlled group of studies used. Actually, roughly three groups of therapists have contributed the bulk of the studies on outcome in psychotherapy. These are the client-centered researchers who have contributed proportionately beyond their number, the behavior therapists who appear to publish with something approaching maniacal zeal, and a third very loosely constituted group that, for want of a better designation, I will call the analytically-oriented-eclectic group. Thus overall judgments concerning the effectiveness of psychotherapy that are at least based on some sort of empirical data are, for the most part, drawn from studies of these categories of psychotherapy.

In order to make more specific the overall statement made in the previous paragraph, let us turn first to a review of some studies of outcome published by Luborsky, Singer, and Luborsky (1975). In comparing the effectiveness of various kinds of therapy, they also constructed a box score for a comparison of the results of psychotherapy in 33 studies in which some kind of control group was also utilized. The latter varied for the different studies and included "no psychotherapy," "a wait group," "minimal psychotherapy," or just hospital care without psychotherapy. In the overall comparison, 20 of the 33 studies, about 60 percent, showed psychotherapy to be significantly more effective than the control condition, in 13 of the studies there were no differences between psychotherapy and controls, and in none of the studies was the control group more effective than the group receiving psychotherapy. This analysis does suggest, therefore, that there is some positive gain to be secured from psychotherapy, although it is not always obtained. It also appears likely that the potency of psychotherapy is not particularly great, since in almost 40 percent of the cases, psychotherapy was no more effective than a no-treatment or control group that did not receive psychotherapy.

Such comparisons of the results secured in a number of different studies tell us something about the possible effects of psychotherapy, but they also leave some questions unanswered. For example, why were positive results secured in some studies but not in others? There are many possible explanations for such a finding, but at present we do not have the answers. Were the results obtained due to more effective therapists or more effective procedures in the more successful studies? Were the successful patients better prepared for psychotherapy or more potentially responsive to the treatment received? Was there a more suitable match between therapist and patient? Were the evaluations of outcome applied more stringently in some studies than in others, or were the differences in the type of control group a factor in the type of results secured? Without more adequate information or intensive analysis, one cannot provide any real answers to these as well as other questions.

Although psychotherapy does appear to produce some positive effects, it is difficult to give a precise estimate of its effectiveness. Overall results pertaining to rates of improvement in psychotherapy also may tend to mask certain kinds of more specific findings which could be of real importance in better understanding and gauging the psychotherapeutic process. In any study appraising outcome in psychotherapy, not all patients show a similar outcome or similar degree of change. For example, if such ratings as "fully recovered, very much improved, improved, no improvement, and worse" are used, the obtained ratings tend to be distributed over the whole range of categories with the smallest numbers usually occurring in the extreme categories. Thus, as in the case of one study (Avnet, 1965), approximately 17 percent and 10 percent of the cases were judged by the patients and the therapists respectively to be "recovered." The fact that the cases so designated by the two different groups of raters were not identical is of no particular concern for the present discussion. The point being made here is that even with the kinds of subjective outcome criteria used in such studies, only a small number of cases are considered to show the really marked improvement subsumed in the category of "recovered." The majority of patients generally show less than maximum improvement. This appears to be a finding of some importance.

It seems fair to say that if most psychotherapists can evaluate their own experience in a reasonably objective manner, they will secure a personal tally which resembles the pattern of results secured in studies of the type referred to above. That is, a small number of the patients treated show very impressive results, a large number show some type of positive gain, although the extent of change may be limited, a small number show very little change, and a possibly smaller number may even appear to be worse off than previously. Although many practitioners may be reluctant to agree, particularly with the last part of this statement, this seems to be supported by several recent reviews of research (Bergin and Lambert, 1978; Lambert, Bergin, and Collins, 1977; Gurman and Kniskern, 1978). To be sure, there may be individual differences among therapists in this regard, with some securing much better results than others, and there may be also some therapists who can be described as psychonoxious (Ricks, 1974). However, the pattern of results for most psychotherapists is most likely to be the one mentioned—a pattern of varying rates of success with only a relatively small number of patients showing marked improvement.

If we accept such a finding as a plausible representation of what occurs currently in psychotherapy, then certain tentative conclusions would appear to have some tenability. On the one hand, as already stated previously, psychotherapy on our overall basis has only a limited power to produce markedly significant positive change in patients. Another possible hypothesis is that our present understanding of the variables that may produce significant change is so limited that these variables come into play rather fortuitously, and thus occur in only a small percentage of the cases. If we could increase our knowledge and more readily pinpoint the significant factors which facilitate change, we might then be able to increase our therapeutic effectiveness. Another possibility is that psychotherapy (or the various psychotherapies) are effective with certain types of patients or problems primarily, and that it is these kinds of patients that give the best results. In partial support of this last hypothesis is the fact that psychotherapy has sometimes been viewed, or tried as treatment, for all types of social and behavioral ills when there was actually little basis for such widespread use. In a similar manner, most psychotherapies have tended to be viewed as "universal" therapies, that is, as good for all types of psychological disturbances. It may be that some are relatively effective with some types of disturbance and not with others. However, since all types of problems tend to be given what is essentially similar treatment, the results are quite variable. These statements are, of course, suppositions, but in the absence of definitive answers they appear to have some plausibility and merit some consideration. Possible answers to such issues or hypotheses would be of some importance in advancing our understanding of the potential effectiveness of psychotherapy.

On the basis of what has just been said, it does seem worthwhile to devote some of our research attention to more specific aspects of outcome in psychotherapy. More attention and intensive study should be devoted to those instances in which very positive results are secured. This would entail detailed study of the clients who exhibit such changes, the kinds of clinical problems presented, the particular behaviors of the therapist and of the procedures used, and the kinds of interactions which took place in therapy. As others have also suggested, it may be worthwhile to study a select group of therapists who obtain, or are reputed to obtain, unusually good therapeutic results (Bergin and Strupp, 1972). Our usual pattern in research has been to focus on group research and to lump the results of many therapists and many clients together, thus glossing over results of smaller groups or individuals which might be of some potential value. We know from research on diagnostic validity that although the overall results of a group of clinicians may be no better than chance, there is extreme variability among the clinicians studied (Chambers and Hamlin, 1957; Holtzman and Sells, 1954). A few were 100 percent accurate, whereas some were off the target 100 percent of the time. Similar studies of psychotherapists would be of interest and value. The retrospective report of Ricks (1974) of two therapists who secured very different results in a well-known children's clinic is an example of this kind of investigation that could be undertaken in a more controlled manner.

NEGATIVE EFFECTS IN PSYCHOTHERAPY

There is another aspect of outcome in psychotherapy to which we have alluded, and that has received attention primarily in recent years. This concerns the matter of possible negative outcome or deterioration in psychotherapy, and it owes much of its impetus to the work of Bergin (1963, 1966, 1971). Like many other areas of psychotherapy, it also has aroused a certain amount of controversy and debate (Braucht, 1970; Eysenck, 1967; May 1971; Rachman, 1973; Strupp, Hadley, and Gomes-Schwartz, 1977). Because of its importance for the whole matter of psychotherapy outcome, it is worth some discussion here.

Bergin (1963) first called attention to the possibility of negative outcomes when discussing the more general issue of outcome in psychotherapy. He, in particular, emphasized the fact that, although the mean gains of treated and untreated control groups were frequently similar, the variance of the former group increased and was larger than that of the control group. He interpreted these findings as indicating that while the group means were similar, more changes had occurred in the treated group but that these tended to balance out. Thus positive gains in the treated group were compensated by some losses. He labeled these latter outcomes as possible deterioration effects.

Since Bergin's earlier work, both he and others have made more systematic efforts to secure and evaluate evidence for deterioration effects in the published literature. Although some have challenged this interpretation (Rachman, 1973; Eysenck, 1967; May, 1971), Lambert, Bergin, and Collins (1977) and Bergin and Lambert (1978) have summarized the results of a number of studies that they feel demonstrate the deterioration effect in psychotherapy. Gurman and Kniskern (1978) also have reported a review of research on marital and family therapy that presents some evidence for deterioration effects in these forms of therapy. Before proceeding to examine some of the results, it can be stated that evidence for a deterioration effect in psychotherapy is not necessarily a pessimistic finding with regard to psychotherapy, as some might assume. Rather, it can also be interpreted as showing that psychotherapy does have some potential potency that may be for the better or for the worse. Any potent drug may have strong side effects or even very disastrous results if misused. A mild drug, however, may have very little effect, be it positive or negative. Thus the matter of possible deterioration effects in psychotherapy is one of some theoretical as well as practical significance.

Bergin (1971), in a review of studies with possible indications of deterioration, estimated that deterioration occurs in about five to ten percent of cases seen in psychotherapy. However, in a more recent review, the statement is made that the range of deterioration among studies is so large that no precise estimate can be given (Lambert, Bergin and Collins, 1977). In their review of the research on marital and family therapy, Gurman and Kniskern (1978) also indicate a probable deterioration rate of five to ten percent. These estimates would suggest then that a small but clinically important portion of those who undergo psychotherapy show some sort of negative outcome. Nevertheless, there is some question about what types of negative outcomes are secured, the seriousness of such outcomes, and their incidence. Bergin has used the term, deterioration, to designate all negative outcome, and this term has tended to be used by others who have been interested in this aspect of outcome in psychotherapy. However, the term deterioration has been used in the past to indicate a rather serious decline or disintegration in an individual's mental and personality functioning, and, as such, it tends to convey a serious worsening in the patient's condition. One can raise the question, therefore, if the negative outcomes secured in psychotherapy are all of such serious proportions and if the term, deterioration, is an appropriate one to use in this regard. The writer has taken exception to this terminology, as have others, and debated the matter with Bergin and Lambert at the 1975 meeting of the Society for Psychotherapy Research. However, Bergin believes that deterioration has now been used to designate negative outcome in psychotherapy and that there is no real need to substitute a new term in its place.

Although one may take exception to labeling all negative outcome as deterioration, the term has been used in this fashion by others and has served to emphasize the possibility and occurrence of negative outcome in psychotherapy. Because of the possible importance of negative effects, an intensive review of the problem was undertaken by Hans Strupp and his coworkers with support from the National Institute of Mental Health. A preliminary report of this work was presented at the 1976 meeting of the Society for Psychotherapy Research by Gomes and Armstrong (1976), and a more complete report has now been published (Strupp, Hadley, and Gomes-Schwartz, 1977). In this latter report these investigators have evaluated critically the 48 studies cited by Lambert, Bergin, and Collins (1977) in their review. Although Strupp and his collaborators have not contested the view that negative effects may occur in psychotherapy, they expressed the opinion that many, if not most, of the studies reviewed had serious deficiencies, and that it was not possible to draw any hard and fast conclusion concerning the frequency of negative effects and the determinants of such effects. They mention that the study by Sloane et al. (1975), which they consider to have the least limitation methodologically, secured relatively low rates of negative change (three to six percent) and that these rates were similar to those secured for the wait list control subjects used in that study. They also refer to the casualties reported by Lieberman, Yalom, and Miles (1973) in their study of encounter groups (nine percent) but take the view that this study was of "subjects" in encounter groups and not of patients receiving psychotherapy.

Thus although the issue of negative effects is an important one for the field of psychotherapy, the conclusions concerning it must still be held in abeyance. Tentatively, it must be admitted that negative outcomes are secured in psychotherapy and that both patient and therapist variables, singly or in interaction, may play a role in such outcomes. For example, borderline or poorly integrated patients who are exposed to certain types of therapists who are overly confrontative and lacking in empathic understanding may be particularly vulnerable. Such an hypothesis appears reasonable on the basis of some clinical reports (Strupp, Hadley, and Gomes-Schwartz, 1977), and on the basis of the study by Lieberman et al. (1973). However, it is clear that much more sound work needs to be done on this problem. Nevertheless, as Strupp, Hadley, and Gomes-Schwartz state: "This is not to suggest that negative effects in psychotherapy do not occur, but that interpretations based on the reported findings must be carefully qualified" (p. 28).

EFFICIENCY IN PSYCHOTHERAPY

There is another aspect to evaluating psychotherapy that has received very little attention, and yet it is of some social as well as theoretical and procedural importance. This concerns the efficiency of the various procedures or approaches used. In most discussions concerning outcome or effectiveness in psychotherapy, almost exclusive attention has been focused on the criteria of outcome or the types of outcome secured with little attention to the time involved. Cost effectiveness, as it were, although occasionally mentioned, has not been considered a matter of great importance. From any vantage point, however, a brief but effective therapy would be much more utilitarian than an equally effective therapy which requires a much longer period of time. Perhaps this lack of concern with efficiency is related to the fact that the dynamic and relationship therapies have traditionally assumed that psychotherapy has to be a long and involved process if it is to be effective, and this view has dominated psychotherapeutic thinking for many years in the past. In fact, because of this view, short-term or brief psychotherapies have frequently been viewed by many therapists with suspicion and have tended to be characterized as superficial therapies. It is time, however, to take a serious look at this matter and to be flexible enough to modify strongly held views when there is no adequate evidence to support them.

It is interesting that, whereas in other areas of human endeavor, including the healing professions, attempts at briefer and more efficient procedures have been eagerly sought and their discoverers have been recognized as making important contributions, such has not been the case in psychotherapy. In fact, in certain quarters, exactly the opposite is the case. It appears as if the longer psychotherapy takes, the more highly regarded it is. Whereas Freud was concerned about the fact that his analyses might run as long as 6 months or a year, the modern version appears to take from 4 to 7 years, or even longer, although accurate statistics are difficult to obtain. In the Menninger study of psychotherapy and psychoanalysis, those patients seen in psychoanalysis were seen for an average of 835 hours (Bergin and Lambert, 1978). It does seem clear that the time required for psychoanalysis and various analytically oriented therapies is at least several years in the United States, and reports of very long periods of psychotherapy ranging up to 20 years or more are appearing in published accounts (Schmideberg, 1958; Kelman, 1971). Although one might have expected that as our experience and knowledge of psychotherapy expanded, we would have been able to streamline and perfect our procedures accordingly, apparently, such has not been the case with the more traditionally insight-oriented psychotherapies. Rather, the opposite seems to have occurred.

This rather unusual situation merits further discussion and appraisal. Why would highly educated and socially oriented individuals be so critical of attempts to shorten the time required for psychotherapy? The only answer I can give is that such psychotherapists have been so strongly influenced and indoctrinated concerning the beliefs they hold about the nature of psychotherapy that they cannot readily shift their views and entertain other possibilities which appear to be diametrically opposed to them. Views about unconscious conflicts, resistance, and insight, for example, are held with strong convictions, and such views appear incompatible with any brief approach to psychotherapy. The latter types of therapy are perceived as superficial, since they do not deal either with the basic conflicts of the client or with the postulated basic features of psychotherapy. A report by Avnet (1965) of a study in the New York City area will illustrate some of the aspects of this phenomenon.

In the report by Avnet 2100 psychiatrists were invited to participate in providing treatment as part of a group health insurance project. The project was a pilot study to appraise the feasibility of providing time-limited psychotherapy as a part of group health insurance policies. Because long-term psychotherapy can be very expensive, the project limited psychotherapy, or any other treatment the psychiatrist chose to use, to 15 sessions. Regular standard fees would be paid to the psychiatrists for these services, and the psychiatrists were apparently eager to have their services included in such health insurance policies in the future. Nevertheless, 900 of the psychiatrists invited to participate did not accept the invitation. Most of these practitioners stated that they only conducted long-term therapy, that they did not engage in short-term therapy, or that they could not help anyone in a short period of time. Implicit in these statements is the belief that long-term psychotherapy is effective and that brief therapy is not.

Two other findings from the study by Avnet (1965) are also of interest. One is that when the amount of therapy provided by the insurance came to an end, further therapy was recommended by the therapist in 94 percent of the cases, reflecting their own views concerning the length of psychotherapy. Most patients, however, did not follow these recommendations. Conversely, when the psychiatrist indicated that no further treatment was recommended, this recommendation was generally followed. A second set of findings are concerned with the evaluations of the time-limited treatment provided by both patients and therapists in a follow-up study 2 years later in which 740 patients were evaluated. In 76 percent of the cases as judged by the therapists, and 81 percent of the cases as judged by the patients, definite improvement was indicated. In fact, 10.5 percent and 17 percent were judged to have "recovered" by the therapists and patients respectively. Although such judgments of improvement are not completely adequate criteria of improvement, the reported results compare most favorably with other results in the literature which have used such criteria. Even though these therapists were not overly favorable toward brief psychotherapy, three-quarters of them judged the results of such therapy to be positive.

Somewhat similar findings are reported in a study by Muench (1965) in which an attempt was made to study the possible effects of time-limited psychotherapy. In this instance, some of the therapists on the clinic staff were very hesitant to participate in a controlled study where some clients would be randomly assigned to time-limited therapy. These therapists believed it would be unfair and possibly detrimental to such clients to have their therapy arbitrarily terminated in this way. As a result, a research design was finally used in which the therapist had the right to go beyond the established time limit if he or she felt this were necessary in the individual case. The study was then carried out and compared the results achieved by three different types of therapy: brief psychotherapy, time-limited psychotherapy, and time-unlimited psychotherapy. Two objective criteria of outcome were used and the following results obtained. There were no significant differences on one measure, and on the other measure used, the brief and time-limited therapies secured significantly more positive results than did the time-unlimited therapy. Thus the briefer therapies were as effective as the longer therapy on one outcome measure, and significantly better on the other. There was another interesting result mentioned in this report. As a result of the findings secured, this particular staff of psychotherapists decided to offer only time-limited psychotherapy of 10 interviews in the future in order to better meet the needs of a larger number of individuals requiring their services. It is one of the few research projects in the field of psychotherapy where the results secured appeared to have a definite effect on practice.

There are also other reports of brief and time-limited psychotherapy that show that, on the whole, such therapies appear to be as effective as therapies that require longer periods of time. One of the earliest and best known studies was reported by Shlien and his collaborators (Shlien, 1957; Shlien, Mosak, and Dreikurs, 1962). In this study time-limited client-centered psychotherapy was compared with time-limited Adlerian and un-limited client-centered psychotherapy, as well as with a control group. A self-ideal correlation based on a Q sort was the criterion measure used. Whereas all three therapy groups showed a significant improvement over the control group, both time-limited groups equalled, or slightly exceeded, the unlimited therapy group at the end of therapy, and this improvement was maintained in a follow-up study. In this study, therefore, the time-limited therapies were judged to be more efficient in terms of time expended than was unlimited therapy.

In their review of comparative studies of psychotherapy, Luborsky et al. (1975) mention eight studies in which time-limited psychotherapy is compared with unlimited psychotherapy. According to these authors, in five of the studies no differences were secured between the two types of therapy. In two, the results favored time-limited therapy, and in one, the results favored unlimited therapy. Actually, they reviewed seven studies but gave two ratings to one study by Henry and Shlien (1958) in which the time-limited group secured a negative outcome on a TAT measure of "affect differentiation," but no differences were secured on three other measures—therapist rating of outcome, a behavioral index, and a Q sort. This was the only study to show a less favorable result for time-limited therapy, and this occurred on only one of the four outcome measures used. Thus the bulk of the evidence does not show time-limited therapy to have any poorer results than unlimited therapy.

The conclusion reached by Luborsky et al. (1975) is "that usually differences in this treatment dimension seemed to make no significant differences in treatment results." Although this conclusion appears reasonable, there is also more that can be said about it which was not emphasized, namely, that if one type of psychotherapy secures comparable results with less time, it should be considered a more efficient type of therapy. This would appear to be an obvious and tenable conclusion to draw, but surprisingly, little has been said along these lines. Part of the reason for this, as mentioned earlier, is the rather negative view that many therapists hold concerning brief therapy. A related factor is also the belief that different types of outcome are secured by the two different therapies, and that the type of outcome secured by longer term therapies is more desirable. Such a claim, however, requires more empirical support than it appears to have.

One other study that has some relevance for this problem is also worth mentioning. This was a study of outpatient psychotherapy in which a variety of outcome measures were used (Garfield, Prager, and Bergin, 1971) and were correlated with length of therapy. Although length of therapy was significantly correlated ($P < .05$) with global ratings of improvement by clients ($r = .38$), by therapists ($r = .37$), and by supervisors ($r = .36$), the correlations obtained were relatively low. Furthermore, length of therapy was *not* significantly correlated with other more independent measures of outcome such as difference scores on the MMPI, ratings of pathology based on tapes of therapy sessions, and a scale of disturbance. It is interesting that, in this study, the most positive outcomes secured were provided by the ratings of clients and therapists made at the end of therapy, and these ratings, as well as those of the supervisors, were the only criteria to be related to length of therapy. Although one can only hypothesize in a post hoc fashion, it is possible that such ratings of outcome constitute in part a justification for the effort expended, the involvement of the parties concerned, and the expectations generated.

Besides these results, there are numerous clinical reports concerning the efficacy of various types of brief, emergency, and crisis-intervention therapies that compare favorably with similar types of reports of longer and more conventional therapies (Butcher and Koss, 1978; Harris, Kalis, and Freeman, 1963, 1964; Phillips and Wiener, 1966). Although the usual limitations of such studies do not offer a sound basis of comparison, they nevertheless raise the possibility that not all individuals may require long-term psychotherapy or that it is not a feasible procedure for most individuals seeking help with a variety of psychological problems.

It is also interesting that results of time-limited brief therapy with other modalities of psychotherapy have also been quite similar to those reported for individual psychotherapy. In their review of studies of marital and family therapy, Gurman and Kniskern (1978) found essentially no difference in the results of time-limited and unlimited therapy reported for these types of therapy. One study reported better results with time-limited therapy, one found a low but positive relationship between length of therapy and outcome, and in six other studies no differences were secured in outcome between the two types of therapy. Gurman and Kniskern's conclusion consequently was: "In sum, *the evidence to date suggests that time-limited marital-family therapy is not inferior to open-ended treatment.*" (p. 879)

On the basis of many different kinds of reports it would appear to be a desirable procedure to start most patients on brief or time-limited therapy and later to decide whether some of them require additional therapy. This would save considerable therapeutic time that would then be available for working with others in need of therapy. Such procedures have been tried in several clinical settings (Harris et al., 1963, 1964; Leventhal and Weinberger, 1975) and appeared to work well. In these reports, approximately two-thirds of the cases seen were dealt with successfully with therapy that lasted about seven interviews, whereas the others were either continued in therapy or referred elsewhere. This seems like a reasonable procedure that could be studied further. What seems to be needed in any event is a more flexible and experimental attitude on the part of psychotherapists and clinical staffs to try out new possibilities and not to cling tenaciously to older views of psychotherapy. Not all new ideas will turn out to be worthwhile, and they will all need to be studied and evaluated. However, some therapists appear to have been so strongly indoctrinated by their previous training or personal therapy that they are extremely resistant to any ideas that imply a change in their approach. The writer has been impressed many times by this phenomenon when he has talked to different groups of psychotherapists both in the United States and Europe. Individuals engaged in long-term psychotherapy convey the impression that any type of briefer therapy is superficial and inferior, and that they will not settle for what they see as lesser goals for therapy. It is as if, to again use a medical analogy, everyone who has a psychological problem has to undergo the equivalent of major surgery. No lesser treatments will be considered! Certainly, it is to be hoped that we will increasingly learn to adapt the treatment to the patient, and that briefer therapies will be used more frequently when they appear to serve as well as longer forms of therapy. In essence, considerations of the effectiveness of treatments must also be supplemented by considerations involving the efficiency of treatments.

SOME CONCLUDING COMMENTS

Although in this chapter we have discussed the rather general issue of the effectiveness and efficiency of psychotherapy, many serious appraisers of this topic have rightfully pointed out that no really adequate answer to this problem can be secured. The main reason is that the question, "Is psychotherapy effective?" is considered to be a poor question and, consequently, can only receive poor answers. Unhappily, this appears to be a reasonable criticism of the situation, and the present writer has indulged in attempting to provide some response to this question because the question, poor as it is, is constantly raised, and various attempts have been made to respond to it. Nevertheless, one must also respond to the reality of the situation.

As was mentioned early in this volume, psychotherapy is not some clearly defined and uniform process. Rather, there are many diverse types of psychotherapies and psychotherapeutic procedures that are provided by a diversity of psychotherapists to individuals with a wide variety of problems. Most of the great variety of psychotherapies have not conducted any systematic studies on the effectiveness of their therapies, nor reported any empirical results on the outcome of their procedures. The fact that practitioners follow certain schools of thought and use certain procedures appears to be primarily a matter of faith or personal judgment. In any event, there is no basis for any objective conclusion concerning the effectiveness of most forms of psychotherapy. The results of relatively systematic studies of outcome in psychotherapy come largely from studies of client-centered psychotherapists, behavior therapists, and a more heterogeneous group that include eclectic and dynamically oriented psychotherapists. Thus any general results attributed to the effectiveness of psychotherapy would appear to be based largely on studies conducted by therapists representing these approaches to psychotherapy.

However, even keeping this delineation in mind, it is still not a very feasible undertaking to attempt to provide answers to very general and poorly formulated questions. Even two practitioners who claim to be adherents of the same school of psychotherapy may actually employ different procedures or function differently in their actual interactions with various clients. Therapists also may perform differently with different types of clients and with different kinds of clinical problems. Thus even to know that a certain type of therapy, or a specific therapist, is successful with 70 percent of the cases seen is not a fully satisfactory state of affairs. What is required is a more comprehensive knowledge of why certain results are secured in certain instances and not in others.

In other words, in order to secure better answers to questions about psychotherapy we must ask better and more precisely stated questions.

Only after this has occurred can we proceed to attempt to devise improved research on the issue of the effectiveness of psychotherapy. To be more to the point, we have to formulate our inquiries more along the following lines: What types of therapeutic procedures will work best with clients with given types of problems administered by what kind of therapists? Instead of dealing with psychotherapy as one uniform process, we have to be concerned with specific therapeutic strategies for specific kinds of clients with certain kinds of therapists. The psychotherapies as practiced today are for the most part seen as universal therapies. Be it client-centered therapy, analytically oriented therapy, or some other kind of therapy, the assumption is made that the particular kind of therapeutic approach is universally suited and beneficial to all individuals with all kinds of adjustment difficulties, with the possible exception of severely disturbed psychotic individuals. This view appears to be an unrealistic and outmoded one that should be discarded. Instead, we must try to individualize our therapeutic procedures and systematically investigate their effectiveness for particular kinds of problems. Only after such an approach will we be anywhere near the position of having some techniques and procedures which have some tested validity for specific problems and which can be selected for appropriate use. At present, the best we can say is that there appear to be some positive gains which accrue from the various applications of the diverse therapeutic approaches now in current use, as well as a much smaller number of negative effects. Furthermore, we are not at all sure as to what variables are responsible for producing the various results secured. Clearly, psychotherapists, as well as the public to be served, cannot be content with the state of affairs that presently exists. The history of medical therapeutics, as well as the history of placebo effects (Shapiro and Morris, 1978), suggests that we are at a relatively early stage of development in psychotherapy, and much more will have to be done before we have developed procedures that have clearly demonstrated therapeutic power and effectiveness. Being fully aware of the problem is the first stage in attempting to overcome it.

REFERENCES

Avnet, H. H. How effective is short-term therapy? In L. R. Wolberg (Ed.), *Short-term psychotherapy*. New York: Grune & Stratton, 1965.

Bergin, A. E. The effects of psychotherapy: Negative results revisited. *Journal of Counseling Psychology*, 1963, *10*, 244–250.

Bergin, A. E. Some implications of psychotherapy research for therapeutic practice. *Journal of Abnormal Psychology*, 1966, *71*, 235–246.

Bergin, A. E. The evaluation of therapeutic outcomes. In A. E. Bergin and S. L. Garfield (Eds.), *Handbook of psychotherapy and behavior change: An empirical analysis*. New York: Wiley, 1971, pp. 299–344.

Bergin, A. E. and Lambert, M. J. The evaluation of therapeutic outcomes. In S. L. Garfield and A. E. Bergin (Eds.), *Handbook of psychotherapy and behavior change*, 2nd ed. New York: Wiley, 1978.

Bergin, A. E. and Strupp, H. H. *Changing frontiers in the science of psychotherapy*. Chicago: Aldine, 1972.

Braucht, G. N. The deterioration effect: A reply to Bergin. *Journal of Abnormal Psychology*, 1970, *75*, 293–299.

Butcher, J. N. and Koss, M. P. Research on brief and crisis-oriented therapies. In S. L. Garfield and A. E. Bergin (Eds.), *Handbook of psychotherapy and behavior change*, 2nd ed. New York: Wiley, 1978.

Chambers, G. S. and Hamlin, R. The validity of judgments based on "blind" Rorschach records. *Journal of Consulting Psychology*, 1957, *21*, 105–109.

DeCharms, R., Levy, J., and Wertheimer, M. A note on attempted evaluations of psychotherapy. *Journal of Clinical Psychology*, 1954, *10*, 233–235.

Denker, P. G. Results of treatment of psychoneuroses by the general practitioner. *New York State Journal of Medicine*, 1946, *46*, 2164–2166.

Eysenck, H. J. The effects of psychotherapy: An evaluation. *Journal of Consulting Psychology*, 1952, *16*, 319–324.

Eysenck, H. J. The effects of psychotherapy. In H. J. Eysenck (Ed.), *Handbook of abnormal psychology*. New York: Basic Books, 1961.

Eysenck, H. J. The effects of psychotherapy. *International Journal of Psychiatry*, 1965, *1*, 97–178.

Eysenck, H. J. *The effects of psychotherapy*. New York: International Science Press, 1966.

Eysenck, H. J. The nonprofessional psychotherapist. *International Journal of Psychiatry,* 1967, *3*, 150–153.

Frank, J. D. Therapeutic components of psychotherapy. A 25-year progress report of research. *The Journal of Nervous and Mental Disease*, 1974, *159*, 325–342.

Garfield, S. L., Prager, R. A., and Bergin, A. E. Evaluation of outcome in psychotherapy. *Journal of Consulting and Clinical Psychology*, 1971, *37*, 307–313.

Gomes, B. and Armstrong, S. H. Deterioration effects in psychotherapy: Once more revisited. Paper presented at the Seventh Annual Meeting, Society for Psychotherapy Research, San Diego, Calif., June, 1976.

Gurman, A. S. and Kniskern, D. P. Research on marital and family therapy. In S. L. Garfield and A. E. Bergin (Eds.), *Handbook of psychotherapy and behavior change*, 2nd ed. New York, Wiley, 1978.

Harris, M. R., Kalis, B., and Freeman, E. Precipitating stress: An approach to brief therapy. *American Journal of Psychotherapy* 1963, *17*, 465–471.

Harris, M. R., Kalis, B. L., and Freeman E. H. An approach to short-term psychotherapy. *Mind,* 1964, *2,* 198–206.

Henry, W. E. and Shlien, J. Affective complexity and psychotherapy: Some comparisons of time limited and unlimited treatment. *Journal of Projective Techniques,* 1958, *22,* 153–162.

Holtzman, W. H. and Sells, S. B. Prediction of flying ability by clinical analysis of test protocols. *Journal of Abnormal and Social Psychology,* 1954, *49,* 485–490.

Kelman, H. *Helping people. Karen Horney's psychoanalytical approach.* New York: Science House, 1971.

Lambert, M. J., Bergin, A., and Collins, J. Therapist-induced deterioration in psychotherapy. In A. Gurman and A. Razin (Eds.), *Effective psychotherapy. A handbook of research.* New York: Pergamon, 1977.

Landis, C. Statistical evaluation of psychothererapeutic methods. In S. E. Hinsie (Ed.), *Concepts and problems of psychotherapy.* London: Heinemann, 1938.

Levanthal, T. and Weinberger, G. Evaluation of a large-scale brief therapy program for children. *American Journal of Orthopsychiatry,* 1975, *45,* 119–133.

Lieberman, M. A., Yalom, I. D., and Miles, M. B. *Encounter groups: First facts.* New York: Basic Books, 1973.

Luborsky, L. A note on Eysenck's article, "The effects of psychotherapy: An evaluation." *British Journal of Psychology,* 1954, *45,* 129–131.

Luborsky, L., Singer, B., and Luborsky, L. Comparative studies of psychotherapies. *Archives of General Psychiatry,* 1975, *32,* 995–1008.

May, P. R. A. For better or for worse? Psychotherapy and variance change: A critical review of the literature. *The Journal of Nervous and Mental Disease,* 1971, *152,* 184–192.

Meltzoff, J. and Kornreich, M. *Research in psychotherapy.* New York: Atherton Press, 1970.

Muench, G. A. An investigation of the efficacy of time-limited psychotherapy. *Journal of Counseling Psychology,* 1965, *12,* 294–299.

Phillips, E. L. and Wiener, D. N. *Short-Term psychotherapy and structural behavior change.* New York: McGraw-Hill, 1966.

Rachman, S. J. The effects of psychological treatment. In H. Eysenck (Ed.), *Handbook of abnormal psychology.* New York: Basic Books, 1973.

Ricks, D. F. Supershrink: Method of a therapist judged successful on the basis of adult outcomes of adolescent patients. In D. F. Ricks, M. Roff, and A. Thomas (Eds.), *Life history research in psychopathology,* Minneapolis: University of Minnesota, 1974.

Rosenzweig, S. A transevaluation of psychotherapy—a reply to Hans Eysenck. *Journal of Abnormal and Social Psychology,* 1954, *49,* 298–304.

Schmideberg, M. Values and goals in psychotherapy. *The Psychiatric Quarterly,* 1958, *32,* 333–365.

Shapiro, A. K. and Morris, L. A. The placebo effect in medical and psychological therapies. In S. L. Garfield and A. E. Bergin (Eds.), *Handbook of psychotherapy and behavior change,* 2nd ed. New York: Wiley, 1978.

Shlien, J. M. Time-limited psychotherapy: An experimental investigation of practical values and theoretical implications. *Journal of Counseling Psychology,* 1957, *4,* 318–323.

Shlien, J. M., Mosak, H. H., and Dreikurs, R. Effect on time limits: A comparison of two psychotherapies. *Journal of Counseling Psychology,* 1962, *9,* 31–34.

Sloane, R. B., Staples, F. R., Cristol, A. H., Yorkston, N. J., and Whipple, K. *Psychotherapy versus behavior therapy.* Cambridge: Harvard University Press, 1975.

Strupp, H. H., Hadley, S. W., and Gomes-Schwartz, B. *Psychotherapy for better or worse: The problem of negative effects.* New York: Jason Aronson, 1977.

CHAPTER 13

Psychotherapy:
A Concluding Note

In the preceding pages the author has attempted to present his views of psychotherapy and the current psychotherapeutic scene. As a practitioner, teacher and, at times, research worker in the field of psychotherapy for over 30 years, my views have, of course, been influenced by my own experience, the observations of others, and by serious attempts to keep up with the vast literature in this field. Some readers, of course, will not agree with my observations and formulations and may view them primarily as representations of the author's biases and narrowness of point of view, or, perhaps, as a superficial approach to psychotherapy. Apart from the evident inadequacies of the author's attempt to order and integrate his views, for which the shortcomings naturally accrue to the author, there may be other reasons as well. As has been mentioned several times, views and allegiances concerning psychotherapy tend to be held on bases other than scientific evidence, and it is not an easy matter to modify views that are held on the basis of faith and related convictions. Nevertheless, in the long run, unsupported statements and assumptions must be challenged and attempts must be made to secure answers and to modify procedures on the basis of empirically derived data.

In spite of what may at times be viewed by some readers as a rather pessimistic appraisal of the status of psychotherapy at this time, the author actually views the possible progress for psychotherapy in the future quite optimistically. Along with the proliferation of psychotherapeutic approaches, and what at times appears to be an emphasis on nonintellectual and noncritical views in psychotherapy, there have been a number of positive and encouraging developments. In addition to a significant increase in the amount of research on psychotherapy, there has also been a greater awareness and acknowledgment of the importance of research in this field. It is fair to state that the great bulk of research and the critical appraisal of psychotherapy have occurred in the last 25 to 30 years—a relatively short period of time. Furthermore, there has been evident a greater degree of sophistication in research in psychotherapy in the last 10 years or so, and most of the sounder studies have appeared during this period of time. Certainly, investigators are much more aware of the problems which need to be considered in planning acceptable research in this area. These are all important signs of progress and augur hope for the future, although much remains to be done.

There has also been evident in recent years a greater desire for experimentation and innovation in psychotherapy, and attempts have been made to devise programs and procedures to better meet the needs of hitherto neglected problems and segments of our society (Butcher and Koss, 1978; Kazdin, 1978; Lorion, 1978). A number of such attempts have also been carried out in such a manner as to provide some kind of systematic evaluative data on their possible effectiveness. As was alluded to earlier in this book, a certain amount of research has been carried out with reference to preparing the patient for psychotherapy. This work was stimulated by the findings reported on a premature termination, particularly with lower class individuals. In one study, a "Role Induction Interview" was developed to provide patients with appropriate expectations concerning psychotherapy in order to facilitate the process and outcome of therapy. The group that received this training significantly exceeded a control group of therapy patients on 6 of 16 criterion measures used, including that of attendance at scheduled therapy sessions (Hoehn-Saric et al., 1964). Strupp and Bloxom (1973) developed a role-induction film for lower-class patients and compared it with a role-induction interview, and with a control film. The patients who received the role-induction film and the induction interview showed significantly greater gains in therapy than did the control group. Holmes and Urie (1975) also reported that children who were given a therapy preparation interview dropped out of therapy significantly less than a control group of children. More detailed accounts of such work are available elsewhere (Garfield, 1978; Heitler, 1976).

Such occurrences are also positive indications of commendable changes. Even the rash of newer approaches can be seen as manifestations of giving up older allegiances to unproductive procedures and trying out newer ones in the hope of increasing one's therapeutic effectiveness, although the lack of any efforts at systematic appraisal of these new procedures does not inspire much confidence in such ventures.

There are other developments currently taking place in the field of psychotherapy that also appear promising and that have been alluded to earlier in this book. The decrease in commitment to a single theoretical orientation with the resulting openness to other formulations and possibilities is one such manifestation. The results of the survey by Garfield and Kurtz (1976), that over half of the clinical psychologists surveyed indicated an "eclectic" preference, is evidence of such a change. Also, an additional study of a sample of these eclectic psychologists indicated that their preference for an eclectic orientation was related to their view that one psychotherapeutic approach was not adequate for working with the wide variety of problems they encountered (Garfield and Kurtz, 1977). Many of them also indicated that different procedures were required for different types of cases, and thus they could not limit themselves to one approach. This, of course, reflects a point of view and an emphasis that is similar to that advocated by the present writer. Clearly, individualizing psychotherapy to meet the needs of a particular client appears to be a necessary and sound procedure, and one which requires the use of techniques and procedures which are not limited to any one school of thought. Although considerable work is required to enable us to know which procedures will work best with what types of individuals and problems, a recognition and acceptance of such a view is a step in the right direction.

Another development noted previously that also appears to offer promise is the appearance of cognitive behavior therapy (Mahoney and Arnkoff, 1978). Although a quite recent development, it has been represented by a number of different therapeutic approaches and procedures, and although all of them may not turn out to be particularly effective, this development may represent a significant change in what many saw as a somewhat parochial school of psychotherapy—behavior therapy. This enlargement and flexibility of orientation, manifested within a relatively short period of time by followers of a young and vigorous approach to psychotherapy and behavior change, is an unusual and potentially important development. Whether or not it really portends a beginning realization of the limitations of a single approach and the possible rapprochement of some of the different emphases in psychotherapy remains to be seen. However, it is a step in this direction and, therefore, a very welcome development. Furthermore, many of the individuals involved in this development are very able, active, and energetic researchers, and one can anticipate continued contributions from them in the future.

There are also other positive developments which hold some promise for the future. Besides some evident loosening of a strict adherence to one school of thought on the part of psychotherapists and a willingness to admit that other approaches also may have some value for certain kinds of cases, publications by well-known leaders in the field of psychotherapy have appeared that convey a more open attitude to developments outside their own orientation and that even question some of the fundamental postulates of their own orientation. Strupp (1975, 1978), for example, although identified for much of his career with psychoanalytic views, has questioned some of the basic tenets of psychoanalysis and psychoanalytic therapy, including the nature of the therapeutic influence in psychoanalysis and the importance of interpretation, as well as perceiving some common elements among psychoanalysis and among psychotherapy generally. Several persons have also made some attempts to bring analytic and behavioral procedures together and to consider some synthesis of these two divergent procedures (Birk and Brinkley-Birk, 1974; Marmor, 1971, 1973; Wachtel, 1977). One paper by Marmor (1971), a psychoanalytically oriented therapist, is a well reasoned discussion of the need for dynamically oriented therapists and behavior therapists to be aware of the overlap and similarities between their two forms of psychotherapy, as well as the need to broaden perspectives so that the most appropriate procedures available are selected for use with particular patients. While pointing out some of the oversimplifications evident in behavioral explanations of the psychotherapeutic process, Marmor also stresses that the "process in both approaches is best explicable in terms of current theories of learning which go beyond simple conditioning explanations and encompass central cognitive processes also" (1971, p. 28). Thus there would appear to be a somewhat similar emphasis in the view expounded by this dynamically oriented psychiatrist and that being advanced by the cognitive behavioral psychologists. Such evidence of a broadening of views by psychotherapists coming from very different theoretical orientations and training is indeed a hopeful sign that narrow sectarian views of psychotherapy may be giving way in some quarters at least to a more comprehensive or eclectic perspective.

Another example of a similar convergence on an aspect of the psychotherapeutic process is the interest and research on the problem of expectancies in psychotherapy, a topic discussed in an earlier chapter. Although first discussed by Frank (Frank et al., 1959; Frank, 1961) and others (Goldstein, 1962) in relation to more traditional approaches in psychotherapy, the role of expectancies in psychotherapy has received considerable attention by behavior therapists in recent years. Several critical reviews of this area of research have been published recently by behaviorists (Lick and Bootzin, 1975; Morgan, 1973; Perotti and Hopewell, 1976), as well as others (Wilkins, 1971, 1973), and the methodological deficiencies evident in a great deal of this research have been discussed at length. The most recent view by Kazdin and Wilcoxon (1976), however, suggests that expectancy effects may actually play a large role in the positive therapeutic results secured by means of systematic desensitization. Regardless of what conclusions are finally reached concerning the role which expectancies play in behavior therapy, the point being made here is that behavior therapists have not only been sensitive to the possible importance of therapeutic variables postulated by therapists outside of their particular school, but they have proceeded in characteristic fashion to investigate them rather rigorously.

Other examples of possible rapprochement and convergence of viewpoints in the field of psychotherapy can also be mentioned. An interesting presentation has been published by Spanos, Moor, and Barber (1973) that examines possible common denominators between hypnosis and behavior therapy. Four specific sets of variables are mentioned as being present in both of these forms of therapy: motivational variables, attitudinal and expectancy variables, the specific working of suggestions or instructions, and circumscribed cognitive processes such as goal-directed imagining occurring in response to the suggestions or directions. These authors also suggest that a free flow of information between these two approaches to therapy could lead to a mutual theoretical enhancement of both. A similar plea for the recognition of similarities between hypnotherapeutic and behavioral methods and the enhancement of both procedures by such recognition has also been made by Weitzenhoffer (1972).

Behavior therapists, as already noted, have also been sensitive to factors other than strictly traditional learning variables. Brown (1967) has also published an interesting analysis of Joseph Wolpe's own behavior in conducting therapy and pointed out the possible influence of Wolpe's own personality and interactions with the patient, as well as the cognitive aspects of his therapy. As Brown points out, "The behavior therapy of Joseph Wolpe is a multifaceted therapeutic tool consisting of his personality, his rapport with patients, his skilled verbal responses, and his specific behavior techniques. To concentrate on the last factor alone produces a disturbing bias" (Brown, 1967, p. 857). Brown (1972) has gone on to describe the various procedures that go to make up what he calls broad spectrum psychotherapy which includes the relationship between therapist and patient, management techniques, behavior therapy, and cognitive therapy. Lazarus (1971, 1973) is an example of a well-known behavior therapist who has broadened his earlier views and procedures to encompass a broad spectrum behavior therapy which also pays attention to cognitive, relationship and other variables.

Several other writers have commented on both the divergencies between the various schools of psychotherapy and the possible similarities and convergencies apparent in these approaches (Patterson, 1967; Tseng and McDermott, 1975). Although Priest (1972) is less hopeful about a possible convergence of points of view, he does feel that a confrontation between approaches might lead thoughtful individuals to examine the evidence for each approach, which is at least a positive possibility.

Thus there appear to be several indications of possible developments among a number of psychotherapists of different theoretical persuasions that could lead to a better integration of procedures and orientations, to less doctrinaire practices, and to some advancement of the field. There also appears to be a clearer recognition of the communalities among the various psychotherapies, as well as of the need to treat specific problems in the most effective and efficient manner possible. This is certainly a much desired development that could do a great deal to spark real progress, particularly if such attempts at the modification of practice are accompanied by systematic attempts to evaluate whatever new procedures are devised and tried out.

In addition to what appears to be a possible ecumenical movement within psychotherapy for less sectarianism, there are other positive indications, mentioned previously, of a greater willingness to break away from older traditions which have dominated the field for many years and which have hindered experimentation and innovation. Whereas a little over 30 years ago there was a very negative reaction to the work of Alexander and French (1946), which presented an approach to a briefer psychoanalytically oriented psychotherapy, today one encounters a very different situation. Not only are some analysts aware of developments within behavior therapy, but as noted, some are even pointing to the value of such procedures and for the need to broaden one's approach. In addition, there have been numerous reports by a variety of individuals of attempts to offer briefer therapies in the hope of meeting long neglected social needs (Bellak and Small, 1965; Harris, Kalis and Freeman, 1963, 1964; Lorion, 1978; Butcher and Koss, 1978). Besides such innovative attempts, there have also been efforts to provide therapy when it is required, to do away with long waiting lists, to prepare patients for therapy, to decrease premature termination, to implement programs for very disturbed individuals, and to devise procedures for a wide variety of specific problems such as obesity, hyperactivity, learning difficulties, family conflict, and the like (Garfield and Bergin, 1978; Kazdin and Wilson, 1978). Although not all of these innovative efforts have been fully successful, such developments are noteworthy. They indicate the initiative of a number of psychotherapists to take a new look at problems, and to try to develop more effective procedures to cope with them. It is this manifestation of experimentation and the desire to deal creatively with problems, which is the refreshing and encouraging aspect of the changes which have been taking place in recent years. Thirty years ago, it would have been impossible to predict the developments which have actually occurred.

Consequently, although one currently cannot make overly strong claims concerning the effectiveness of various psychotherapies, one need not necessarily be unduly pessimistic. There are a number of trends evident today which at least offer some promise and prospect for potential progress in the future—and most of these are of fairly recent origin. This, of course, is not to say that everything in the future appears unusually promising, for such an inference is not obviously warranted. Before we conclude this chapter, we will also discuss some other problems that are with us today, and that probably will continue into the relatively near future. Nevertheless, many positive changes have occurred and there are clear possibilities for additional changes inherent in the current scene.

SOME REMAINING PROBLEMS

Although there are many encouraging trends discernible in the field of psychotherapy, there are also a number of problems which remain. Besides the continuing need for more research leading to a greater specification of the kinds of therapeutic procedures required for the most effective treatment of the wide variety of psychological problems presented by clients, there are several others. One concerns the broad issue of who shall provide psychotherapeutic services. Another concerns the necessary qualifications for the psychotherapist, and a related one has to do with the proper training of those who practice psychotherapy. As pointed out in Chapter Four, there are many unsettled issues in this domain, and there do not appear to be any easy solutions. These are also problem areas which are found in other countries besides the United States.

Because of the way psychotherapy has evolved over the years, there is no recognized profession of psychotherapy that sets up and regulates the standards and qualifications for its practice. Instead we have a number of separate recognized professions, as well as other groups, which engage in some type of psychotherapeutic practice. Professional standards, training requirements, and codes of ethics are thus regulated by the separate professions, and psychotherapy constitutes just one of the activities of the established professions. In spite of some attempts to consider the setting up of a distinctive and separate profession of psychotherapy (Kubie, 1955, 1971; Holt, 1971), little progress toward this objective has been attained, and its ultimate success does not seem very likely, for reasons which have already been discussed previously. The only real hope is for the setting up of appropriate standards by the established professions, by adequate policing within these professions, by careful peer reviews, and, hopefully in the future, by some sort of interdisciplinary attempts at setting up procedures for examinations and periodic appraisals of those engaged in practicing psychotherapy. Although the latter development may appear to be a somewhat utopian goal, it is not completely impossible, particularly if some of the hoped for developments in psychotherapeutic procedures do indeed take place.

Progress in the identification of the necessary personal requisites of psychotherapists for effective psychotherapy will also depend on renewed research attempts to relate such attributes to positive outcome in psychotherapy. We must move beyond merely listing the ideal characteristics of the psychotherapist to studying what kind of personal qualities and interactions are positively related to outcome. Furthermore, successful completion of training programs that include psychotherapy as an important part of the program should be based on clear demonstrations of skill and successful outcome measured in some objective manner. Anything less than this leads primarily to the perpetuation of the supervisor's biases, and a certification of adequacy which is based on criteria other than psychotherapeutic competence. There will also have to be a clearer recognition by all of the established professions that include psychotherapy as one of their main functions of the fact that individuals who do not demonstrate a clear competence in psychotherapy must not be graduated or certified as possessing these skills. This objective will not be easy to accomplish because each of the professions is made up of skills and knowledge besides those pertaining to psychotherapy. Consequently, an individual who is bright and otherwise capable, will usually not be held back because of inadequate or deficient skills in psychotherapy. The hope is that such individuals will engage in other professional functions and not in psychotherapy, but this does not always follow, and there are no current procedures for handling such a problem. However, a problem it certainly is, and each of the recognized mental health professions has an obligation to the public at large to do something about it. Generally, a bright graduate student or psychiatric resident who has little apparent aptitude for psychotherapy will be allowed to complete his or her program and to engage in the practice of psychotherapy unless the person is grossly psychotic.

There are also problems of individuals who are not members of the established mental health professions, but who engage in various kinds of psychotherapeutic activities. Because there is no clear-cut and universally accepted definition of psychotherapy, and also because it is very difficult to delimit psychotherapy from other kinds of genuine and positive human relationships, it probably will not be possible to exercise control over all possible interactions which may resemble psychotherapy, and which possibly may be therapeutic—and this is not necessarily to be decried. However, in the more formal treatment and care of those who seek psychological treatment, there are some features which deserve comment. Do all individuals who engage in psychotherapy need to be those who have M.D.'s or Ph.D.'s after their names? Although it is not easy for most professional psychotherapists to give an objective answer to this question, it is a perfectly reasonable question, and the answer is best provided by research. Although not a great deal of research has been done on this matter, what research has been done does suggest that psychotherapists do not necessarily have to go through current professional programs to become competent therapists, nor that long periods of training are required (Durlak, 1979). The experimental program devised by Margaret Rioch and her collaborators at the National Institute for Mental Health to train "middleage" housewives to become psychotherapists is one source of data (Rioch, 1967; Rioch, Elkes, and Flint, 1965). These housewives received the equivalent of one year of intensive training in psychotherapy, spread over a period of 2 years, and became the most intensively studied and evaluated group of psychotherapists ever. In terms of a variety of criteria, they performed at least as well as the average professional psychotherapist, even as judged by professional colleagues. In fact, even psychiatrists rated them as performing as well as the average psychologist or social worker, although not quite as well as the average psychiatrist! The study currently being conducted by Strupp (1977) and his colleagues of trained professional therapists and untrained therapists suggests surprisingly little difference in outcome between the two groups of therapists. This is a most intriguing state of affairs, and if these preliminary results are maintained and confirmed, we shall have to take a closer look at what kind of therapist variables are important in psychotherapy.

To the extent that individuals with certain personal qualities, but less than full professional qualifications, can perform satisfactorily as psychotherapists, serious questions can be raised concerning the current modes of training and entry into the practice of psychotherapy. In the light of such findings, we will not be seen as serving the public's interest by attempts to be overly restrictive in terms of who can function in a psychotherapeutic role. With the current needs for services and the relatively high cost of such services, restrictions concerning the practice of psychotherapy which cannot be strongly supported by empirical evidence will be seen correctly as the manifestation of a guildist orientation. At some point, this issue will have to be faced and handled appropriately. In clinical settings where adequate supervision from competent and experienced psychotherapists is available, there should be no real difficulty in utilizing nonprofessional therapists who have received some training and have been screened as being potentially capable therapists. The real problem is one of maintaining adequate standards so that the individual's performance as a psychotherapist is adequately evaluated in terms of adequate outcome criteria, and as already mentioned, this applies to professional therapists as well. Until adequate procedures for periodic appraisal of psychotherapists generally are developed, such nonprofessional therapists would be restricted to appropriate clinical settings with adequate supervision.

Another aspect of providing psychotherapeutic services that is already evident is the matter of accountability in providing such services. Many clinics supported by public funds are increasingly being asked to provide some indication that their services are in effect serving the function that they are supposed to be serving. In essence, are these services or treatments effective? Are programs for delinquents, alcoholics, drug addicts, and the like actually effective in meeting their stated aims? Do treatment programs for disturbed children help in preventing later adjustment problems?

What appears to be asked for increasingly is evidence that programs and attempts at treatment are really effective and deserving of the support they have received—and most clinical operations have been deficient in providing adequate data on such questions. Most institutions will provide various kinds of information such as number of clients seen, number of treatments given, average length of stay, number of referrals made, and the like, but generally will not make any systematic attempts to appraise the adequacy of their services. Much more could be done toward this end with comparatively little extra effort, but it has usually not been done. With a little planning, most clinics could develop forms which would allow them to collect some basic data systematically which could be used in attempts to better evaluate the services they are providing. Such forms could provide data which would indicate the frequency of missed therapy interviews, the number of patients seen for specific lengths of time, the extent of early termination, etc. Such data could also provide some information on how different therapists perform, as well as information about the performance patterns of different groups of patients. Standard rating forms for evaluation of therapy by therapists and patients would at least provide somewhat better information than is usually available in the case files. Furthermore, such data gathering might also help to focus attention on possible problems such as premature termination or difficulties with certain types of patients, as well as stimulating possible interest in the staff to initiate some potential research projects arising out of these preliminary investigations. All staff members should be interested in the effectiveness of their psychotherapeutic work and in its evaluation. Ideally, they should also have some interest in improving the quality of their work.

Another aspect of psychotherapy that needs greater attention concerns the matter of training. Although it is difficult to make any really adequate appraisal of this area, the impression one gets is of a somewhat loosely organized or haphazard system of didactic and practical training, depending upon the local resources available. A certain amount of it is also sectarian in that some training centers only provide training in a particular type of psychotherapy. How adequate the training an individual secures is thus frequently a matter of chance. In addition, in many situations a supervisor is not selected on the basis of his or her proficiency as a teacher or as a psychotherapist, but merely on the basis of his/her position on the staff which is providing the training.

Besides the importance of utilizing adequate outcome in psychotherapy as a criterion of the efficacy of training, many other steps need to be taken to improve the training of would-be psychotherapists. The first would be to select teachers and supervisors who themselves have clearly demonstrated competence in the activity which they are to teach others, instead of selecting people who are available or who are merely "experienced" psychotherapists. In terms of prevailing practices, this would be a rather revolutionary change. However, something along this line needs to be done if we are to improve existing standards of practice as well as teaching. Otherwise mediocrity, or worse, gets passed on from the teachers and supervisors to their apprenticed learners. A second prerequisite would be to enlarge the techniques and approaches which are taught in order that the training be broadened, and that what amounts to sectarian indoctrination be diminished. Another emphasis that needs to be incorporated in psychotherapy training programs is the importance of evaluating the effectiveness of one's own clinical work, as well as of the clinical center as a functioning unit. Evaluation and research must be viewed as basic parts of one's professional responsibility and not as something which is separate from the actual carrying out of psychotherapy. Research appraisal should not be seen as something that only research specialists do, but as something which is required of all participants in order to provide feedback on what is being done and ultimately to improve the level of service.

Finally, in training, adequate emphasis should be placed on the actual operations and interactions which occur in psychotherapy, and not primarily on theoretical formulations and speculations. Anyone who has sat in or participated in clinical case conferences should be aware of the speculations and flights of fantasy which occur in such meetings with little regard for facts or data. Speculations tend to be treated as facts, and there appears to be little awareness of the amazing range of interpretations that are offered by the various participants, some of which are not only far removed from the actual clinically reported events, but which can neither be verified nor rejected. Reports by therapists of what took place in psychotherapy should be replaced by taped recordings of actual sessions so that the perceptions and interpretations of the therapist can be separated from the actual behaviors which occurred. The availability of video equipment for training in psychotherapy allows for an improvement of training so that the operations of therapy can be grasped more readily, and the modeling of appropriate behaviors more easily accomplished. A number of innovative uses of such equipment have already been made, although many of them have been limited to a particular orientation (Garfield, 1977).

CONCLUDING COMMENTS

A few final words can be added in closing. Psychotherapy has developed from a number of different sources over a period of years and has gradually come to be recognized as a group of procedures and practices devised to help people with a variety of problems encountered in their daily lives. At different times it has been practiced in different ways and under different auspices. A variety of individuals and professions have offered psychotherapeutic services in a variety of social and cultural contexts ranging from priests, shamans, and witch doctors to physicians, psychologists, psychoanalysts, trainers, and even "quacks" (Frank, 1973; Kiev, 1964). It would appear that people have had a need to confide in others, to talk over problems, to receive advice and suggestions, and even to adhere to certain rituals or modes of treatment. Not only during the comparative present, but even in more remote periods of time, there were different schools of psychotherapy, although they were not so designated, and they differed from those of the present day. Most of these forms of therapy apparently also claimed to be effective, and the successful healing procedures were passed on to a group of loyal devotees and disciples.

It seems likely that a number of these earlier "psychotherapeutic" systems utilized some of the same common, and even some of the specific, factors which appear to be operative in most current psychotherapies (Frank, 1973; Torrey, 1972). Later psychotherapies have followed in the path of some of these earlier forerunners, although they have cloaked their procedures with different formulations. To be sure, there have been some new and unique procedures developed, and there is currently more awareness of the possible factors operating in psychotherapy, as well as more sophisticated evaluations of the effectiveness of psychotherapy. Although what have been termed "placebo effects" (Shapiro and Morris, 1978) may have played an important role in the results secured by most of the psychotherapies, we are much more aware of such effects at present, and in comparison with other older forms of therapy, we need not be overly apologetic or beset by feelings of inadequacy. As pointed out by Shapiro and Morris (1978), "Since almost all medications until recently were placebos, the history of medical treatment can be characterized as the history of the placebo effect." (p. 370) They also point out that "Patients took almost every known organic and inorganic substance—crocodile dung, teeth of swine, hooves of asses, spermatic fluid of frogs, eunuch fat, fly specks, lozenges of dried vipers, powder of precious stones, bricks, furs, feathers, hair, human perspiration, oil of ants, earthworms, wolves, spiders, moss scraped from the skull of a victim of violent death, and so on. . . . Throughout medical history patients were purged, puked, poisoned, punctured, cut, cupped, blistered, bled, leached, heated, frozen, sweated, and shocked" (Shapiro and Morris, 1978, p. 370). Although one can, perhaps, draw some partial analogy to certain aspects of psychotherapy, on the whole, psychotherapists have used less fearsome methods of treatment. It should also be pointed out that with the increase in scientific knowledge and the improvement in medical training resulting from medical schools becoming affiliated with universities, medicine has shown remarkable progress in the past 50 years or so, and as a profession can be justly proud of its achievements.

Psychotherapy, in spite of some of its current manifestations, has also shown significant progress in recent years and has the potential for even more important advances in the years ahead of us. The investigative spirit is strong, the hold on the field of traditional approaches has noticeably diminished, and there has been a trend for both experimentation and an open eclecticism that is conducive to change and possible progress. Some of the rivalry between the important fields of psychiatry and clinical psychology has noticeably lessened, and there is an increased cooperative spirit and recognition of quality work, regardless of professional field. This is particularly evident in the annual meetings of the Society for Psychotherapy Research, a multi-disciplinary organization in which many of the leaders of all professions engaged in research on psychotherapy exchange their views and are concerned with the common goal of advancing our knowledge of psychotherapy.

We have adequate research sophistication at present to develop research projects which can provide answers to many of our present questions. There is also a greater awareness than ever before of the possible factors which may be operative in facilitating change by means of psychotherapy. Coupled with this, there is also a clearer recognition of our social responsibility for providing as efficient and effective psychotherapeutic services as possible. Thus, whereas our current knowledge and our current procedures are modest in comparison to what we would ideally prefer, we have a reasonable basis for optimism in the future. If psychotherapists can accept the fact that our knowledge is relative and that we must not only anticipate change, but actively seek it in order to improve our level of practice, then progress will be secured more readily and with less apprehension and concern. In the final analysis, the society we serve and the individuals we seek to help will be the recipients of our efforts to face reality squarely and to improve the work that we do.

REFERENCES

Alexander, F. and French, T. M. *Psychoanalytic therapy.* New York: Ronald, 1946.

Bellak, L. and Small, L. *Emergency psychotherapy and brief psychotherapy.* New York: Grune and Stratton, 1965.

Birk, L. and Brinkley-Birk, A. W. Psychoanalysis and behavior therapy. *American Journal of Psychiatry*, 1974, *131*, 449–509.

Brown, B. M. Cognitive aspects of Wolpe's behavior therapy. *American Journal of Psychiatry*, 1967, *124*, 162–167.

Brown, B. M. The multiple techniques of broad spectrum psychotherapy. In A. A. Lazarus (Ed.), *Clinical behavior therapy.* New York: Brunner/ Mazel, 1972.

Butcher, J. N. and Koss, M. P. Research on brief and crisis-oriented therapies. In S. L. Garfield and A. E. Bergin (Eds.), *Handbook of psychotherapy and behavior change,* 2nd ed. New York: Wiley, 1978.

Durlak, J. A. Comparative effectiveness of paraprofessional and professional helpers. *Psychological Bulletin*, 1979, *86*, 80–92.

Frank, J. D. *Persuasion and healing: A comparative study of psychotherapy.* New York: Schocken Books, 1961.

Frank, J. D. *Persuasion and healing,* 2nd ed. Baltimore: The Johns Hopkins Press, 1973.

Frank, J. D., Gliedman, L. H., Imber, S. D., Stone, A. R., and Nash, E. H. Patients' expectancies and relearning as factors determining improvement in psychotherapy. *American Journal of Psychiatry*, 1959, *115*, 961–968.

Garfield, S. L. Research on training the professional psychotherapists. In A. Gurman and A. Razin (Eds.), *Effective psychotherapy. A handbook of research.* New York: Pergamon Press, 1977.

Garfield, S. L. Research on client variables in psychotherapy. In S. L. Garfield and A. E. Bergin (Eds.), *Handbook of psychotherapy and behavior change,* 2nd ed. New York: Wiley, 1978.

Garfield, S. L. and Bergin, A. E. (Eds.), *Handbook of psychotherapy and behavior change*, 2nd ed. New York: Wiley, 1978.

Garfield, S. L. and Kurtz, R. Clinical psychologists in the 1970s. *American Psychologist*, 1976, *31*, 1–9.

Garfield, S. L. and Kurtz, R. A study of eclectic views. *Journal of Consulting and Clinical Psychology*, 1977, *45*, 78–83.

Goldstein, A. P. *Therapist-patient expectations in psychotherapy*. New York: Pergamon, 1962.

Harris, M. R., Kalis, B., and Freeman, E. Precipitating stress: An approach to brief therapy. *American Journal of Psychotherapy*, 1963, *71*, 465–471.

Harris, M. R., Kalis, B. L., and Freeman, E. H. An approach to short-term psychotherapy. *Mind*, 1964, *2*, 198–206.

Heitler, J. B. Preparatory techniques in initiating expressive psychotherapy with lower-class unsophisticated patients. *Psychological Bulletin*, 1976, *83*, 339–352.

Hoehn-Saric, R., Frank, J. D., Imber, S. D., Nash, E. H., Stone, A. R., and Battle, C. C. Systematic preparation of patients for psychotherapy. I. Effects on therapy behavior and outcome. *Journal of Psychiatric Research*, 1964, *2,* 267–281.

Holmes, D. S. and Urie, R. G. Effects of preparing children for psychotherapy. *Journal of Consulting and Clinical Psychology*, 1975, *43*, 311–318.

Holt, R. R. (Ed.), *New horizon for psychotherapy*. New York: International Universities Press, 1971.

Kazdin, A. E. The application of operant techniques in treatment, rehabilitation, and education. In S. L. Garfield and A. E. Bergin, (Eds.), *Handbook of psychotherapy and behavior change*, 2nd ed. New York: Wiley, 1978.

Kazdin, A. E. and Wilcoxon, L. A. Systematic desensitization and nonspecific treatment effects: A methodological evaluation. *Psychological Bulletin*, 1976, *83*, 729–758.

Kazdin, A. E. and Wilson, G. T. *Evaluation of behavior therapy: Issues, evidence, and research strategies*. Cambridge, Mass.: Ballinger, 1978.

Kiev, A. *Magic, faith and healing. Studies in primitive psychiatry today*. New York: Free Press of Glencoe, 1964.

Kubie, L. S. The pros and cons of a new profession: A doctorate in medical psychology. In M. Harrower (Ed.), *Medical and psychological teamwork in the case of the chronically ill*. Springfield, Ill.: Charles C. Thomas, 1955.

Kubie, L. S. A doctorate in psychotherapy. The reasons for a new profession. In R. R. Holt (Ed.), *New horizon for psychotherapy. Autonomy as a profession*. New York: International Universities Press, 1971.

Lazarus, A. A. *Behavior therapy and beyond*. New York: McGraw-Hill, 1971.

Lazarus, A. A. Multimodal behavior therapy: Treating the "basic id." *Journal of Nervous and Mental Disease*, 1973, *156*, 404–411.

Lick, J. and Bootzin, R. Expectancy factors in the treatment of fear: Methodological and theoretical issues. *Psychological Bulletin*, 1975, *82*, 917–931.

Lorion, R. P. Research on psychotherapy and behavior change with the disadvantaged. In S. L. Garfield and A. E. Bergin (Eds.), *Handbook of psychotherapy and behavior change*, 2nd ed. New York: Wiley, 1978.

Mahoney, M. J. and Arnkoff, D. B. Cognitive and self-control therapies. In S. L. Garfield and A. E. Bergin (Eds.), *Handbook of psychotherapy and behavior change*, 2nd ed. New York: Wiley, 1978.

Marmor, J. Dynamic psychotherapy and behavior therapy. Are they irreconcilable? *Archives of General Psychiatry*, 1971, *24*, 22–28.

Marmor, J. The future of psychoanalytic therapy. *The American Journal of Psychiatry*, 1973, *130*, 1197—1202.

Morgan, W. G. Nonnecessary conditions or useful procedures in desensitization: A reply to Wilkins. *Psychological Bulletin*, 1973, *79*, 373–375.

Patterson, C. H. Divergence and convergence in psychotherapy. *American Journal of Psychotherapy*, 1967, *21*, 4–17.

Perotti, L. P. and Hopewell, C. A. *Expectancy effects in psychotherapy and systematic desensitization: A review*. Paper presented at the 7th Annual Meeting of the Society for Psychotherapy Research, June 18, 1976, San Diego, California.

Priest, P. N. The destiny of psychological therapies: Convergence or divergence. *British Journal of Medical Psychology*, 1972, *45*, 209–220.

Rioch, M. J. Pilot projects in training mental health counselors. In E. L. Cowen, E. A. Gardner, and M. Zax (Eds.), *Emergent approaches to mental health problems*. New York: Appleton-Century-Crofts, 1967.

Rioch, M. J., Elkes, C., and Flint, A. A. *National Institute of Mental Health project in training mental health counselors*. Washington, D.C.: U.S. Department of H.E.W. Public Health Service Publication No. 1254, 1965.

Shapiro, A. K. and Morris, L. A. The placebo effect in medical and psychological therapies. In S. L. Garfield and A. E. Bergin (Eds.), *Handbook of psychotherapy and behavior change, 2nd Ed.* New York: Wiley, 1978.

Spanos, N. P., Moor, W., and Barber, T. X. Hypnosis and behavior therapy: Common denominators. *American Journal of Clinical Hypnosis*, 1973, *16*, 45–64.

Strupp, H. H. Psychoanalysis, "Focal Psychotherapy," and the nature of the therapeutic influence. *Archives of General Psychiatry*, 1975, *32*, 127–135.

Strupp, H. H. The Vanderbilt psychotherapy process-outcome project. Paper presented at the 8th annual meeting, Society for Psychotherapy Research, Madison, Wisconsin, June, 1977.

Strupp, H. H. Psychotherapy research and practice: An overview. In S. L. Garfield and A. E. Bergin (Eds.), *Handbook of psychotherapy and behavior change*, 2nd ed. New York: Wiley, 1978.

Strupp, H. H. and Bloxom, A. L. Preparing lower-class patients for group psychotherapy: Development and evaluation of a role-induction film. *Journal of Consulting and Clinical Psychology,* 1973, *41,* 373–384.

Torrey, E. F. What western psychotherapists can learn from witchdoctors. *American Journal of Orthopsychiatry,* 1972, *42,* 69–76.

Tseng, W. and McDermott, J. F. Psychotherapy: Historical roots, universal elements and cultural variations. *The American Journal of Psychiatry,* 1975, *132,* 378–384.

Wachtel, P. L. *Psychoanalysis and behavior therapy. Toward an integration.* New York: Basic Books, 1977.

Weitzenhoffer, A. M. Behavior therapeutic techniques and hypnotherapeutic methods. *The American Journal of Clinical Hypnosis,* 1972, *15,* 71–82.

Wilkins, W. Desensitization: Social and cognitive factors underlying the effectiveness of Wolpe's precedure. *Psychological Bulletin,* 1971, *76,* 311–317.

Wilkins, W. Expectancy of therapeutic gain: An empirical and conceptual critique. *Journal of Consulting and Clinical Psychology,* 1973, *40,* 69–77.

Author Index

Subject Index